The Family in the Welfare State

The Family in the Welfare State

Alan Tapper

ALLEN & UNWIN

Australian Institute for Public Policy

First published in 1990 by
Allen & Unwin Australia Pty Ltd
8 Napier Street, North Sydney, NSW 2059, Australia

in association with the
Australian Institute for Public Policy
23 Mount Street, Perth WA 6000, Australia.

National Library of Australia
Cataloguing-in-publication entry:

Tapper, Alan.
The family in the welfare state.

Bibliography.
Includes index
ISBN 0 04 442309 8

1. Public welfare. 2. Family. 3. Social Policy.
I. Australian Institute for Public Policy. II. Title.

362.828.

Set by AIPP in 10/11 Times Roman
Printed by Chong Moh Offset Printing Pte Ltd, Singapore

Contents

The Author

Dr Alan Tapper's main interests are in philosophy and history, particularly the history of philosophy in the eighteenth century. He currently teaches philosophy at the University of Western Australia. He claims that his best qualification for writing on family policy is that he spent about ten years at home looking after his three children while his wife Robin earned the family income.

Foreword

This book originated in discussions within the Australian Institute for Public Policy in 1987. Numerous aspects of modern society—the divorce rate, the gradual weakening of the legal distinctions between marriage and cohabitation, juvenile homelessness and crime, the apparent increase in the incidence of child sexual abuse, to name but a few—seemed to suggest that 'the family' was in trouble. It also appeared that these changes had coincided with the large expansion in Australian welfare programs since the early 1960s. Similar things seemed to have happened in the United States since the 'Great Society' programs of the 1960s, and indeed in countries such as the United Kingdom and Sweden.

The possible links between these phenomena seemed to demand investigation. In the US, Charles Murray had shown in *Losing Ground* that people do respond to some extent to the financial and other incentives placed before them by welfare programs, and that a supply of welfare payments to some extent creates its own demand.

Little if any comparable work was under way in Australia. Such writing as there was on the role and functioning of the family appeared to us to be either from a traditionalist Christian, usually Roman Catholic viewpoint, or from a 'progressive' socialist or feminist sociological viewpoint. These two schools of thought have little common ground, and, we felt, little appeal to the non-devout, non-radical majority of the population. The policy proposals of both schools typically involve greater government intervention and government spending. Despite pretensions to be 'radical', proposals from the socialist and feminist side in fact just call for more of the same welfare state programs that are a partial cause of the evils they seek to alleviate.

Both sides, moreover, tend to deprecate or ignore economic considerations, both in the micro sense of how people respond to incentives and in the macro sense of what Australia's economy can afford. The impact of family problems on the economy is substantial, most obviously via government spending and the associated taxation. A frequent outcome of family breakdown is of course that one parent and the children rely for their income on the welfare system. Other calls on the public purse linked with family breakdown include the family law system, refuges and other support for the homeless, and the costs of the police, courts and other institutions that deal with juvenile crime.

Ignoring the problem of paying for all this may reflect well on one's good-heartedness, but it also shows a depressing lack of practicality. To discuss welfare without paying sharp attention to micro- and macro-economic factors is like carving a statue without paying sharp attention to the strength of the material and the distribution of the weight. Get these things wrong and the statue will break or fall over even before it's finished.

Nevertheless, the family is not just an economic institution. It is a complex of biological, emotional, economic, legal, and other kinds of relationship. Investigations that forget this—and many do—are almost certain to omit some vital consideration.

All in all, there seemed to be a crying need for some radical thinking about the whole matter of welfare and the family; radical, that is, in the sense of 'from the roots up', and not of 1960s political activism. Although the Commonwealth's Social Security Review was in progress, there seemed no likelihood that its recommendations would extend much beyond fine-tuning the existing system. We therefore decided to commission a book-length study of *The Family in the Welfare State*. We chose Alan Tapper for the job because we wanted someone good at careful research and careful thinking, but without previous 'form'. We gave him an open brief and—when asked—such assistance as was in our power. We expected that as a philosopher and historian he would think clearly in this very complicated and often emotion-laden area, while life as a family man and sometime 'house-husband' would keep his feet firmly on the ground. The finished work, I feel, justifies this confidence, although readers are reminded that (as with our other publications) opinions expressed herein are not necessarily endorsed by the Australian Institute for Public Policy.

John Nurick

Acknowledgements

The original idea for this book came from the Australian Institute for Public Policy, which had the enterprise (or foolhardiness) to take on an unknown and—in crucial respects—unqualified author..

John Hyde and John Nurick of AIPP gave me the freedom to think for myself. They were encouraging when encouragement was needed, critical when criticism was warranted, and remarkably patient when patience was a virtue. Such conditions are rare. John Nurick was especially helpful with the technicalities and conceptual difficulties of Chapter Six.

Without the support of my wife Robin the project would have come to nothing. Occasionally she even seems to agree with some of my conclusions. My children Alison, David and Nicholas have taught me many lessons of the sort that only children can teach. In part the book attempts to take a child's-eye view of Australian social policy, so in some ways it is their book too. Writing about family matters also made more than usually conscious of my debt to my own parents. I hope that some of what they stand for is in this book.

My own thinking has grown out of many years of talking with Julius Kovesi. Though we did not much discuss the subject of this book, much of whatever may be good in it is in one way or another the result of his friendship, humour and wisdom. It would be a better book had he been able to comment on more of it. His death in August 1989 was a loss to everyone who knew him.

The book itself will show which writers and researchers I have found most constructive and interesting. I am particularly indebted to those people—perhaps a dozen in all—who gave me their opinions on many of the topics dealt with in the book. Without their encouragement I would not have had the confidence to trespass in so much unfamiliar territory. I hope that I have articulated some of their concerns.

I also wish to record my thanks to the long-suffering Australian taxpayer, who supported me through my earlier studies in philosophy and intellectual history. I would like to think that this book shows that years of wandering in remote centuries may eventually yield practical results.

In controversial matters it is more than usually necessary to emphasise that the arguments used and the conclusions reached are mine alone, and that therefore the errors are also mine alone.

Alan Tapper

On behalf of the Australian Institute for Public Policy I would like to express our gratitude to the following organisations, whose generosity made this project possible and who backed the idea before a word had been written.

ALCOA of Australia Ltd
Elders IXL Ltd
Hospital Benefit Fund of WA
Mutual Community Ltd
The Perron Group Trust
Western Mining Corporation Ltd

We hope they like the result. Nevertheless, the fact that they supported the project does not mean that they agree with what the book says.

John Nurick

1 The Politics of the Family

'The Personal is Political': it was with this mysterious slogan emblazoned across their breastplates that twenty years ago the early feminist leaders marched into battle against the serried ranks of male chauvinism. Even now it is not very clear what the slogan means, or meant; but it has not quite lost its capacity to sound revolutionary, or at least provocative. Had the slogan read, 'Some Aspects of Personal Life are Related to Some Aspects of Politics', the effect would have been lost, even if truth had gained. But perhaps this mundane truth is an important one. Amongst the multiple meanings that might be fixed to the not-very-illuminating words is the claim that the relation between the public and private worlds is more complex than is allowed by the orthodox distinction between state and citizen. If this was roughly true twenty years ago, it is very much more apposite now. The private world, against which the feminists were in rebellion, is largely—but of course not wholly—the domain of the family. And the domain of the family is now very much a matter of political controversy. Any survey of the boundaries of that domain is necessarily in part political.

Until recently, very little thought has been devoted to the relation between family policy and welfare policy. Whole shelves of books have been written on welfare matters with barely a passing mention of the family. Even the notion of family policy is relatively novel, at least in the Australian context. Indeed, it will be an underlying tenet of this book that astonishingly little serious thought has ever been devoted to the role of the family in society, and that we are now reaping some of the effects of that neglect—but a defence of this ambitious claim would require a separate and very different work. This book's focus is contemporary and its intention is practical. If it does no more than to collate some of the main questions that need to be considered under the heading of 'family policy' it might serve a useful purpose. If in passing it also manages to raise some of the larger and more puzzling questions about the relation between family and society then that will be incidental to the main design.

Family policy matters are now inescapable even for the most hard-headed and practical-minded of politicians and policy-makers. It is no longer possible to regard family questions with the easy-going acceptance or indifference of earlier generations of social thinkers and planners. Brigitte and Peter Berger exaggerated very little when in 1983 they entitled a book *The War Over the Family*. The battle has been much more violent in America, which was their main subject, but it is acute enough in Australia. The basic issues are the same here as they are in all advanced Western societies. The following list of Australian family policy problems—in no particular order—would probably be easily recognisable in a dozen other countries:

- General assistance to ordinary families with children has tended to decline over time. Those who wish to curtail welfare spending see family allowances as a prime target for further reductions. Many parents feel a sense of financial crisis and believe that they need (and even deserve) greater social support in the form of increased allowances or tax relief.
- In response to this sense of financial difficulty the Family Allowance Supplement has been created to assist low-income working families. The allowance is also designed to improve the incentives for families to take poorly paid work in preference to welfare benefits, but in pursuing this aim it has also created 'poverty traps'—high effective marginal tax rates with significant workforce disincentives.
- The divorce rate has tripled in the last twenty years. It is estimated that between a third and two fifths of all recent marriages will end in divorce, many within the first ten years, many involving children and many resulting in loss of contact between the children and their non-custodial parent.
- A high percentage of divorced couples re-marry, indicating that the institution of marriage is still popular, but the break-up rate for these couples is slightly higher than that for first marriages, suggesting that the difficulties of sustaining marriages are often too deep to be solved simply by a change of partners.
- Divorce law has been shifted from a fault basis to a no-fault basis, but 'easy' divorce has led to no noticeable reduction in the ill-will and hurtfulness generated by the divorce process. Post-divorce property settlements and issues about access to children are frequently controversial and sometimes end in violence and suicide.
- The Sole (formerly Supporting) Parents Benefit, introduced to assist sole parents at the beginning of the rapid growth in the divorce rate in the 1970s, has now become a major part of the welfare budget.

- A more rigorous system of maintenance payments has had to follow (though very belatedly) the Supporting Parents Benefit, as increasing numbers of non-custodial parents refused to support their children and the cost of Supporting Parents Benefit became increasingly burdensome to the community.
- The rapid increase in unemployment and the divorce rate in the late 1970s has put many families, and thus many children, close to poverty. Long-term dependency upon welfare payments has become chronic for some families, and may be passed on from generation to generation. Many families have found it difficult to work their way out of poverty, because of high effective marginal tax rates. The combination of Unemployment Benefit and Supporting Parents Benefit is such that in some circumstances it favours couples who choose to separate. The more basic question of how to prevent child poverty by helping families to stay together has been studiously avoided by those in a position to influence policy.
- The number of children born without a father available to support them has increased nearly threefold since the mid-70s.
- The proportion of abortions to live births has risen rapidly. For every three children now born, one is aborted.
- Women, the traditional mainstays of family life, are now choosing to devote a much larger portion of their lives to the paid workforce, even to some extent when they have young children. The reasons for this change are partly economic and partly to do with personal fulfilment. This has been accompanied by an increasing demand for taxpayer-funded childcare services to assist the workforce participation of women.
- Many women who choose to stay at home with their children feel that their choice is belittled and neglected. Underlying this feeling appears to be a major decline in the social status of family life and the work done by parents to sustain families and marriages.
- Feminism, which has dominated discussion of many family issues, is frequently hostile to the family, and portrays the family as a bastion of male privilege.
- Domestic violence, typically the violence of men against women, is now an important issue for social policy.
- Sexual abuse of children is becoming recognised as a major problem, though the question of how much this phenomenon is to be thought of as an intra-family problem is at present controversial.
- The fertility rate is now at an all-time low, and has fallen below the replacement rate. Some welcome this as a necessary recognition of the limited resources of an overpopulated planet and a dry continent. Others see it as a failure of confidence in our social future.
- As the proportion of young members of the population declines, the proportion of the old increases. This increasing longevity poses a question about the capacity of the working population to support the old at

the levels presently accepted. At the same time as many of the elderly are enjoying an unprecedented opportunity for independence and leisure, some seem consigned to lives of loneliness and neglect.

- In a period in which expenditure per child on education has doubled and yet serious doubts exist about whether educational standards have risen, debate about education has begun to take an interest in the interaction between families and schooling.[1]

Not all these questions will be discussed in this book. The rights or wrongs of abortion is the most notable omission, though not of course because it is any less important than the topics which are dealt with. Child sexual abuse is a subject for specialists with wide experience in child health and welfare. Domestic violence is discussed only briefly, and then only in the most general way. Little is to be said about fertility and population size. The remaining matters are material enough. The book will attempt to serve both as a survey of current thinking on the topics covered and as an independent critique of existing policy and practice. The first four chapters attempt to clear the ground, by putting aside a variety of feminist and welfarist preconceptions which cloud the real issues. The next four chapters deal with the central topics of the book, money and marriage. The last three consider life-cycle stages—childhood and old age—and their place in social policy.

In matters as hotly contested as these all are, it is difficult, perhaps impossible, to state the issues without seeming to prejudge their evaluation. To make matters very much worse, policy-making requires some grasp of how these elements interact. The developments mentioned are, though familiar, still relatively recent ones from a longer historical perspective, and some of them lack any historical precedent. We can expect that the process of coming to some understanding of them will be a slow one, and that it will require intelligence, imagination and freedom from ideology. A variety of viewpoints will be required, for no-one has a monopoly of wisdom in these matters.[2] Certainly, the old approaches of Left and Right are unlikely to be of much help. Any new approach will need to be sensitive to the wishes and aspirations of families as they actually are, but what this entails in practical terms is very far from clear. If some of the positions taken in this book seem to the reader extreme, two points need to be kept in mind before judgement is passed: one is that the book may sometimes go to those extremes partly in reaction against what seems to the author as the premature fossilisation of debate imposed upon the subject by welfarist and feminist premisses; and, more importantly, that the real test of an argument is not whether it is 'extreme' or 'orthodox' (or 'fossilised') but whether it is well grounded and well reasoned. Wherever possible the claims to be

1 For a very fair-minded and cautious survey of the international trends see Popenoe, *Disturbing the Nest*.

2 Readers are recommended to consult Eastman's *Family: The Vital Factor* for another recent, interesting analysis of Australian family policy issues.

made here will rest upon assumptions, authorities and evidence accepted by those who may not share the conclusions drawn from them.

Social theory is a matter of following the argument wherever it leads. Social policy is to some extent a different matter, involving compromise with those who do not see the issues in the same light. This book attempts to be uncompromising about substantive questions, but it need not be read as unwilling to compromise in practice. Most of all, however, it seeks to avoid the combination of rudderless pragmatism and ideological huffing, puffing and bluffing which has bedevilled discussions of this subject matter.

The domain of the family

Remarkably, after all that has been said against the family, and all that is manifestly or apparently problematic about it, the great majority of the Australian population continue to identify with the battered old model. After all the social changes of recent times, and despite the undeniable evidence of considerable breakdown in many families, this central allegiance has changed very little. The staying power of this institution is beginning to be reckoned with. 'The family' is now busily being 'discovered', at least by some of those for whom it was somehow mysteriously lost. This is probably no bad thing; but having for so long been ignored and neglected, families are unlikely to be carried away by the new-found enthusiasm of those previously indifferent or hostile to family interests. After two decades of 'liberation movements', most of them raucous and some of them savage, the notion of a 'family liberation movement' has a distinctly comical sound to it, however appropriate the substance of such a movement may be.

Governments, always on the lookout for new and appealing slogans, are already starting to dress up their old programs in the clothing of family policy, and there will be a rash of family policy tokenism in the next few years. We should not be taken in by this, however well-meant it may be. The danger is that cosmetic alterations will be passed off as real improvements. What we need is some hard thinking about what a really family-centred society would be like. And because the subject has been for so long ignored, there are no ready-made answers to this question. Good answers will have to accept the fairly rigorous conditions of proof now properly required by economically responsible or 'dry' governments. This book will try to make out a strong case for generous public support for families. But in passing it will try also to weed out weak and partial special pleading for family policies. Not everything that calls itself a family policy is designed to help all families. To be successful the argument will have to establish that families are not yet another special interest group lining up for a government handout.

Three cardinal principles will inform the argument of this book. The first is that the family is a miniature society, a social unit. The second is that in producing, caring for, and educating children the family contributes to the good of the wider society. The third is that in caring for dependants—young or old—the family is a welfare institution. All three principles, stated simply, may seem innocuous, but the consequences which follow from them are likely to be regarded as controversial. They certainly conflict with much of our present practice in this area. The principles themselves may also turn out to be controversial when the consequences become apparent, so it will be part of the book's strategy to argue not just *from* but (as far as possible) *for* first principles. The public good and welfare aspects of the family will be considered in later chapters. Since we are here thinking about the relation between the state and the family it is appropriate to think for a moment about the family as a social unit.

Amongst the many matters of family policy which require serious thought is the general question of the domain of the family. Very little has been said about this in policy discussions, yet it is of considerable importance. Like states, families are social units. They have their own boundaries, their own domestic policies, and their own foreign relations. A conceptual border exists between the family and the state, and between the family and the individual. To obliterate these distinctions is in effect to pretend that the family does not exist; but it is no more accidental that we have families than it is that we have states.

This point may be clearer if we think about cases where the family trespasses on the domain of the state. When family-based organisations such as tribes, clans and mafia-type syndicates evolve their own legal and policing machinery we quite properly protest that they are setting up as 'a state within the state'. Similarly we would protest against nepotism if we suspected family favouritism in appointments to the public service, though the same sort of favouritism is unobjectionable in a family business. But we are far less sensitive to interference by the state in the internal life of the family. We do not, although we should, protest against the state setting itself up as 'a family within the family'.

The operations of clans and mafia are perhaps not current problems in Australia, but the trespasses of governments are certainly of topical interest. Should, for instance, government policies be designed to help mothers join the workforce? Or should they be designed to encourage women with dependent children to stay at home? These questions are very similar to the question whether warrior tribesmen should be allowed to carry weapons. To recognise that there are boundaries here is to accept self-denying ordinances. As a tribal warrior I may think that I could do a better job than the police. As a feminist or anti-feminist policy-maker I may think I know what is best for families. I may even be right. But a boundary is not a boundary if it does not permit people to be foolish, wrong-headed and perverse. And in any case there is no good reason to expect that in general policy-makers will possess greater insight into most family issues than that already possessed by family members themselves.

To argue in this way is not to say that the state should never interfere in the family. Membership of a family is not a licence to practise murder, violence or sexual abuse on fellow members of the family. Likewise, it seems very plausible to argue that the whole of a society, as embodied in the state, has a responsibility to give all children a fair start in life beyond that which their family can give them. Children are as much the future members of the whole society as they are future adult members of the family into which they are born. But while there are grounds for state intervention in extreme cases, there are in fact many matters in which we readily agree that there is no role for state interference in family decisions. The state should not decide how many children we should have, except perhaps in situations of famine or disease. It should not dictate how we bring up our children, except to prevent extreme abuse. It should not attempt to settle ordinary domestic disputes. It should not prevent mutually agreed divorce, though it does have some role in seeing that children of divorcing couples do not suffer too greatly from the outcome.

A similar set of questions arises about the relations between families and individuals. All family members are also individuals, and all have interests of their own separate and distinct from the interests of their family. A family which did not recognise this would be oppressive, just as would a state which did not recognise the separate interests of individuals and families. A family which assigns all the drudgery to the mother without permitting her to foster her talents is an obvious example of such injustice. But it can just as easily be the case that individuals can harm their family by pursuing their own interests. Parents can do this by becoming engrossed in their careers, or even in housework, forgetting the needs of their children or their own parents. Children can do it by becoming selfish and grasping.

Whether in any particular case family relations have become unbalanced is often difficult to determine even by the family members themselves. Friends of families know how much caution and tact is required before they risk intervening. Social workers and teachers face the same dilemma. Exactly the same tact and caution, only multiplied many times over to allow for the imbalance of power in one direction and knowledge in the other, should be demanded of the state when it decides to intervene in family affairs. Respect for this principle will incline us to put the onus of proof that intervention is required on the state. The general rule should be that the state may intervene only in extreme cases. Put in this form the rule seems unobjectionable. Applied to actual situations it leads immediately to controversy.

Consider the following question: Should the state take up a moral stance in favour of the 'traditional' two-parent family or should it aim to be neutral between different family forms? The above rule suggests that it should be neutral, but the result conflicts with current practice. Since changes to divorce legislation and welfare benefits policies in the mid-1970s it is not at all clear that the state does anything to sustain the two-parent family. It can be argued that in providing benefits to custodial single parents that are not given to dual-parent families, public policy is far from neutral about family form. At present total annual Commonwealth expenditure on single-parent families exceeds that for assistance to two-parent families, although the children in the latter outnumber children in the former by about eight to one.[3] (In fact, as Chapter Five will show, the position of two-parent families is far worse than this contrast suggests.) The obvious replies to this claim are not very convincing. Supporting Parents Benefit, it will be said, aims to assist with the costs of children or to compensate for the custodial parent's difficulty in joining the workforce. But dual parents have the same costs and one partner has the same difficulties. It will be said that (barring unemployment) the two-parent family at least has one income. But there is no clear reason why a separated or divorced couple cannot still share an income. To argue this is not to claim that there should be no payments for single parents, only that if we are to have such benefits then on equity grounds similar assistance should be extended to two-parent families. This argument will be pursued more fully in Chapter Eight; it is introduced here merely to illustrate the way in which family policy questions return us so rapidly to first principles.

To treat the family as a social unit is most likely to be resisted by those most committed to change (of whatever sort) in the internal structure and behaviour of families. How families are changing, and how they ought to change, are matters in which we all have some interest. Active social research and lively public debate, in which a wide variety of viewpoints is encouraged, can only be beneficial. However, a vital distinction needs to be drawn between influencing family change by public discussion and causing changes by public policy action. It is often taken for granted that a good case for change is a good case for government action which favours

---

3 In 1987–88 Family Allowance expenditure amounted to $1355 million and Family Allowance Supplement $213 million, about 85 per cent of which would have gone to two-parent families. The budget for sole parent families included $1525 million for Supporting Parents Benefit and Allowances, and an unknown proportion of the $1000 million outlay for the Widows Pension Class A. (How many Class A recipients are widows, and how many are divorcees or never-married sole parents, is not disclosed by the Department of Social Security. The Class A pension has recently been subsumed under what is now known as the Sole Parent Benefit.) At the time of the 1986 census about 5,500,000 children were living in two-parent families and 550,000 in sole parent families (*Census 86—Australian Families and Households*, ABS Catalogue No. 2506.0, Figure 1.1.) Adding the taxation contributions to the sole-parent/two-parent comparison would only accentuate the disparity between the two: two parent families are generally high tax payers, and sole parent families pay little in tax.

such change. This would be unobjectionable if it could be done in such a way as to expand the options of all families. In practice it usually requires action which restricts the freedoms of some families in order to expand the freedoms of other families. Change by persuasion is so much to be preferred to state-imposed change that the latter, however well-meaning, should be considered only as a last resort.

The family and the interest groups

Family policy is, inevitably, political, though how it relates to the traditional divisions of political debate is an open question. To understand the political fortunes and prospects of the family we need some wider context. A brief sketch of the political and ideological changes in Australia of the last two decades is unavoidable. Matters of family and welfare policy are not merely technical questions for specialists. They affect us all. Changes in these matters become part of our social history. Without some picture of our recent social history we cannot see where we have come from, nor where we ought to be going, yet the question of where we have come from is always as difficult and controversial as the question of where we ought to be going to. The following sketch lays no claim to detailed verisimilitude; it attempts only to put a point of view different from that found in conventional accounts of the matter.

For a very long time the political world has been neatly divided into two parts, quaintly known for historical reasons as the 'Right' and the 'Left'. The average voter may have found it difficult to define these terms, but he or she knew that they roughly corresponded to a division in the social order between the middle and the working classes. The aim of the Right was to preserve and enhance the achievements of the propertied business and farming sector, seen as the domain of the middle class; the aim of the Left was to promote the interests of the workers and to protect the poor. This was an immensely convenient fiction. It was relatively easy to know where you stood on most issues. It was relatively easy to know who was with you and who was on the other side. The mythology sometimes came with a standardised catalogue of heroes and villains. However acrimonious divisions within each party at times may have been, the metaphors of Left and Right were thought to mark a major rift running across the political and social landscape which could be taken for granted by all participants.

Yet while this dichotomy dominated political debate and allegiance, the political and social behaviour which took place under its auspices gradually came to exhibit some very powerful convergent tendencies. In almost every corner of society the attitude grew that government existed to be exploited for all it was worth. It became the overriding aim of innumerable interest groups—some enormously powerful, some minuscule—relentlessly to persuade and pressure governments and parties to provide for their own particular and eminently worthy 'needs'. A magical, new word—'funding'—entered common parlance to symbolise this trend. Tariffs, subsidies, regulations, grants, concessions, rebates, services, reductions, discounts, favours, positions, privileges, committees of enquiry, advisory bodies, and many other 'lurks and perks' proliferated, until the art of politics became that of being seen to be doing something for everyone, where 'everyone' consisted of the collective membership of these innumerable lobby groups. And for all practical purposes it must have seemed that everyone did belong to one group or another. The list was impressive enough: big businesses, big unions, farmers, students, environmentalists, age pensioners, feminists, sporting bodies, professional groups, multiculturalists, teachers, Aborigines, welfare organisations, animal liberationists, old Uncle Tom Cobleigh and all. It used to be said that the preferred social policy of the farming community was to individualise its profits and to socialise its losses; this now became the primary strategy of anyone with the power to put it into practice. At the same time each group cultivated its own rhetoric of 'rights', until the moral universe was populated by as many rights as there were good causes.

The proliferation of interest groups in recent times has been an international phenomenon, but in Australia it has been aggravated by the unique centralised wage-fixing system—an Antipodean freak of social evolution—which has functioned as a parallel polity, with exactly the same weaknesses as the official political structure. The system is quasi-judicial rather than democratically elected, but this distinction has made no discernible difference. In this period (at least until the 1985 Wages Accord) the Arbitration Commission was bombarded with demands for pay rises which bore little relation to the harsh realities of stagflation and high unemployment. The Commission could no more resist the demands of the entrenched interest groups—both unions and employer organisations—than could the elected representatives.

Even with the wisdom of Solomon, no politician—or Arbitration Commissioner—could be expected to adjudicate intelligently between all these conflicting claims. With the rather ordinary quotient of wisdom that politicians enjoy, the results were very predictable. Total public sector outlays as a proportion of GDP grew from 28 per cent in 1970–71 to 33 per cent in 1975–76, 35 per cent in 1980–81, and 38 per cent in 1985–86.[4] Commonwealth social security and welfare expenditure grew more or less in parallel to this expansion, from (in 1986–87 dollars) $6.4 billion in 1970–71 to $12.9 billion in 1975–76 to $16.1 billion in 1980–81 to $20.5 billion in 1985–86.[5] It is hard to avoid the conclusion that the growth of government, and not any item from the agenda of one or other of the parties, is the central political event of the last twenty-five years.

4 See Hyde, *Deregulate or Decay*, 37.

5 See Hendrie and Porter, 'The Capture of the Welfare State', 24.

There was one small logical difficulty in all of this: if everyone gets something from government then in effect no-one gets anything, for whatever government has to give away it must first take from those who seek to benefit. The difficulty was swept aside. All it showed was that all parties should renew their efforts to get a little bit more than anyone else. But the greater the demand for funds, the harder it was for government to meet it. The high tax rates required encouraged creative accountancy: at all levels of society, from the unemployed to small self-employed tradesmen to family farmers to highly-paid professionals to big corporations, an enormous amount of mental energy and financial ingenuity was devoted to the gentle art of avoiding taxation. The process was self-generating: the success of the unscrupulous lowered the ethical barriers of the moderately self-interested which in turn made the more high-minded wonder why they should stick to principles recognised only by themselves. The growing demand for government spending was a major reason for the huge budget deficits of the 1970s and most of the 1980s. These deficits were only partly funded by selling government bonds; printing paper money for the remainder was government's own creative accounting. The consequent inflation both whittled away governments' accrued debts and introduced Australians to the phenomenon of bracket creep, the insidious increase in revenue arising from the failure to index income tax thresholds.

In this stampede of self-promotion and self-interest two groups were left behind: the PAYE taxpayer and the person with a family to support. And the burden was borne most heavily by the PAYE taxpayer with a family. The PAYE taxpayer, however virtuous or villainous he or she might aspire to be, could do very little about the taxes extracted directly from his or her pay packet. As a consequence the proportion of PAYE tax to total Budget receipts grew from under 25 per cent in the mid-1960s to pass 30 per cent in 1970–71 and peak at 43 per cent in 1981–82, since when it has declined slightly. (Chapters Five and Six will seek to show that the Australian taxation and welfare systems are considerably biased against families with children, particularly two-parent families.)

The stampede of the 1970s, while it has not quite run out of steam, is gradually losing momentum. Economic reality has begun to intrude, and necessity is beginning to make us if not virtuous then at least relatively prudent. The pork barrel has been scraped to the bottom. Government, we have discovered, is not an endlessly self-regenerating Magic Pudding. The old clear-cut Left/Right dichotomy no longer dominates political argument. The differences within each of the two main parties are now greater than the differences between them. It is less interesting to know whether a person or a politician is Liberal or Labor than to know what kind of Liberalism or Laborism he or she supports. It is also less important to know whether someone is a 'worker' or an 'employer' than it is to know whether he or she favours a more efficient and internationally competitive economy. Much of the traditional 'conflict' between 'labour' and 'capital' was (and still is) a highly elaborate form of shadow-boxing, more appropriately judged as a theatrical genre than as a representation of social reality. The long history of collusion between big business and big labour unions whereby each in turn employs government to protect its own interests against those of the ordinary consumer, the ordinary worker and the ordinary family is, with any luck, coming to an end. A deregulated society, if we achieve one, is likely to be less exciting for those who find the theatre of politics exciting; but it is also likely to be better at maintaining average living standards, thereby allowing us to pursue other, more exciting and civilised interests.

The confidence that the Left once placed in government as the instrument for controlling and correcting the alleged imbalances of a market economy has been eroded. It is now widely believed that a productive economy is not incompatible with the interests of the working class. Deregulation and privatisation are gaining acceptance as possible strategies for improving living standards for all. All parties accept that the current account deficit must be brought back to earth. An efficient public service is considered a high priority. Tax avoidance and evasion are being brought under control, and the tax base has been broadened. Wage rises have been kept within some limits. These changes have not yet brought about any great alteration in the structure of politics or the economy. Savings remain inadequate and productivity growth is minimal; the high current account deficit is evidence of these unsolved structural problems. But at least we are no longer dominated by the blind conviction that any such changes will be automatically disastrous. Economic deregulation has to be preceded by this kind of ideological deregulation.

At the heart of this process of ideological deregulation are two conflicting theories: the theory of market failure, and the theory of government failure. It was Adam Smith who observed that 'People of the same trade seldom meet together, even for merriment and diversion, but the conversation ends in a conspiracy against the public, or in some contrivance to raise prices'. Two hundred years later we know there is equal truth in the proposition that people engaged in the process of government seldom meet together, even for merriment and diversion, but the conversation ends in a conspiracy against the public, or in some contrivance to raise taxes. The choice between markets and governments may be seen as a choice between two different kinds of 'conspiracy'. The real question is which is more easily detected and controlled. There are good reasons for thinking that in general markets are better at controlling prices than governments are at containing taxes. The much-derided competition that markets entail is both more efficient and more humane than competition for the spoils of government.

It was the idea of market failure (with some assistance from Keynesian economics) that cleared the ground for post-war large-scale government intervention in the economy and in social affairs. The idea was that in many matters markets do not operate efficiently to serve the general interest. The particularities of this thesis matter less here than the once commonly-accepted assumption that government is, in general and all other things being equal, more rational than market processes. Because they usually do not involve conjoint deliberation, markets and market prices appear irrational. Governments, on the other hand, do involve centralised decision-making and deliberation, and thus appear to be rational institutions. This contrast is a conceptual illusion. All else being equal, conjoint deliberation is no more likely to be rational than the multitude of decisions which go into market processes. Indeed, the presumption should be the other way round: very much more deliberation, cumulatively, goes into the setting of market prices than can possibly pass through the narrow bottle-neck of government. Also, the quality of information about people's needs and wishes is superior in market decisions, because each person knows his or her own needs and wishes better than can any person representing them. And, further, people are more careful about what they do with their own money than they are about what they do with other people's. On grounds of both quantity and quality of deliberation, then, we can assume that market decisions tend to be more rational than those made by governments.

Government failure is a theory forced upon us by two or three decades of experience of governmental attempts to correct what was perceived as market failure. The theory (made familiar through the television series *Yes, Minister*) contends that government employees—public servants—are no more altruistic than any other kind of employee or employer. They are as much committed to securing their own advantage as to promoting the good of the public. This is not to say that they do not serve the public, only that they do so within a certain framework. Public servants, for instance, do not recommend the abolition of their own positions, even if those positions have ceased to serve any essential purpose. The public service unions make it practically impossible to lay off any workers, no matter how redundant they may have become. Public service management has an interest in expanding the programs it supervises and maximising the number of persons who work under its supervision. Because its efforts are dictated by political considerations rather than economic necessity, it has difficulty in setting and policing standards of efficiency. Because its internal structure involves no close connection between performance and reward there are few incentives to find new, cheaper or otherwise better ways of achieving the goals of the organisation.

But perhaps governments are more humane, even if less efficient, than markets? Perhaps sometimes they are; but, phrased this way, the question is being begged. Efficiency and humanity are not necessarily mutually exclusive. Socialist societies are notoriously inhumane, not just in the sense of being very often brutal, but also in the more mundane sense of requiring shoppers to spend half the day queueing to buy a small quantity of poor quality food or clothing. This form of inhumanity has little to do with economic incapacity and much to do with government inefficiency. The limitations of socialism are now apparent even to many socialists; by comparison commercial societies look like lands flowing with the milk of human kindness, even though markets require little sense of mutual goodwill between participants. The point is borne out by the contrasting standards of living enjoyed by ordinary workers in East and West Germany and in North and South Korea. These examples do not show that some hybrid of government and market societies is not more humane than the pure form of either, but any argument along these lines needs to show that the hybrid will not inherit genetic defects from its government component which will override the genetic strengths of markets.

Government failure has not gone unnoticed by the electorate. As a result, governments have now discovered that they can do things which once would have seemed electoral suicide. They are not locked into ideological stereotypes. They can over-ride the pleas of narrow interest groups. Short-term pain will be borne by voters if there is a reasonable prospect of long-term gain. There is more to good political leadership than buying the maximum number of votes at the lowest possible price. All this is of vital importance in determining the future of welfare policy. There is no painless solution to welfare problems. There are justifiable long-term approaches to the issues but to achieve them will require resolution and intelligence of the kind now slowly beginning to be applied to our economic ills. This intelligence will not come from thinking conducted in the hardened old ideological categories. A rethinking of welfare matters will require the same sort of mental flexibility.

The discoveries here referred to were made by a Labor government, as recently as 1984–85.[6] It need not have been Labor that made this discovery. In the 1950s and 1960s it was the Left which supplied most of the ideas for changing society and the Liberals who implemented them; today ideas for social and economic change come from the Right but are put into practice by the Labor Party. The preceding Fraser Liberal government talked some of the rhetoric of the New Right, but the almost universal hostility to economic rationalism that it encountered amongst manufacturers, trade unions, the welfare lobby and the press persuaded it to return to the ways of its predecessors.

A new set of distinctions is needed to understand this change. The central metaphors of the new politics are 'wet' and 'dry', or big and small, government. (Perhaps 'drunken' and 'sober' might be more descriptive.) These concepts measure a government's resistance to expenditure pressures, whether they come from the Left or the Right, from labour or capital, from the poor or the rich. Wet and dry governments operate with

6 It will be remembered that the change of mind took place almost exactly at the time when senior members of the Labor Party were doing their best to vilify 'the New Right' whose ideas they immediately set about borrowing.

quite different public expenditure criteria. Under the downpour of wet government the reasoning was that if *X* is a good thing then *X* is a good thing for governments to do (and, equally important, be seen to be doing). Dry government asks the simple question, 'Yes, but why should it be the government that does it?' This question is not easy to answer.

Governments, we would all agree, have a responsibility to care for the public interest. What is needed here is the ability to distinguish sharply between special interests and the public interest. The problem is by no means purely theoretical. Every special interest naturally (sometimes even sincerely) attempts to represent its cause as being in the public interest. The public interest is by its very nature such that no-one can be taken as its authorised spokesman. And it needs to be borne in mind that the public interest often might be best served by government doing nothing at all.

But further than that, we need to come to grips again with the notion of social justice. Without this central concept we cannot hope to develop impartial public policies. For some time now the dominant notion in social advocacy has been that of a 'right'. This term has now been exploited and abused so comprehensively that it would be better if we could delete it from the lexicon. A few decades of peace and quiet would do the word a world of good. The notion of a right is the natural rhetorical ploy of every special interest group because the concept allows us conveniently to overlook the question of what that right is based on. Rights, after all, are rights. If I have a right to do or get *X* then I have that right and there's no more need for discussion. Or so we assume, though the argument is blatantly question-begging. The fact that my opponent cannot see that I have this right is taken to be neither here nor there. The fact that the notion of a right is necessary primarily to distinguish between the claims of two plausible but conflicting proposals is somehow forgotten. The fact that rights can be forfeited goes by the board. And the fact that rights entail responsibilities is equally downplayed.

A reduction in the dominance of interest group politics, while necessary on both economic grounds and as a matter of justice, is also an important goal for anyone interested in the welfare of families. It might be going too far to imagine a constituency of virtuous hard-working families struggling to raise children in the suburban mortgage belts who were left behind in the rush for the spoils of government. Some who fit this description were also members of the grasping interest groups. But many were not, and for obvious reasons. Political activism requires an economic base, as radicals so often remind us. At the end of the day—for parents of young children the phrase is more than a cliché—raising a family does not leave much spare time, energy and money for political wire-pulling. Perhaps also the inclination to engage in such gamesmanship diminishes as other responsibilities crowd in. Many who fall into this category have no deep convictions about old-style Left/Right partisanship, which they observe like side-on spectators at a not very exciting tennis match.

In the seventies, raising a family, though still the preferred mode of life for most of the populace, was not an activity which commanded much social or political status—nor does it now, for that matter. Indeed, it would be difficult to name a politician, a party faction, a political lobby group or a social 'movement', in that era of lobbies and 'movements', which spoke up for the interests of families (the Australian Family Association and the Australian Institute of Family Studies were begun in the early eighties). The exception who proves the rule here is B.A. Santamaria, a figure whose unflagging advocacy of family interests made him seem eccentric and unfashionable to moderates and outrageously provocative to radicals. But the political weakness of families in this period is a natural consequence of the growth of interest group competition.

There are also deeper structural reasons at work here, the logic of which has been clarified by American economist Mancur Olson. Olson argues for the paradoxical conclusion that relatively unrepresentative groups are usually more effective in manipulating the state than are widespread but diffuse interests. His detailed explanation of this apparent paradox, and the historical evidence for its truth, is presented in his *The Rise and Decline of Nations*. Here we are concerned only with its practical implications. Olson notes, for instance, that

> In no major country are large groups without access to selective incentives generally organised—the masses of consumers are not in consumers' organisations, the millions of taxpayers are not in taxpayers' organisations, the vast number of those with relatively low incomes are not in organisations for the poor, and the sometimes substantial numbers of unemployed have no organized voice.... By contrast, almost everywhere the social prestige of the learned professions and the limited number of practitioners of each profession in each community has helped them to organize.[7]

On Olson's account, industry associations and trade unions are at the same end of the spectrum as the professional bodies; and clearly (although he does not discuss this case) families are at the dispersed, disorganised and diffuse end. The exception to this rule—an exception which tends to confirm the rule—is the single parent family, the interests of which are protected by the well-organised welfare lobby. (The evidence for these claims does not need to be taken on faith here—it will be presented more fully in Chapter Five.) Whether the rise of the elderly as an interest group can be accounted for by Olson's account is perhaps more doubtful. The age pension seems to provide a focal point for joint action which otherwise would not be possible.

Olson's theory is a theory about political life between elections, and in a democracy the voter can to some extent restore the balance which is threat-

7 *The Rise and Decline of Nations*, 34f. See also Olson's *Australia in the Perspective of the Rise and Decline of Nations*. It is notable that consumers, families and the unemployed have never been represented in the deliberations of the Arbitration Commission (now the Industrial Relations Commission).

ened by the natural tendencies of the pressure group process. However, even democracy does not serve family interests particularly well. Children do not vote: this fact is both blindingly obvious and universally overlooked. It is one of those facts so much taken for granted that it is never mentioned, much less justified. Yet children are individuals and they have needs and interests. If the purpose of democratic politics is to represent the needs and interests of individuals then there would seem to be a good case for enfranchising children as well as adults. This vote would have to be exercised for them by their parents, but a proxy vote is certainly better than no vote at all, particularly if it is exercised by those best placed to understand the child's interests. With growing maturity children could make their views known to their parents, and the process of discussion between parent and child would play an important part in their political education. Such an extension of the franchise would also do much to restore the political balance back towards those who do the once-respected work of raising the next generation.

Iconography and family values

So far in this discussion two general claims about the 'politics of the family' have been made: that families tend to suffer when governments take it upon themselves to interfere in their internal affairs; and that families tend to suffer in societies organised into interest groups competing for the spoils of big government. Later in this book these points will be taken further. Here a third and final political point might be made: 'the family' is not a symbol which belongs to any one party or position on the political spectrum, nor need it have any special ideological affiliations, and there is nothing in the ordinary traditions of both 'Left' and 'Right' politics to justify the ideological suspicion and hostility to the family which have been so prevalent in recent times.

Of all the political options currently available, concern for the family is usually identified as a preoccupation of the so-called 'New Right'. ('So-called' because what is referred to under that description is neither new nor Right. It would be better known as the Old Centre.) Many family policy issues, it is true, do lie in the borderlands between liberalism and conservatism. When free market thinkers start to talk about the social importance of the family they are immediately confronted with what seems to their assailants as a nice knockdown argument which attempts to pit their liberalism against their conservativism. Michael Stutchbury puts the argument this way (referring to Liberal Party leadership difficulties):

> As fashionable economic dries, the Liberals are supposed to worship laissez faire—individual freedom, diversity and heterogeneous outcomes. This tends to be how markets work best. But, as social conservatives, they are drawn towards prescriptive moralising, curbs on individual behaviour and rigid homogeneous

> outcomes.... Social conservatives tend—sometimes cynically—to exploit 'the family' as some sort of idealised social norm.[8]

If this is a fair description, is there a contradiction here? The argument assumes that to be committed to a free market economic philosophy entails a commitment to free market thinking in all areas of life. But maybe the family is not to be thought of as a kind of market arrangement? Maybe freedom is not the only social good? Perhaps markets work best in one way and families in another. This does not seem too outrageous a claim. Perhaps stability and security are important in private life, and especially in the care and upbringing of children. Families, after all, need to manage children who have not yet acquired the independence of adulthood. If the family is a welfare system, then perhaps it is not a market system. Few, if any, libertarians would deny the need for some social welfare system, though they may prefer it not to be state-run.

Commitment to a family does entail some curbs on individual behaviour, but who would claim that it does not? But then, if family life is not reducible to the pursuit of individual self-interest, perhaps markets are not so different. Markets also require restrictions. A free market philosophy might maintain that people should uphold their private commitments, just as they should honour their promises in the market. On the other hand, families are free to adopt their own ways of doing things in many aspects of life: support for 'the family' does not require prescriptive moralising about how to run a family. Nor is it obvious that families produce 'rigid homogenous outcomes', whatever they might be. As almost everyone grows up in a family it is hard to see how 'the family' might be accused of stifling diversity. Some family policies might be designed to increase the range of choices open to families, and could be seen as libertarian.

Australian society does not dragoon people into starting families; it is very hospitable to the decision not to have children. But most people do choose to form families of their own. To express some support for this decision can hardly be construed as defiantly or daringly conservative. Most Australians favour parliamentary democracy, but it would not be thought remarkable if a politician said he thought their preference a good one. Is democracy an 'idealised social norm'? No doubt democracy is flawed, and so too perhaps is the family, but their popularity and the absence of any remotely credible alternative ensures that they both merit a central place in our society.

Unfortunately, Stutchbury's remarks are typical of the way in which some journalists comment on this subject. It is they, rather than the public, who are the victims of stereotyped thinking; and it would be a pity if sensible family policies had to be delayed until such people managed to struggle free from such self-imposed intellectual limitations. A more serious cause of delay might be the assumption, which Stutchbury makes,

---

8 *Australian Financial Review*, 17 August 1988.

that family policy is somehow the prerogative of what he thinks of as 'the Right'. Suppose it were the case that conservatives had given more thought to family matters than the so-called Left. So what? If a policy is a good one then who cares who brings it in? In a world no longer regimented by the ideologies of the past, Labor should not feel inhibited about borrowing 'conservative' family policies. Contrary to the conventional iconography of this subject, there is no reason at all to regard support for the family as conservative. It is a long-standing part of working class traditions, in Australia and elsewhere. If Labor wishes to regain contact with its traditional constituency, and with its own tradition, it could hardly do better than to start here. But, in any case, no party in Australian politics has given much serious thought to family issues. The field is wide open for anyone with the imagination and initiative to take it up.

The argument of this book will make quite a lot of the ethical importance of family and work. When this sort of notion gets discussed in the press—in connection with Mrs Thatcher's references to 'Victorian values' for instance—the tone of the discussion is usually one of condescension or ridicule. The not-so-veiled implication is that these values are perhaps fit for shopkeepers' daughters, but they bear little relation to the enlightened world of the late twentieth century. Work and family, we are being asked to believe, are merely the totemic cults of the petty bourgeoisie. But are they? Of course they are not, as anyone who stops to think can see. It is a fair bet that few of those who write in this vein could bear to be deprived of their work or of their families for a year or even a month. Most people who face enforced idleness hate it, and few who choose idleness voluntarily make any creative use of it. This is not surprising—it is the way things have always been in most societies. The only exceptions are tribal societies, where commonly the women did almost all the work, and aristocratic societies, where the men cultivated a military ethic. Neither is a very attractive alternative.

Such attitudes ought to have no place in left-wing thinking. No social movement has emphasised the importance of work more than has socialism—it even claims to derive all value from labour. The socialist tradition has had much less to say about love and family life than about work and production, but it has not neglected them altogether. Engels' anger at what he saw as the forced disintegration of working class family life in the Manchester slums in 1844 fed into the *Communist Manifesto*. And, at another level, the young Marx aspired to assess all human relations by the criterion of how well they compare with the natural relationship between man and woman.

> The immediate, natural and necessary relationship of human being to human being is the relation of man to woman.... From this relationship one can, therefore, judge man's whole level of development.[9]

9 'Private Property and Communism', 154.

How much can be read into this cryptic but suggestive section of the *Early Writings* is difficult to say because the thought in them is not expanded or followed through elsewhere, but it can hardly be insignificant that it immediately precedes his first full high-flown description of 'Communism' as 'the genuine resolution of the conflict between man and nature and between man and man, the true resolution of the strife between existence and essence, between objectification and self-affirmation, between freedom and necessity, between the individual and the species'.[10] If Marx thought that all of this is encapsulated or foreshadowed in the natural relation between men and women then he rated the importance of that relation, and presumably also of marriage and family life, very highly indeed.

It is interesting to turn from Marx to another patron saint of twentieth century thought, Sigmund Freud. Erik Erikson tells us that

> Freud was once asked what he thought a normal person should be able to do well. The questioner probably expected a complicated answer. But Freud, in the curt way of his old days, is reported to have said: 'Lieben und arbeiten' (to love and to work).[11]

If Freud is right, the capacity to love and the capacity to work are the basic elements of sanity. Freud was thinking of individual sanity but there is no reason why the same test might not be applied to measuring the sanity of a society, just as Marx also argued from the relation between individual men and women to wider social relations. One need not be a great admirer of Freud or Marx in any other respect to see that their judgements are not to be lightly dismissed.

However, yet another 'eminent Victorian', one more unreservedly deserving of our admiration, is worth hearing on these questions.

> You cannot bring about prosperity by discouraging thrift. You cannot strengthen the weak by weakening the strong. You cannot help the wage-earner by pulling down the wage-payer. You cannot further the brotherhood of man by encouraging class-hatred. You cannot keep out of trouble by spending more than you earn. You cannot build character and courage by taking away a man's initiative and independence. You cannot help men permanently by doing for them what they could do for themselves.[12]

The speaker is Abraham Lincoln. Lincoln's attitude to family matters is aptly symbolised by the occasion when, during the deliberations of the Civil War, his young sons interrupted a Cabinet meeting by opening mock fire upon the officials with a toy cannon, and Lincoln as Commander-in-Chief of the Army and Navy had to restore peace. A good deal of his greatness lay in his refusal to allow politics and public life to take itself too seriously or to interfere with his domestic and family affections.

---

10 *Ibid.*, 155.

11 Erikson, *Childhood and Society*, 229.

12 Quoted in Conway, *The End of Stupor?*, 144.

Lincoln, Freud and even Marx, it appears, did not share the now common disdain for 'Victorian values'. (The term is itself a misnomer, since the values are not exclusively Victorian, nor were they particularly well exemplified by the Victorians.) We need not contend that these values were universally esteemed until recent times—we know too little about intellectual attitudes to the family, in particular, for confident generalisations. All that is being claimed is that blanket presumptions against family and work are alien to our main traditions. The sentiments expressed by Lincoln, Freud and Marx may be platitudes but they are platitudes which have now been the subject of strenuous efforts aimed at their refutation. It may be that they have now stood the test of time better than their negations. We do not need to accept them in their finest details to allow that in general they manifest a better grasp of the large questions of social policy than do those negations. Indeed, it is very difficult to imagine a society in which the values of work and love, of creation and procreation, are not central for most of the population. They are the values which the great majority of Australian people—whether 'working' or 'middle' class—practise and affirm.

Any defence of the importance of the family in personal and social life is, tediously, guaranteed to produce the accusation that the defence is nothing more than nostalgia for some past time, usually thought of as the 1950s. This objection is itself a device for avoiding real debate. It reduces discussion to the level of mere imagery and style, as if social policy decisions are tantamount to the judging of a fashion parade. This stratagem is characteristic of the 'New Class', a category whose members might be defined by their distaste for 'capitalism' and 'the family', a legacy from the radicalism of the 1960s and 70s.

Sometimes the 'nostalgia' objection is fleshed out with details of all that was wrong with life in the 1950s—the conformism, the anti-intellectualism, the xenophobia, the sex role stereotypes, the backbreaking drudgery performed by women in the home. This version of the argument seems to invite a response in kind, as if defenders of the family must show that these complaints are invalid. It is tempting to return the compliment: Is not the New Class itself conformist (in a fashion-conscious way), anti-intellectual (style substitutes for argument), xenophobic (it seems actively to dislike anything 'Anglo'), stereotyped (women must on no account be seen to be doing anything domestic), and in favour of drudgery (the 'Feminist Mystique' requires women to prove themselves in the workforce at whatever cost to their private lives)? Mirror images of ugly objects are not themselves usually very attractive.

But it is better to decline this gambit altogether. The objection is simply irrelevant. There is no necessary connection between a belief in the importance of family life and any of the things complained of above. Les Murray captured the flavour of 'New Class' politics in a 1976 essay which is still remarkably apt. Murray's remarks are worth quoting in full:

> The new class is the natural upper class of a socialist world order, and has come into existence as it were in anticipation of that order. In it, tertiary education plays a part analogous to that played by land ownership in past ascendencies: it is a central but not an entirely exclusive organizing principle. Just as a university degree or some ability in the general field of letters or the higher fornication could gain one a place in the English gentry of two centuries ago, a certain radical style can get one into the new class now. Style, in fact, is probably the broadest common denominator of the new ascendancy, and one of its most important cohesive principles. Another feature that is diagnostic for the whole class, above and beyond all of its apparent divisions, is its tendency to see all opposition to it as being right-wing, and to use fashion as a weapon of defence and attack.[13]

Murray added that 'The new ascendancy has, if we want to be dramatic about it, captured most of education, much of the arts, and much of fashion in Australia'; and he predicted that it would 'get into the corridors of power again', though perhaps not under the aegis of Labor. Its survival skills, according to Murray, involve 'a powerful psychological safeguard built into its belief system, the image of itself as a valiant, downtrodden band bearing aloft the torch of enlightenment against all oppression'. Murray thinks that 'We have reached the age of privileged, often subsidized martyrs'.[14]

The 'New Class' phenomenon Murray describes is familiar enough, not least in the world of welfare policy and practice, and his speculations about it are interesting; but the notion is perhaps unlikely to figure strongly in any would-be scientific sociology. As a device in argument the concept is as obviously ad hominem as the comparable usage of the term 'the right' about which Murray properly complains. What is needed most in discussions of 'the politics of the family' is a refusal to use fashion and style as weapons of defence and attack. Sociological aesthetics is no basis for social policy.

The remainder of this book will endeavour to concentrate on matters of substance. In this chapter three main claims have been made. One, that families are social units possessing a degree of autonomy, which governments should respect. Two, that families with dependent children are not well able to compete for the spoils of big governments, and they tend to fall behind in periods of intense interest group competition. Three, that there is nothing in the mainstream Australian traditions ('Left' or 'Right') to warrant the now-common suspicion of families or to warrant the neglect of family interests which—it will be argued—is now built into the Australian social system. But before pursuing the question of family interests, we need to examine the fortunes of the other major welfare institution, the welfare state.

---

13 *The Peasant Mandarin*, 148.
14 *Ibid.* 149.

2 Welfarism

The purposes of welfare

The Welfare State is an attractive notion. Here, it seems, is the ultimate ideal—the most powerful of all social agencies harnessed to the most beneficent of all possible aims. At last we have created a society which functions as a true community, caring for the weak, the old and the poor, and at the same time considerate of the interests of all. Indeed, the state now seems like one big happy family, the family at its best, warm, accepting, generous and kind. Better than a family even, because it transcends the family, overcoming the pettiness, the privacy and the emotionalism of family life. The Welfare State is the family writ large, but writ according to impartial and publicly-ascertainable rules. It provides something for everyone, at little or no obvious cost.

And yet there is no doubt that the Welfare State is beginning to lose some of its appeal. In Britain and the United States debate has raged back and forth for a decade now about the merits of welfare systems. In Australia, it is true, we are more circumspect: little work has been done from a sceptical viewpoint, and most criticism is dismissed on moralistic grounds, as if suspicion about such a noble enterprise could only derive from base motives. Yet even democracy, the best of our social achievements, is only the least bad form of government. Defences of the Welfare State should be aimed at showing it to be not the best of all possible societies, but the least bad of all possible arrangements. That way we might be able to get a clear idea of its weaknesses, and perhaps learn to adapt to them. Analysis of the Welfare State must aim to show not merely that it has good intentions, nor that it partly achieves good ends; it must also consider its failings, and weigh them up against other ways of achieving the same ends.

One of the most striking features of the Welfare State (and perhaps of any state) is that it has a real talent for disguising its costs and failings. When, for instance, a major review of the social security system is announced by government, and dozens of capable researchers are assigned the task of analysing the system from every possible angle, somehow we can know in advance that no major criticisms of the status quo will emerge in the final deliberations, nor will basic doubts be lavishly entertained and vigorously argued along the way. The federal government's Social Security Review (now in its fourth year of deliberations) will cost the Australian taxpayer something over $15 million, but it will not reach any incisive or decisive conclusions. At most, we know, such a review will recommend that the system remain the same, only more so. The underlying principle is Colonel Blimp's 'Gad, Sir, reforms are all right as long as they don't change anything'. Such caution is not necessarily a bad thing, nor is it done through any ill-intent. It may be a side-effect of the way welfare systems are structured: the attempt by welfare systems to do two things at once, to save the poor and weak and to insure the fit and strong, makes it practically impossible to discover how well it is managing to do either. What is clear is that sceptical analyses of welfare realities will have to come from outside the system. Such analyses will necessarily lack the statistical wealth and research resources of government-sponsored work. What they can do is focus attention on the central question: is the welfare system really helping the disadvantaged? To answer that question we need to grasp the complexities of the wide-ranging international debate about welfare, and attempt to measure Australia's welfare achievements and failings in the light of those arguments.

There are perhaps two main views about the development of the Australian welfare system. Commentators sometimes contend that the system has changed very little since the main categories of pensions and benefits—child endowment, unemployment and sickness benefits, pensions for widows and deserted wives, and automatic cost-of-living adjustments to age and invalid pensions—were laid down in the mid-1940s. The history of Australian welfare written from this perspective would see it as running parallel to the British welfare state. This viewpoint tends to hold that the rapid growth in welfare expenditure in the early 1970s was the product of demographic and economic changes. It will concede that payment levels for unemployment benefits also grew rapidly in that period, and that a new category, the supporting parents benefit, was created at that time; but it will see these as responses to social causes rather than causes themselves of social change. The Australian welfare system also tended not to follow the more complete commitment to universalism of Britain and the European social democracies—in that respect we have been closer to the minimalist tradition of the United States. Henry J. Aaron's summary of the Australian income support system seems a fair one. He regards it as a hybrid between a universal benefits system and a system which regards the state as a repairman or an agent-of-last-resort 'called upon to act only if all voluntary or private measures have failed'. The Australian system follows the repairman model in that payments are flat and income tested. But, he adds, 'some benefits under some programs (age pensions, for example) are high enough so that most people eligible on non-economic criteria also qualify on economic grounds. Other programs (unemployment benefit and supporting parents benefit, for example) have some features that are quite generous, at least by US standards'.[1]

An alternative view would look at the past two decades in Australian welfare history as running parallel to the American experience when Americans set out to overthrow their traditional minimalism. It could be argued that since the 1972 election of the Whitlam government Australia has attempted its own 'War on Poverty' similar to that launched by Presidents Kennedy and Johnson. The scale is very different but the aims and ethos have been comparable. The general expenditure picture—counting education as a form of welfare expenditure—is summarised by Butlin, Barnard and Pincus as follows: 'The share of all governments' outlays devoted to welfare (excluding housing and grants for private capital purposes) rose from an average of a quarter in the second half of the 1930s to a third during the 1960s and a half in the 1970s'.[2] Between 1966 and 1986 government spending on welfare and social security (not counting education) rose from 3.5 per cent to 7.5 per cent of gross domestic product.[3] It is this rapid rise which is in question here, and which might be thought of as constituting Australia's 'War on Poverty'. Some of the optimism and idealism of the American effort surrounded the Henderson Poverty Commission. The underlying belief that poverty could be eradicated by generous social support was the same. There has been a similar interest in guaranteed minimum income schemes. State welfare bureaucracies also grew rapidly.

The crucial difference, of course, is that the ten-year time gap between the American and Australian examples meant that the stagflation of the mid-1970s hit our effort before it could get off the ground. It is an important fact about the Australian welfare effort that its most rapid growth has coincided with a period of economic slowdown. Unemployment benefit payment levels increased rapidly just as unemployment rates rose. (Similarly, benefits for single parents were expanded just as divorce was made easier.) This may not seem surprising because hard times make for increased welfare needs. But welfare spending need not correlate with economic decline. It may grow out of prosperity. To discover what might have happened here had we enjoyed the prosperity to carry through a US-style anti-poverty campaign we would need to look at the American experience

1 Henry J. Aaron, 'Social Welfare in Australia', 384.
2 Butlin *et al.*, *Government and Capitalism*, 194.
3 See EPAC Council Paper 35, Chart 2.1.

between 1965 and 1975. The American welfare debate has centred on the question whether, controlling for changes in general economic conditions, working-aged poverty has increased or decreased with increases in welfare expenditure. Many have now concluded that, paradoxically, welfare expenditure increases have caused an increase in poverty. Understanding how this result might be possible is now a major focus of thought about welfare systems, and forms the central question for what will be called in the next chapter 'welfare scepticism'.

Many in the welfare industry now think that the economic slowdown and consequent cutbacks have been the principal reasons why we do not seem to be making much headway against poverty in Australia. But whether these are the reasons is very debatable. Popular wisdom on this matter tends to disagree with the welfare consensus: it is commonly thought that welfare assistance is as much part of the problem as it is part of the solution. It may be that the assumptions and methods upon which our welfare efforts are based are as much at fault as the general state of the economy, particularly the assumption that more is better. In any case, as the Social Security Review demonstrates, it can hardly be said that the welfare industry is alive with new ideas and approaches to this ancient problem. And this is surprising because there are many ways of viewing the phenomenon of poverty. This survey of the welfare debate will try to sketch some of them. To do so will require us to go beyond the narrow horizons of conventional welfare discussion.

Loss of faith in state welfare is far from universal, and there are varying degrees of support for the different elements of the system. Before we can be more particular here we need a rough taxonomy of welfare structure and aims. The first and most obvious distinction to be drawn is between government welfare transfers and government welfare services. The transfer system has three main functions: poverty alleviation, social insurance and 'horizontal equity'. The first two concepts correspond very roughly to the contrast sometimes made between 'welfare' and 'social security', with the former including unemployment and sickness benefits and the latter old age and widows pensions. There is no ultimate distinction between transfers and services. The difference has to do with the manner of funding and the degree of choice allowed to the consumer. Exactly the same questions about aims and justice arise for welfare service funding criteria as arise for welfare transfers. State welfare services are especially vulnerable to the theory of government failure. Both are susceptible to interest group analysis.

Poverty alleviation is often referred to as 'vertical equity', equity between the relatively well-off and the relatively poor. Exactly what 'equity' means and whether it is being correctly used in this context is rarely discussed. The standard assumption is that equity requires that the distribution of social goods be in some proportion to needs. Needs are usually taken to be a function of income and wealth per person dependent on those resources. This test, very deliberately, takes no account of how that poverty was caused, but the question of causation is ethically important. Poverty can be chosen—for religious or ideological reasons, for instance—or it can be assumed as a means of living off others, or it can be simulated. Whether poverty alleviation is to be defended on grounds of justice or equity for the victims of society or is to be seen as an act of compassion and humanity permits of no single answer because the nature of the poverty depends in part on its origins. 'Equalisation' is a less morally loaded and question-begging term than 'equity', and from here on it will be used in preference to 'equity' except when the stricter moral implications of 'equity' are intended.

That welfare spending serves an insurance function is sometimes denied on the grounds that most or many recipients take more out of the system in benefits and pensions than they put in in taxes. Whether this is so is not easy to determine in a system where welfare monies come out of consolidated revenue and not out of individual accounts or ear-marked budgets. Australia is unusual in having no ear-marked welfare spending (the Medicare levy is the closest we come to this). Yet it seems hard to deny that our old age pensions are analogous to compulsory government-administered retirement insurance. It might be objected that our pension system is not sufficiently like a genuine insurance scheme, or that we should move towards compulsory private insurance. But these objections make sense because the present system is sufficiently similar for such comparisons to take hold.

Some of the contingencies against which we use the state as an insurance agency are relatively predictable, such as old age. Others, such as disability, are not. Both the risk of disability and the chances of reaching old age are fairly evenly spread across the community (although women live longer than men). Whether unemployment benefits can be seen as a form of income insurance is more doubtful, since the threat of unemployment is spread unevenly across the workforce. Unemployment benefits are more like a transfer to the vulnerable. Whether we could move towards a private system of unemployment insurance depends upon whether it is reasonable to expect the high risk group to bear the cost of self-provision. More generally, while the insurance function of state welfare systems might be replaced by (perhaps compulsory) self-provision through the private sector, it is more difficult to see how poverty alleviation can be handled privately. To what extent these two functions can be disentangled is a matter which requires careful thought and analysis.

'Horizontal equity', which is also sometimes listed as one of the goals of a welfare system, is a notion even more resistant to easy definition than vertical equity. The basic idea is that social policy ought to treat like cases alike. The usual application of this notion is to taxation, where it is said to be 'horizontally' inequitable for some taxpayers to be able to spread their taxable income across their dependants while others with the same gross income and family responsibilities are unable to do so. By extension the notion has been applied to justifying any policies which take account of the number of dependants affected by it. While 'equity' can be correctly used in the taxation context, in the extended sense of the word it is preferable to use 'equalisation', for the same reasons as applied to the vertical concept.

All three welfare aims are in some way relative to the whole pattern of a person's life. Poverty and need can be short-lived, or they can be chronic and inter-generational. Assessments of need, in the course of assessing the urgency of need, must choose the time-span over which need will be measured. Responsibilities for dependent children are a temporary phase for most of us. Because of this, horizontal equalisation becomes in effect a cross between vertical equalisation and an income insurance scheme. Horizontal equalisation equalises income across the life-cycle, making us more self-supporting in those periods when our income would be inadequate to our family needs. In a sense, then, horizontal equalisation is a compromise between poverty alleviation and insurance. It is the latter two which seem to be the basic functions of welfare systems.

Although most matters in this field are controversial, there is general agreement that the most urgent and most perplexing poverty issues today concern children and families. The primary emphasis of this book will be on 'thc family in the welfare state', taking that phrase to refer to families with children. However, issues of old age and the extended family network may also come under that description. For the most part, as an issue in welfare policy old age is regarded as a matter for a 'social insurance' approach, whereas issues to do with children and their parents fall under the headings of 'poverty alleviation' and—as this book will emphasise—'horizontal equity'. Old age can then be treated as a separate matter, and will be discussed in Chapter Eleven. The remainder of the book, and the remainder of this discussion of the wider welfare debate, will mainly concern dependent children and their parents.

'Poverty'

Welfare spending, however much it has grown in the past two decades, is still only one segment of total government expenditure, and the taxes collected to pay for it are still only one part of total revenue collection. It is generally accepted that welfare spending has to be viewed within the whole framework of government taxing and spending. Thinking along these lines suggests the conclusion that the purposes of welfare spending reflect the general purposes of government taxing and spending.

The main purpose of government is the provision of public goods, goods which individuals cannot supply by and for themselves, goods which can be had only by communal effort. Defence and foreign relations, public order, a system of justice, and many but not all public works (altogether about 40 per cent of all government outlays) are taken to fall into this category. Using government taxing and spending as a form of social insurance—as distinct from a form of redistribution—is, rightly or wrongly, to treat that insurance as a kind of public good, even though to some extent the benefits could be provided by individuals for themselves.

Most of us accept that government has some role to play in redistributing income from the relatively rich to the relatively poor, and we support welfare transfers, government services and progressive taxation on the grounds that they are structured so as to tend towards achieving that end. Welfare spending to alleviate poverty serves as the most direct application of this principle. So too does spending on education, health, housing and employment. Together social security, education, health, housing and employment outlays constitute more than half of all government expenditure. If the principle that personal income taxation (PIT) should be progressive is controversial, the argument is mostly about the degree of progression appropriate and about the counter-productive effects of high marginal tax rates on personal income. As a matter of fact, the total Australian tax system (as distinct from PIT) is proportional, not progressive—a point which will be elaborated upon in Chapter Six. However, because most government services and welfare payments are allocated 'progressively' so that they favour the poor, the lack of progressiveness in the total tax system does not defeat the poverty alleviation objective.

Until recently, little was known about the degree to which public policy succeeded in redistributing income from rich to poor. This deficiency has now been corrected (so far as such complex questions can ever be resolved) by the work of the Australian Bureau of Statistics in conducting Australia's first ever fiscal incidence study, published in 1987 under the title *The Effects of Government Benefits and Taxes on Household Income*.[4] This study enables us to measure with some degree of confidence the net effect of government on material well-being, and to compare its impact on different segments of society. It is based on a variety of sources: an analysis of the 1984 Household Expenditure Survey which covered 10,000 households; estimates of direct and indirect taxation paid by those households; and ABS public finance data covering the consolidated outlays of all three levels of government (federal, state and local) in the four main social expenditure areas: education, health, housing and social security and welfare. The study excludes outlays and revenues which cannot be allocated to individual households, such as those from defence, law and order, company tax, and the operations of public trading enterprises.

The most important results for our purposes are shown in Figure 2.1. It appears that a substantial redistribution of income takes place through the Australian tax and welfare system. All household income deciles (tenths of the population) get roughly equal benefits from government, with most

4 ABS Cat. 6537.0. For some general cautionary comments on statistics of this sort see Piggott, 'Statistical Incidence Studies: An Economic Perspective'.

going to the second and third deciles; but the cost of these benefits is borne roughly in proportion to income rather than in proportion to apparent need.

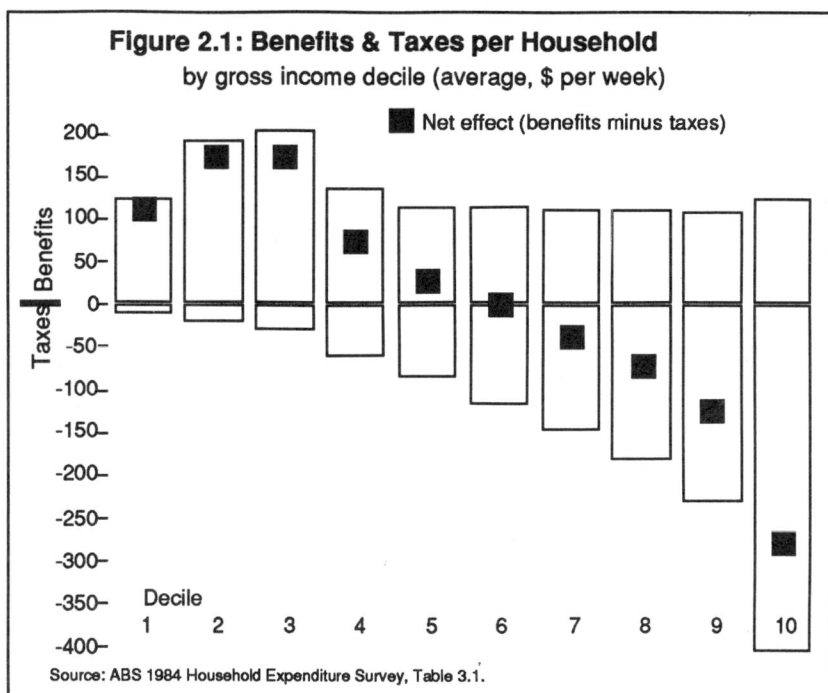

Figure 2.1: Benefits & Taxes per Household

by gross income decile (average, $ per week)

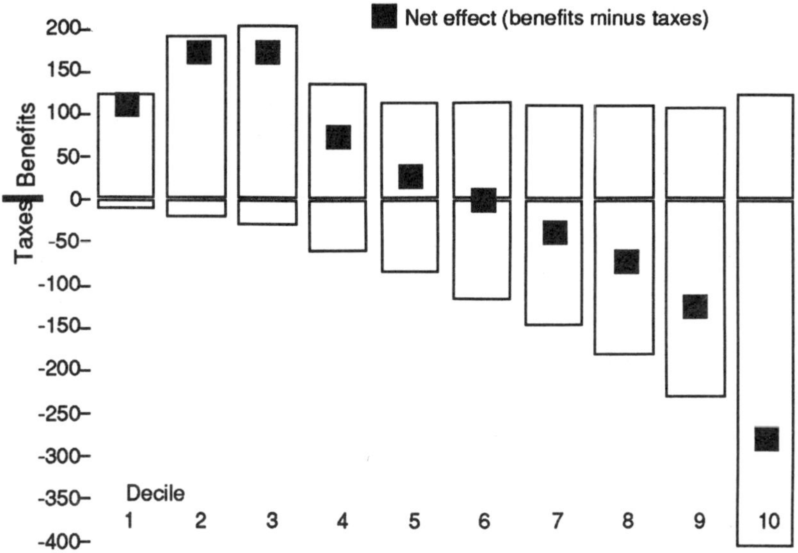

Source: ABS 1984 Household Expenditure Survey, Table 3.1.

This, however, is not the whole story. In a broader perspective it is not too much to say that 'the Australian social welfare system is pervasive throughout the Australian economy'. This observation is made by P.P. McGuinness, who adds that 'social welfare is the sole justification for the enormous network of regulations in Australia. They are always defended because of their impact on social welfare and their presumed redistributive effect in favour of the poor'. McGuinness lists tariffs, farm product stabilisation, minimum wages, interest rate controls, housing for the poor, free education, various fringe benefits and concessions for pensioners, and publicly subsidised child care as instances of such quasi-welfare expenditures and regulation. As McGuinness points out, economists tend to argue that such intervention and regulation very often favour the relatively well-off rather than the poor.[5] The economic effects of some of these forms of regulation are not likely to be captured well by the ABS study.

The primary purpose of redistribution and welfare spending is to prevent or at least alleviate poverty. But to do this with any confidence we

5 P.P. McGuinness, in *Conference Discussion Relating to the Paper 'Social Welfare in Australia'*, 60.

need some account of what poverty is and some understanding of what causes it. This first problem, the definition of 'poverty', is very much more vexed than is commonly realised.

What is poverty? Consider a variety of possible candidates for the description:

- students living away from home with no family assistance, but with good job prospects in a year or two;
- unemployed teenagers living at home, receiving the dole and help from their families, paying no rent;
- a farmer in a bad year, with no income at all but with perhaps $1,000,000 worth of assets;
- a family of newly arrived migrants, from a country in which their income was lower than Australian minimum wages, prepared to work long hours at low wages in their new home;
- Aborigines on a reserve outside a country town, some chronically alcoholic, others willing to do some seasonal work but often living off unemployment benefits for long periods of time;
- a large, lower-working-class family, relatively happy and stable, with the father in continuous but low-paid work;
- old age pensioners, with low incomes but with a modest, fully paid-for suburban house;
- a depressed, bored fifty-five year old single man who gave up his job to go on unemployment benefits, who has saved nothing, and who rents a room in an inner-city boarding house;
- a childless couple buying and running a suburban delicatessen, working long hours and clearing little profit, with uncertain future prospects;
- a well-qualified middle-class family man, living for a few months on unemployment benefits while looking for a more attractive job than the one he has just given up;
- a young sickness beneficiary with a dubious case of 'back trouble';
- a young sickness beneficiary with agonising back trouble;
- a businessman bankrupted by injudicious share dealings;
- an angry, disturbed homeless twenty-year-old living in a squat, supplementing the dole with petty theft to pay for his drink and drugs;
- a middle-class single parent with one school-age child living for a number of years on state benefits in low-rent shared accommodation;
- a young couple attempting to live self-sufficiently on a few acres of marginal farm land;
- a school-leaver or a person just reaching retirement age who is in the workforce for only part of any one year;
- any long-term resident of prison, hospital or mental institution.

Which of these persons is poor? According to the dominant definition of the term, in which poverty is simply low income relative to the number of dependants supported by that income, they all are. But very obviously these categories have almost nothing in common apart from their lack of income. Disregard that single characteristic, lump them together, and the result might well be in every other way an ordinary cross-section of the Australian population. They might have as much in common as all left-handed persons or all persons with good singing voices have in common. It would be absurd to devise social policies for left-handed persons. It might be equally absurd to devise comprehensive policies to deal with 'poverty'. At least, any such policies will need to recognise the enormous variety of cases which fall under that description, and to be prepared to differentiate between them.

The notion of poverty conceals other conceptual illusions. In most accounts poverty is defined in relation to average earnings. This seems at first reasonable, until it is realised that on this definition (all other things being equal), the faster the growth of the economy and of average earnings, the faster may be the increase in those defined as being in poverty. Even worse, some definitions tie the notion to average *household* earnings. The problem here is that household earnings rise with women's workforce participation, not just with average weekly individual earnings. In a period in which women's workforce participation has risen steadily the definitional increase of those in poverty must also rise. But the increase is merely definitional. Actual living standards for the lowest ten per cent of the population may well have risen at the same time as these accounts show poverty to be increasing. The effect is that of a hall of mirrors in which the same figure appears larger looked at in one way and smaller viewed in another.

Poverty-line statistics similarly fail to make the distinction between short-term and long-term poverty, a distinction which makes a world of difference. They do not usually include as income the market value of government-provided in-kind assistance and services such as housing, health care or education. By this way of reckoning the matter, people may have all their needs catered for and yet still be counted as poor because they earn no income. The focus on monetary income also means that no account is taken of a person's non-monetary resources—fixed assets, education, qualifications, family support and social status. A person may be income-poor but resource-rich, and it is not at all obvious that a resource-rich person is in need of 'income support'.

Income relativities are of little interest for another equally compelling reason. The fact that one group of incomes is rising faster than another group does not by itself show that it is rising at the expense of the other. The two groups may be quite independent of each other. The arrival of computers, for instance, provides a lucrative opening for a whole class of persons who would not have done so well in a world dominated by conventional literacy and numeracy skills. If the incomes of the middle class are rising faster than those of the poor this may be due to the advantages of such innovations. And the composition of the newly wealthy class may be quite different from that of the old. Good social policy will do what it can to open up these opportunities to the poor; but this can be done only if we are able to identify where these opportunities lie, and this information is not to be acquired from bald income statistics.

If our aim is to minimise and alleviate poverty we need some accompanying theory to account for changes in the 'gap' between rich and poor. Only then can we hope to be able to devise appropriate policies to help the poor. It is these theories which are crucial, and which are so difficult to establish. Suppose the gap is widening. This may just show that excessive wage rises have put more people out of work, or it may show that more people are becoming chronically dependent upon welfare benefits. Suppose it is narrowing. Then—it can be claimed—we can see that free enterprise does tend to raise the relative position of the lowest income groups.[6] These are not conclusions that welfarists are accustomed to draw. But unless we concentrate our efforts on understanding the mechanics of poverty, they are just as good as any other theory.

None of this is to be read as showing that there is no poverty, or at least serious hardship, in Australia. What it does show is that the orthodoxies of welfarism provide us with no credible means of measuring its real extent, though we can at least be sure that it is very much less than the figures commonly produced by welfare advocates. One British assessment of poverty, using not income statistics but a standardised list of household 'necessities' such as a refrigerator, annual holidays and new clothes, seems to show that only 1.5 per cent of the British population is poor.[7] Australia is generally assumed to have less poverty than Britain, but welfarists do not speak of a poverty rate of one per cent.

We may also be led to suspect that poverty is not a one-dimensional function of low incomes, but—as we shall suggest—a complex social and personal phenomenon.

Causation and theory

The question of the causes of poverty is even more contentious than that of its definition. It is, unfortunately, not enough to assume that because poverty is an absence of adequate income it can be cured simply by supplying 'income support'. If we are mistaken about the causes then any intended cure may simply make the problem worse. There are in fact quite a few moderately plausible theories about the causes of poverty, and about

6 It is interesting to note that, among the rapidly growing economies of East Asia, the country with the least government economic and welfare intervention, Taiwan, seems also to be achieving the most equal distribution of the benefits of growth. See e.g. Kasper, *Accelerated Industrial Evolution in East Asia*.

7 This is the average of the third column of Mack & Lansley's figures shown in Saunders & Whiteford, *Measuring Poverty*, Table 2.

the justification of welfare spending, and the conflicts between them cannot be ignored. The most general causes of poverty are no great mystery. Unemployment. Family breakdown. Old age. Chronic illness and disability. Alcoholism. Drug abuse. Laziness. Welfare dependency. Educational deprivation. Cultural demoralisation. Racial and sexual discrimination. Political persecution. Observers will rank these causes differently. Even more difficult is to get some grasp of the interaction between these elements. It may be that there are no valid generalisations in this field. Many people face poverty because of a combination of these factors; many others experience the same conditions and yet manage to overcome them.

Considering the complexity of these possible causes, it is surprising to find so much agreement about basic matters of principle amongst those who shape welfare policy and advocate on behalf of welfare recipients. For convenience this consensus can be designated 'welfarism'. Angered at the existence of poverty in a prosperous society, welfarists conclude that economic growth by itself is no solution to the problem. 'Poverty is not just a personal attribute; it arises out of the organisation of society', as the Henderson Report put it.[8] Others go further and contend that the causes of poverty are not in any way personal: to suggest otherwise is to indulge self-righteously in 'blaming the victim'. Poverty, we are told, is 'structural'; it arises out of the 'social system'.

Unfortunately, the metaphors of 'system' and 'structure' are not very helpful. These terms have been so prevalent but have remained so opaque that it is difficult to avoid the conclusion that welfarism lacks any discussable social and economic analysis. Such analysis as welfarism supplies usually consists of attacks on the greed of other interest groups. However justifiable these criticisms might be, they do not by themselves lead to the desired conclusion that the illicit gains of these other groups ought to be transferred to the welfare budget. (The Henderson Report is an exception to this rule because it rightly took inflation very seriously as a threat to the welfare of the poor. It wanted both greatly expanded welfare spending and controls on inflation. But how these two aims were to be reconciled it did not explain.) While it very probably is true that a society dominated by narrow interest groups is unhealthy for the poor (just as it is unhealthy for families), so far welfarists have not drawn the obvious conclusion that we should move towards a deregulated society in which economic well-being depends more upon effort than on access to government.

For a long time now criticism of the welfare system has been stifled and obstructed by moralistic counter-objections. Welfarists have been able to divert attention from any failings of welfare practice by accusing the critics of meanness and greed. The objections are moralistic rather than genuinely moral because they rely for their effect upon an artificially restricted moral vocabulary. The argument is patently *ad hominem*, but it is not less effective for that. All too often debate in this area sinks to a level where it seems

8 Henderson Report, **1**, 1.

as if welfare supporters need an enemy of this rampaging ogre-like kind—Margaret Thatcher, Ronald Reagan and Malcolm Fraser have all been fitted out for the role, none of them very plausibly—to restore their faith in their own failing solutions. The fact that per capita welfare expenditure has continued to rise seems not to register in their calculations.[9]

Beyond attacking other interest groups, welfarism seems barren. It becomes reduced to seeking solutions to welfare problems from entirely within the framework of the existing welfare system. The universal remedy seems to be bigger welfare budgets, with a few percentage increases in payments here and another few million dollars' worth of services over there. No doubt keeping track of the ever-shifting 'needs' of the community is a necessary exercise, but when 'needs' seems always to increase it becomes difficult to know whether this whole approach is really achieving what it says it aims to achieve. Maybe instead of more welfare we need more thought about the origins of real wealth and well-being. Instead of grimly pursuing the same old one-track solutions we ought to be opening up new lines of thought, new theories and new hypotheses. The orthodox theory of poverty itself suffers from a poverty of theory.[10]

Marxist theory has exercised a strong pull on welfarist thinking, mainly because welfarism lacks any strong or distinctive framework of its own. The welfare state, some have gone on to claim, is only one stage in the long march of the working class towards equality and justice. Society's debt to the poor goes beyond the mere prevention of pauperism or the mere provision of opportunities for self-improvement. The social order itself must be restructured. No real change can be expected until this is done, and indeed welfare assistance may merely delay the onset of genuine advances.

Marxists are divided at this point between those who accept the welfare state as a necessary but temporary expedient and those who see it as a bribe by the rich to prevent the poor from recognising that their real interests lie

9 See Hendrie & Porter, 'The Capture of the Welfare State', 20: 'per capita real expenditures (1986 dollars) on social security have risen from $514 in 1970–71 to $1300 in 1986–87, ... with similar escalations in spending on health and education, in the name of the less advantaged'. Daryl Dixon has shown that under the Fraser Government the number of social security pensioners and welfare beneficiaries rose by almost one million, whereas under the Hawke Government it has fallen by 77,000. He adds that 'In only one of the seven Fraser Government budgets was welfare spending cut in real terms' (*IPA Review*, March–May 1989, 5).

10 This conclusion is not idiosyncratic. The most recent work on the subject, Saunders and Whiteford's *Measuring Poverty*, seems to share this sense of frustration with the existing poverty measurement techniques. They speak of the 'risk of undue obsession' with details, and complain about 'the almost total lack of effort put into developing an alternative' to the Henderson poverty line. They emphasise the weakness of taking money income as a measure of well-being. Their own discussion, like most others, has nothing to say on the causes of poverty. See *ibid.* 34.

in class struggle. The best-known Marxist work on the subject, Ian Gough's *The Political Economy of the Welfare State*, ends with a distinction between those who see the welfare state as 'a socialist island within a capitalist sea' and those who see it as 'a creature of capital, pure and simple, [and] will have nothing to do with extending or defending it'. Gough thinks that the concept of 'human needs' helps to clarify what is positive and what is negative in the welfare state, yet the substance of his book does nothing to justify this claim, and the concept seems impossibly general to perform such a task.

Reading Gough, it soon becomes apparent that this ambivalence is no temporary difficulty but is rooted in an ambivalence towards the state itself which goes back to the initial premisses of Marxism. In Marx the state is at once both an 'epiphenomenon' and an instrument of class domination. It will become the instrument by which the proletariat sets the world to rights, and yet it will wither away as an unnecessary fiction. Marxism has difficulty supplying a coherent account of the welfare state because the welfare state throws its historical scheme into confusion. If we presently live in the bourgeois era—as we must because the means of production are mostly still in private hands—then the state cannot really be aiming to raise the well-being of the working class. But if the welfare state is a foretaste of socialism then it cannot suffer retrenchment and must be carried forward with the march of history towards the future full triumph of socialism.

Marxist optimism about the welfare state is intellectually unsatisfying: it simply asserts something which contradicts Marxist premisses. Marxist pessimism about the welfare state goes further than most welfarists are prepared to go, partly because it seems too cynical (radical libertarians may find it more congenial), and partly because it leaves welfare agencies with no useful role to play. Pursuit of a consistent Marxist theory ends only in intellectual schizophrenia. The difficulty for those who resist Marxist conclusions is to define the causes for which their activities are meant to be the cure. Here welfarism has bogged down. It is no longer adequate to talk abstractly of 'society' or 'the system', yet a class analysis leaves welfare with little role to play.

The Marxist contention that welfare assistance serves the needs of 'capitalist society' is not wholly mistaken. Our form of capitalism is democratic capitalism, and it may be that welfare provision has a special role to play in a democratic society. A democracy which allowed some of its members to degenerate to the point that they became incapable of playing their part as competent citizens would to that extent be failing as a democracy. Citizenship requires, at the very least, basic literacy; to be uneducated in a modern society is to be disenfranchised. It was Aristotle who first observed, in his *Politics*, that in a democracy it 'is in the interests of all classes, including the prosperous themselves' that 'measures should be taken to ensure a permanent level of prosperity'. Far from being a devious and sinister form of exploitation by the ruling classes, as it sometimes is made to appear, this is a feature of our society which should be welcomed and supported. The real difficulty is in how to achieve it, not whether to try to achieve it.

There are two other voices to be added to the welfarist consensus, those of the feminist and the Christian. It is increasingly being recognised that women bear the burden of poverty more acutely than do men. Perhaps it should be added that women increasingly bear this burden more than men, for the evidence suggests that the proportion of women in poverty is larger than it was in the past. There are a number of partial explanations of why this is occurring. Bettina Cass has listed these as: 'women's discontinuous workforce participation, lower rates of full-year, full-time employment, lower pay when in work, responsibility for child care and the ideology of women's dependency on a male income earner'.[11] A strictly feminist account would want to reduce the first four factors here to functions of the fifth. Cass omits to mention one other obvious factor, divorce and family breakdown.

Usually, however, feminist accounts of the causes of poverty are not sharply distinguished from the more general welfarist position, and it is as difficult to discover any distinctively feminist social theory as it is to discover any distinctive welfarist theory. Feminism, like welfarism, has tended to rely on other theories such as socialism to provide it with an account of the causes of women's economic vulnerability. But, as some feminists have noted, it is not at all obvious why male socialists should be friendlier to women's interests than any other group of men.

Many who enter the welfare field do so from motives of Christian charity and compassion. They may see welfare work as a practical extension of the commands of the gospels. In this they stand in a long and continuous historical tradition. The Churches have always been the main source of voluntary welfare workers in Western society, and they still are today. (Even the term 'the welfare state' seems to have been coined by Archbishop William Temple.) However, whether there is a distinctively Christian view of poverty and society is very doubtful. 'Blessed are the poor'. 'The poor will be with you always'. 'Consider the lilies of the field'. 'If any will not work, neither shall he eat'. Christian origins and tradition are in this matter, as in much else, fairly complex. Nevertheless, in recent years most Christian discussion has been from a welfarist viewpoint. If the poor are 'blessed', as the Beatitudes insist, then blaming them for their sufferings will seem at once both uncaring and un-Christian. (Few Christian spokesmen seem to ask whether the decline in Christian belief and affiliation might not be an important cause of social disarray and deprivation, though this hypothesis is not obviously more implausible than any other.) The New Testament ethic on poverty is matched by an equally categorical position on divorce. Considering the demonstrable connections between poverty and family instability it may be apposite for the churches

11 Comments in *Targetting Welfare Expenditure on the Poor*, 4.

to consider whether there are internal connections between these two ethical imperatives. Liberal church leaders tend to emphasise one, evangelicals the other, and both seem smaller than the original.

What Christianity might also contribute to welfare discussion is some understanding of the nature of compassion, upon which Christian faith is founded. Compassion is easy to feel but difficult to practise, and not just because it involves self-sacrifice: it may be misplaced, and its misplacement may be destructive. It is also subject to the 'small is beautiful' principle. Institutionalised compassion is necessarily depersonalised compassion, and may not count as compassion at all. In many of life's crises what is needed is not money but the patient care even of someone who is otherwise a stranger. In the past Christians have understood these matters and specialised in their practice; but to the extent that they now turn to 'social justice' as their central tenet they cease to contribute what once made them a distinctive presence in society.

Need and equality

If welfarism is not illuminated by its intellectual allies, Marxism, feminism or Christianity, what content can we give to the notion? Two deep-seated moral convictions hold welfarism together. One is the belief that under no circumstances must commentary on welfare matters engage in 'blaming the victim'. This view is often asserted but rarely examined or discussed. The phrase 'blaming the victim' derives some of its power from the fact that it comes close to being tautological. If a person really is a victim of society then of course it would be reprehensible to blame them for their situation. The difficulty is to know whether they are or are not to be thought of as a victim. The fact that they are at the bottom of the social pile is no proof that they are the victims of those above them. The causes may lie in their own actions, or there may be no particular causes. Any society which does not enforce perfect equality will have some 'above' and some 'below'.

The second binding assumption of welfarism is a belief in the moral importance of equality. Welfare politics is dominated partly by the notion of rights, but even more by the notion of equality. A great deal of comment and research on poverty in Australia is preoccupied with the question of whether incomes and wealth are or are not becoming more equal. But the question of equality is, by itself, of little interest. There is no good argument to show that equality is by itself morally desirable. Sometimes it is desirable, as in equality before the law; at other times it is not, as in the awarding of prizes after a race. If equality were intrinsically desirable then it would be impossible to account for those cases in which clearly it is undesirable.

Rights, including welfare rights, if they exist at all and if they are to be more than just assertions of wishes, must be based on some deeper and more useful moral criterion. So also must the notion of the public interest, if it is to be distinguished from the multitude of special interests masquerading as public. So too must the notion of equality, if we are to determine which forms of equality are desirable. That criterion is justice. This is a conclusion which welfare advocates might happily accept, for many of them feel that welfare systems are aimed at providing 'not charity but justice', but this assumption is very doubtful. The beauty of the concept of justice is that it ties together two apparently disparate notions: needs and deserts.[12]

We commonly assume that justice is about needs. At the back of our minds we perhaps have the slogan 'From each according to his abilities, to each according to his needs'. Unfortunately, applying this principle by itself would devastate the living standards of the Australian poor in very quick time. Our planet contains perhaps a billion inhabitants whose needs are, by any objective measure, very much more urgent than those of the poorest of the Australian poor. If justice is about needs then their needs come first. Very few of us believe that they do come first, and even fewer of us put that belief into practice. Perhaps the world's poor should take precedence. But, at least, we cannot justify anything like our present preference for helping our fellow countrymen first on the simple ground that justice requires us to help the needy.

What is it that creates obligations to our fellow Australians stronger than those to starving Sudanese or homeless Bangladeshis? Is welfarism just a species of moral parochialism? The fact that Sudan and Bangladesh are relatively remote is irrelevant: there are many destitute in Indonesia and New Guinea to whom we feel very little national sense of obligation. The only possible answer seems to be that those who benefit from the Australian welfare system would, if they could, willingly contribute to the well-being of other Australians. If an unemployed or disabled Australian suddenly came into a fortune he might expect to pay out a large part of the windfall in tax. If Sudan suddenly became rich in oil or gold it would not be expected to do more than pay off any debts it may have to those countries who previously gave it assistance. It is of course morally plausible and logically consistent to argue that we should seek to eliminate world poverty before we worry about the considerably lesser hardships of Australian citizens, but that line of argument will not be pursued here.

Welfare entitlements within the Australian system, if they have any moral foundation, must rest on the recipient's willingness to become a

---

12 In *Giving Desert Its Due*, Wojciech Sadurski provides a full-scale defence of a needs-and-desert account of justice (one quite independent of the partly *ad hominem* argument to be offered below). For a well-argued attempt to rehabilitate the notion of rights (partly against the kind of arbitrariness which fails to distinguish between wants and rights) by tying rights to social roles, see Ewin's *Liberty, Community and Justice*. (Both Ewin and Sadurski are Australian philosophers.)

welfare contributor. Needs should be regarded as deserving of recognition only when the person in need has shown himself willing but unable to be self-supporting. We presume that net beneficiaries are willing but not able to be net benefactors. It is for this reason that the question of why someone is unable to contribute is morally sensitive. A claim upon the system of benefits requires a demonstration of willingness to contribute as well as a demonstration of need. A person may be unable to contribute because he (or she) is disabled, though many disabled can undertake some kinds of work. He may be unable temporarily to find work, though many unemployed could contribute to community projects or voluntary welfare activities of the kind promoted by 'workfare' programs.

Justice, then, involves effort, or at least willingness to contribute. Need alone may supply a reason for being generous, but it alone does not establish entitlement to benefit. The distinction between the deserving and the undeserving poor, which welfarists have so often regarded as obnoxious, is inescapable if we are to regard welfare as a matter of justice and not as a matter of charity, which they also regard as unacceptable.

Nor can welfarism fall back comfortably upon the claim that its purpose is to equalise incomes. Exactly the same objection to needs-based policies applies to equalisation strategies. The most conceptually-articulated discussion of equality in Australian welfare writing is that to be found in Alan Jordan's contribution to the Social Security Review, *The Common Treasury: The Distribution of Income to Families and Households*. Jordan himself prefers to start from the egalitarian proposition that 'none of us owns, as of prior right, that whose possession denies others the possibility of as good a life'.[13] Positively, Jordan's egalitarianism amounts to

> a feeling of solidarity based on each person's rational belief that on balance his life is as good, and worth as much, as other people's, that any dissatisfaction is either within his power to overcome or results from accidents that can happen to anybody and not from unfair treatment, and that he can enter into transactions with others not as a supplicant but as one who asks for no more than he can give.[14]

But (following Ronald Dworkin) he is prepared to subject this preference for equality to an 'envy test' to ensure that differences in ambition and different tastes for leisure are taken into account. From this it follows (as he notes) that inequalities of income 'do not necessarily represent or correspond to inequalities in a more basic sense'. He also recognises that 'many of the relevant inequalities [that egalitarians wish to minimise] originate or can be redressed only outside the actual and proper domain of public policy'.[15] The obligations of public policy are to ensure equal access to education, equal access to careers and to a minimum income, conceived

---

13 Jordan, *The Common Treasury*, **2**, 203.
14 *Ibid.* 206.
15 *Ibid.* 206, 204. See also Dworkin, 'What is Equality?'.

as a form of collective insurance policy against the contingencies of talent and fortune.

All this is arguably fairly close to the institutional arrangements that we presently have. Jordan allows that

> We may, like Pareto, argue that historically the condition of the poor has been improved by economic growth rather than the redistribution of existing wealth and therefore that the best distribution [of incomes] is whichever maximises work incentives, capital accumulation and so on, or argue that the important value is not equality but equity and therefore that a fair distribution is whatever results from fair rules of allocation.[16]

These would not be egalitarian positions, though he offers no reason for thinking of them as less plausible than egalitarianism, and there is considerable overlap between their practical implications. What Jordan's position—like other forms of egalitarianism—lacks is any reason for restricting an equalisation program to Australians alone. And related to that, he has no account of the obligations entailed by membership of a mutually-supportive society. Jordan quotes Dworkin's judgement that a person can demonstrate need 'by attempts to find employment that have failed, or by evidence of less than average general physical and mental abilities, and so forth'.[17] The vagueness of these criteria hardly does justice to the importance of the issue. It makes a very large difference whether or not the benefits of society's support systems are available irrespective of effort and willingness to contribute. Someone who holds that 'a fair distribution is whatever results from fair rules of allocation' can argue that society need only supply the opportunity for self-sufficiency. Egalitarians who want to go beyond equality of opportunity seem committed to the implausible view that society must assist a person regardless of his willingness to support himself.

Showing that 'equality' is by no means synonymous with 'equity' does not by itself show that we should not pursue social policies which tend in some degree to equalise the well-being of persons who would otherwise be markedly unequal. What it does show is that the pursuit of equality is not a goal binding upon governments. Likewise, there are no 'welfare rights' which arise solely out of 'need'. Governments may well wish to eliminate poverty, though more from motives of charity, prudence and a sense of social solidarity than from obligations arising from a sense of justice. The importance of this is that it introduces an element of discretion into policy-making which would not obtain if welfare was straightforwardly a matter of seeing that justice be done. Under this way of thinking the primary consideration is the pragmatic question: what works? If a policy visibly tends to reduce poverty in an enduring way or if it promotes family success and stability, then very probably it will win strong support from the

16 *Ibid.* 202.
17 *Ibid.* 201.

taxpaying electorate. But if it tends to have the opposite effects then the electorate will be well within its rights to seek to veto such a policy. And the question of what works is an empirical question, the answer to which has to be discovered by trial and error and by relevant description of the phenomena.

Description

If welfarist writing is lacking in argument, it is also surprisingly deficient in description. It is often almost impossible to see beyond the veil of statistics to the life stories which the statistics purport to describe. To take a simple example, it would be impossible to discover from the orthodox writing on one-parent families that female sole parents are (with the exception of a small sub-population) just an ordinary cross-section of the female population, with exactly the same educational and vocational qualifications as their contemporaries. They are not generally resource-poor, whatever their income statistics might suggest. Similarly, welfarists rarely discuss the relation between welfare dependency and crime, alcoholism or domestic violence, though analysis of possible connections between these is commonplace in the welfare literature of other countries.[18] Saunders and Whiteford report that they know of no work in Australia 'exploring the relevance of the behavioural approach embodied in the concept of the underclass, or applying the methodology developed overseas to investigate whether an Australian underclass exists'.[19]

Exceptions to this rule are rare but they do exist. Jean McCaughey's *A Bit of a Struggle: Coping with Family Life in Australia* is one model of how it can be done. McCaughey's work is set in Geelong, and describes the lives of sixty-four families most of whom were not well-off and who made use of the welfare system in one way or another. The general picture which emerges is of a stable society with functioning family networks and a relatively modest usage of welfare services and income support, but the detailed evidence can be read in a variety of ways. In summing up, McCaughey comments, 'It often seemed that the families whose needs were greatest received the least help, and the very problems which created the need, such as alcoholism and domestic violence, were among the chief causes of their isolation'.[20] This might be taken as evidence of a poorly-targeted welfare system. She reports that many respondents chose not to use community facilities even when they were eligible to do so, preferring help from within their families if they could get it, and sometimes retreating into their own lives if they could not. But she also notes many cases of

18 See, for instance, Wilson & Herrnstein, *Crime and Human Nature*, 315–35.
19 Saunders and Whiteford, *Measuring Poverty*, 34.
20 *A Bit of a Struggle*, 219.

persons living for long periods, and for no obvious reason, on welfare benefits.

The distinction between welfare services and welfare benefits is a crucial one here. Australian welfare expenditure for families is heavily skewed in favour of spending on unemployment and supporting parent benefits rather than on local-level services for people with a variety of needs. McCaughey's respondents disliked the large impersonal bureaucracies, particularly the Department of Social Security and the Commonwealth Employment Service. On the other hand, she found that ethnic clubs, sporting organisations, churches, childcare cooperatives, financial counselling services and neighbourhood houses played a vital part in supplementing family resources and opening up opportunities for their members. The message here is certainly that small is not only beautiful but very likely more effective. The small voluntary welfare agencies were thought to be helpful, innovative and imaginative, and in no way demeaning. Although such agencies have been for long unfashionable there is considerable evidence now, from both here and overseas, that they work very well.

McCaughey notes also—as others have found—that deprivation is intergenerational and is bound up with poor family relationships. On this evidence there are good grounds for thinking seriously about how to help families improve those relationships, difficult and delicate though that task may be. Even with 'long-standing and intractable problems such as alcoholism, domestic violence or psychiatric illness', she sees self-help organisations as vitally important, because they provide friendship and mutual support. Yet, as she observes, these organisations are 'still the Cinderellas of both State and federal governments and can be cut by arbitrary decisions'.[21] McCaughey includes childcare as one of these essential family support services, though she notes that most families had little wish to use it when it was available.

The importance of family life is also painfully evident in the more desperate existences described by John Embling in his book *Fragmented Lives*. Embling works in west Melbourne with the children, teenagers and mothers of broken families, providing in his Families in Distress Foundation a relatively stable home and refuge for many local youths, the calm eye in the centre of a social cyclone. Violence, suicide, crime, promiscuity, drunkenness, drug addiction and aimlessness are routine in Embling's world. In his rare spare moments Embling has given a great deal of thought to the causes of and possible cures for this chaotic condition.

The most instructive lesson here is the way Embling tries to reproduce in almost impossible circumstances the moral order that most parents convey almost without thinking about it to their children, which he describes as 'a pragmatic blend of love and discipline'.[22] Without this central struc-

21 *Ibid.* 229f.

22 *Fragmented Lives*, 100.

turing experience, he has found, all else is a waste of effort. The people he works with may be poor and may lack community facilities, but that is not their essential problem. What they lack most of all is the inner stability which comes from receiving and learning to practise that crucial combination of authority and affection. Embling believes that easy-going liberalism is often deeply destructive:

> I hate the old-style authoritarianism, but some of the freedom-at-any-cost brigade are even more repressive in their own licentious way. They free children to destroy themselves. That's not freedom, it's an outburst of infantilism.[23]

This important point has implications for welfare policy. He accepts that 'handouts are necessary in a crisis, but I don't believe it is healthy to treat them as a matter of course'.[24] The Foundation's motto is, very aptly, 'No Rights Without Responsibilities'.

A third example of illuminating welfare writing is David Pollard's *Give and Take. The Losing Partnership in Aboriginal Poverty*. The title is well chosen, reflecting as it does the importance of reciprocity in constructive welfare practice. His book is an attempt to understand why extensive funding for Aboriginal welfare seems to have done so little to lift the recipients out of persistent poverty and dependency, 'the reappearance—generation after generation—of almost identical indicators of social deprivation'.[25] In Pollard's view, the key mistake has been the absence of a realistic appraisal of Aboriginal skills and of Aboriginal aspirations.

> Policy making has now to come to terms with the lack of communal skills among Aborigines, collectively, and their desire, individually, for participation in mainstream social experiences, especially workforce participation.... Aboriginal employment has, until the 1986 Miller Report, only rarely been addressed in the Commonwealth literature as the key issue affecting dependency.... It may be the advent of stable or declining funding which acts as a spur to putting into place programs which actually deal with the clearly expressed needs for work and other forms of social participation. It may be the relative shortage of resources which contributes to ending the dependency that so characterises Aboriginal history.[26]

Pollard rejects mystificatory talk about Aboriginal unity and the assumption that the channelling of funds to Aboriginal 'community' organisations will by itself permit 'self-determination'. Aboriginal society is not, he says, 'a seamless garment linking leadership to people, community to community, and community to community-based organisation'. The 'chief constraint' upon Aboriginal advancement is the lack of Aboriginal 'managerial expertise'.[27] He argues that we should emphasise the differences between

23 *Ibid.* 16.
24 *Ibid.* 23.
25 *Give and Take*, 126.
26 *Ibid.* 132–34.
27 *Ibid.* 118, 123.

black and white poverty less, and stress the similarities of circumstance and ambition more.

There will be no special discussion of Aboriginal welfare issues in this present book. Interested readers should refer to Pollard's work, which is perhaps the most astute white analysis of the subject. There is of course plenty of important Aboriginal description of the failures of past white policy, though rather less has been said about the ill-health, alcoholism, petrol-sniffing, educational failure, welfare dependency, factional conflict, poverty, unemployment and general demoralisation still suffered by many Aborigines.[28] This dark side is far from being the whole story, however. Pollard argues that Aborigines are gradually finding a place in the larger society, a place closer to that envisaged by the old integrationist position than to the separatist vision implied by some of the land rights and self-determination rhetoric. In Pollard's view, 'large sections of the Aboriginal community wish to enjoy the same benefits from society that whites are perceived as enjoying. In expressing these needs—a steady job, a good house, a real education—Aborigines are expressing an implicit intention of conforming to the sets of white values associated with them'.[29] A realistic policy should seek to build upon this wish, in order to combat the legacy of demoralisation and displacement.

What McCaughey, Embling and Pollard describe is real lives, not ideological abstractions or statistics. But when we see these lives close up we begin to see that their problems are rather different from those depicted by the welfarist consensus. Large and vague generalisations about 'society', 'class', 'gender' and 'poverty' are replaced by particularity and variety. The main social failure, in their accounts, appears to be not a lack of 'income support' but our inability or unwillingness to provide access to work. The agency most closely involved, the Commonwealth Employment Service, is held in low regard. And our system of almost unlimited access

---

28 See also Collman, *Fringe-Dwellers and Welfare*. Collman's description of life on the fringes of the outback towns is realistic and penetrating. In his view, 'The basis of Aboriginal ingenuity with respect to whites is a battery of techniques whereby they gain access to white-controlled resources but minimise their debt to, and involvement with, white [welfare and other] agencies' (8). The irreverent, cliché-free style of the book is suggested by the following: 'The Mt Kelly people describe their escapes from the welfare authorities with great enthusiasm and they boast of houses they have rejected or destroyed. They deny that they are poor and take great pride in the amount of money that flows through the camp. They are conscious and inveterate spendthrifts. Many Mt Kelly people spend large amounts of money on items most white officials consider wasteful, particularly liquor' (108). The book includes important discussions of family structure and of the social role of drinking. However, Collman's 'Epilogue' (entitled 'The Bureaucratic Expropriation of Aboriginal Culture') has little to offer towards the improvement of welfare policy.

29 *Ibid.* 122.

to welfare benefits for the workforce-aged appears to be a highly dubious solution to the problem.

If any single valid generalisation emerges from McCaughey's and Embling's work (Pollard's subject is rather different) it is the overwhelming importance of family life in preparing people for the adult world of work and marriage. If welfare policy is to match the realism of this writing then it will have to take those matters as seriously as it presently takes the secondary question of income support. There are some signs that the more thoughtful and perceptive of welfarists are beginning to take an interest in these issues. Adam Jamrozik, for instance, has argued that welfare debate should concentrate on 'the forces at play' which lead to poverty.

> In the prevailing perspectives in social research and in social policy the focus of attention tends to be on the outcomes of these forces (whatever they are) but not on the forces themselves; that is, the focus is on the outcome of inequality rather than on the mechanisms that lead to inequality.[30]

In another paper Jamrozik has cautiously approached the thorny question of the family. He concludes his discussion by observing that

> If ... it is true that a high proportion of families and children who need attention and assistance from State and non-governmental welfare agencies come from one-parent families, it then would seem logical, for social and economic reasons, to allocate more resources to the two-parent low-income unit so as to maintain its economic viability and thus lessen the need for some of the remedial measures which are now used after that family unit breaks down.[31]

Jamrozik argues that we need to rethink the treatment of the family unit in the taxation system. He believes that fairness for low-income families requires an adjustment of tax thresholds. However, he regards any proposal for family unit taxation as 'a utopian suggestion, because, for political reasons, no government would consider it'.[32] About this, however, opinions are changing. A National Social Science Survey in 1987–88 found that 74 per cent of Australians would prefer tax cuts to increased spending on social services.[33] This is not because Australians are an ungenerous people—a survey reported in the same paper showed that they give $869 million a year to charities, or about $70 per adult annually, the second highest level of giving of any country. Disillusion with our present welfare expenditure policies rests not on selfishness but on the suspicion that the present forms of spending are not giving good value or serving desirable social ends.

Supporting the low-income two-parent family through the welfare and taxation systems does now appear to be a high priority, but getting the best combination of policies without creating poverty traps is no easy matter.

30 Jamrozik, 'Are there Alternatives to the Welfare State?', 136f.

31 Jamrozik, 'Social Security and the Social Wage', 27.

32 *Ibid.* 21.

33 *The Australian*, 11 December 1989.

Whether the present Family Allowance Supplement will achieve that goal is still highly debatable. Later chapters in this book will attempt to unravel the complexities of these questions. But before tackling them we need to pursue further the alternatives to welfarism.

3 Welfare scepticism

There is by now a formidable body of writing which is deeply sceptical about the welfare state, going beyond the piecemeal criticisms of welfarism touched upon in the previous chapter. The purpose of describing it here is to exhibit its general outlines, to show the variety of forms it has taken, and to make it better known, for so far little of it has been absorbed into Australian thinking. Mostly this scepticism has come not from 'outsiders' but from people involved in the practice and theory of welfare systems. Formidable though the criticisms are, they need not be taken as the last word on the subject. Whether and to what extent they are true is more a question of fact than of theory—but like all good theories they may help us to see things that would otherwise be missed or to question assumptions which have never been fully tested.

There are three main rivals to welfarism. The first is economic rationalism. Economists draw attention to the hidden costs and lost opportunities of welfare expenditure. They remind us that every transfer of wealth is a transfer away from some other, possibly more productive use, a use which might be more generally beneficial. They remind us that government is typically a relatively inefficient deliverer of services, including welfare services, and they usually favour private provision or self-provision of welfare needs. Economic rationalism does not reject welfare expenditure outright, but it scrutinises it with a rigour that is rarely applied by people who are primarily concerned with the welfare of the poor. It takes seriously the theory of government failure, and argues that the capture of welfare funds by middle-class interest groups is a real threat to the genuinely needy. Its ambition is to restrict welfare expenditure to a minimum, and to provide that minimum to those, but only those, whose needs are most urgent.

The second rival to welfarism is not so much concerned with the efficiency of government or the size of the budgetary deficit. Rather, it focuses on the question of incentive effects and employs the techniques and assumptions of orthodox microeconomics to predict the behavioural effects of welfare policy. Its overriding concern is with the effects of welfare on the poor themselves, and equally importantly, on that class of persons who manage through effort and self-respect to keep themselves out of welfare dependency.

The third rival to welfarism will be termed 'civic conservatism'. This view takes seriously the reciprocal obligations entailed by membership of a democratic political community, and particularly the obligations which arise from the use of a welfare system in such a community. Its ambition is to devise a welfare system which enforces these obligations in a manner which is both benevolent and directive.

This chapter will consider each of these perspectives in turn. It will then go on to outline in the broadest way the possible relations between the family and the welfare state, taking some account of the complexities of the debate about welfare policy.

Before going further, however, it needs to be emphasised that few if any sceptics regard poverty with indifference. This point has to be made only because it is very easy to portray any view other than the standard welfarist line as rationalisation for self-interest. Cartoonists delight in depicting such self-deception, but good intentions bear no necessary relation to good results, and often enough good intentions themselves lead to self-deception. The argument is primarily about what public policy is in the best long-term interests of the poor.

Efficiency

Economic reality is a subject with which people on low incomes are painfully acquainted. The decline in Australia's international economic competitiveness is a fact of life which presses hard upon them. Its effects are beginning to be felt in welfare budgeting, though the welfare budget has not been 'slashed' as is sometimes claimed. Welfarists are not great enthusiasts for economic realism. They fear that as the economy gets worse and taxpayers feel the pinch, they will transfer the pain to those least able to resist or bear it. Taxpayers in turn feel that if they have to suffer reductions they don't see why welfare expenditure should not also come down to the same degree.

There are some important misconceptions here which seem to prevail in welfarist thinking. Anyone concerned about the welfare of the poor has a very powerful additional reason for wanting an efficient economy. These two are not at odds. Our capacity and our willingness to support a welfare budget are both directly proportional to our economic productivity. But more than that, economic inefficiency itself creates poverty by causing unemployment, as many know from first-hand experience. The welfare industry ought to be whole-heartedly behind efforts to improve productivity and export industries. If a deregulated economy is more efficient than a regulated economy then it is the poor who stand to gain as much as anyone from a deregulated economy.

As was noted in the previous chapter, much regulation and government intervention is intended to have social welfare benefits, but many economists believe that such regulation, even when designed to assist the poor, often has contrary effects. Mancur Olson contends that

> the orthodox assumption of both Left and Right that the market generates more inequality than the government and other institutions that 'mitigate' its effects is the opposite of the truth for many societies, and only a half-truth for the rest.... In reality many, if not most, of the redistributions [of income] are inspired by entirely different motives, and most of them have arbitrary rather than egalitarian impacts on the distribution of income—more than a few redistribute income from the lower to higher income people.... There are innumerable tax loopholes that help the rich but are without relevance for the poor.... There are minimum wage laws and union-wage scales that keep employers and workers from making employment contracts at lower wages, with the result that progressively larger proportions of the American population are not employed.[1]

Arguments of this kind might give substance to the welfarist contention that it is 'society', and not the individual, which generates poverty. 'Society' in the context of Olson's argument is the network of 'distributional coalitions' which capture the political process and which, because of their capacity for tight organisation, enjoy comparative advantages in the cut and thrust of interest group competition.

Olson's argument is particularly focused on wage regulation. In his view the failure of Western economies in the 1970s—the rise of stagflation and unemployment—and the inability of Keynesian economics to predict, explain or remedy this failure has much to do with the unresponsiveness of the wage-fixing system to economic signals. An equally trenchant critic of this tendency is American economist Thomas Sowell. Sowell's particular interest has been the effect of regulation on poor American blacks.[2] Certainly Australian society, its labour market especially, is more heavily regulated than the United States.

Australian economist Wolfgang Kasper puts these general points well:

> Some social regulations applying to health and safety and the environment do have to be accepted. But many of the existing regulations of this kind are really only a smokescreen for redistribution in favour of powerful groups. And *on no account* can economic regulation be justified by reference to 'social equity'. The evidence, in Australia and overseas, shows that such regulation either succeeds, but leads only to equal poverty, or fails, leading to greater social inequality....

1 *The Rise and Decline of Nations*, 173f.
2 *Minorities and Markets.*

> The only definition of equity that is compatible with [economic] growth is equality of opportunity. Many regulations grossly violate this, such as minimum wage regulations and business licences.[3]

Though economists generally recognise the reality of these barriers to greater adult self-sufficiency they are rarely discussed by welfarists. The Social Security Review, for instance, nowhere discusses this issue.

Just as economic regulation may produce unintended and undesirable effects, so too taxation may involve unintended costs which can outweigh the intended benefits of the programs it pays for. Virtually all taxes cause people to choose second-best courses of action—to do things they would not otherwise have done, or not do things they otherwise would have done—and this is a direct loss in well-being. High effective marginal tax rates also affect people's willingness to work (this is discussed in Chapter Six). The way in which costs can swamp benefits is perhaps best highlighted by the many cases in which people are simultaneously paying income tax and receiving income support such as family allowance or the age pension. Taxing Peter to pay Peter—known in the literature as 'churning'—incurs direct administrative costs and the indirect costs of distorted behaviour for no direct benefit whatever.

Econometric modelling of these unintended effects is necessarily a complex business, but the consensus now appears to be that the deadweight losses in the tax/transfer process are far from negligible, although studies have produced widely varying estimates. If there is a consensus in the field, it is that the deadweight costs of collecting taxes are around the 40 per cent mark. As Australian economist Terry Dwyer puts it, this means that each extra dollar of taxation 'should yield social and economic benefits in excess of $1.40 to be socially worthwhile'.[4] This formidable requirement puts the onus of proof on those who seek to promote such transfers, to show that their preferred programs are really worthwhile.

The question of efficiency arises also *within* welfare programs. Without doubt the taxpaying public would be far more willing to support welfare efforts if they were sure that the welfare industry was ruthless in its elimination of waste, fraud, cheating and badly designed benefit guidelines, but the defensiveness of welfarists on these matters is not reassuring. Taxpayers need to be able to see that the industry is aimed at making the able-bodied self-sufficient, at getting them back into the workforce. There are limits to what can be done to this end from within the welfare world but it needs to be clear that that goal is foremost in welfare strategy.

To contend that there is no room for improvement in the design of welfare benefits or the delivery of welfare services within the present budgetary framework is to do a disservice to those whose needs are greatest. There can be feather-bedding in a large and cumbersome welfare system

---

3 Comment in James (ed.), *Restraining Leviathan*, 175.

4 EPAC, *Working Papers to Council Paper No. 35*, 48; see his whole discussion, 43–57.

just as there can be in industry, and every dollar of benefits that goes to someone who does not need it is a dollar that someone who does need it misses out on. To claim that such inefficiency does not exist is like pretending that tax avoision does not occur.

Neal Gilbert has observed of the growth of the American welfare system:

> Lacking synoptic vision of the social market and its relation to the market economy, the liberal approach generated a vast number of programs intended to solve social problems and to alleviate the needs of various groups. In the absence of a comprehensive perspective on the social market, these programs multiplied with relatively little thought or measurement of their cumulative impact. There was no conceptual map of the welfare state with boundaries, however tentative, beyond which programmatic expansion had to be carefully charted.[5]

Gilbert's comment has been echoed even more sharply in the Australian context by Ronald Mendelsohn:

> It is astonishing that so pervasive an activity as welfare can continue to be so planless, so haphazard, so nakedly devoid of feedback, of any indication of whether the programmes are achieving their objectives—whatever those objectives may be.... No private manager could survive a single year on the feeble lack of plans and objectives which characterises our welfare services.[6]

This is from a defender of the system, who had observed its workings at the highest level.

Admittedly, efforts at evaluation have improved somewhat since Mendelsohn was writing in 1980. But, as Digby Anderson has observed of the British welfare system, 'it is dangerous to make calls for the critical evaluation of a bureaucracy, for bureaucrats are skilled in using such criticism to initiate change in one direction only—expansion'. He adds that 'If the evidence demanded of current critics of the welfare state had been demanded of its instigators, there would be no welfare state to criticise'. In Anderson's opinion the 'welfare debate' is not so much an intellectual disagreement as 'an encounter with clever and adaptive people, webs of vested interest, uncritical idealism, committed ideology and labyrinthine bureaucracy'.[7]

One particular form of inefficiency arises from the nature of state welfare provision. Gilbert's 'axioms of social service allocation' are relevant here:

> Less troublesome clients will be served before more troublesome ones. Those who can pay will be served before those who cannot. Higher status clients will be served before lower status clients. Middle-class clients will obtain more knowledge about social service resources to meet their needs than lower-class

5 *Capitalism and the Welfare State*, 178.
6 Mendelsohn, 'A Sharing, Caring Community'.
7 Anderson *et al.*, *Breaking the Spell of the Welfare State*, 13, 27, 22.

> clients. When both middle-class and lower-class clients know where resources are available to meet their needs, the middle-class clients will be more effective in getting at the head of the line.[8]

Economic rationalists take seriously the theory of interest group capture of government spending. Why it is that welfarists are not usually very vocal about this is not clear, for the theory ought to fit their belief in the poor as victims of the affluent. One view would be that those who are employed in the welfare industry themselves have vested interests and themselves stand to lose most from any rigorous application of economic criteria. In this respect economic rationalism is similar to Marxism: both threaten to leave much of the welfare industry redundant.

State welfare is undeniably cumbersome and clumsy. The administrative costs of state welfare (about $850 million annually for the Commonwealth Department of Social Security alone) are a dead weight on the economy, the taxpayer and the needy. Much might be done to streamline the existing system. We could reduce the multiple assets and income tests, and we could convert various in-kind fringe benefits to cash. The complexity of state welfare is confusing and irritating to the mostly not well educated population who use the system. It is at once both remote and intrusive, and is felt to be intimidating in both its remoteness and its intrusions. Above all, it is impersonal.

Incentives

There is a more important point to be made here about economic and welfare efficiency, which brings us to the second main alternative to welfarism. The gradual realisation in the last decade that the Australian economy is running precariously close to disaster has forced us to rethink the question of incentives and their effect on human behaviour. We can now see that this question is more complex than we had thought, and that to get it right is a pre-requisite for any successful social policy. Our wages system has been structured to protect the worker against exploitative employers; but in doing this it very often has failed to promote the enthusiastic and capable worker against the mediocre one. Our school system has been designed to protect the average or less than average student against the stigma of failure; but in doing so it has tended to abolish the distinction between success and failure, and has thus lessened the rewards for effort at all levels. Our welfare system has aimed to protect the vulnerable; but in doing so it has failed to reward those who struggle to avoid poverty and welfare dependency, or who fight their way out of them.

In all of these cases we have chosen to consider needs, at the expense of rewarding efforts. Too often the effect has been to make failure rewarding and success unrewarding. We are back with the distinction between needs

8 Gilbert, *Capitalism and the Welfare State*, 70.

and deserts. A theory of justice which considers needs alone becomes prey to those who have no interest in real fairness. We cannot conveniently assume that programs intended for those who are genuinely needy will not be exploited by those who are perfectly capable of looking after themselves. Following this line of thought, the central issue of welfare policy becomes that of designing a system of incentives which reward socially appropriate responses without creating unintended incentives for counterproductive behaviour. The question of incentives is one made familiar by debate about taxation policy but its implications extend in every direction. Above all it raises the question of welfare dependency. If the benefits of a welfare system equal or nearly equal those of paid work, what incentives are there to become or remain self-supporting? In highlighting the importance of incentives in enhancing or reducing effort, this view focuses most on those aspects of the welfare system in which effort can reasonably be expected. It has little to say about the very old, the genuinely sick and the severely disabled, except perhaps to warn us that people will be attracted to simulating sickness and disability.

John Nurick has framed the central issue as well as anyone:

> At the heart of welfare policy is a dreadful paradox: everything done to ease the lot of poor people reduces the incentive to escape from poverty by one's own efforts. There is no escape from this. We cannot dismiss the matter of incentives, both because the country cannot afford to provide a comfortable income to everyone whether they choose to work or not, and because of the importance of work in people's lives....[9]

John Embling asks similar questions, though with a more personal focus, reflecting his experience of the difficulties of welfare practice:

> How do you best maintain regular contact with damaged, discriminated-against people in a way which, (a) adds dignity to them and their position, (b) gives practical assistance and support and, (c) assists them to cope with the realities, harshness and heavier aspects of their everyday lives without crippling or diminishing their capacity to act for themselves? How can you be sympathetic and supportive on the one hand but honest, fair and, if necessary, firm on the other? You can't play God.[10]

These are perennial questions of welfare policy.

The most articulate account of this form of scepticism is that to be found in Charles Murray's *Losing Ground: American Social Policy 1950–1980*. Murray contends that the massive 'War on Poverty' launched by the Johnson administration in the 1960s succeeded only in deepening poverty and dependence. Although US federal spending on the poor grew in real terms by more than ten per cent per year between 1965 and 1974 there was, he claims, no visible improvement in the lot of the target population. The explanation for this is not that upward movement was impossible, because

9 *Wealth and Power*, 11.
10 *Fragmented Lives*, 20.

the civil rights movement had removed many of the racial barriers to black advance and many employed blacks were able to take advantage of this. According to Murray, before the 'War on Poverty' began blacks were steadily narrowing the economic gap between them and the white population. But the anti-poverty programs had the effect of bifurcating the black population. The position of one group, stable, educated, employed blacks (perhaps about 60 per cent of the black population), continued to improve; but amongst the remainder—most of them young, welfare dependent, ghetto blacks—poverty and family instability increased and deepened. 'A profound irony of the trends of the sixties was that growing numbers of blacks seemed to give up on getting ahead in the world just as other blacks were demonstrating that it was finally possible to do so'.[11] The explanation for this irony, in Murray's view, must be sought not in racial discrimination nor in general economic trends, but elsewhere.

Murray's position rests partly on the empirical interpretation of the first decade of the 'War on Poverty' but also, and equally importantly, on 'experimental' evidence. In the past two decades welfarism and economic rationalism, or at least some representatives of these schools, have at times converged in agreement over some form of guaranteed minimum income (GMI) or negative income tax (NIT) schemes. A NIT proposal was a central recommendation of the 1975 Henderson Poverty Commission. Something similar to Henderson's proposal has been advocated by economists Colin Clark and Wolfgang Kasper (and before them by George Stigler and Milton Friedman). One large attraction of these schemes is their administrative efficiency: they abolish all the complex categories and criteria that make the Department of Social Security such a massive, unwieldy and costly bureaucracy. GMIs are also attractive to welfare recipients and welfarists because they seem to minimise the stigma of welfare assistance.

The NIT/GMI idea is more than just a moral ideal or an academic debating point. In what Murray has described as 'the most ambitious social-science experiment in history', NIT and GMI were put to the test—and the results were disappointing even to the most enthusiastic proponents of the idea. The biggest series of experiments lasted ten years and involved 8700 low-income people, mostly in Seattle and Denver. Those in the experimental groups were given a guaranteed minimum income at the poverty line, usually for three years. The control groups had no such assistance. The intention of the schemes was to provide a platform from which the poor could work their way up out of poverty, yet one detailed analysis of the results concluded that the income guarantee led to an average reduction of work effort of 51 per cent.[12] The economists assumed that the income guaranteed would be low enough to act as a spur to effort; welfarists assumed that it would be high enough to lift the recipients out of poverty and set them on the road to self-sufficiency. The failure of these

11 *Losing Ground*, 85.

12 *Ibid*. Chapter 11.

schemes supplies what seems to Murray (and other commentators) direct evidence of the inadequacy of the welfarist assumption that generous benefits will—either immediately or eventually—eradicate poverty. On this evidence incentive difficulties are very much more intractable than was once thought.

The third component of Murray's argument is his analysis of the ground-level situation faced by a person having to choose between welfare dependency and low paid, unattractive work. Murray maintains that we do not need to postulate any 'breakdown in the work ethic' or any 'culture of poverty' or any tendency towards 'shiftless irresponsibility' or any failure in family life—though all these may be part of the whole story—to explain the rapid growth in welfare dependency between 1960 and 1970. So great was the change in incentives available that the choice of the welfare option should be seen as 'the behaviour of people responding to the reality of the world around them and making the decisions—the legal, approved, and even encouraged decisions—that maximise their quality of life'.[13] The dollars-and-cents details of his analysis are irrelevant here. His general point is that the welfare system provides single men and women with an alternative to tedious, apparently prospectless work; and it provides couples with an alternative to marriage, allowing men to leave when the relationship palls and permitting women to use their children as a form of economic insurance more stable than that provided by the men.

Murray is as much concerned to explain why the War on Poverty failed as he is to show that it failed. He sees welfare policy as caught in a dilemma between making its intentions effective and producing unintended adverse effects. For example, training programs to help the poor acquire job skills rely upon the voluntary cooperation of the beneficiaries and thus can employ only positive inducements; but this means that the inducements must be large and generous.

> Theoretically, any program that mounts an intervention with sufficient rewards to sustain participation and an effective result will generate so much of the unwanted behaviour (in order to become eligible for the program's rewards) that the net effect will be to increase the incidence of the unwanted behaviour. In practice, the programs that deal with the most intractable behaviour problems have included a package of rewards large enough to induce participation, but not large enough to produce the desired result.[14]

Murray denies that eligibility rules can be devised so as to screen out those who do not need assistance.

> Any criterion we specify will inevitably include a range of people, some of whom are unequivocally the people we intended to help, others of whom are

---

13 *Ibid.* 162.
14 *Ibid.* 217.

> less so, and still others of whom meet the letter of the eligibility requirement but are much less needy than some persons who do not.[15]

In earlier times, Murray says, the attitude was 'better to deny help to some truly needy persons than to let a few slackers slip through', but when we adopt the reverse assumption that 'no moral cost is incurred by permitting some undeserving into the program' then no scalpel exists sharp enough to excise only those who do not genuinely need the help being offered.

The ultimate effect has been to undermine the traditions of independence and personal responsibility which have long been central to working class life. It achieves an 'homogenisation of the poor', so that all became 'victims' alike, and no distinction could be drawn between the perennial battler who fights to remain respectable and the person who neglects his or her job, spouse and children. Government assistance takes away respect, dignity and status in their local communities from those who struggle to stay self-supporting, and it pays for its programs partly out of the taxes of that self-supporting group.

Murray believes that American social policy since 1964 failed because it chose to ignore three basic principles:

- People respond to incentives and disincentives.
- People are not inherently hard working or moral.
- People must be held responsible for their actions.[16]

All three accord with popular (and particularly working class) wisdom, but professional social analysts and well-meaning social reformers tend to find them either too simple or too pessimistic to be true.

Economic rationalism and a concern about incentive effects are by no means the same thing. Economists tend to believe that welfare spending is justified if it is aimed at the 'genuinely needy'. They concede that targeting creates 'poverty traps'—or welfare-created disincentive effects—which make it difficult for the poor to work their way out of poverty. A policy of targeting seems to cater for needs at the risk of creating welfare dependency. Poverty is for many who suffer it only a temporary phase of their lives. They will often work their way up into economic independence. But if they as the target population for welfare spending are dissuaded from making this effort then they will remain poor and a burden on others.

Those who take seriously the incentives argument tend to be sceptical about the genuineness of the category of the 'genuinely needy'. If poverty is rewarded many who would otherwise fight to support themselves at a minimal level will be tempted to relax their efforts and seek welfare assistance. Others with high earning capacities but low living requirements will use the welfare safety net as a hammock. The targeting of welfare may succeed but only at the price of attracting a new population of 'needy'.

15 *Ibid.* 212.
16 *Ibid.* 146.

On Murray's view, economic growth in combination with welfare assistance will leave the poor just as deeply dependent as ever. On the welfarist view only economic growth aided by welfare assistance (and perhaps even assistance without growth) will lift people out of poverty.

On the other hand, economic rationalism and concern about incentives share a scepticism about large government and high levels of social regulation. Murray reached the conclusion that the best thing that can be done for the welfare of the American poor is to abolish the 'the entire federal welfare and income-support structure for working-aged persons'.[17] Welfare assistance should be devolved to the local level and handed over to private charities. Economic rationalists have reached similar conclusions but from different premisses. On their view the biggest barrier to the welfare of the poor is not just state welfare, but the whole apparatus of state intervention in and regulation of society. Liberation of the individual from government will liberate productive energies at all levels of the population.

Ethics

Welfare policy is unavoidably value-laden, and welfare debate is necessarily debate about moral matters, yet both economic rationalism and, to some extent, the microeconomic concern for incentives tend not to make much of the moral dimension of welfare policy. Murray's emphasis on the ethos of independence and personal responsibility certainly takes the moral issues seriously. But his account of the choice between welfare and work is described in terms of rational self-interest, not communal obligations; and his deep scepticism about what he calls 'the constraints on helping' lead to the view that welfare systems can do nothing to shape and direct an ethic of communal obligation. The third alternative to welfarism does not share this agnosticism. Its credo might be that chosen by Embling's 'Families in Distress Foundation': 'No rights without responsibilities'.

The strongest spokesman for this viewpoint is another American policy analyst, Lawrence M. Mead. In his *Beyond Entitlement: The Social Obligations of Citizenship*, Mead claims that

> the main problem with the welfare state is its permissiveness, not its size. Today poverty often arises from the functioning problems of the poor themselves, especially difficulties in getting through school, working, and keeping their families together. But the social programs that support the needy rarely set standards for them. Recipients seldom have to work or otherwise function *in return* for support. If they did, the evidence suggests they would function better, bringing closer an integrated society [18]

This thesis, like Murray's, is essentially a very simple one, and, like Murray, Mead pursues it with intellectual clarity and thoroughness. Mead

17 *Losing Ground*, 218.
18 *Beyond Entitlement*, ix.

describes his position as 'civic conservatism', and distinguishes it sharply from what he calls (in American usage) 'liberalism'—or 'welfarism' in my terminology—and 'conservatism', which is roughly Murray's position, and which is better known as 'classical liberalism'.[19]

Mead contends that American liberalism (welfarism) and conservatism (classical liberalism) have one crucial common characteristic: they both reject the use of government authority to control and direct the beneficiaries of social programs. Welfarists (switching here to my terminology) reject this for optimistic reasons, because they regard it as unnecessary, assuming that the 'victims' of poverty will automatically respond appropriately to society's offer of assistance; classical liberals take a pessimistic view, regarding regulation for moral ends as impossible, partly because anyone determined to evade such regulation can easily do so, and partly because classical liberals tend to assume that those in positions of power are unlikely to possess greater moral insight than the general population. And insofar as welfarism and classical liberalism share a strand of libertarianism, both can unite in rejecting government intrusion into what can be seen as the private morality of its citizens.

Mead argues that poverty policy went astray in the 1960s when economists took over social planning in the Washington bureaucracy and proceeded to abolish the previous assumption that 'the poor were in some ways less deserving or competent than other people'. As Mead puts it, 'The abstract psychology of economics eschewed such judgments'. The economists' solution to work avoidance was 'work incentives or some other device such as a wage subsidy that would strengthen recipients' interest in jobs'. Other schemes, modelled on the negative income tax proposal, attempted to build a combination of tax and welfare incentives which would favour work over welfare. But, Mead says, 'While each incorporated a work incentive to *motivate* work, none actually required employables to work on pain that aid would otherwise be denied'. The economists' attempts at welfare reform in the 1970s died in Congress, essentially because no agreement could be reached on the necessity of stringent and compulsory work requirements. In the end the work tests which Washington attached to American welfare programs were, in Mead's phrase, 'profoundly half-hearted'.[20]

---

19 No attempt can be made here to describe the transition from 18th-century liberalism to the modern sense of that term, but, as Clifford Orwin has observed, the story would involve 'post-Christianity, sanctifying each soul but no longer willing to make any demands on it; cultural relativism, denying that any way of life is more dignified than another; compassion, uneasy with the severity of the older standartds of dignity; the "therapeutic ethic", insisting that society has a duty to make us feel as good as possible' ('Welfare and the New Dignity', 26).

20 Mead, *Beyond Entitlement*, 99, 101, 169.

For our purposes it is worth pursuing further Mead's description of the intellectual sources of this failure. Mead quotes Daniel Moynihan's harsh judgement on the economics-trained planners who ran federal welfare programs: 'These bureaucrats were *idiot savants*—a term the French use to describe a witless person who exhibits skill in some limited field'. Until the mid-70s Moynihan himself had approached welfare issues in the economists' manner, but he came to believe that the incentives design approach avoided confronting the crucial behavioural problems. Economics, Mead observes, is a science of means but not of ends; and its inability to determine social goals renders it deficient as an instrument of policy analysis. But this agnosticism about ends only reinforced a pre-existing American political culture which itself minimises the role of authority in public policy. American government tends to be of, by and for the people, but not government over the people, even when it is a matter of deploying federal authority for democratic ends. Mead's view is that welfare policy will succeed only when the scope of governmental authority matches the scale of the government programs. The challenge is to 'use authority in social policy in a benevolent *and* directive way'.[21]

To persuade the public that this can and should be done requires an insistence on the moral issues which goes beyond the straightforwardly economic questions. It involves seeing society as a network of reciprocal rights and obligations. It is this conception which makes Mead's position a form of *civic* conservatism. (Its historical affinities are with the 'civic humanist' or 'republican' tradition which grew out of the Renaissance.) Full membership of society requires a willingness to acknowledge these reciprocal social obligations quite as much as they require mutual political or legal recognition. The specific requirements entailed by this conception are listed by Mead as follows:

- Work in available jobs for heads of families, unless aged or disabled, and for adult members of families that are needy;
- Contributing all that one can to the support of one's family (but public assistance seems acceptable if parents work and cannot earn enough for support);
- Fluency and literacy in English, whatever one's native tongue;
- Learning enough in school to be employable;
- Law-abidingness, meaning both obedience to the law and a more generalized respect for the rights of others.[22]

Mead and Murray, though both deeply sceptical about present welfare practices, make an interesting contrast. The questions they address are similar. Both want to know why the American Civil Rights movement was not followed by comparable economic achievements by the whole black population. It is in their preferred remedies that they differ. Mead rejects Murray's abolitionist or minimal-government approach to state welfare. He

21 *Beyond Entitlement*, 182, 215.
22 *Ibid.*, 242.

argues that in matters 'where public standards are indispensable to order', such as welfare, education and law enforcement, 'either governments set requirements or no one does'.[23] Murray might reply that, if the state were to bow out of welfare provision, economic necessity and natural family obligations will set their own requirements, as (in his view) they did in the relatively law-abiding and economically successful decades before the state entered the welfare scene. If Murray is correct then it is impossible to institutionalise Mead's 'civic obligations', and attempts to do so will lead only to further expensive failures. If Mead is correct then only concerted social action can prevent further deterioration in the lives of the welfare underclass. This fundamental clash between the classical republican and the classical liberal approaches to social policy is perhaps the most urgent issue in welfare policy today.

Mead and Murray are, nevertheless, united in challenging the moral assumptions of current practice. The welfarist vision of the welfare system might be likened to some Western attitudes in the 1960s to the use of technology in eliminating Third World poverty. The technologists assumed the overwhelming moral superiority of what they had to offer, but they were often blind to how that technology was to function in detail in particular cultures. Welfarists assume a similar moral superiority about their general goals but adopt a similar indifference to the actual effects of their social interventions. What Mead and Murray are calling for is comparable to the 'appropriate technology' attitude now favoured for Third World development. Appropriate welfare policy is policy which builds on the moral assumptions recognised in functioning working class communities. To achieve this involves analysis which focuses not on intentions and inputs, but on effects and social mechanisms. It also involves tackling the gigantism of the welfare bureaucracies, for bureaucracies cannot hope to hear the opinions of their clients' communities or see the effects of their actions in those communities.

Mead and Murray's insistence on the moral importance of self-reliance is not an eccentricity of 'right-wing ideologues' but a belief which crosses conventional boundaries. The denial that society should insist upon strenuous effort to be self-supporting is central to welfarism. In this welfarists are at odds with an unlikely coalition of traditional Christians, old-style liberals, libertarians, down-to-earthers, Marxists and conservatives, not to mention most Asians and Jewish people. F.D. Roosevelt spoke for them all when he maintained that to dole out regular unemployment relief without insisting on some effort in return 'is to administer a narcotic, a subtle destroyer of the human spirit'.[24] It is certainly arguable, as some Marxists do argue, that welfare payments serve a palliative and pacifying function. It is remarkable, surely, that the rise of high levels of unemployment has not led to massive social protest. One need not be a radical to conclude that

23 *Ibid.*, 252.

24 Quoted in *ibid.*, 129. See also Green, *Social Welfare: The Changing Debate.*

concerted, peaceful protest by the unemployed would be far preferable to the passivity, despair and counter-productive forms of protest such as crime and welfare cheating which are presently generated by the welfare system in combination with a highly regulated labour market. Such a protest, to be effective, would need to be directed at the real cause of the problem, the system of regulation which limits entry to the workforce.

Relevance to Australia

Although Murray and Mead (and other welfare sceptics like them[25]) have not yet made much of an impact in Australia, and although American welfare analysis is dominated by the problems of black poverty, much of their work is readily applicable to the Australian scene. The issue of race does not obscure the general question because, if Mead and Murray are right, black poverty arises more from failures of public policy than from racial discrimination. American black poverty is only partly analogous to Aboriginal poverty in Australia (the situation of American Indians is a far more appropriate comparison) but the depths of black poverty can at least serve as a warning to Australian policy-makers. While it is impossible to spell out the relevance of welfare scepticism to Australian policy and practice in any detail here, some general indications are worth mentioning.

The Australian welfare system suffers, like the American, from bureaucratic gigantism. It entails no reciprocal obligations (such as workfare) which might bind recipients into the political community. Its attempts at work enforcement have been (in Mead's phrase) 'profoundly half-hearted'. We permit people to get the dole even if they leave a perfectly good job out of boredom or laziness. Cheating and fraud are commonplace. Rates of unemployment and family breakdown grew rapidly in the mid-1970s just when the level of benefit payments was increased and the scope of coverage enlarged. Average duration on benefits has increased at an extraordinary rate, suggesting that chronic welfare dependency is now well entrenched. (Even in the mid-70s, at the time of the Henderson Poverty Commission, six weeks was thought a long stay on unemployment benefit; the median duration is now about 48 weeks.) An income maintenance experiment conducted by the Brotherhood of St Lawrence in Melbourne in the 1970s produced results quite as disappointing as the American experiments reported by Murray. And the level of benefit payments in Australia is such that there is often little or nothing to be gained financially in moving from welfare to work.

---

25 See also Butler & Kondratas, *Out of the Poverty Trap*, and Danziger & Weinberg, *Fighting Poverty: What works and what doesn't*. For a recent encounter between American and Australasian welfare sceptics see James (ed.), *The Welfare State: Foundations and Alternatives*.

Welfare scepticism is rarely represented in Australian debates, but Peter Sawyer's *Dolebludging—A Taxpayer's Guide* is an important contribution to the genre (notwithstanding its author's subsequent ventures into conspiracy-theory politics). Three years in the Department of Social Security convinced Sawyer that in Australia 'we don't really have a welfare system'; what we have instead is 'a structured method of making payments to people willing to tell the right stories'. His book documents this contention. In 1985, according to Sawyer, the Department had to handle 50,000 cases of misrepresentation, only 1800 of which went to court because an arbitrary quota of prosecutions permitted action to be taken against only a few 'literate, fluent English-speaking males between the ages of twenty-five and forty-five, usually on Unemployment Benefits'. In 1986 the then Special Minister of State, Mick Young, admitted in Parliament the existence of a departmental report detailing welfare fraud at $300 million a year. Sawyer does not quite conclude, as Murray does, that it is impossible to distinguish administratively between genuine need and plausible but fraudulent story-telling. He maintains, rather, that 'If people in Benefits Control [the claims-checking section of DSS] wrote, or had any meaningful input into the writing of Social Security legislation, there would be no glaring loopholes....' Resistance to the exposure of these loopholes, and of the people who use them, came from further up the public service hierarchy, and also, he believes, from a more general political 'lack of vertebrae'.[26]

Welfarists, of course, will dispute all these sceptical claims, yet they commonly do so by artificially restricting the terms of discussion. On the crucial question of incentives, for instance, Bettina Cass can assert that 'Fewer than one per cent of full-time wage earners would receive an income from employment that was less than they could receive from unemployment benefit'. She also calculates that 'A married person with a dependent spouse will generally be at least 25 per cent better off financially in a low paid job than on unemployment benefit'.[27] Professor Cass reaches these conclusions by playing down many of the permanent costs associated with taking a job, such as travel, compulsory superannuation costs or union dues; by not counting the fringe benefits in cash and kind that go with beneficiary status; by not counting the free zone of earnings permitted to beneficiaries; by making no mention of cash-in-hand work in the black

26 *Dolebludging—A Taxpayer's Guide*, 117, 99ff, 126, 104..

27 Cass, *Income Support for the Unemployed in Australia: Towards a More Active System*, 79. The then Minister for Social Security, Brian Howe, calculated that from July 1, 1989 (following the May 1989 taxation changes) a two-child family of an unskilled worker earning $300 per week will be $65 a week better off than on being on unemployment benefit (Letters, *The Australian*, June 12th 1989). This calculation leaves out the same factors overlooked by Cass. It takes little imagination to see that that $65 will be easily eaten up by those factors.

economy; and by forgetting that for some the leisure of unemployment can be both attractive and profitable. When these facts and figures are added in to the equation it begins to look as though *all* the unemployed might be better off on benefits than they would be in a basic job. Even if we agree with the obviously true proposition that most workers would be worse off if they went on the dole, it may still be true that many unemployed would be worse off if they went back to work. Most of the long-term unemployed do not have readily saleable skills, or have lost whatever skills they once had; most came from low-paying jobs; most will have to re-enter the labour market at the bottom level; and many have lost the will to succeed. The best they can hope for from forty hours work is a few tens of dollars above what they would have received for no effort and inconvenience at all.

Cass's calculations look convincing but they collapse under scrutiny. They bear little relation to the actual situation as perceived from the position of the unemployed themselves. It takes a very resolute species of idealism to believe that these perverse incentives will have no effect on people's behaviour. It seems obvious that many people will take advantage of the system given half a chance, just as many will use tax loopholes given half a chance. We do not necessarily have to think of such people as parasites, though some undoubtedly deserve that description. We may think of them as behaving according to what they perceive as the dictates of rational self-interest. More importantly, a life of useless leisure can be paralysing rather than attractive, because it produces a double-bind mentality of despair and resentment, a mentality in which the recipient both blames society for his plight and loses all confidence in his own ability to act even when opportunities exist to break out of the situation. Unfortunately, no amount of 'income support' can unravel this twisted response pattern, the characteristic form of iatrogenic illness incurred as a result of prolonged stays in the welfare state hospital.

A similar defence of each of the sceptical claims made above about Australian welfare might be mounted, but this chapter is aimed at outlining the general picture, not at detailed documentation. All that is being claimed is that the conditions exist to make possible the kind of negative dynamic —welfare policies which reduce the long-term well-being of those they seek to benefit—which welfare scepticism seeks to describe and explain. It is not being claimed, straightforwardly, that welfarism is mistaken and welfare scepticism true. It may be that some welfare recipients are 'victims'. There are good grounds for insisting that labour market rigidities, restrictive work practices and other inefficiencies, poor quality management, and protectionist trade policies reduce the general level of demand for labour, and thus help to put and keep people out of work. Other recipients may be victims of racial discrimination or short-sighted or exploitative employers, though it is hard to believe that any fair-minded worker would be unable to find any work anywhere.

But it is at least equally plausible to claim that a great many welfare recipients are not 'victims' in any sense except the sense in which existing welfare practice encourages a person to pursue short-term gains which are not in his or her long-term interest or in the interest of their society. Exactly how many suffer in this way cannot be determined a priori. The figure may be very large. Welfarists presume it is small but they do so without, apparently, considering the appropriate kind of evidence. Those in the best occupational position to interpret that evidence, social workers, are either dominated by unexamined welfarist assumptions which they simply repeat, or else they take no part in the welfare debate, perhaps feeling that what they have to say does not fit the dominant paradigm and is therefore not 'real' knowledge. Nothing would be more refreshing in this whole discussion than to see social workers describing in some depth the situations with which they deal, in the manner pioneered by John Embling, but readers will search in vain through the *Australian Journal of Social Work* for anything like Embling's penetration and realism. Of course a person's professional standing may be damaged if she says things which are heresy from the highly moralistic standpoint favoured by welfarist orthodoxy; and in any case it is personally difficult to reconcile welfare scepticism with the self-image of moral concern and humanitarianism which (very properly) motivates people to enter social work in the first place. So the silence of the social work profession is, though disappointing, perhaps understandable. Nor, unfortunately, can it be said that social work training teaches students to question welfarist assumptions or to have confidence in their own native intelligence or natural moral sense. Yet without such critical self-confidence social workers cannot hope to handle the tangled problems of welfare dependency which are very often the first difficulty with which they have to deal.

However, these no doubt controversial claims are outside our present ambit. The crucial contention is only this: that welfare scepticism is a viewpoint which is internally consistent and credible; which fits much of the available evidence, including Australian evidence; which is backed up by the experiential evidence of the income maintenance experiments; which has never been falsified at any essential point; which is close to the general beliefs of the working population; and which is frequently dismissed out of hand by those who ought to consider and weigh its claims objectively and at length. Welfarism, on the other hand, is a paradigm which, although it is subscribed to by the great majority of welfare practitioners and has available massive resources to propagate its point of view, usually fails to engage closely with the relevant evidence; no longer throws up new and illuminating hypotheses or data; often misdescribes the *kind* of evidence relevant to the central questions; lacks theoretical power in its usual versions (often resorting to the semi-tautological accusation of 'blaming the victim' to deflect criticism); gains theoretical power only in versions which welfarists either choose to ignore or do not notice; provides welfare workers with little practical guidance or intellectual insight; and presents itself to the general public in a manner which is tendentious, moralistic and high-handed. In the terminology employed by philosophers of science, welfarism has to be described as a degenerating research program. Sometimes in the history of science similarly decrepit paradigms continue to hold the field for a long time, even when plausible alternatives exist, so there is no reason to predict the demise of welfarism—the Social Security Review is not its last gasp. But it is certainly time that we viewed the issues through more than one set of preconceptions, according welfare scepticism the generosity with which welfarism has been favoured, or else demanding of welfarism the same stringency that has been employed to talk down the claims of sceptics.

There are many arguments for and against the welfare state: welfarism, Marxism, economic rationalism, the incentives argument, libertarianism, feminism, and the democratic defence of welfare. No doubt there are others. What is clear is that the welfare state does not rest on any comfortable consensus about its aims, justification or chances of success. Any discussion of welfare and any welfare policy unavoidably takes sides in this complex debate, even if only by choosing to ignore some of the other ways of viewing the evidence. But it would be a mistake to portray these schools of thought as in conflict at every point, and it is useful here to see where they agree, or might agree.

All schools of thought continue to believe in the traditional liberal ideal of equality of opportunity. Even Murray, who is unremittingly hostile to the principle of equality of outcome, fully endorses the principle of equality of opportunity: 'billions for equal opportunity, not one cent for equal outcome'.[28] All schools of thought seem to accept that for this reason children are an especially appropriate focus for social expenditure. As Murray puts the general view, 'There is no such thing as an undeserving five-year-old'.[29] It is generally accepted that the best form of assistance to children is education paid for from public funds. Most would now agree that child poverty is a matter for serious concern, though there is no more agreement about the causes and cure of child poverty than there is about poverty in general. As to whether the state has an obligation to assist children or their parents beyond the provision of a basic education and the alleviation of poverty, this is a matter of disagreement.

All groups would agree that steady employment is vital to a person's chances of escaping poverty. On the welfarist view unemployment is usually said to result in some unspecified way from the unregulated play of 'market forces'. Economic rationalists argue that unemployment basically arises from the over-pricing of labour through excessive wage demands or awards. In this they share with welfarists the assumption that unemployment has (at least in part) social causes. Murray argues that sectional

28 Murray, *Losing Ground*, 233.
29 *Ibid.* 223.

unemployment can increase quite independently of the general state of the economy and wages. He contends that black unemployment increased most sharply at a time when the US economy was booming. In this view it was the War on Poverty which, paradoxically, produced this result.

But not all groups agree about the place of the family in the welfare system. 'The family' is far from being a 'motherhood' subject in the way that employment and opportunity are. This subject raises complexities which require us to go even further than the sceptical analyses of Murray and Mead, while building on their insights.

In Chapter One it was argued that the family has to be thought of as a small social unit within a larger society. Nothing was said there about what sort of unit the family is—what purposes it serves. Something was said about the boundaries between these two bodies, but nothing about the interaction between their characteristic functions. These topics now need to be considered. The aim here is to set the stage for a more detailed consideration of the role of the family in the welfare state in the later chapters. It will be a central contention of this book that the family must be thought of as a welfare institution, perhaps as the primary welfare institution. This point is obvious if we remember the simple fact that many societies have only minimal state welfare systems, but all have family welfare systems. The full implications of this claim will take some time to emerge, but three points are immediately important, and all are directly related to the three forms of welfare scepticism considered above.

- If we are interested in promoting social well-being and preventing poverty we need to think seriously about what makes for stable and successful family life.
- We need to ask whether the welfare state as it presently exists—and the predominance of narrow interest groups in the welfare state—supports or undermines the family.
- If the state and the family are both welfare institutions then they must be to some extent in competition with each other as well as at times in cooperation. Such competition need not be unfriendly or destructive. But the fact that they are different approaches to the same task leads to the question of comparative advantage and to the conditions of fairness in competition. It requires an analysis of the choice between approaches, and between centralised and decentralised decision-making.

The discussion here will reverse the order followed earlier in this chapter—going from ethics to incentives to economics.

Family ethics

Is there a distinctive family perspective on welfare policy? If the family is the primary welfare institution of society then it would not be surprising if there were such a viewpoint. Suppose that much of our social failure comes from the failure of our society to support the institution of the family. If this is a root cause then its reversal will require a reappraisal of the social role of the family. At least there may be one more voice to be added to the welfare debate. Neither welfarists nor (until recently) economists have shown any particular interest in the family, beyond the bare recognition that raising a family creates additional needs and entails extra costs. Usually these extra costs have been calculated only for the purpose of setting appropriate levels for welfare benefits and pensions. Little thought has been given to the question of what constitutes a successful family, or what social conditions foster such success.

If we are to have a state designed as a super-family the question remains: what sort of family is it to be? Some families are generous, easy-going and endlessly forgiving; others may be illiberal and demanding. In some respects the welfare debate can be seen as a conflict between different styles of family life. The position to be taken in this book is that effective family life requires a combination of authority and love, and that something analogous to this is necessary in welfare arrangements.

It would be very surprising if the ancient tradition of family welfare had not built up an accumulated body of wisdom about how to care for dependants. These skills and practices need not correspond to what passes for public knowledge in these matters. They may exist only in anecdotes and oral traditions, as much knowledge does. People (mainly women) who possess such wisdom and skills may not even think of them as knowledge. They may exist only rather tenuously today, when so much emphasis is placed on certificates and credentials and, it should be added, fashionability. As with all such informal traditions they are easy to caricature and belittle. But they should not be forgotten: we may decide we need them only when it is too late to recover them.

The significance of family practices would be more obvious were it not for the fact that the question of how best to care for children has itself been the subject of a controversy which has run parallel to that about public welfare policy. 'Liberals' have prided themselves on their 'progressive', non-authoritarian practices; 'conservatives' have tried to show that 'discipline' is sometimes necessary and usually not half as harmful as liberals believe. Undoubtedly, in the past two decades the pendulum has swung towards the non- or anti-authoritarian approach, to such an extent that some children now receive little direction from their parents. However, this progressive/conservative polarisation is perhaps more a conflict of opinions than of practices, for very few parents would deny the importance of love for children and very few succeed in never losing their temper with the children whom they nevertheless love. The polarisation is a distracting way of perceiving these issues, drawing attention away from the common ground shared by the great majority of parents.

We now have good academic authority (if such is needed) to indicate that it is a blend of the two approaches which best caters for children's need to mature to independence. Moira Eastman has surveyed the psychological literature on this subject very usefully in her *Family: The Vital Factor*. She reports on one study which found that 'authority in superior families was exercised discreetly, with humour, flexibility and affection, and with children learning early that they are to share in it as they grow to deserve it'. She also notes that (according to another study) 'some social welfare professionals did not appreciate the role of authority in family life and were unable to tell a healthy family from a dysfunctional one'. This incapacity to distinguish between authority and authoritarianism is, Eastman suggests, related to the 'narcissism' which Christopher Lasch has depicted as the characteristic personality style of today, a style which indulges children without providing genuine warmth, which refuses to accept responsibility, and which eventually manifests itself as 'a pervasive jealousy and rage'.[30]

Perhaps the most succinct summary of family welfare practice is John Embling's phrase, 'a pragmatic blend of love and discipline'.[31] The phrase suggests that families typically operate with an ethic analogous to Mead's 'civic conservatism'. They aim to be 'both benevolent and directive', to 'set standards as well as provide benefits', in the manner which Mead would like public welfare policy to adopt. Mead himself quotes Edward Wynne on human well-being: healthy human beings, Wynne maintains, are the product of 'engagement, caring, persistent attention, and—most importantly—of demanding relationships'.[32] The present welfare state, in Mead's view, makes no meaningful demands and permits an unhealthy disengagement from sociability. Its form of 'welfare' is itself socially unhealthy. On this account, the welfare state reproduces just those one-sided, unstructured relationships which are characteristic of unhealthy families, and which often enough lead to welfare dependence in adulthood.

These questions have an important political dimension. Commitment to the adult community grows out of commitment to a family. A child's successful development—where 'successful' is defined (as Freud defined it) as enjoying the capacity to love and work—depends upon anchorage in a family. Children have a very strong desire to know where they come from. As none of us existed before conception we need to know what there was before we came into being and how that world relates to us. Perhaps only family memories and continuity can provide that primary sense of belonging. It is from these memories that children's curiosity can grow to take in some sense of our wider social history. With this sort of security behind them they can expand their interests to becoming part of the adult social world. When this basic sense of anchorage is missing the social conse-

30 Eastman, *Family: The Vital Factor*, 79. See also Lasch's *Haven in a Heartless World* and *The Culture of Narcissism*.

31 *Fragmented Lives*, 100.

32 Mead, *Beyond Entitlement*, 248, quoting Wynne, *Social Security: A Reciprocity System under Pressure*, 138.

quences are not desirable. Most, perhaps all, juvenile offenders who repeatedly get into trouble come from seriously disturbed family backgrounds. If there is a valid general rule here then we have some reason to fear that the disintegration of families will tend to lead to a parallel social and political disintegration.

Not all moral debates require black-or-white answers. Hard-line libertarianism resembles hard-line Marxism, in that neither has any time for palliatives and partial solutions. Both put their total faith in the unaided capacities of their favoured category, the self-reliant individual or the self-created working class. What both lack is an adequate sense of the confusion and twistedness that occurs in a world where people grow up without the moral order provided by family life. They run the risk, as John Embling puts it, of using 'the lives of troubled, knotted, desperate kids to suit and serve their ideological purposes. Then they dump the real people when they can't come to grips with the confusions and convulsions that are simply human beings'.[33] But the difficulties in attempting to provide a social substitute for the family are great. Robert Nozick is pessimistic about this. Radicals, he says, are ambivalent about the family:

> Its loving relationships are seen as a model to be emulated and expanded across the whole society, at the same time that it is denounced as a suffocating institution to be broken and condemned as a focus of parochial concerns that interfere with achieving radical goals. Need we say that it is not appropriate to enforce across the wider society the relationships of love and care appropriate within a family, relationships which are voluntarily undertaken?[34]

'Enforce' here is the crucial word. Love and care may not be enforceable, but there are differences of degree rather than a difference of kind between the voluntary and the enforceable. Notions such as civility, respect, kindness and practical helpfulness mediate and soften the sharp contrast between voluntary love and involuntary imitations of love. In the most difficult cases, however, it may be that Embling and Nozick are both right: nothing except a voluntary and whole-hearted commitment of the kind found within families is likely to undo the damage suffered by those who missed out on such love in their youth.

Incentives

Whether or not there is a distinctive family view of welfare policy, it is at least clear that the effects of welfare policies on families must now be very carefully scrutinised, and some social theorists interested in incentive effects have taken seriously effects on the family. Murray, in particular, has drawn stark attention to the evidence of family failure in the USA,

33 Embling, *Fragmented Lives*, 96.
34 *Anarchy, State and Utopia*, 167.

notably the alarming rate of illegitimate births to black teenage girls, which in 1983—other sources suggest—reached 88 per cent of all births to that group.[35]

Losing Ground is significant partly because it sees chronic unemployment and family breakdown not as separate social processes but as aspects of a single phenomenon. Murray dates the rapid rise in black illegitimate births and poor or low-income single-female households from the mid-1960s, at precisely the beginning of the anti-poverty campaign. He notes that 'The number of poor families headed by a female increased dramatically, not just as a proportion of people living in poverty but in absolute numbers as well, and these numbers were out of proportion to increases in the overall population'.[36] In this period better-off women entered motherhood later, had fewer children and usually re-married after divorce; poorer black women had more children than before, had them earlier, and did not usually re-marry after divorce. The proportion of black children with low birth weight actually rose, against the general trend, between 1950 and 1980.

Similar evidence of family breakdown is now coming from some of the most 'advanced' welfare states, notably affluent Sweden.[37] In both cases family breakdown is usually seen as in part a side-effect of perverse welfare incentives, which in attempting to help those who are out of work or whose marriages have broken up only increased the incidence of unemployment and family failure. What the incentive effects would be in a welfare system which aimed to support families and keep them together we perhaps do not know. Such a strategy has not been tried in Britain, the United States or Australia.

Economics

It follows from the fact that the family is the primary social welfare institution that, conceivably, all the welfare functions of the modern state might be handed over, or handed back, to the family. When, occasionally, this suggestion is made, it is usually greeted with alarm by defenders of our present welfare agencies. Even the simple recent decision to deny unemployment benefits to sixteen- and seventeen-year-olds, and to require them

35 See *A Community of Self-Reliance*, Table A-13, 225. The figure for white teenagers was 39 per cent. In 1960 the figures were 7 per cent for whites and 42 per cent for non-whites.

36 Murray, *Losing Ground*, 132. Daniel Patrick Moynihan drew attention to this phenomenon as early as 1965, but his report *The Negro Family: The Case for National Action* was met with indifference. He has recently attempted to reopen the discussion in his *Family and Nation*, 1986. See also Eastman's survey of the question in *Family: The Vital Factor*, Chapter 9 and McLanahan, 'Family Structure and the Reproduction of Poverty'.

37 See Popenoe, *Disturbing the Nest*, 85–258, particularly 237–247.

to depend upon their families, met with this reaction. Yet it is not at all obvious why we should fear such a transfer of functions. Such a family-centred society may include something like the present redistribution of income, at least between income-earners. As each family would enjoy a larger disposable income each would be better able to assist the needy in their immediate family, in their extended family and in their vicinity. Those who had no family to turn to, or were rejected by their family, need not be neglected by the community at large. What is needed here is some way of weighing up the general gains and losses which such a shift of emphasis would entail.

To consider the interactions between family and society involved here we need some larger theoretical framework. Economic theory might provide one such framework, but the family and the household economy are entities which fit rather awkwardly into standard economic theory. As Amartya Sen has written,

> The family is a remarkable institution. And a complex one. Indeed, so complex that much of economic theory proceeds as if no such thing exists.... The individual owns resources, sells them, earns an income, buys goods and services, and has utilities. The firm buys resources, makes commodities, sells them, makes profits, and gives incomes to individual owners. So the story runs, with no family in sight—and children neither seen nor heard.[38]

In so far as family activities are quantifiable at all they resist measurement by the methods employed for the public economy. According to Australian economists Butlin, Barnard and Pincus,

> We know virtually nothing about charity dispensed through families or through voluntary organisations. To ask the extent of help given to unemployed people by near relatives; to ask how many orphaned children are cared for by families; to ask how many aged parents live with their children: these questions merely indicate the extent of our ignorance.[39]

And in large measure family activities are fuelled by motives and wishes which cannot be quantified at all. However, while it is true that the family no longer serves as the basic unit of economic organisation, having been replaced by the company, it continues to play a vital part in economic life.

Sen's assertion that much of economic theory proceeds as if the family does not exist was made in 1983. Since that time 'the economics of the family' has become a central interest for many economists. A recent article on the subject opens with the remark that 'Over the last decade, there has been a growing awareness that many important public policy issues turn critically on the assumed nature of economic relationships within the family'.[40] Much of the new writing is of a technical nature, and has not yet

---

38 Sen, 'Economics and the Family', *Asian Development Review*, 1983, 14; quoted in Burns, 'Mother-headed households: what is the future?'.

39 Butlin *et al.*, *Government and Capitalism*, 204.

40 Bernheim & Bagwell, 'Is Everything Neutral?'.

been translated out of economese into the language of general public debate. However it seems a fair generalisation that there are two main strands to this new-found interest: one is an attempt to bring to light the world of domestic economic activity, to quantify that activity and to analyse its interaction with the public economy; the other is an attempt to apply standard microeconomic techniques to family-related behaviour which would not normally be thought of as economic activity, such as marriage, divorce and child-bearing decisions. Both enterprises tend to see the household as a centre of production rather than as merely a centre of consumption, as was the tendency in older economic thought.

The first enterprise is a matter of setting on non-market activities an equivalent to a market price, a difficult enough task, involving many questionable assumptions. The importance of this for welfare policy can be illustrated by considering the rise in married women's workforce participation in recent years. In part this rise reflects the fact that labour-saving technology has taken some of the drudgery out of housework and made it less time-consuming. Thus far there is a pure gain either to the total leisure or, if the homemaker enters the workforce, the total income enjoyed by the family. If, however, a mother enters the workforce out of a sense of economic necessity, this may indicate a net loss in family well-being, though it will appear in the public side of the economy as a substantial gain. Work once performed in the family economy, such as caring for children, invalids, the disabled and the elderly, may now be performed by the public welfare system in hospitals, nursing homes and childcare centres. Employment in both the woman's chosen occupation and that of nurses and childcare assistants will rise. Taxes collected from their wages will increase but outlays will also rise to meet the costs to the public welfare system.

The care of the elderly illustrates clearly some of the issues here. There seem to be only two main possibilities: either the frail aged are cared for by their kin, or they are looked after in publicly-funded nursing homes, hostels or C class hospitals. In the first case the cost is borne by the family—particularly women—in the form of forgone earnings and expenses incurred; in the second case the cost is borne by the same family—including women—in the form of higher taxation. At the social level, as distinct from the economic, there are also costs to be borne either way. Institutions are impersonal; homes are personal but relationships are sometimes strained by the difficulties of aged care. Thus far there is perhaps no obvious general advantage either way. At this point the issues takes a different turning. The question becomes not 'Which solution is the best in general for our society to adopt or favour?', but 'Which do I (the elderly person) or we (the elderly person's family) prefer in our particular case?' Public policy, if it can discover no good general reason for favouring one approach over another, should be resolutely neutral about the family's decision; but being 'neutral' involves providing exactly the same resources for one option as for the other. In practice this will mean supporting those who choose the family solution at exactly the same level as those who (in the same circumstances) choose to use state-funded public or commercial institutions. Until recently, however, public policy has been conducted as if families did not exist.

The point of this example is not to debate the particulars (which will be considered in Chapter Eleven), but to emphasise the pattern of argument. It is a pattern repeated in every case where the welfare functions of state and family overlap. A second example, education, casts a somewhat different light. While a few families favour home education, the great majority of parents prefer to send their children to school. At the same time, it is obvious that a great deal of education takes place in the home through the work of parents. In this situation we would expect to find strong bonds and busy interaction between homes and schools, a partnership in which both family and state (in the case of state schools) work together in a common task. Yet as a matter of fact this has not been the case. Home and school relationships have been distant at best, even when families have been supportive of the school's efforts. This disengagement is not easy to explain, but it suggests that powerful forces are at work which operate to the detriment of school, family and child. Understanding how this disjunction occurs is a primary goal of educational thinking, and perhaps of more general social thought, if similar examples are apparent. This theme is taken up again in Chapter Ten.

One important reason why imbalances such as these arise between state and family policy decisions is that usually the contributions of families, in a quite literal sense, 'do not count'. Public policy decisions are made on the basis of measuring activities in the public domain only, and sometimes only activities in the domain of governments. If an economics of the family succeeds in finding ways of correcting this bias it will have served a very useful purpose. One glaring example of this error is provided by those welfarists who rank the various welfare states according to their level of public welfare expenditure, thereby obtaining an 'international league table' of welfare 'leaders' and 'laggards'.[41] No proof is offered to show that increases in public expenditure imply proportionate increases in social well-being. The increased public expenditure may simply substitute for private expenditure. (It may also be spent on socially undesirable ends or merely be given back to those from whom it came in the form of family allowances or welfare expenditure, but those are other kinds of objection.) Of course increased public expenditure *may* produce a net increase in social well-being, but that claim requires a proof of its own which cannot be derived simply from public expenditure figures.

The second enterprise of the 'new economics of the family' is even more methodologically adventurous. It starts from the standard micro-

41 See for instance Frank Castles, 'Thirty Wasted Years: Australian Social Security Development 1950–80 in Comparative Perspective'.

economic assumption that each individual acts to maximise his or her own well-being or 'utility'. But, interestingly, at least in the version defended by Gary Becker, it takes one of the distinguishing features of family life to be 'altruism', defined as an increase in one's own well-being or 'utility' with an increase in the well-being or 'utility' of other family members.[42]

On a very pure form of this assumption, 'all for one and one for all', the relative well-being of each family member, and possibly—if all members of society are linked by a network of family ties—everyone, will remain unaltered whatever circumstances obtain. Well-being will have its own natural level and it will seek that level through the agency of the family, however much the actions of natural forces or governments may appear to disrupt that equilibrium. This thesis, though moderately plausible, runs counter to the claims made immediately above about imbalances which arise between state and family. On this account there can be no such imbalances because private actions will step in to correct the distortions of state policy. Social security provides a case in point. Suppose that the payment level of the old age pension was doubled overnight. To pay for this increase taxes would need to be raised very considerably, but an unknown proportion of this burden would be compensated for by transfers within the family from the elderly to the taxpaying younger generation. Suppose then that old age pensions were halved or abolished overnight. Presumably something similar—though again to an unknown degree—would take place in reverse.

This is certainly a consoling perspective for anyone who has no high regard for the rationality of governments. It might also prove attractive to those who regard markets as riddled with 'failure'. But it has some obvious vulnerabilities: in particular, everything in the argument depends upon the initial assumption of family altruism. This assumption decreases in plausibility as the strength of the claim increases. In its pure form the thesis has no credibility at all; but in a moderate form which allows for innumerable exceptions it seems reasonably acceptable—in general family members do tend to care for one another more than do persons unrelated to each other.

Our inability to estimate the extent and strength of family altruism is comparable to the difficulties in measuring factors in the household

42 See Becker, *A Treatise on the Family*; Becker & Murphy, 'The Family and the State'; and Willis, 'What have we learned from the Economics of the Family?'. The assumption of family altruism is an old one. David Hume, for instance, contemplating the possibility of a society governed by mutual benevolence, remarks: 'In the present disposition of the human heart it would, perhaps, be difficult to find complete instances of such enlarged affections; but still we may observe, that the case of families approaches towards it....' (*An Enquiry concerning the Principles of Morals*, Section III, Part I.) For a study of this aspect of Hume's thought see Baier's 'Hume—the Women's Moral Theorist?'. Mark Blaug makes some interesting criticisms of Becker's application of the economic approach to family issues in *The Methodology of Economics, or How Economists Explain*, 240–49.

economy. Work of this kind is in its infancy, and long neglect of these questions has left us ignorant about many of the most elementary features of our own social life. The new economics of the family is likely to go some way to expanding our self-understanding, though we cannot expect immediate results, and it is doubtful whether the work is presently applicable to public policy problems.

The evidence adduced by feminists of the 'feminisation of poverty' can also be viewed from a family perspective. Bettina Cass's list[43] of the ostensible disadvantages suffered by women—limited paid work opportunities, relatively low pay, childcare responsibilities, dependence on male earnings—may all be seen as consequences of women's role in the family. The real issue is the role, and not the gender of the person who plays the role: the disadvantages are little different for a man who takes on that role. And male parents also suffer related disadvantages compared with men without families to support.

The thesis that family relationships tend to be altruistic is only another form of the claim that families are welfare institutions. Much has been said about the family by feminists, and most of it has been hostile. Why this has been so, and whether it need be so, will be discussed in the next chapter. Before we can take our analysis of the family as a welfare institution any further we need to consider the objections to the family as a social institution.

---

43 Quoted on page 37 above.

4 The ideology of the family

Love and marriage, according to the old song, 'go together like a horse and carriage'. The song was popular in the 1950s, which as we all know was the heyday of family ideology, the era of motherhood and the baby boom and all that. Since then we have got over our infatuation with family life, and we now take a more realistic look at what goes on within families—the power struggles, the pettinesses, the tedium, the distortion of personalities, the unequal division of labour, and much else besides. Family issues come to public attention usually in connection with questions of domestic violence, the oppression of women, broken homes, child abuse, child sexual abuse, youth suicide and youth homelessness. Statistics are regularly turned out to show that now only *x* per cent of children live with both their biological parents.[1] The family, it seems, is as out of date as the horse and carriage.

Or so we are sometimes told. Yet the family is still central to our lives and our values, and it always has been so. Far from being (as some accounts would have it) a freakish deformation produced to satisfy the exigencies of industrial capitalism, it now appears that the 'nuclear family'—the triangle of forces binding together two parents and their children—goes back to the origins of man, and may have played a crucial part in human evolution. In a survey of current research evidence on this subject, the biological anthropologist C. Owen Lovejoy has put forward the proposition that the nuclear family, characterised by 'intensified parenting and social relationships, monogamous pair bonding [and] specialized sexual-reproductive behaviour' actually pre-dates and partly explains the advanced material culture and rapid brain development which are distinc-

1 The correct figure is hard to ascertain but is probably around 75–80 per cent.

tive of our species.[2] The slow but profound human maturation process required its own special social arrangements, of which the family is the most important. An institution as old and as basic as this probably has something to be said in its favour. There is, we might suspect, no other successful way of raising children, nor perhaps are there many attractive alternative ways of sustaining close relations between men and women. In short, in so far as any society manages to foster love and caring for others, it very likely does so in and through the family. Not, of course, only in the family—but without a foundation of good relations within the family it may be that the quality of relationships in the wider society tend to deteriorate.

These, at least, are beliefs that we act out in much of our lives, but for reasons difficult to understand we like to think otherwise. It is the thinking and talking classes, the 'New Class' of academics, teachers, journalists, policy-makers, activists and social reformers, who for a long time have been telling us that the ideology of the family is a form of false consciousness. This chapter will argue that the boot is on the other foot. The anti-family standpoint is 'ideological' because it cuts itself off from common understandings and practices, rather than expanding and building upon them; because it seeks to close off discussion, allowing only one acceptable viewpoint; and because, often enough, it masks the class interests of those in the welfare and other professions who seek for their own purposes to minimise the importance of families in shaping the well-being of their members. In so far as it employs reasoning it is commonly of the Queen of Hearts' 'Sentence first—verdict afterwards' kind, which Alice rightly found so objectionable.

The issue here is by no means merely academic. In the past two decades strenuous efforts have been made to find some alternative to the nuclear family, but it now appears that these have come to almost nothing. The general intention of these efforts was to extend the range of adults available to children beyond the constraints of the traditional two parent family. They failed because they were unable to supply the enduring for-better-or-worse commitment that parents routinely provide. Sadly, the one major and lasting change to family form in this period has tended to narrow rather than extend the family: the rise of the sole parent family represents a splitting of the nucleus of the nuclear family. Similarly, the attempt to break down rigid sex role stereotyping—a moderately successful and benign social change—has been accompanied by a decrease in the richness of role models available to children in their closest and most important relationships. A third apparent contradiction occurs in the conflict between the new-found (and well-founded) emphasis on the importance for babies and young children of emotional 'bonding' with their parents and the increased willingness on the part of parents to break those bonds when they seem restrictive. In this same period much has been said about the unfortu-

2 Lovejoy, 'The Origin of Man'.

nate effects of the past practice of separating Aboriginal children from their parents; adopted children and their natural parents have been seeking out and rediscovering each other; and enthusiasm for family history has never been livelier—yet in public debate and policy we seem to put almost no value on the integrity of existing intact natural families.

Those who dislike what they see as the narrowness of the nuclear family ought to be even more concerned about the deficiencies of the single parent family, but reason is sometimes the first casualty in discussions of these topics. It is common to contrast the 'deficiencies' of the nuclear family with the 'richness' of the extended family, and to attribute nuclear family breakdown to the alleged decline of the extended family. These claims are rarely supported by evidence. This book will take the (now well-attested) view that Anglo-Saxon societies never had a tradition of co-residential extended family life; that there is no evidence that extended family networks are in serious decline; and that the contrast between nuclear and extended family relationships has been greatly over-stated. Those who praise the extended family by contrasting it with the nuclear family are usually those who deplore family 'authoritarianism' and 'patriarchy', overlooking the fact that these characteristics have been more commonly associated with extended than with nuclear family life.

In recent years it has been feminism which has prosecuted the case against the family most zealously, and an English feminist, Wendy Clark, provides a catalogue of the many failures for which the family is ritually blamed.

> The family has become a catch-all phrase for everything that we, as feminists, condemn in our society. Family equals oppression, patriarchy, psychosis, neurosis, domestic labour, role stereotyping, gender-specific definitions, stifling relationships, fathers, mothers, sisters, brothers, children, financial dependence, marriage, sexual repression, sexual activity, heterosexuality, growing up, living, dying, tradition, delinquency, love, hate, incest, violence, battering and bad eating habits.[3]

This last reference at least suggests that the author has a sense of humour, a quality often lacking in the dreadfully serious tirades which she has accurately characterised. There is much else that is commonly said against the family, and not just by feminists. Family life is isolated, private, secretive, inward-looking, cut off from the public world, shallow, stuffy, narcissistic, greedy, claustrophobic, over-emotional or under-emotional, manipulative, possessive, conservative, bourgeois, suburban, conformist, materialistic, and so on.

The feminist critique of the family has been usefully summarised by Ailsa Burns. She lists nine objections:

- Marriage and family life involves women's acceptance of male authority and supremacy.

---

3 Clark, 'Home Thoughts from not so far Away', 170.

- Family life involves a sexual division of labour under which housework and child care is [sic] relegated to the wife/mother, classed as non-work, and accordingly devalued, despite the fact that it may consume 80 hours and more per week and if costed at market rates, would cost more than the husband's salary.
- Because of the above attitudes and arrangements, it continues to be the case that where a wife/mother is in the workforce (now true of almost 50 per cent of Australian married women) she will continue to perform her normal unpaid labour at home (the 'double load'), whereas her husband will at most make a modest contribution to 'help her out'.
- Marriage and family life involves (at least in Western societies) a cultural assumption that mothers do and should carry most of the responsibility for children.
- Among the 'helping' professions, there is a refinement of the above attitudes, such that mothers are scapegoated for health and adjustment problems of their children.
- Despite all of the above, the family ethos is such as to stigmatize spinsterhood as a low status, unfulfilled and unfortunate fate....
- In consequence of all these forces, there is an early assumption by the majority of girls growing up within families that for them too the family rather than the workforce will be their major life commitment.
- [T]he woman whose husband is violent is likely to find the community unwilling to offer her the protection and support that it would accord to anyone else that her husband attacked.
- Where the partner who specialised in 'breadwinning' (i.e. the husband/father) deserts, divorces or dies, the homemaking specialist (i.e. the wife/mother) and the children suffer the consequences of her specialisation in the non-waged job—poverty.[4]

It is convenient to take Burns's objections one by one. In doing so the purpose is not to attack one person's position but to offer an alternative to the standard feminist line. Though she describes the feminist objections as 'devastating' the remainder of Burns's essay shows that she too is moving away from some of the familiar feminist orthodoxies. Complex arguments of this kind involve points of detail, large, difficult-to-determine questions of substance and interpretation, possible errors of omission, issues of logical consistency and matters of moral principle. The questions are hotly contested, and no one account is likely to be very satisfying.

Male supremacy

It is certainly true that in the past the husband has been (in Burns's words) 'the person to whom government, financial and commercial agencies address themselves on the assumption that he is the person "responsible" for the family', an arrangement which caused a nineteenth century feminist

4 Burns's argument is close to that of Barrett & MacIntosh in *The Anti-Social Family*.

wit to remark that 'Under the laws of England man and wife were one person, and that person was the husband'. In other words, traditionally men have conducted the family's 'foreign affairs', while women have taken charge of the internal conduct of family life. This pattern has been for so long the norm that it was usually entered into with little thought. But it is certainly no longer the case that women sacrifice all connection with the public world when they marry and have children. Nor is it at all certain that such a public/private division of roles by itself constitutes proof of male supremacy. To make good this claim it needs to be shown that the external affairs of the family are more important than the internal.

Burns goes on to contend that as well as controlling external matters, men dominate women within the family. Wives, she says, 'pay far more attention to their husbands' moods than vice versa; do most of the conversational spadework; [and] occupy less (or no) private space in the house'. Feminists have made much of points such as these, yet the same writers may also object that men play little or no part in the family. The objection might be that men make all the important decisions in the family and leave to the women the drudgery required to carry them out. However, there is good evidence that in Australian families most decision-making also falls to the mother. A 1957–58 study by an American, Dr Dan Adler, coined the term 'matriduxy' to describe the dominance that women exercise in Australian homes. Adler's contention that the mother made most decisions in 50 per cent of homes is brought up to date up by Ronald Conway, who observes that 'the urban Australian family has been shaped by the emotional pressures generated by the mother in over 75 per cent of cases'.[5]

Matriduxy, or male supremacy? Burns's version seems far too simple. Conway insists that 'In the 1980s, with divorce rates, de facto mating and the new demand by women for equality in workplace and society, "headship" in most households is becoming an irrelevant concept'.[6] It may or may not be true that we are moving towards the 'symmetrical family' heralded by Young and Willmott in 1973, in which family decision-making is shared equally between spouses, but it is certainly not the case that the family is by and large a bastion of male power. On this perennial subject Ambrose Bierce was certainly wittier and probably more accurate when he defined marriage as 'A community consisting of a master, a mistress and two slaves—making in all two'.

Both liberal and socialist feminism hold that traditional male dominance of the public world is proof of male power and male oppression. The usual fallacy at this point is to equate, without discussion, public with strong and desirable, private with weak and exploited. It ignores the complex varieties of power that are available in varying degrees to both sexes: emotional, intellectual, sexual, physical, financial and political. 'Private' is not

---

5 Adler, 'Matriduxy in the Australian Family'; Conway, *The Great Australian Stupor*, 71–75.

6 Conway, *The Great Australian Stupor*, 73.

synonymous with 'powerless'. Some feminists (fewer now than 10 years ago) would not regard the shaping of children as a way of shaping the world, but the hand that rocks the cradle may have at least some influence in building a creative and peaceful future. Not that all women should have children, or that all who have them should care for them full-time. But children are the future, and caring for them well is in its own way a species of power.

The sexual division of labour

'The position of women in the family makes it possible for men to pursue careers and interests unencumbered by the need to provide care for their children', Burns complains. The reversibility of this familiar feminist proposition often goes undiscussed, yet it is of course equally true that the position of men in the workforce makes it possible for women to pursue homemaking and childcare unencumbered by the need to earn an income to pay for their family's needs. Or more generally, families very often employ a male/public–female/private division of labour. It is not clear why this should be regarded as anything more than a statement of the obvious. If the woman in this arrangement is economically dependent on the man, the man is also dependent on the contribution of the woman, and he will often value her contribution as much as she will value his. The feminist's real objection must be not to the division of labour as such, but to either the rigidity of male/female stereotyping or to the devaluation of work in the home—two quite distinct complaints which should be discussed separately.

Why is it that the home role is usually allocated to women and the paid work role to the man? Is it because men treat the paid workforce as their exclusive preserve? Burns is correct when she remarks that 'Until recently in Australia women were formally barred from entry to many ... career structures', but she also notes that 'Most of these formal barriers have now been lifted....' However, she adds, 'the indirect and informal barriers remain enormous'. What are these barriers? They are, very simply, children. 'Parenting responsibilities in an employee are ... defined as illegitimate, and those people bearing such responsibilities described as unreliable and lacking in commitment to the job'. But if this is so then the real issue is not essentially a male/female one. The barriers will exist for a man who cares for children, and not for a woman who does not have childcare responsibilities. It becomes a male/female issue only in so far as childcare is assigned on grounds of gender.

The paid work role is usually allocated to the man not because men want to keep women out of the workforce but because women usually take responsibility for the children. But why do women do this? There are three possible kinds of answer here: one, they are better at it than men; two, it is more efficient for women to combine childcare and homemaking with child-bearing and lactation than it is to divide these tasks and assign the latter to women and the former to men; three, it is a menial and tedious job beneath the dignity of men.

Both of the first two explanations seem plausible enough. Taken just as they are, women do seem better at caring for children than men. (If the familiar feminist complaints against men—laziness, insensitivity, arrogance—were even half true, it would be a rash woman who would entrust her children to one of them.) To say this is not to say that men cannot become as good as women at the job—no doubt many can. Male rhesus monkeys do not normally care for the young, but a solitary male if persistently exposed to an infant will soon learn to nurture it as a mother would.[7] Perhaps the same is broadly true in the human case.

It is certainly true that in general human males spend very much more time and energy caring for their offspring than do most other males. As Robert Trivers has noted, the usual pattern in nature, especially strong among mammals, is that

> females do all the [parental] investing, males do none of it.... Females suffer the cost of pregnancy, the cost of nursing, and the additional responsibility of protecting the young and showing them a place in the world. The male's contribution to this entire enterprise is the sperm cell, weighing on average one 10-trillionth of a gram.[8]

The human male's active involvement with his offspring is 'a surprising feature of human life, something we share with male sea spiders, butterflies, birds, and wolves but not something we share with our closest living relatives, the great apes, nor the monkeys closest to them'.[9] If men are anomalous in this way it would not be wholly surprising if their attachment to their families tended to be slightly less tenacious than that of women. Sociobiological arguments of this kind are usually dubious because they select the animal evidence to suit the preferred human conclusion. Trivers' evidence is based on a wide range of data, and so is not selective in this biased way. Since there is no way of testing the claim that there are biological differences of this kind between men and women, the argument may be of negligible significance, but then again it may not. Lovejoy's thesis suggests that, from an evolutionary viewpoint, male parental investment has been crucial to the success of the human species.

From an evolutionary viewpoint it would be very surprising if women did not have some natural maternal inclinations, in the sense of a general desire to produce children, to bond with them emotionally, and to protect, nurture and educate them. Without such inclinations it is hard to imagine how a species as defenceless and with such a slow maturation process as

7 Peter van Sommers, 'Male and Female Body and Brain: The Biology of Sexual Differentiation', 88.

8 *Social Evolution*, 207.

9 *Ibid.* 239.

homo sapiens could possibly have survived. Such tendencies need not be automatic, infallible or rigidly specific in the range of behaviour they generate. Nor need they be confined to women or to the biological mother. But, as Midgley and Hughes put it, 'On any view, at least up to the stage where social conditioning may be supposed to take over, the survival of our ancestors depended, as much as or more than that of other mammals and birds, on strong, natural parental motivation'.[10] The fact that women have had the primary parental role leads us to expect that these skills will have been passed on from mother to daughter across the generations. Feminists have tended to regard this transmission as mere 'conditioning', but there is no reason why it ought not to be thought of as education. If there are such skills then they need to be preserved. It does not follow that because girls receive such training they are therefore dissuaded from taking up other kinds of work, nor does it follow that boys ought not to be given similar training.

The efficiency explanation of sex role differences is often underrated, yet it makes considerable sense. Both the pursuit of a career and the care of children are often demanding and complex activities. The skills which each requires do accumulate with experience. This need not be so in all cases: some jobs can be dropped and taken up at will, and there is more than one way of seeing that childcare needs are met. The desire and capacity to be flexible about these matters will vary from family to family and from time to time in each family. However, it is absurd to suppose that many parents do not very willingly choose to specialise in the roles they adopt.

The third explanation, that childcare is regarded by men as beneath their dignity, cannot be dismissed *a priori*, but neither can it be demonstrated by mere assertion. Burns maintains that homemaking is 'devalued and unwaged', and that women are 'relegated' to this kind of work. Her only proof of 'relegation' is from the fact that the work is low in status—she does not show that women are forced to take this role. There is no doubt that homemaking is now a low status occupation in our society. The Victorian Women's Consultative Council's recent report on *Woman in the Home*, which obtained questionnaire responses from 1000 women, is now the best source of information on these topics. In ranking the difficulties encountered by homemakers it found that 'lack of status' was listed as the second most frequent complaint, behind 'lack of personal income', and closely followed by 'lack of leisure'. In ranking the main difficulty each respondent faced, 'lack of status' again came second behind 'lack of personal income', on a par with 'family poverty'.[11]

Even so, an occupation can be low in status and yet intrinsically valuable. It needs also to be asked: how did this come about? and what can be done to remedy it? Has the feminist movement played no part in this devaluation? And has it recommended anything to improve the status of

10 *Women's Choices*, 211; see also Wolgast, *Equality and the Rights of Women*.
11 Victorian Women's Consultative Council, *Women in the Home*, Table D.

homemakers? Readers can form their own opinions about these questions. It is far from obvious that this aspect of the feminist critique of the family does not rebound on those who are making the criticism. The women surveyed in *Women in the Home* 'overwhelmingly believed that attitudes to women in the home should change'. When asked to particularise about this, 62 per cent said that the community at large needed to develop a better appreciation of women at home, but only 6 per cent felt that 'men, and particularly spouses and partners, should give greater respect to women in the home'.[12]

The issue here is one of considerable practical importance, and one which will reappear a number of times in this book. The general notion that a society should in some way help families with dependent children commands almost universal, though often half-hearted, support. One very basic reason why so little is done to implement policies aimed at providing such assistance is that those most interested in articulating such policies cannot agree on how to go about it. The question of how to support families produces divisions within feminist ranks and cuts off many feminists from potential support in the wider population of women. While the movement has been forceful in its advocacy of subsidies for work-related childcare, it has done little or nothing to promote the idea of comparable financial assistance for homemakers. Even the obvious resolution of this dilemma, a system of general assistance which leaves families free to use it as they see best, is regarded with suspicion. Certainly some of the issues raised by the notion of family assistance are sensitive and some are complex, but they are not made easier by the partisanship which pervades debate in this area.

Liberal, professionally-oriented feminists argue that the best solution—the only solution, on some accounts—to the difficulties of life in the home is to encourage women to stay in the workforce, but in promoting this viewpoint they have fostered some strange opinions about the joys of life in the paid workforce which are at odds with the viewpoint of their socialist-feminist confreres. Burns speaks of men 'pursuing their careers and interests' as if life as a bureaucrat or bus driver or boilermaker were an uninhibited pursuit of self-fulfilment. This ignores the pressures, the monotony and the health risks which often attend both professional and non-professional work. On almost any standard health indicator—cardiovascular disease, arteriosclerosis, cancer, asthma, emphysema, alcoholism, cirrhosis of the liver, ulcers, accidental injury—men suffer more than women, and live shorter lives. By standard feminist reasoning this would have to be the result of their oppression by women, but of course the reasons for the differences are many and complex. Not the least disadvantage, moreover, of spending most of one's life at work is that it means missing out on close daily contact with young children. If one partner to a marriage (not necessarily the wife) is at home this experience can be enjoyed vicariously. Again, it is not necessary to advocate this way of

12 *Ibid.* 34.

dealing with the issue as the 'best' solution: there is no single solution which will suit everyone.

What feminism routinely fails to notice is that this conflict—or choice—is nobody's fault. It is not the work of 'capitalism' or 'patriarchy' or of any other bogeyperson. It is just a natural consequence of the fact that any society has two main tasks, to reproduce the species and to maintain a reasonable standard of living. There are dozens of ways of negotiating between the demands of domesticity and the opportunities open in the workforce, and no one of them is the right or the wrong way to manage the issue. Solutions have to be responsive to families' particular circumstances and personal preferences, and public policy-makers have no special insight into these matters. Feminist attempts to portray these issues as elements in a grand-scale moral drama fall down when we attend more closely to the details of the case. Some people are sympathetic to women's choices and regard them as difficult; others, both men and women, are relatively indifferent and think there are far worse problems in the world.

Perhaps historian Kathleen Fitzpatrick has put this whole matter as sanely as it can be expressed. She says:

> I am inclined to quarrel with the question 'Why do so many [women] fall by the wayside?' because it seems to impute failure to those who undertake professional life and do not persist in it, whereas I am inclined to regard this as a choice they have made for reasons which may be perfectly valid. There are women who combine the role of wives, mothers, housekeepers and professional women successfully: I admire them unreservedly but regard them as superwomen and therefore necessarily few. As for the many women who would also like to combine the traditional woman's role with a professional career but lack the physical strength, iron self-discipline, cooperative husband and exceptional planning ability required, I see as yet no satisfactory solution. There are solutions that are partly satisfactory, such as part-time work and junior appointments, but the achievement of professional excellence is a full-time job. Most women have to make a choice and every choice involves a renunciation.[13]

She goes on to add that male prejudice in the professions does persist, 'based on fear that life is going to become more uncomfortable for men if

13 In Grimshaw & Strahan, *The Half Open Door*, 132. Leaving aside male prejudice in this matter, the practical difficulties in trying to have the best of both public and private worlds at once should not be underestimated. The most constructive and optimistic guide here is Apter's *Why Women Don't Have Wives*. By showing what some outstanding women have achieved, and how, she offers inspiration—and perhaps some false hope, for not everyone can live up to the standards they set. The sky may be the limit but not everyone can fly in such a rarefied atmosphere. Hewlett's *A Lesser Life: The Myth of Women's Liberation in America* shows—not altogether intentionally—how very unprepared many highly-educated young American women are for making this combination of public and domestic life. See also Cardozo's *Sequencing*, the theme of which is summed up by the sub-title *Having It All But Not All at Once*.

the traditional pattern of family life is changed'. Prejudice of this kind, like all of the many such prejudices we carry around with us, has to be fought on a case-by-case and person-to-person basis.

The real power base of feminism is of course in the professions, not in the working class. There is no need here to enter into the debate between liberal and socialist feminists, which is on the whole just the old debate between liberalism and socialism. As Miriam Dixson remarks, those who have reaped the most benefit from the movement have been 'women in the bureaucracy, polity, media, teaching and helping professions, and less noticeably, in management'.[14] Not the least achievement of the movement has been the creation of a great many comfortable jobs in the Commonwealth and State public services, particularly in the welfare sector.[15] The attachment that some feminists have to socialism seems more tactical and self-interested than a principled commitment to the values and interests of working-class women. And the common feminist faith that their goals can be best achieved through the state is dubious at best. Feminists, as Dixson observes, 'display few reservations in committing themselves to an unlimited growth of government and hence to an accelerated erosion of women's, as of every citizen's, autonomy. This massive contradiction is the more powerful because it is so deeply repressed and angrily denied'.[16] Feminist over-statement is a nice illustration of Marx's thesis that each new class seeks to 'universalise' its own concerns.

Women who are serious about being entirely independent of men should be wary of exchanging dependence on a man for dependence on the state. Most of the state's money comes from taxes paid by men. Accepting social security payments, for instance, is just a way of becoming dependent upon a multitude of men, which may be worse than being dependent on just one of them. Such feminists should also be wary of joining the paid workforce, for most paid employment happens to be structured and controlled by men. Anyone really seeking independence would be best to start up their own business. They could then choose their clientele. If they then regarded the relation between sellers and buyers as one of exploitation they could choose to deal only with customers of the opposite sex; if they regarded it as one of mutual support they could choose same-sex customers. In this way capitalism is friendlier to separatist feminism than is socialism. In a state-run system women would have no choice but to work under and alongside men. Feminists in Russia and China commonly regard the right

14 Miriam Dixson, 'Gender, Class, and the Women's Movement in Australia, 1890–1980', 15.

15 'Sixty-two per cent of all women and thirty-six per cent of all men with tertiary degrees or equivalent qualifications are employed in health, education or welfare', according to Adam Jamrozik ('Social Policy: Are there Alternatives to the Welfare State?', 126).

16 Dixson, *op.cit.* 23.

to have time with their children as their first priority, though they and their families also suffer from the poverty endemic in state-run economies.

Domestic drudgery and the double shift

Discussions of the relative work effort which men and women contribute to the family are full of traps. The question is not one of how much housework or childcare each partner performs, but it includes all the work—both paid and unpaid—that goes into raising a family and running a household. When in 1973 Young and Willmott attempted such a complete computation they concluded that men working full-time, women working full-time and women working part-time each contributed about 60 hours per week, and women not in paid work about 45 hours per week.[17] Their analysis involved 350 (English) parents using self-recorded time-budget diaries. The fragmentary nature of much childcare and housework may have led to an underestimation of the work done by the women at home.

Burns refers to no Australian studies which will show that this pattern does not hold in this country. Later in her essay she does report on Australian research—the J. Walter Thompson survey—which indicates that 'between one-quarter and two-thirds of husbands (as reported by wives) helped out "actively and consistently" with such tasks as looking after small children, shopping, cooking and cleaning'.[18] This takes no account of men's contribution to gardening, home repairs, car maintenance etc. The report found that men helped more with housework when their wives were also in the paid workforce.

The most authoritative research on this general question, the *Time Use Pilot Survey* conducted by the Australian Bureau of Statistics in Sydney in 1987, shows that non-employed married women average 48 hours per week on unpaid housework, shopping and childcare; employed married men contribute about 15 hours to the same tasks; and employed wives about 35 hours. However, when their total contributions are calculated the study shows that employed, married men and women work (at work and at home) almost identical hours per week and enjoy almost identical time for volunteer/social/leisure activities.[19] This research supplies no reason to think that in general women work more than men. Counting both paid and unpaid work, married men on average work a 64-hour week, employed married women work 65 hours, and non-employed women 48 hours—results very close to Young and Willmott's findings. These figures relate to all married men and women, and do not measure directly the relative workloads of parents of dependent children, but there is no obvious reason to suppose that the married population is greatly different from the population

17 Young & Willmott, *The Symmetrical Family*, 113.
18 Burns, 'Why Do Women Continue to Marry?', 225.
19 ABS Cat. 4111.1, 1987, 36.

of parents. Of course, if we assume that housework and childcare are inferior activities then it will appear that women have been 'relegated' to them, but it is this assumption which is at issue. If, equally arbitrarily, we adopt the opposite assumption, then we will get the opposite result. In the absence of any overriding argument, the only reasonable assumption must be that people are dividing their labour in ways which happen to suit them best.

In saying this we need not deny that in some households the workload is not shared at all equally. (Amongst the unemployed, for instance, there is a large discrepancy between the workloads of women and men, with the women working 40 per cent more than the men. Sole fathers, on the other hand, worked 30 per cent longer than sole mothers on total labour force and household activities.[20]) But it need not be inferred from these isolated cases that the family is a device for the oppression of women by men. Families are very much more than arrangements for running households. Even some feminists have grown tired of the obsessive focus on housework. One critic, American sports journalist and post-feminist Hilary Cosell, has observed how all discussions of marriage eventually 'seem to shrivel into one topic: the division of labour'. She maintains that a woman who accepts the heavier workload is not necessarily selling out on the fundamental principles of sexual politics. Realism sometimes requires compromises (and sometimes it is men who make the compromise). Such realism is not incompatible with self-confidence, assertiveness and a refusal to be brow-beaten by opinionated men. Cosell looks forward to the day when 'dishwashing will finally resume its proper perspective in American life: a subject largely unworthy of debate'.[21]

The domestic drudgery objection also fails to acknowledge the obvious truth that domesticity is now very much less demanding than it has ever been at any time in human history, most particularly because the birth rate has fallen very markedly in recent decades. Indeed, this decline in domestic demands is an essential premise of one whole strand of feminist argument which Burns fails to mention. It was Betty Friedan's insistence that the home no longer needed to absorb all the best energies of women which set much of the movement in motion.

House arrest and maternal guilt

As an addendum to her complaint about women's confinement to the childcaring role, Burns adds that marriage and family life 'can result in near house-arrest of mothers of young children living in poorly-designed housing in areas deficient in community and transport facilities'. It also 'sheets home to mothers responsibility for any poor outcomes among their

20 *Ibid.* 36, 42.
21 *Woman on a Seesaw*, 115.

children'. These are two very different objections, and they need to be considered separately.

The 'house arrest' complaint is a variation on the familiar feminist theme of the suburban isolation neurosis. There is no doubt that many women with the care of young children feel that they suffer from loneliness and isolation, and in some cases the effects can be serious, but the issue needs to be kept in some perspective. *Women in the Home* found that 'social isolation' ranked fourth in the list of homemakers' difficulties and fifth in the list of main difficulties. It is not clear from this report that lack of transport, which appeared seventh in the list of difficulties, is the main cause of this isolation. No doubt many women do not have use of a car during the day, and public transport may not provide ready access to family and friends. For some, isolation can result from a move into a new State or a new suburb, in pursuit of jobs or better housing. A further factor here is that as more women take more part in paid work, those who remain at home find they have a diminishing range of potential social contacts.

It is true that many suburban areas lack much sense of community focus, apart from the local shopping centre. Government-initiated attempts to 'build community' are fraught with difficulties, but the case may not be entirely hopeless. The Western Australian Government is attempting to improve this situation by setting up 'Family Centres' in such suburbs, facilities which will include playgroups and other community activities, and which will be managed by local people. Other states have experimented with 'neighbourhood houses'. It would be useful to monitor and compare the progress of these attempts.

In passing here, it is worth noting the implausibility of the common claim that strong family relationships tend to weaken community bonds. There is good evidence that many community organisations—sporting clubs, churches, service clubs and the like—are led and run by people with the self-confidence which comes from strong family support.[22] Social workers in areas in which family breakdown is prevalent do not report high levels of community-mindedness and participation.

Burns's 'maternal guilt' objection—the alleged blame which attaches to mothers if their children go off the rails—involves questions about which it is almost impossible to generalise. Do women get the credit when their children turn out well? Is this credit or blame much different from that which men or women experience when things go right or wrong in their paid work? Do we not make allowances for the fact that children are born with personalities of their own which function independently of the efforts of their parents? Anyone who thinks there are clear-cut answers to these questions is looking at the world through monochrome spectacles.

22 See O'Donnell, 'The Social World of Parents'.

Unhelpful helpers

The failings of the helping professions can hardly be counted as grounds for complaint against the institution of the family, which is itself often an important source of resistance to excessive interference in people's lives by well-meaning but self-interested professionals. There is no doubt that in recent years families have been besieged by advisory organisations telling them how to bring up their children, what foods to eat, etc. Some observers of this trend think there has been a causal relationship at work here: as the prestige and importance of these groups has grown, so the status and self-assurance of the family has fallen. These may or may not be causally connected. The most basic issue here is that of consumer sovereignty.

Actually, well-meaning intrusion into the internal affairs of families is not confined to the helping professions. Few of these have been as dogmatic and bossy about the conduct of family life as has the feminist movement.

The stigma of spinsterhood

According to Burns, this stigma has lessened in recent times, but 'it is still something to be reckoned with'. Yet although she gives the subject no further discussion it is, when taken in conjunction with her next objection—family or workforce?—in some ways at the heart of the whole debate.

The family or the workforce?

The question here is this: do women have a real choice about whether or not to marry and have children? Feminists commonly make it sound as if this is not a real choice. Both early conditioning and later social pressure, we are told, leave no option for the majority of women. The fact that most women do marry and have children is taken to show just how effectively they are socialised and how powerful is the pressure. They rarely encounter models for other modes of life.

What this argument obscures is the fact that whether or not something counts as 'conditioning' or 'pressure' depends in part upon whether it is, or is believed to be, a genuine good. Consider an analogy: a child is brought up to appreciate good music. Her parents encourage her to sing, to attend concerts, to learn an instrument, to listen to the classics. On becoming an adult she decides to give it all up, against the wishes of her parents and contrary to the advice of her friends. Has she suffered 'conditioning' or 'pressure' in her upbringing? If the terms can be used to cover this sort of case then they have lost all the negative force which they are usually thought to carry. But suppose she carries on and becomes a moderately competent trombonist. Has she had no real choice about this? The analogy with getting married and having children requires no labouring. Only if we assume that these are not satisfying ways of life can we show that they result from adverse kinds of causation.

Contrary to the whole tenor of feminist thought, it might plausibly be argued there has never been a time when less effort was made to prepare people for marriage and parenthood than at present. And the opportunities open to 'spinsters' are now very great, both in work and in private life. According to Burns, girls are conditioned to lack interest 'in acquiring the attitudes and jobs that might open up a "male" career'. However, 61.8 per cent of females but only 53.4 per cent of males completed secondary education in 1988; in 1987, 71,300 females but only 67,400 males were attending universities and colleges of advanced education.[23] By the reasoning commonly employed by feminists these differences would have to be construed as evidence of discrimination against males. (Further evidence of the subjugation of boys might be sought in their heavy predominance in remedial classes or in the fact that they are subject to far more disciplinary action than are girls.) If the emphasis is placed upon the fact that women do not often end up as architects, managers, mathematicians and accountants, then any explanation will need also to explain why so many of them are now succeeding as lawyers and doctors. If the question is why so many women work in service industries and clerical work and not in heavy industry, labouring or trades then perhaps the answer is that they are better suited to that kind of work.

Writing of the first feminist movement, G.K. Chesterton commented that 'twenty million young women rose to their feet with the cry *We will not be dictated to*: and proceeded to become stenographers'.[24] Some will read this as a cheap sexist jibe; others might see in it a defence of the role that women play in the home, which was probably Chesterton's intention. More usefully, it might serve as a reminder that for most people most of the time the decision between work in the home and paid work is a rather pragmatic and mundane adaptation to a complex of circumstances, and has little to do with 'liberation' from the 'tyranny' of domesticity. The feminist retort to this is of course that women are given only the low-paid low-status jobs left over after men have had first choice. To establish this claim it would need to be shown that women who pursue full-time careers with the same tenacity and skill as men do worse than men do. Whether or not this is so is not a matter for armchair philosophising, and it would be foolish to pronounce upon it without good evidence. There may not be any clear-cut generalisations possible here: the truth may be that it is true in some places and not in others.

At this point it will be alleged that 'structural' discrimination against women is demonstrated by the fact that in general men earn higher wages

23 ABS Cat. 6227.0, May 1989, Table 13.

24 Quoted by Canovan, *G.K. Chesterton: Radical Populist*, 55.

than women. Here it is possible to refer to some figures. In the last quarter of 1988 men earned an average of $512.10 and women $427.20 when employed full-time for an ordinary week's work. In other words, on average women earned 83 per cent of the male wage. Other figures suggest that this ratio is strongly related to age: young women earn almost as much as young men, older women earn considerably less than older men. In the 15 to 19 age group the difference may be as little as five per cent.[25] The most obvious explanation or partial explanation of this increasing disparity with age is that children disrupt women's careers and thus limit their chances of promotion. Another explanation is that younger women are better educated, more highly qualified and more career-minded than their predecessors.

Whether evidence of unfair discrimination against women can be derived from these figures depends on how heavily we choose to weight the disruption effect. It is commonly believed that women's work as homemakers disadvantages them when they return to the paid labour market, but a recent analysis of women's lifetime earnings found, rather surprisingly, that this is effect is minimal. An econometric study of 2500 women by John J. Beggs and Bruce Chapman, entitled *The Forgone Earnings from Child-Rearing in Australia*, concluded that although children—particularly first children—substantially diminish women's labour force participation 'the consequences of children on women's hourly wage rates are negligible'.[26]

The assumption that women are 'conditioned' to adopt certain sorts of work, like the assumption that they are conditioned to raise children, rests on the further assumption that what women choose to do is inferior to the alternative choices they might have made. Whether it is inferior is little more than a matter of opinion—the answer will vary from person to person. It seems best to conclude that the women themselves are better judges of the kind of work that suits them best than are the feminist theorists. In any case, the only real issue for public policy is whether any artificial barriers are placed in the way of anyone's choice of occupation.

It can be plausibly argued that if people thought only of their own interests they would probably not have children at all, such is the range of other ways of life now available. We know that most couples find it very difficult to articulate why it is that they decide to have children.[27] The explanation for this may be simply that the desire to reproduce the species is a biological imperative which manifests itself in ways which are not readily rationalised.

---

25 See Anstie *et al.*, *Government Spending on Work-Related Child Care: Some Economic Issues*, Table 2, 8.

26 Beggs & Chapman, *Forgone Earnings from Child-Rearing in Australia*, 4.

27 See Richards, *Having Families*, on this theme.

The privatisation of violence

'Only a minority of men are violent', as Burns allows, so the fact of domestic violence cannot by itself be used as evidence against the family. The real issue is why violence occurs in some families and not in so many others. Burns's objection is rather that, when it occurs, domestic violence is treated by both the police and neighbours as a purely private matter. The objection is partly about when an outsider should intervene in family conflicts, but underlying it is perhaps a more general issue concerning the boundary between a family and the rest of the world.

Critics of the family very often dislike the privacy of family life. The value that is placed upon privacy or sociability will vary very much from person to person (and from culture to culture), and it makes little sense to think of one choice as better or worse than another. Consequently, it makes no more sense to criticise family life for involving privacy than it does to criticise a commune for lacking it. Families do have boundaries: without them they could have no autonomy and thus no identity. The flexibility of these boundaries will vary from family to family. Such boundaries are not justifications for any sort of behaviour which goes on behind them, but neither can they be crossed by anyone who just happens to dislike the way people behave in their own homes. Sometimes outsiders—including the police—will intervene when they should not; at other times they will stand back when they should have intervened. Often, as police find, it is a no-win situation, but just because this is the case it is foolish to blame people who would like to be helpful but don't know when or how to be so.

Much thought is presently being given to these issues in connection with domestic violence, and most of the credit for this can be given to the feminist movement. But the tendency to overdramatise the issue—to use it as a stick with which to beat the institution of the family—appears difficult to resist. Even Don Edgar, the Director of the Australian Institute of Family Studies, can remark in this context that 'Reasoning, explanation, controlling anger and conflict management do not typify the average home'.[28] The only evidence adduced for this surprising claim is Paul Amato's study *Children in Australian Families* suggesting that 70–80 per cent of parents sometimes slapped, spanked or yelled at their children. This tells us nothing about relations between spouses, which has been the real issue for feminists.

Amato's results do show that all forms of 'violence' towards children are more likely to be practised by women than by men—not surprisingly, as women spend more time with children than men do. But the results also fail to establish Edgar's contention. Only if we assume that spanking etc. are not accompanied by reasoning, explanation, the controlling of anger and conflict management can we draw that conclusion. Amato claims but

28 Edgar, 'Family Disruption and Violence', *Family Matters* **22** (1988) 13; Amato, *Children in Australian Families: The Growth in Competence*.

does not show that physical punishment and other forms of discipline such as sending a child to its room are 'coercive, power-assertive forms of discipline that are quite different from forms of control based on love and reasoning'.[29] He tells us nothing at all about the circumstances or the frequency of such actions, though his figures show that physical discipline drops off to about 20 per cent for teenagers. He also found that about 6 per cent of children had at some time been told by their parents that they did not love them, which may be thought a more disturbing statistic than the 70–80 per cent of slapping and yelling. Putting the two sets of statistics together what we find is that most parents sometimes yell at and hit their children but never tell them they do not love them. Is this the best method of rearing and caring for children? Perhaps not, but it is very easy to be pharisaical in these matters. In any case, it is clear that they cannot be construed as an explanation of violence between men and women without torturing the data to death.

Analysis of the question of child sexual abuse is still in its infancy, but the first careful study of proven cases, based on Victorian Police statistics, by Geoffrey Partington, found that only about ten per cent of cases took place within the family. Twenty per cent was perpetrated by strangers. But in a massive seventy per cent of cases the offence was committed by someone professionally responsible for the care of children, such as a teacher or a welfare worker.[30] Within the family, step-fathers were found responsible for under two per cent of cases and fathers also for under two per cent. If these figures are accurate reflections of the causes of child sexual abuse, natural fathers are (after mothers) the least of our worries in this area. And perhaps the 'stranger danger' campaign should be revised to teach children to beware of professionals. It is also worth noting that professional social workers who, on the flimsiest grounds for suspicion, interrogate children about events within the family and refuse to take the child's denial of maltreatment as good evidence, may sometimes do as much harm to the child as actual molesters. Of course, even if Partington's figures are underestimations of child sexual abuse within the family, that would not even remotely show that the family is an inherently abusive institution, just as his actual figures do not remotely show that welfare professionals are inherently dangerous to children.

An equally surprising discovery made by two leading American researchers, Straus and Gelles, is that violence within the home and spousal homicide are as often perpetrated by women upon men as by men upon women, at least in the sample analysed in their study.[31] In Australia the

---

29 Amato, *op. cit.* 79.

30 Reported in *The Bulletin*, 27 September 1988. On the medical and social complexities of this subject, the indispensable authority, which supersedes much previous guesswork and speculation, is now Wakefield and Underwager, *Accusations of Child Sexual Abuse*.

31 Straus & Gelles, 'Societal Change and Family Violence'.

spousal homicide ratio is three murders by husbands to one murder by a wife, so perhaps the physical violence ratio is something similar. If so then we can say that the problem is not simply a male one. Edgar mentions the American result, but he goes on to claim that 'Central to the problem of socialised aggression is the accrual of a massive power base of resources by males'.[32] He adds that 'there can be no doubt that men have more to lose from the breakdown of the family than women'. If men have such resources and such interests, and assuming only that they possess a modicum of rationality, it is hard to see why they would commit acts of violence likely to jeopardise the stability of their family. It is equally difficult to explain the reported level of violence by women against men (in America) or by women against children.

What is needed here is not global and unprovable generalisations about men and women, but insight into the dynamics of particular deteriorating relationships. And there is good reason to be hopeful that we are coming to understand something of these dynamics. Work by Ian MacDonald of the Queensland Marriage Guidance Council, for instance, suggests that chronic violence by men against their partners does conform very closely to an identifiable pattern—a 'Cycle of Violence'—and that it can be cured. MacDonald's method has been to help men understand the dynamics of this cycle and to teach them stress and anger management techniques. 'Our experience has been that it will take up to 6 months in the [therapy] group before a man can say with confidence that he is violence free', he reports.[33] MacDonald himself conceives this task as that of undoing a lifetime of sexist socialisation. He asserts that 'Men's power over women is enshrined in almost every area of life in the community', but the fact that he has such success seems to suggest otherwise. No doctor would expect success if the disease he had to cure was all-pervasive in the community. In any case, what matters is the success itself. As he rightly says, 'Progress with violent men is hard-won, but the benefits for this generation and for following generations are inestimable'.

While the progress of these programs will need to be monitored, the general aim of curing violence is a cause well worth public support. At the same time women's refuges—whatever the faults some of them may have—will continue to be needed. Refuges and therapy can be supplemented by legal prohibition, law enforcement measures and court-issued restraining orders, and in the recent public awareness campaign these have been the main focus. While legal restraints are necessary in some cases, this strategy has important limitations. What makes domestic violence different from ordinary criminal violence—what makes it more tragic than malicious—is that it takes place between two people who, in most cases,

32 'Family Disruption and Violence', 14.

33 Macdonald, 'The Cyclic Pattern of Abusive Relationships' in Crawley (ed.), *Counselling and Domestic Violence*. See also Jean Beck's perceptive 'Wounded Men: The Hidden Face of Violence' in the same volume.

believe they love each other and want to go on living together. Often also the perpetrators themselves have been victims, of abusive parents, of bitter divorce struggles between their parents, of school playground bullying, of wartime traumas. For these reasons the emphasis should be as much on cure and rehabilitation as on prevention by deterrence and restraint.

Feminists have not shown any commensurate interest in the emotional violence which commonly accompanies marital breakup and divorce, particularly the disruption suffered by children, yet if a campaign comparable to the domestic violence effort was applied to family breakdown we might manage to alleviate this form of suffering.

Divorce and the feminisation of poverty

Burns objects to the 'structural inequity' which befalls women when their husband deserts, dies or divorces. This is a large subject, to be dealt with in two chapters of this book. All that needs to be said here is that it is about three times more common for women to initiate a divorce or separation than it is for men to do so.

Rethinking family achievements

If Burns's analysis is a fair average quality sample of the feminist critique of the family then clearly it contains little to cause the ordinary suburban homemaker to think that her life has all been a dreadful mistake. It fails quite markedly to show that women in general are the victims of opression. Two matters of importance arise from it, both of them obvious: the fact that homemaking is a low-status occupation, and the fact that it is difficult to combine responsibility for children with ambitions for a career, especially a full-time career.

A number of methodological points should be made about the 'critique' of the family. The anti-family literature fails to be properly critical because it never makes the effort to see why we have families and what it is they really do; because it constantly generalises from examples of family failure to the failure of the family as a whole; because it has no account of how and why some families manage to be relatively successful; because it has little respect for people's ordinary aspirations; and because it has nothing to put in the place of the family which embodies those aspirations. We easily believe almost anything about what governments can do to improve the world, or what can be done by the individual in pursuit of his or her own self-fulfilment, but we apply much more stringent standards when judging the achievements of families. The tendency has commonly been to blame the family for as much as possible, however ludicrous. We need to distinguish what happens in a family from what happens because it is in a family. The two are quite different. Much that goes wrong in families would happen in some other way were the persons concerned not members of any family. It may be that their being in families actually prevents further and more serious disintegration.

The critics have got one thing about family life right: it is a low-status business. Part of the reason for its lack of status is that it is the subject of so much ill-informed and ill-intentioned 'criticism', and it would help matters somewhat if this were to die out. But part of it is in the nature of the thing. Much of the work of family life is rather tedious. Housework and childcare especially are slow, day-to-day activities, and the results are nearly invisible. The critics do not ask creatively what might be done to make them easier. But more importantly, status is a device for regulating relations between people who are strangers to each other. It is, in other words, a public phenomenon. Families cannot use this device, quite simply because they know each other too well.

It is usually those who are hostile to the family who do most to perpetuate the sentimental image of family life, for the purpose of creating a straw target.[34] The truth is that we do not have to take this 'critique' half as seriously as it takes itself. There are things which are problematic about every family, just as there are about all states, societies and people. But families are as different and as varied as are people and societies. There are many signs that this anti-family propaganda is in decline, but we do not yet have any convincing picture of what it is that families really do. And without such a picture we cannot hope to understand or prevent family breakdown, much less eliminate child poverty, which is so often a consequence of family breakdown.

So far the argument will have seemed hostile to feminism. But not all of feminism is hostile to family life, and it may be that a rehabilitation of our understanding of families can be drawn partly from feminist sources. Feminist hostility to the family can be partly explained on various grounds. One is that the problems which feminism has with the family may just mirror, perhaps grotesquely, the general awkwardness our whole culture has here. But also, as Kathleen Fitzpatrick suggested, it is difficult to combine household and childcare responsibilities with a desire to do something in the public world. We might learn ways of making this easier. That the burdens of domestic life are usually borne by women should not be discounted as unimportant. These considerations make the strains in feminist rhetoric and argument at least partly explicable. Nor is it too much

---

34 Actually, this 'critique' of the family is mostly very old: there is little that can be said against the family that was not said long ago by Plato in *The Republic*. Anyone interested in the long history of wrestling between the pretensions of public life and people's natural preference for their own private world should read Mount's *The Subversive Family: An Alternative History of Love and Marriage*. See also Jean Bethke Elshtain's *Public Man, Private Woman: Women in Social and Political Thought*.

to hope that something of lasting importance for the understanding of our relation to the family may eventually come out of the movement, or at least from its more clear-thinking and self-critical exponents. 'The Personal is Political' slogan, which was intended to convey a sense of public anguish at private wrongs, can take on a different twist. It might be used, contrary to its original intention, to make the public world more aware of the importance and value of the private world. For lack of any better terminology this strand of argument might be known as 'conservative feminism'—assuming of course that a set of ideas can be conservative without being hidebound or illiberal.[35]

Where liberal feminism wants women to achieve in public life, conservative feminism wants public recognition of private achievements; it wants a revaluing of the importance of home and family; and it portrays the child-rearing skills as central virtues: empathy, forbearance, nurturance, support, and patience. But the image is often somewhat stuffy; it makes women seem secondary, selfless, and dull. Its central claims are that private achievements within the family have public value; and that you can have both love and equality between men and women, if you work at it; but it rarely argues for these with sufficient force. Its position gets patronised, or matronised, and its voice is rarely taken seriously.

As an example of a kind of conservative feminist argument, consider the following feminist attack on the ideals of liberal individualism by Mary Midgley:

> The whole idea of a free independent, enquiring, choosing individual ... in spite of its force and nobility, contains a deep strain of falsity, not just because the reasons why it was not applied to one half of the human race were not honestly looked at, but because the supposed independence of the male was itself false. It was parasitical, taking for granted the love and service of non-autonomous females (and indeed often of the less enlightened males as well). It pretended to be universal when it was not. This equivocal, unrealistic attitude to the mutual dependence central to human life does not just inconvenience women. It falsifies the whole basis of life. Morality becomes a lop-sided melodrama. The virtues and qualities we need for love and service are uncritically despised, while those involved in self-assertion are uncritically exalted (except when it is women who are doing the asserting).[36]

This is interesting for a number of reasons. In the first place it applies very well as a description of what is wrong with much contemporary feminism as well as traditional male attitudes. Feminists have very often exalted independence, despised self-sacrifice and pretended that their claims and

35 That conservatism is not intrinsically objectionable is shown by the environmental debate. Conservationists are ecological conservatives; conservatives are social conservationists.

36 Midgley, 'Sex and Personal Identity. The Western Individualistic Tradition'. For arguments from a similar perspective see Eastman's *Family: The Vital Factor*.

demands were universal when they were not. Women, because their work had no place for it, were once far better than men at detecting cant and hypocrisy. This is no longer true. But also, insofar as liberal feminism is individualist, Midgley's objections hold good against feminism.

The comment focuses on male/female relations. In a manner all too characteristic of feminist writing (though certainly not of Midgley's other writings) the passage makes no mention of children, yet it might be applied even more strongly to family life as a whole. Family members are individuals and they do have interests of their own, but it is hard to conceive of a family which operated predominantly on those individualistic assumptions. (This holds true also for friendship, and for teamwork in all its various manifestations, but it has special importance in the long-term context of family life.) Midgley's remarks help to mark the boundary between an individualist ethic of self-fulfilment and an ethic based on the 'mutual dependence central to human life'.

It is useful to distinguish here between dependence and mutual dependence. Dependence as such is the condition of young children and sick, disabled and very old adults. Mutual dependence is an adult possibility. It entails mutual support, yet it is not inconsistent with self-reliance, a quality which both some conservatives and some radicals properly admire. The family involves both mutual (husband/wife) and simple (parent/child) dependence. The traditional purposes of marriage are the creation and nurture of children, sexual mutuality, and companionship between husband and wife. The old Anglican marriage service speaks of 'the mutual society, help and comfort that the one ought to have of the other, both in prosperity and adversity'.

An ethic of caring for dependants is dismissed by some militant feminists because it seems to them to be itself a form of exploitation. There is a grain of half-truth in this: people occupied in caring for others (both women and men) cannot look after their own interests as well as the rest of us can, and they are therefore vulnerable to exploitation. This is one reason why families require some social support, though all such outside assistance can easily become outside interference. Any shift to re-emphasise the importance of homes and families is open to the objection that it thereby devalues the public gains made by women in the past two decades. But there is no theoretical conflict here. Both are good, and the world will be richer if we can maximise both. (In that sense Midgley has not shown that there is anything wrong with liberalism or individualism as public philosophies—only that they cannot accommodate private life.)

The ethics of the family are very different from the ethics of public life, where the interests of the individual tend to predominate. Marriage is entered voluntarily; children are sometimes planned. But we do not choose where, when and to whom we will be born; and once having produced children of our own we are more or less stuck with them through thick and thin, whether we like them or not. Traditional marriage likewise assumed permanence, no doubt partly because care for children requires long-term commitment. The basic purpose of the family is to bring the next generation into being, and transmit to it self-confidence, competence and respect for others. This much should be obvious, though it is not often said. The fact is that to a remarkable extent families do this, and do it moderately well. The fact is extraordinary because to do the job at all well requires considerable quantities of care, consideration, patience, self-sacrifice, humour, flexibility, self-assurance, not to mention a good deal of time, labour and money.

The scale of this commitment is such that a visiting Martian who knew nothing about human reproduction and life-cycles would surely wonder why we go to so much trouble for so little reward. Parents sometimes ask themselves the same question. Of course there are great rewards and pleasures in family life, but many of them are not the standard kinds of pleasure that we tend to seek as adults in search of self-fulfilment in our careers or our leisure activities. To a large extent the pleasures consist in taking pleasure in someone else's happiness, growth or achievement. They are the second-order pleasures of altruism. It is this familial altruism which is the primary form of love and which is essential to personal and social sanity. It is this altruism which comes to the fore when, for instance, family members suffer serious illness or disability. It is of course a very different thing from the sentimentalised accounts of the nature of love which somehow predominate in our culture.

In saying this there is no need to deny the genuine danger that parents may be too altruistic for their own good, by seeking to give their children everything for nothing. There is in every family a complex interplay between parents and children which amounts to the process of moral education. Clearly, it is within the family that children learn most of what they ever learn about respect for other people. It is by playing a part in the mini-society of the family that they learn to play a part in the larger society of adults. Public affections and commitment do not come wholly naturally and without effort. They have to be learned by being practised in a manageable and friendly environment. And that involves bumping up against others with conflicting interests and desires, and learning to respect those desires and interests.

The family also acts as safety valve for the pressures and stresses generated elsewhere in society. This is one reason why family life does not, cannot and should not conform to the sentimentalised image propagated about it by its enemies. To understand why people—both men and women—sometimes seem to behave worse at home than they do in public we need to be sensitive to the safety valve aspect of family life. They behave worse there because they know that there at least they will be accepted with all their faults. It is not family life which puts up a false front, it is public life—and our real selves have to emerge somewhere. These things should be kept in mind when we are thinking about the serious issues of child abuse and domestic violence. They are of course not an excuse for such abuse or violence but only a partial explanation of it. To say this is not to deny that families sometimes generate their own, perhaps unnecessary, crises. And sometimes these need help from outside the family. But most intra-family problems, and a great many which originate outside the family, are dealt with inside the family. The unconditional for-better-or-worse commitment of traditional marriage is a recognition that we need someone to be there when all else fails, or when we ourselves fail. As Robert Frost remarked, 'home is the place where, when you have to go there, they have to take you in'.

Furthermore, marriage and family life are compatible with feminism. As Hilary Cosell puts it, marriage

> satisfies and fulfils the need for intimacy in ways other relationships can't.... The unwillingness to admit this, to find ways and means for women to create successful personal lives built on their visions of themselves as females, as well as successful business lives, is the termite of the feminist soul.... The concept that a professional identity and success is a substitute for a female identity—consequently a marital and/or motherhood identity—ignores the basic need for companionship all people feel. It ignores the peculiarly female complications of the need and assumes any differences between females and males are merely environmental, culturally programmed, solely the result of custom.... [W]hen women live in a world where they are fearful and ashamed to admit that they want to marry and have children, when women live in a world that indicts them for wanting to not only marry and have a child, but remain at home to oversee raising that child, then this new order doesn't offer much of an improvement over the old.[37]

The work of American feminist and sociologist Alice S. Rossi reinforces this conclusion. She rejects the view, 'fashionable nowadays, that family systems victimise and oppress women', and argues that marriage and family life are generally good for both men and women. Her claim is based on research evidence of psychological differences between men and women. Women, she believes, are more naturally sociable than men: 'they tend to seek out other people; they form quasi-sisterly relations with other women; and they turn to parents, adult children, and siblings to satisfy their social and emotional needs, all of which further reinforce their embeddedness in social institutions, a pattern men do not show to nearly the same extent'. Rossi interprets this as suggesting that 'a critical function of family systems is to bind men into the social collective'. The advantages of this binding to women, children and men are, she implies, very great. 'All the sociological literature on social deviance lends support to this interpretation, for young, unattached males predominate in sexual violence, alcohol and drug abuse, crime and terrorism'.[38] She adds that only for a

37 Cosell, *Woman on a Seesaw*, 109f.

38 Rossi, 'Sex and Gender in an Aging Society', 158ff. See also her 'Gender and Parenthood'.

small minority of men does work provide a comparable force for social integration.

Australian figures on suicide tend to corroborate the view that families are important support systems. An analysis of ABS data on suicide and marital status between 1971 and 1986 by Trevor Chambers (a researcher for Care and Communication Concern) shows that both men and women who never marry are about three times more likely to suicide than those who are married. After divorce women and men are about four times more likely to suicide than women and men who are married. This last figure probably underestimates the disparity because the figures for spouses who are separated are included in the figures for those who are married, and data from Britain which distinguishes between separated and living-together married couples indicates a very high suicide rate amongst separated spouses. As Chambers observes, 'This suggests that, for Australians, the "most suicidal" group is hidden in the statistics among the marrieds'.[39]

Contrary to the sentimentalised version of family life, the family is a sceptical institution. It is not starry-eyed and self-admiring. It has little place for appearances and style. People are known in their families in ways in which they cannot be known elsewhere. The principle that no man is a hero to his valet is crucial to the understanding of family ethics.[40] Families rarely need to debunk the flightier pretensions of their more ambitious members, for they know without needing to say so how limited public success is. No man or woman is a public figure to his or her children. This ethos needs to be cultivated rather carefully now when the traditional guardians of this scepticism, women, are themselves seeking greater public recognition.

Defence of marriage and the family should not need to appeal to any elevated ideals. The case stands or falls on their ordinary operation. But marriage and the family do have their own built-in ideals, and institutionalised ideals are more susceptible to a certain sort of criticism than are more down-to-earth social arrangements. The fact that we don't live up to the ideals can be used to show either that they are not good ideals or that those who espouse them are hypocritical. This sort of criticism is all too easy; and the conclusions do not follow from the premise. A world without ideals is not necessarily better than a world with only half-realisable ideals. In practice we do need to learn to live with the fact that reality rarely measures up to the ideal, and sometimes we might decide to abandon the ideal itself, but it should not be for the easy reason that it is after all only an ideal. We learn to live with similar ideals in many other parts of our

39 Chambers, 'Psychosomatic Suicide', 4.

40 The maxim comes from Montaigne, and the source is interesting: 'Men have seemed miraculous to the world, in whom their wives and valets have never seen anything even worth noticing. Few men have been admired by their own households'.

lives—in art, in attitudes to nature, in religion, even sometimes in politics. Marriage and family life require the same kind of adaptability.

Such is the long history of hostility to the family by intellectuals that it will be no easy matter to learn to think both realistically and appreciatively about the institution. The twin facts that it is still the preferred mode of life for most people and that we have great difficulty in managing family life makes it important that we do learn this. Ferdinand Mount, who has done much to document this hostility, concludes his *The Subversive Family* by asking: 'Why do people still wish to submerge, at least partially, their personalities in marriage and devote a great part of their lives, perhaps the major part, to "working at" this battered old form of human relationship?' His hesitant answers are worth quoting.

> With all its tediums and horrors, [marriage] has both more variety and more continuity than any other commitment we can make.... Its passions, both of love and hatred, are more intense. Its outcomes—children, grandchildren, heirlooms of flesh and blood—stretch away over the horizon; they are the only identifiable achievements which most of us are likely to leave behind us, even if, like many achievements, they are liable to be flawed and only partially within our control. Marriage and the family make other experiences, both pleasant and unpleasant, seem a little tame and bloodless.[41]

This passage does combine realism and idealism. It may even contain an element of truth.

Having been critical of some feminist attitudes and arguments it is perhaps appropriate to end this chapter by quoting an Australian feminist, Ann Curthoys. 'It's time', Curthoys says, that

> feminists began sweeping the ground from under the feet of the Right, not by defending 'the family' per se, but by defending those values which it is held to represent: long-term relationships, emotional commitment, kinship ties, and especially the importance of the close bonding which occurs between parents and children.[42]

It is difficult to know whether this is feminism sweeping the ground from under the feet of 'the Right', or the Right having swept the ground from underneath feminism, but either way it doesn't much matter. The important thing is our common commitment to these values, which transcend partisan and factional considerations. However, if these are appropriate goals then we need social policies which support them, or at least do not undermine them. The two most notable policy areas concern the financial viability of families and the processes involved in maintaining the long-term relationships central to family life. The next four chapters will seek to show both that at present we do not have policies which support the objectives outlined by Curthoys, and that if we value those goals we can find ways to assist in achieving them.

---

41 Mount, *The Subversive Family*, 256.

42 *For and Against Feminism*, 66.

5 Family finances

Family incomes

The most original, substantial and interesting contribution to the Social Security Review is Alan Jordan's two-volume analysis of incomes in Australia, entitled *The Common Treasury: the Distribution of Income to Families and Households*. Jordan set out to apply the techniques of computer-based cluster analysis to the data from the 1982 ABS Income and Housing Survey, covering 15,000 households and 21,000 income units, with a view to illuminating some very old questions about human well-being. He lists the questions he has in view as follows:

> How are differences in the incomes of individuals and families to be measured? Why do they matter? Are we concerned with income as an end in itself, as a means to other ends, as one good among many? How is income related to other things people value? Which individuals and families have higher and lower incomes, and why? How do their incomes vary over time? Do the inequalities correspond to discernible structures and processes? When are inequalities to be considered both unnecessary and unacceptable? Are we concerned only about poverty, or with inequality in general? In so far as we are concerned with poverty, how do we know whether an individual or family is poor? If existing inequalities appear to be unjust, what can be done about them?[1]

Economists and other social theorists have attempted to deal with these questions for a very long time, and many have been prepared to accept defeat in the face of them. Casting their loosely-woven conceptual nets at random into a sea of plankton-sized data, it is not surprising that the nets returned to the boat with little more than the occasional red herring.

1 *Common Treasury*, **1**, 1.

Jordan's work is now a useful starting point for discussion of these topics. His results are significant not just because he has successfully dredged through the data; he has at the same time raised the standard of interpretation of the subject to a level commensurate with the complexity of the questions. Previous income analyses have been bedevilled by the fact that the researcher has had to select *a priori* the criteria deemed likely to reveal significant results. The Henderson Poverty Commission, for instance, attempted to discover levels of poverty in a select range of 'disability groups'—'fatherless families', 'the unemployed', 'aged couples', etc. Jordan's cluster analysis makes it possible for the first time 'to sort individuals, income units or households into groups having as much similarity as possible within and as much dissimilarity as possible between groups' with a minimum of rigid presupposition about which categories will and will not produce the most revealing results.[2]

The other difficulty which has bedevilled this sort of enterprise is to find some way of comparing people in families with individuals outside the family. As Jordan observes, 'Many more people depend on than receive incomes, and the actual standard of living of the recipient depends on how much goes to the support of dependants, that of dependants on how much benefit is passed on to them'.[3] To come to terms with the asymmetry between earners and dependants it is necessary to introduce the concept of 'equivalent income'. This notion attempts to provide an approximate measure of standards of living. To do this it must supply a formula which reconciles three conflicting tendencies: to allow for the degree to which an income is shared between dependants; to allow for the different needs of adults and children; and to allow for the economies of scale enjoyed by those who share a household. Equivalence scales are calculated not simply on the actual expenses of living, which will vary greatly between rich and poor families, but on the costs of basic needs such as food and housing. They attempt to measure some minimum standard of living. For this purpose the needs of wealthy children are regarded as the same as those of poor families.

Jordan adopts the square root of family size as his index. As he puts it, 'The simplest statistic having the desired characteristics is the square root of size of the unit and the simplest method of calculating equivalent income is therefore to divide unit income by square root of unit size'.[4] On this reckoning a family of four requires about twice the income of a single person to sustain the same standard of living, and a family of nine three times the same income. Jordan's formula has, quite by happenstance, the advantage of being a very convenient mathematical simplification, but other measures might have been adopted, and some of them may be superior. The ABS equivalence scales, for instance, rank the first child as

2 *Common Treasury*, 23.
3 *Ibid.* 10.
4 *Ibid.* 12.

approximately 40% of an adult, second as 20%, third as 15%, fourth as 10%.[5] We shall adopt Jordan's formula in the remainder of this book, not because it is demonstrably better than any other index, but because it seems to be as good as any other. One might reasonably suspect that the economies of scale alleged by both Jordan's and the ABS formula are somewhat exaggerated, and thus biased against families—the last child in a family of nine might well feel hardly done by on these calculations. But the general reliability of these scales is a complex question and it is convenient to take Jordan as our authority on the matter, allowing that future research may come up with a better formula. (We can note in passing that the cost of child care—opportunity cost for the parent who stays at home, actual cost for the family that pays for child care—is not counted in either the ABS scales or Jordan's scheme.)

Jordan's *Common Treasury* is as notable for what it does not prove as much as for what it does. Although the questions being asked are ambitious, he is admirably cautious about the limitations of his techniques. The data available for cross-indexing against (pre-tax) income include age, family status, educational qualifications, occupation, accommodation, and dependency on social security. Jordan makes it very clear that such research cannot take direct account of personal differences such as motivation, ambition, intelligence, talent or taste. Nor can it include family characteristics such as inherited wealth, intra-family transfers and quality of family relationships. Even more overtly social phenomena such as quality of schooling or income minimisation for tax avoidance purposes also slip through the net. And Jordan freely allows that income and welfare are by no means synonymous. As he observes, 'Inequalities of income do matter, but ultimately only because of their relationship to the distribution of social goods more important than money'.[6] Within such limitations Jordan's conclusions are of necessity modest ones. Indeed, he can say that

> Ultimately, only partial answers can be supplied to the question of why some people are better off materially than others. Describing and explaining the distribution of the sum of material and immaterial benefit is impossible.[7]

In the end, Jordan's 'partial answers' revolve around three concepts: social class, stage in the life cycle and age cohort. The age cohort effect—whether one grew up in the Depression or the post-war boom or the 1970s economic slowdown—is the least predictive of the three, and need not enter into this discussion. But Jordan's conclusions about social class do bear repetition here, as it is commonly assumed by people concerned with social welfare issues that Australia is in some significant sense a class society. The notion of class is notoriously elastic, and any discussion of the subject must be imprecise. Jordan does not deny that there are class differ-

5 Cass, *Income Support for Families with Children*, 24.
6 *Common Treasury*, **2**, 231.
7 *Ibid.* 180f.

ences in this country, but he emphasises the permeability of those differences. The differences are differences of median income, but they do not appear to be strongly underpinned by other differences. As he puts it,

> We have demonstrated no sharply-defined strata within which people lead different lives. None exist in Australian society. Whatever the imprecision of our groups of higher and lower status, one characteristic that may be accepted as an accurate representation of reality is that their incomes overlap.[8]

Even among the highest income groups, Jordan found, surprisingly, a significant number of persons without formal educational or occupational qualifications. When classifying income-earners by occupation he found that the 9 per cent of earners with tertiary degrees had an equivalent income of 388; the 15 per cent of semi-professionals 286; the 23 per cent with trade qualifications 247; and the 53 per cent with none 232.[9]

Even at the bottom end of the social spectrum, Jordan concludes, the working poor 'with lowest earned incomes can no more be seen as a permanent and homogeneous underclass than the people at the other extreme can be seen as a superior caste'.[10] The difference between the gross, pretax equivalent incomes of the top 20 per cent of income-earners and the bottom 20 per cent is a ratio of three to one. After tax the difference between the two would be further reduced. And even those dependent on welfare transfers do not constitute a clearly-demarcated social stratum.

> As compared with the working population, non-aged recipients of government benefits tend to have characteristics generally associated with low income—relatively low educational status and rates of home ownership, for example—but not in such a degree as to set them apart from people whose incomes are much higher. That is, they are an underclass in terms of income but not, as far as one can tell, in terms of other characteristics....[11]

In other words, the unemployed male is likely to be almost indistinguishable from his employed next-door-neighbour, and the female sole parent almost indistinguishable from her married neighbour. This suggests that what makes a person a welfare recipient is to be found either in those personal and family characteristics which slip through Jordan's net, or else is a matter of chance. The implications of this for welfare policy can be postponed until we come to discuss sole parenthood directly. All that needs to be noted here is that assistance to the welfare population does not seem to require wholesale social change of the kind that (for instance) Marxists would like to see.

It might be insisted here by those who favour class analyses that wealth and not income is the appropriate measure of class differences. Wealth does not fall within Jordan's purview. Attempts to estimate wealth differ-

8 *Common Treasury*, **2**, 179.
9 *Ibid.* **1**, 75.
10 *Ibid.* **2**, 164.
11 *Ibid.* 226.

entials are sometimes simplistic. As with income, wealth comparisons need to be corrected for life-cycle effects. John Nurick has shown that in a perfectly egalitarian society with no inherited wealth and with everyone receiving the same weekly income from age 17 until death at age 75, if everyone saves 5 per cent of their income at 5 per cent compound interest then the poorest 10 per cent of the population—young adults—will have about 0.4 per cent of the wealth and the richest 10 per cent—the elderly—will have nearly 30 per cent of the wealth.[12] He also points out that calculations of wealth may omit items which should be counted: the family home, superannuation entitlements, life insurance, the contingent value of social security benefits, the value of one's publicly paid-for education, shares in government assets such as defence, roads, hospitals, schools, and publicly-owned enterprises. Only once all of these complexities have been taken into account can any conclusions be drawn from wealth distributions about the structure of society. In the meantime we are confined to discussions of income.

But if Jordan's de-emphasis of class differences is unexpected, his emphasis on life-cycle differences is equally surprising. His three-to-one ratio of equivalent income for top and bottom quintiles of the working population cannot be taken at face value as a direct indication of class differences because it is affected by life-cycle differences. The bottom twenty per cent are likely to be mostly young working-class families, and the top twenty per cent middle-aged middle-class couples whose children have left home or are living at home and in well-paid employment.

To compare classes it is necessary to compare like with like. When Jordan analysed married-couple income units with children he found the population tended to divide into two groups, presumably reflecting class differences; but the interesting discovery here is that the median equivalent incomes of the two are in the ratio of 3:4—not a difference that can be held up as an example of a class society.[13] Some other categories of the population produced sharper income contrasts, others produced less demarcation; the 3:4 ratio seems a reasonable summation of the whole picture. Yet, when he examined life-cycle differences, he found that a very similar order of magnitude holds here. For instance the equivalent income ratio of all working families with dependent children to all working individuals including those with families is 4:5.[14] But this underestimates the difference: to be more exact here it would be necessary to exclude families with children from the second population and to hold age and class (as measured by education and occupation) differences steady. Jordan's methods did not permit such a disaggregation because, as he remarks, 'Single adults are not a definable stratum of the population'.[15] However, if we can assume that

12 Nurick, *Wealth and Power*, 28f.
13 *Common Treasury*, **2**, 175; Jordan's exact ratio is 158:207.
14 *Ibid.* 171f; the exact ratio is 192:244.
15 *Ibid.* **1**, 70.

family formation and family size are class-neutral, then some rough comparison might be drawn between the equivalent incomes of those who do and those who do not have children. The ratio turns out to be 3:5.[16]

Of course the population of persons without dependent children is a heterogeneous one, ranging across young adults before they begin a family, older couples whose children have left home and the stratum of permanently childless. Families with children are located in the life cycle between the first two of these groupings, and it might be guessed that their average gross incomes (not equivalent incomes) would be about equal to the weighted average of the gross incomes of those two groups. This is a complicated comparison. Earnings for primary earners are usually lowest at the beginning of a person's career, and tend to level off at about age 45. For women, most of whom interrupt their careers to have children, earnings are much more variable, but are on average lowest during the childbearing and child-rearing years. And incomes fall dramatically for both men and women at retirement age, though this is to some indeterminate extent cushioned by accumulated wealth and assets. The 3:5 ratio, then, cannot be taken as anything more than the roughest of guides to family standards of living. The reality may be higher, or it may be lower.

Further consideration of these figures suggests that there will be some even sharper distinctions to be drawn. Childless couples, for instance, can be expected to enjoy very high equivalent incomes, not just because they will both enjoy uninterrupted careers, nor simply because they do not share their incomes with dependants; they also have the advantage of the economies of scale that come from shared living. It might be expected that they would typically enjoy a standard of living at least twice as high as that of families with children. At the opposite end of the scale, single income families will enjoy equivalent incomes considerably lower than the median for all families with children, though again Jordan's analysis does not permit any quantification of this difference. Contrasting these two opposite ends of the spectrum—the double income couple without children and the single income family—it is easy to arrive at an equivalent income ratio of about three-to-one, the same ratio Jordan found between the top and bottom equivalent income quintiles for working income units. In other words, the decision to have children and to have one partner caring for them full-time at home is a decision to lower one's standard of living to about a third what it could otherwise be.

The main general conclusion of this analysis is that families with children seem to operate on an average standard of living about three-fifths that of the rest of the working community. As Jordan observes, 'those on whom the community depends for its continued existence—its children—are allocated low equivalent incomes, at birth perhaps the lowest of their lives....'.[17] Or to put the same point differently, those on whom the com-

16 192:322; calculated from the population proportions at *ibid.* 170f.
17 *Ibid.* 179.

munity depends for the continuation of the species—its parents—have low equivalent incomes, at the birth of their children perhaps the lowest of their lives. Raising a family is a costly business.

Jordan's description can be supplemented by the results of Beggs and Chapman's analysis of *The Forgone Earnings From Child-Rearing in Australia*, which calculated that 'Relative to the lifetime earnings of childless women, one, two and three children reduce earnings by about 53, 61 and 67 per cent respectively'. On average women forgo about $400,000 in lifetime earnings in order to care for children. If this hypothetical woman had been able to invest these 'earnings' at five per cent per annum interest, the lifetime sum forgone would be closer to a million dollars.[18] These sums, large though they are, by no means measure all of the time and money that parents put in to their work as parents. One calculation estimates the forgone earnings costs to be 70 per cent of total child-rearing costs.[19]

From all this it seems clear—even when the necessary cautions and qualifications are added in—that life-cycle differences are on the whole just as marked as differences of class in Australian society. Of course, anyone who denies that justice, prudence or charity require any form of redistribution from rich to poor may also wish to deny that government ought to adjust gross incomes so that people on the same earned gross incomes but with different family commitments enjoy similar living standards. However, the considerations which support the former may not be the same as those which support the latter. Indeed, it may be easier to accept the latter. Equalising the living standards of people on similar incomes seems less likely to set up adverse incentives, and it is perhaps more compatible with rewards for ability and effort.

Families and government

Jordan's *Common Treasury* is an important addition to our knowledge of incomes, and particularly of family finances. But it deliberately excludes consideration of the impact of government and taxation on income. It is commonly assumed that government does redistribute income to families. The most visible mechanisms for doing this are through the tax and welfare systems, and most discussions of the subject proceed to list as examples of Australian family assistance the Family Allowance, the Family Allowance Supplement for low-income working families, the Dependent Spouse Rebate, the Sole Parent Rebate, the Sole Parents Benefit, and the additional payments for children of other kinds of pensioner or beneficiary.

---

18 Beggs & Chapman, *Forgone Earnings from Child-Rearing in Australia.*

19 Espenshade, 'The Price of Children and Socioeconomic Theories of Fertility'. See also his *Investing in Children: new estimates of parental expenditure.*

Rebate, the Sole Parent Rebate, the Sole Parents Benefit, and the additional payments for children of other kinds of pensioner or beneficiary.

Discussions along these lines are, however, of very little interest in themselves. The Family Allowance, for instance, constitutes about $1350 million in the Commonwealth Budget, an impressive-looking sum until it is translated into the dollars and cents of the family housekeeping budget. As Peter Whiteford pointed out in 1986, 'In effect, the family allowance program provides no more than a payment of between 25 cents and 50 cents for each meal that a child has in a week'.[20] In fact it is much less than this: about half of the allowance is already paid for by the average family itself in its taxes, and along the way some of the money is lost in administration costs (not to mention other deadweight losses caused by disincentive effects). Probably most children get more in pocket money from their parents than the family gets from government in its 'allowance'.

To appreciate the total impact of government on families we must look beyond personal income taxation and social security spending. What is needed is a full-scale analysis of the interaction between government and different kinds of income unit, and, fortunately, the Australian Bureau of Statistics fiscal incidence study gives us, for the first time, a clearer picture of this interaction. The results are just as surprising as those from Jordan's research. We now know that, taking into account all government services and benefits and deducting all direct and indirect taxes, there is no net transfer to families with dependent children. In other words, everything that families get from government—including the most costly item, education—they pay for themselves. Indeed, they pay for slightly more than they receive. The only transfer to poor families comes from better-off families. There is no transfer to families with children from those who never have children. And for those who do have children there is no transfer from the periods before and after they have children to that period in the middle when their needs are greatest.

The Bureau's findings on the interaction between government and families are summarised in Figures 5.1 and 5.2, which rely on a paper by the Australian Statistician, Ian Castles.[21] Castles selects ten broad, mutually-exclusive household types from the survey population, defining them in terms of family structure and age of household members (explanations beneath Figure 5.1). The charts show the average benefits received and taxes paid per household for each of the household types, and the net effect. Figure 5.1 shows dollars per week (in 1984), and Figure 5.2 shows

20 Whiteford, *Issues in Assistance for Families— Horizontal and Vertical Equity Considerations*, 31.

21 'Government Welfare Outlays: Who Benefits? Who Pays?'. Remarkably this evidence, though it is crucial to family assistance questions, and though it has been available since 1987, has nowhere been taken into account or even mentioned by the Social Security Review.

Figure 5.1: Benefits & Taxes per Household

for selected household types (average, $ per week)

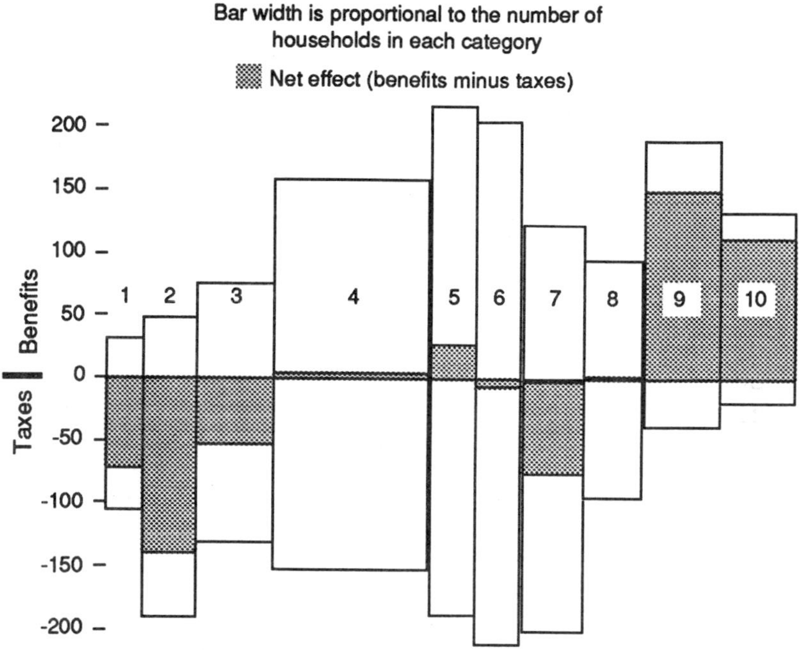

Composition of the selected Household Types:

1 Young single (one person living alone, age under 35).
2 Young married couple (no children, household head aged under 35).
3 Couple and child(ren) under 5 years.
4 Couple and child(ren), eldest aged between 5 and 15).
5 Couple and dependent child(ren), eldest aged 15 or more.
6 Couple and both dependent and non-dependent children (but no other household members).
7 Couple and non-dependent child(ren).
8 Middle-aged couple (head aged between 55 and 64).
9 Elderly couple (head aged 65 or more).
10 Elderly single (one person living alone, aged 65 or more).

Source: Table A in I. Castles, Government Welfare Outlays: Who Benefits? Who Pays?, *Canberra Bulletin of Public Administration*, March 1987.

Figure 5.2: Benefits & Taxes per Household
as per cent of final income, for selected household types

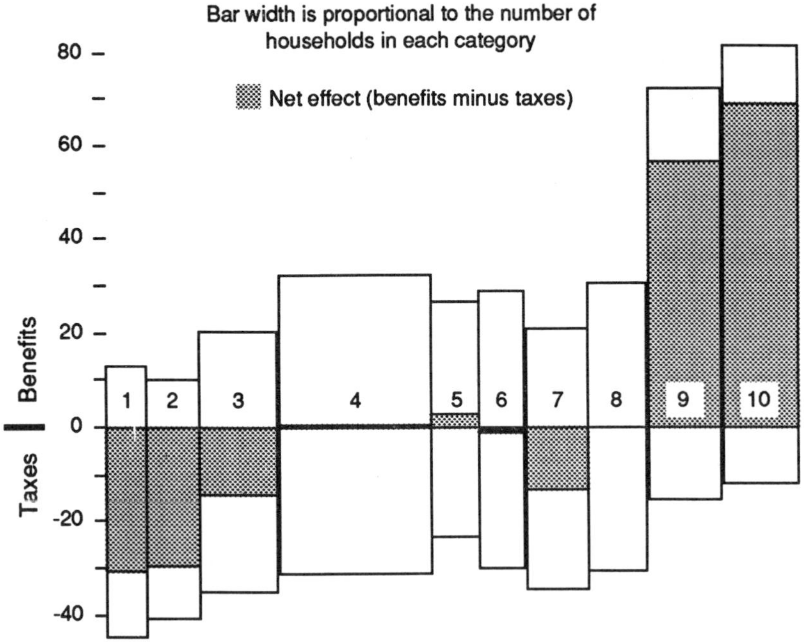

See Figure 5.1 for information on household composition.
Source: See Figure 5.1.

the amounts as percentages of final income. The width of each column in the figures is proportional to the number of households in each category (though not to the numbers of persons in each household type).

The Bureau found that the total revenue taken from direct and indirect taxes roughly equalled total government 'social' expenditure—that is, outlays on such items as education, health, housing and social security, each of which is substantially a private good. Conveniently for our purposes, the remaining expenditure—the 'public good' budget—can be thought of as coming out of other forms of taxation. Taken overall the graph indicates that the main net transfer in the Australian social system is from young to old. Pensions and health services for the aged are paid for mainly by income earners below the age of 35, some of whom have young children.

Our particular interest is in households with dependent children—types (3), (4), (5) and (6)—amounting to about half the selected households. As the shaded net effect areas show, these groups taken together give more to governments than they get back, and the major contributors are families with young children. The only net beneficiaries are type (5), couples with older children of secondary school or tertiary education age. The charts enable us to modify Jordan's broadly-correct observation that 'society is not much concerned with young children, shows more interest when they go to school, and invests most heavily in those who, the time approaching for them to become independent agents, disclose plausible claims to higher status'.[22] Society does indeed allocate its resources in this way, but the resources are those it has taken directly from the families themselves. Education is the only major item of government spending which goes primarily to families, and both primary and secondary education are paid for entirely out of family taxes.

The ABS fiscal incidence figures can be supplemented to some extent with information about changes in personal income tax payments, as collated in a recent EPAC paper, *Income Support Policies, Taxation and Incentives*. No straightforward connections can be drawn between the two sorts of data because income tax figures tell us nothing about government spending. One social group may have its tax payments increased and yet be a net gainer if government spending is directed towards it and away from other sectors. And vice versa: a group may enjoy tax reductions and yet still lose out if government spending is directed away from it.

In 1954–55 a single taxpayer (someone with no dependants) earning average weekly earnings paid 9.60 per cent personal income tax; an earner with a spouse and two children to support paid 4.96 per cent, but after child endowment payments are taken into consideration this amounted to only 0.57 per cent. In 1964–65 the same comparison gives figures of 14.36 per cent, 9.32 per cent and 6.57 per cent. In 1974–75 the figures have jumped to 21.96 per cent, 17.30 per cent and 16.29 per cent. Ten years later the figures are 24.59 per cent, 19.96 per cent and (we are now counting Family Allowance, not child endowment) 16.97 per cent.[23] Another way of putting this is to say that after family assistance is taken into account, the proportion of tax paid by average-income families to that paid by average-income single persons is 6 per cent in 1954–55, 46 per cent in 1964–65, 75 per cent in 1974–75 and 69 per cent in 1984–85.

Between 1964–65 and 1984–85 the net tax (counting family assistance) paid by average single persons increased by 71 per cent and that by average (two child) families by 158 per cent. If we compare individuals and families on 0.75 average earnings then the contrast is even more dramatic: 78 per cent and 325 per cent. At 1.50 times AWE (61 per cent and 102 per cent) and at 2.0 times AWE (58 per cent and 84 per cent) the comparison is somewhat less stark, but the same trend is clear. While the 1989 May Economic Statement, which increased and indexed Family Allowances, will have made some slight difference to these figures, the difference does not significantly alter the long-term trend.

22 *Common Treasury*, **2**, 189.
23 EPAC Council Paper 35, 86.

The taxation picture can be further sharpened if we distinguish between two-parent and one-parent families. An earlier EPAC publication, *Aspects of the Social Wage*, demonstrates that whereas two-parent families are net contributors to government (thus confirming the ABS finding), sole parent families receive in government benefits four times as much as they contribute in taxes.[24] Since one segment of the population of families with children is so strongly favoured by government assistance, and as families on the whole get no net benefits from government, we can conclude that two-parent families generally lose from their interaction with the tax/transfer system.

International comparisons are sometimes employed to support the conclusion that Australia gives little support to families with dependent children, but this evidence is misleading. Carol Oxley surveyed the international family assistance scene for the Social Security Review. Her contribution, *The Structure of General Family Provision In Australia and Overseas: A Comparative Study*, provides evidence for the conclusion that (contrary to common belief, and contrary to Oxley's conclusion) Australia appears to be, by international standards, not ungenerous to families with children. The belief that Australia is ungenerous rests on a comparison between levels of universal family assistance in the OECD countries.[25] On this comparison Australia ranks twelfth in a list of sixteen countries, providing about half the international average level. A more revealing comparison, also based on 1984 figures, is that between the levels of family disposable income after tax.[26] On this way of reckoning the matter Australia ranks sixth in a list of thirteen, considerably higher than Sweden and the Netherlands, who far outrank us in the previous table, and not far behind Belgium and Austria, the top two in the first table. Even more curiously, Spain and Canada, who were last and thirteenth in the first table, come out fifth and third in the second table.

Oxley does not discuss these remarkable transpositions. One obvious interpretation is that those countries who rank highly in the first comparison but low in the second, such as Sweden and the Netherlands, give generously to families but then tax back almost as much as they give, a perfectly pointless exercise known to policy analysts and economists as 'churning'. On this comparison Australia's low level of family assistance at least can be credited with being well designed, relative to international standards. However, the best test of family assistance levels can come only from full fiscal incidence comparisons, and (as we have seen) Australian governments provide no net assistance to families. If this fact is reflected in Australia's ranking in Oxley's second table then it would appear that many

---

24 EPAC Council Paper 27, 38 & Chart 11.

25 Oxley, *The Structure of General Family Provision in Australia and Overseas*, Table 1 (derived from OECD, *The 1982 Tax/Benefit Position of a Typical Worker in OECD Member Countries*.

26 Oxley, *op. cit.*, Table 4.

advanced countries are even less helpful towards families than we are. But, as Oxley observes, these figures take no account of whether or not government spending favours families. In general it seems best to conclude that the international comparisons presently available are difficult to interpret and of little value for policy purposes.

What is clear is that the extraordinary growth of government in Australia in the past few decades has been financed disproportionately out of family earnings, particularly the earnings of two-parent families on PAYE taxation. Much of this growth has taken place in the welfare sector, if we interpret that term broadly, to cover health, housing and education as well as income transfers and welfare services. The paradoxical conclusion suggested by the above evidence is that the expansion of the welfare state in the past two or three decades has been paid for mainly by the primary welfare institution, families with dependent children; but in return for their contribution they have received very little, even after taking into account the rapid increase in expenditure on education. In other words, one welfare system—the state—has tended to displace or impoverish another—the family. If, however, we attribute the growth of government to a more general process of capture by interest groups or (in Olson's terms) 'distributional coalitions', of which the welfare industry is only one amongst many, then the evidence reinforces the argument of Chapter One that families are poorly equipped to compete in this sort of politicking. This trend away from universal family assistance runs counter to the general trend which Goodin and LeGrand have described as 'creeping universalism in the Australian welfare state', as evidenced by trends in the age pension and the invalid pension.[27] A further generalisation suggested is that, while Australia is not a class society, it may have an unbalanced allocation of resources between the generations, making the child-rearing years even more difficult than they intrinsically are. This point will be pursued in the later part of this chapter. Chapter Six will consider some of the further implications for taxation policy.

Coping strategies

So far, then, we have found—with as much assurance as any such matter can be known—that families operate on about three-fifths the equivalent income of the rest of the community; that they get no net advantage from

27 The family assistance trend poses an interesting explanatory problem. Goodin & LeGrand ('Creeping Universalism in the Australian Welfare State') provide four good reasons to *expect* universalism to flourish: 'boundary problems' in distinguishing poor from non-poor; bureaucratic empire-building; behavioural responses; and political pressure. Why have these not operated to expand universal assistance to families with dependent children? Why, indeed, has family assistance steadily dwindled in this period?

government; and that the personal taxation system has been steadily eroding whatever advantages families once enjoyed. At this point, however, opinions diverge even amongst those who will accept this description of the situation. Some will come to the conclusion that this is a society which wants to make parenthood as economically unpleasant and unattractive as possible. Others mount a case for saying that this is how the social system should be arranged. But before we enter this debate it is necessary to note the way in which, in the absence of any social support, families have responded to the economic difficulties they face.

There are four obvious strategies that couples can adopt to cope with these economic pressures. One is not to have children at all; another is to limit the number of children they have; a third is to delay having children until an adequate capital base has been built up; and the fourth is to take a second job while caring for children. It is the last of these which has occasioned most discussion, though all four have become evident social trends at least since the early 1970s when economic growth began to slow down. While it cannot be assumed that these trends are caused solely by economic factors, there is no reason to doubt that economic factors play some part in bringing them about.

The first two of these strategies is indicative of a world-wide trend amongst industrialised societies towards population deceleration or decline. The full explanation of this trend is far from clear, and its interpretation from a policy viewpoint is also the subject of discussion in some countries, though not yet in Australia. Whether social policy should—or can—play some part in preventing population decline is a question which might become more urgent if the present trend continues. A book like this is not the proper place to enter into this debate. The only assumption which will be made here is that Australia, which presently has an active immigration program, can at least seek to sustain something close to its present population level. In other words, a policy which supports families need not be feared on the grounds that it will contribute to the depletion of resources. Family support policies are known from European experience to have rather little effect on these trends.

The third family strategy is postponement of parenthood. The trend has been for teenage birth rates to fall slightly but steadily, for birth rates for women in their twenties to remain stable, and for the birth rate of women in their thirties to rise steadily but slowly. Over the whole life span of any particular family there is presumably no net economic gain from this postponement, for the early completion of the child-rearing phase brings compensating gains to those who have their children when they are young. Postponement does have the advantage of making the child-rearing years economically easier, though it is, even so, an advantage of limited duration.

Women in the Home (the Victorian Women's Consultative Council's 1986 report mentioned in Chapter Four) found, as we saw, that the most pressing problems of homemakers are lack of money, especially lack of personal income, lack of status and lack of leisure. Money and status correspond to the difficulties of family economics and the decline of family morale which are central themes of this book. Complaints about lack of money should not necessarily be taken at face value—experience sometimes suggests that the more money people have the more they complain about the lack of it. But if, as we saw, the average family operates on an equivalent income three-fifths that of the average person without dependants it seems plausible that this reported 'lack of money' is not merely the self-interested or self-indulgent grumbling which most of us engage in from time to time.

It might seem that the reported lack of personal income is best solved by encouraging women to enter the workforce, and there is no doubt that many women who do take a job appreciate the financial independence that a second income brings. However, although 'lack of personal income' appeared as the most frequent complaint overall and 'family poverty' as only the fifth most frequent complaint, when we examine the ranking of 'main difficulties' 'family poverty' rates almost as highly as 'lack of personal income' (still the highest). There is, it seems, no clear distinction between personal and family hardship. If the somewhat artificial distinction between the two sorts of need is removed then the combined category ranks far above all others.

Furthermore, and surprisingly, a second job was not listed by these homemakers as a priority. This may be a consequence of the design of the questionnaire, which did not specifically ask respondents about aspirations to employment; it did, however, leave space for open-ended comments, and some of those comments indicated some concern about loss of self-confidence about returning to the workforce. However, although we have little reliable research on this subject, other studies tend to reinforce the conclusion that many mothers who are working would prefer to spend more time caring for their family. The 1984 Clemenger/Reark study of working women (not specifically mothers) concluded that 64 per cent worked to earn an income and 36 per cent for career reasons.[28]

The extent of women's entry into the paid workforce is often misconstrued. Discussions of this subject need to distinguish between part-time and full-time work, and between workforce participation by all females, by married women, and by mothers of dependent children. The most commonly mentioned statistic is the fifty-something per cent of married women in paid employment, a figure that has risen steadily in the past three decades. This figure may disguise as much as it reveals. What is less well known is that only about 12 per cent of mothers with children under five years of age work full-time, and only about 25 per cent work part-time. Less than 50 per cent of all mothers of dependent children are in the

28 Edgar, 'Volunteerism and the Changing Pattern of Women's Lives', 32.

workforce, only 20 per cent of them full-time and 27 per cent part-time. A few per cent are classified by ABS as 'discouraged job seekers'.[29]

As a general policy prescription for family needs, 'Let them get a job' has all the subtlety and appropriateness that Marie Antoinette's 'Let them eat cake' had for an earlier generation of housewives. To ignore the wishes of homemakers in this matter is to continue to belittle their status in the manner deplored by the women respondents to *Women in the Home*. If they do adopt this solution they may merely substitute emotional and physical stress for economic hardship. Even the financial gains of this strategy are often rather limited after childcare costs are taken into account. Many mothers work more from necessity than preference, and to add another job to the family workload does not make the primary job go away, however it may be shared between husband and wife. To say this is in no way to denigrate mothers who make the decision to work primarily for their own needs and interests; it is only to mark a distinction which is essential to understanding the present situation of the majority of families. Rather than offering a generalisable solution to family financial difficulties, entry into the workforce is often like stepping onto a treadmill where, as in Alice's Wonderland, it takes all the running you can do to stay in the same place.

In considering this topic Jordan observes that, although 'the employment or non-employment of married women is a very important determinant of the relative incomes of families, [it] has not been and is not an unambiguous indicator of welfare. It can indicate poverty....' He goes on to add that

> The working woman's net contribution cannot be assessed, and neither can the net effect of employment on her own level of welfare when, as seems to be true of every country in which female labour-force participation has risen in the last generation or so, domestic demands have not declined in proportion to external activity. Probably, that is to say, the visible economic gains have often been offset by a loss of leisure.[30]

Writers on this subject often assume (though Jordan may not) that the alternatives here are work and leisure, but a woman who takes a job to supplement the family income may be losing other things even more valuable to her and her family, such as time with her children. Whether or not this time is to be deemed 'leisure' is a question of linguistic nicety, but the substance of the distinction is a very much more important matter.

---

29 ABS Cat. 2506.0, 1989, 27–30. These figures are a little out of date, and may need to be revised upwards by a few per cent. See also the discussion of workforce participation in Chapter Eight below.

30 *Common Treasury*, **1**, 9.

Family assistance

It seems then that there are no easy ways for families to offset the costs of children which can be implemented by families themselves. But as we have seen the disparity between the 'needs' of individuals and those of families is not—or not any longer—given any special recognition in wages, in government expenditure, in the taxation system, or in the welfare system, except in the form of additional assistance to pensioners and beneficiaries with children and in the Family Allowance Supplement for low-income working families. All other government concessions to families or expenditure on families are likely to be wholly paid for out of the taxes of the recipients.

Although this belief is no longer embodied in our taxation and social welfare system, most people assume that family assistance is a justifiable form of social expenditure. An AGB McNair survey for the Australian Institute of Family Studies, for instance, found that eighty per cent of respondents agreed that families with children should get more tax relief than families and individuals without children.[31] The explanation of the discrepancy between common belief and current practice is perhaps threefold: the disadvantages suffered by families (as detailed above) have not been made widely known; the political process (as was argued in Chapter One) has been commandeered by lobby groups with interests indifferent to family needs; and (as was suggested in Chapter Four) the 'New Class' elite of policy-makers and opinion-formers has often been unfriendly to family aspirations and achievements. In such a situation what was once taken for granted must be defended.

One way to approach this issue is to argue that the conventional criteria of good tax design, in particular the commitment to horizontal equity, require a system which recognises family needs. This is the approach taken by Jordan, and it will be pursued further in the next chapter, but before taking up that theme it is necessary to look at the question of family support in a broader perspective. In the larger framework there are two questions which must be answered: Is it fair in welfare and tax policy to recognise the costs which are peculiar to families? And is it prudent to do so? Realistically the second question is the more important of the two. The suggestion that those who do not have children might support those who do, however persuasive, is not likely to raise much revenue by itself.

Family support can be viewed as a life-cycle transfer. This amounts to a 'childhood pension' something like the age pension. The taxpayer effectively uses the tax and welfare systems to equalise his or her standard of living across the life-cycle. The proportion of permanently childless in the population is small, amounting to about 15 to 20 per cent of childbearing age adults. Most of the support for people with dependent children will have to come from those income earners who have not yet begun families

31 *Australian Institute of Family Studies Newsletter* **18** (1987), 23.

of their own and from those earners who have finished raising their own family. But these are the very people who will benefit in future or who have benefited in the past from family support schemes. As a matter of prudence the balance of gains and losses from such a scheme needs to be calculated rather carefully. Economists argue that all income transfers entail both macro- and micro-economic losses; we need to make some estimate of the net benefits that might result from a proposal such as this.

Before considering the question of economic costs we need to lay out the advantages of the proposal. This is a matter we might have expected the Social Security Review to have discussed very thoroughly, yet it nowhere attempted to weigh up the merits of any substantial system of family assistance. An early Discussion Paper by Ann Harding announced that 'The question of the appropriate balance between universal and income-tested family assistance programs ... will receive detailed consideration during the Review', but this promise was never carried through. A subsequent paper by Peter Whiteford specifically on *Issues in Assistance for Families—Horizontal and Vertical Considerations* made no attempt to consider the case for a very much more substantial system of horizontal equity assistance than that presently in existence.[32] Considering the resources available to the Review, this general timidity seems quite unaccountable.

The obvious rationale for family support has to do with the nature of the human life cycle. For most people becoming a parent entails a financial crisis brought about by four factors: children themselves involve special needs and recurrent costs; at the same stage the family's 'capital' costs of housing are at their most acute; with the birth of children it becomes difficult, and in many cases not desirable or desired, for both parents to be in the paid workforce; and at this time the main breadwinner is usually at the beginning of his or her career, and is thus not likely to be earning a high income. The problem is essentially biological: if parenthood was normally entered in one's forties or fifties, no such crisis would arise. The financial crisis is, however, only a cash-flow problem. Over the whole life cycle almost all families are capable of being financially independent. A system of family support would even out the cash-flow difficulties. It would benefit us all when we are children; and it would benefit parents of dependent children when their income is low relative to their needs. It thus makes families not less but more self-supporting.

Family assistance is both a subsidy from later life to the child-rearing years and a form of compulsory saving before becoming a parent, and both of these aspect require consideration. It is an important fact that most parents earn a higher income in later life than they do in early adulthood, especially if in in later life both are in full-time employment. The only other way to achieve this kind of subsidy would be as a loan on future

32 Harding, *Assistance for Families with Children and the Social Security Review*; Whiteford, *Issues in Assistance for Families*.

earnings, and, since few young adults would have the resources to back a loan of this kind, it is unlikely that a bank would accept such an arrangement.

Discussion of the compulsory saving aspect should keep in mind the small fact that age tends to bring maturity and wisdom. Many parents no doubt regret the money that slipped through their fingers when they were young. The ABS Household Expenditure Survey found that adults under thirty save only 0.7 per cent of their income, the lowest savings level of all age groups apart from the 55–65 age group (many of whom are using lump-sum superannuation benefits to finance early retirement). Jordan found that young adults before becoming parents enjoyed relatively high equivalent incomes.[33] Some of this group will be using their savings to buy a house, but this does not explain how it is that the 30–44 age group, most of whom also have dependent children and high housing costs, have a much higher savings rate of 3.4 per cent. Paternalism perhaps has a place here.

Libertarian opposition to family assistance entails also the elimination of age pensions, which are themselves a form of compulsory saving. It is not impossible that in a purely libertarian society, a society which abolished the whole creaking, rickety Heath Robinson apparatus of state-funded welfare (from age pensions and tax-supported superannuation down to discounts on bus rides for school children), the great majority of families would be better off than they presently are in a Welfare State which recognises all sorts of needs except those of families with dependent children. However, it is not easy to know much about a state of affairs so radically different from that which presently obtains, and there is little political will to abolish all state welfare (a point well made by Lawrence Mead against abolitionists like Charles Murray), so the issue is somewhat academic.

The present trend, particularly amongst the more highly educated, to later marriage and postponement of child-bearing expresses in part a desire to provide well for their future family. Family assistance would make the accumulation of wealth before having a family both more difficult and less necessary. (Only those who thought they were saving for a family and then later decided not to have children would lose by this proposal.) This trend is also in part the result of a desire to get established in a career before facing the 'interruptions' of parenthood. There would be no net cost imposed on any person who took this course, but they would suffer a loss of choice in how their savings could be invested. The loss of choice in investment is balanced by the gain in choice about when to have one parent at home full-time. This option would not exist if family assistance had to be privately funded. One (perhaps minor) benefit of family assistance is that it makes easier the opposite decision, to have children early and pursue a career later in life. At forty a person still has about twenty working years ahead of them, and the advantages of added maturity. Whether at present

33 EPAC Council Paper 29, 34; Jordan, *Common Treasury*, **2**, 190.

employers can see these advantages is perhaps questionable; it is reasonable to think that, if they are in their interests, they will in time come to see them.

In the phase-in stage those who have finished raising a family would lose from the scheme. It would require some sacrifice on their part, perhaps motivated by memories of the stringencies they experienced as parents. Most of the present older generation enjoyed the low tax era of the fifties and sixties, but they will still remember vividly the general difficulties of parenthood and could see the scheme as a form of assistance for their own grandchildren. The AGB McNair survey mentioned above found, surprisingly, that people over 45 were as likely to support tax relief for families with children as were the families with children themselves.[34]

Objections to family assistance

We can turn now to the economic case against family support. Before entering into the detail of this issue it is worth remembering that social practices vary widely between societies. Some societies such as France, without any apparent loss of economic efficiency, employ generous family assistance schemes. Australia, which does not have a good record for economic efficiency, has a social system which provides very little family assistance. On the face of this evidence there would seem to be no direct relation between the two. But we need to look at the issue in greater detail.

At the macroeconomic level there is obviously reason for considerable caution about any large social policy changes. With a net external debt equivalent to more than $6000 per head of population we need to be sure that nothing is done to exacerbate our precarious economic situation. As we have seen, most of the growth of government has been financed out of family earnings; but much also has come from government borrowings. In effect this has jeopardised the economic future of the present younger generation. It might seem that, through the imprudence of government in the past two decades, we are now faced with a cruel dilemma. A policy which has reduced the means of families unjustly and unwisely should but cannot be undone because the cure will be even more ruinous than the disease. This objection requires that we take seriously both the macroeconomic and the microeconomic consequences of any policy changes. And it suggests that perhaps the best reason for economic reform—debt reduction, productivity improvements, export campaigns, tariff reductions, wage restraint, labour market deregulation, tougher scrutiny of the welfare system—is to restore equity to family finances.

The microeconomic objection to family support can be put as follows. The costs of such support require tax increases, which will raise the effective marginal tax rates (EMTRs) for persons without dependants and

34 *Australian Institute of Family Studies Newsletter* **18** (1987), 23.

perhaps also for families or secondary earners in families. Higher marginal tax rates lower labour supply, as people come to prefer leisure to work. The net effect is a loss to both the givers and the receivers, and a loss to the economy as a whole. The details of this argument are a technical matter, but some general comments can be made about the hidden assumptions at work here.

There are two such assumptions. One is that primary income earners with dependants to support are more likely to lower their labour supply than individuals without dependants. Take two people earning the same income, one with five children and the other with none. The first enjoys a standard of living less than half that of the other, even (under the present regime) after tax. Their EMTRs are identical (except for those low income taxpayers receiving the Family Allowance Supplement). Who is more likely to take on some offered overtime? Very obviously the first. Much as he (or she) will value the possibility of some leisure time with his family, their very pressing needs will force his decision. But suppose we make significant welfare transfers to him, so that his net income gives him and his family an equivalent income about two thirds that of the other person. His EMTR is increased by the income tests (if any) that govern the welfare payments, and is now significantly higher than his colleague's. Who now will take the overtime? It is not clear that even now the person with dependants is less likely to do so than the other person. And of course if the transfers are made in the form of tax concessions then his EMTR will stay as before. So there does not appear to be any necessary loss of efficiency at this point.

But families contain two potential income earners. Maybe it is the effect on the actual or potential secondary earner which causes the loss. Here the second assumption comes into play. She (or he) will be making a choice between working at home and working in the workforce. Is this choice to be thought of as a choice between work and leisure? Homemakers with dependant children do not commonly think of their efforts as leisure.[35] It seems then that any change in her EMTR will affect only her choice between one kind of work and another. There is no reason to assume that one is 'real' work and the other not, or that shifts between one and the other in either direction add to or subtract from the net wealth of society. The fact that only one kind is counted in the GDP is little more than an indication of the limitations of national accounts.

Of course it may be in some particular cases that a mother would be better off in the paid workforce, but economists are in no position to estimate how many such women there are in the community. And to count such cases fairly we would need to count also those women who are

35 One—who had spent ten years in the paid workforce—is reported as saying 'I have never experienced such emotional and physical exhaustion, or such little recognition for what I do on a daily basis': Victorian Women's Consultative Council, *Women in the Home*, 25.

presently working but would be better utilised at home. Until economists know as much about what goes on in the ordinary family home as they do about the business world they should leave judgements about such decisions to the persons who make them. If it is the case that some parents would be more usefully employed in the home than in the labour force then there would be some economic gains from family assistance. Apart from the advantages of improving the quality of life within families it might also lower unemployment by making available jobs presently held by two-earner families.

Other efficiency gains may be achieved by channelling family assistance through the tax system instead of through allowances. Economic losses caused by 'poverty traps' which deter welfare beneficiaries from seeking employment are difficult to calculate, but in a society with some 700,000 workforce-aged unemployed and sole-parent beneficiaries—nearly a tenth of the labour force—the advantages of eliminating these disincentives should not be underestimated.[36] This theme will be pursued further in the next chapter.

Fairness

The second question concerns the fairness of family assistance. Claims about the importance of the family sometimes figure prominently in the rhetoric of politicians, and will probably do so with increasing frequency in the next few years. 'The family is the basic unit of society', we are told, but it is not at all clear how rhetoric of this kind translates into useful and fair social policies. In particular, it is not easy to see how a system of life-cycle transfers to help families through the child-rearing stage can be implemented without taxing those who never have children to help pay for the system, and it is difficult to see how those taxes are to be justified if they are unavoidable. At issue here is the question of whether assistance to families with children is anything more than an arbitrary imposition by yet another special interest group upon that section of the public who for whatever reason remain childless. There seems to be a clash here between the economic interests of children, which might be assisted by government policy, and the economic interests of the childless, which unlike the interests of children are catered for in the market. Can this clash be mediated and moderated by rational argument? The question requires us to

36 See Dixon, 'How Mr Hawke has Cut Welfare Dependency', Table 2. In 1988 there were 475,000 unemployment beneficiaries, 183,000 sole parent beneficiaries, 143,000 'widow' pensioners, as well as 388,000 invalid pensioners and 75,000 sickness beneficiaries (who—presumably—are unable to work). Altogether, with their dependants, they would make up a population about the size of Melbourne.

ask some further difficult questions about the nature of families and about basic principles of public policy.

In our society it is basically families which create the next generation; without their work there would be none, and no social continuity. Some families do this job better than others, and a few do it badly, but most try to do it well and the majority succeed in what can be an exceedingly difficult task. But if this is so then it seems plausible to suppose that those who do not have children owe a debt to those who do. Social continuity is valuable to everyone who hopes to see the achievements and projects of their lifetime preserved and perpetuated. Thus, given the assumption that most families do in fact contribute positively to society, one kind of case for family assistance is based on the work which families do.

It is difficult to see how an argument of this kind could be adjudicated, but one way to consider the question is to ask whether there is any realistic alternative to the family. Some alternatives have been tried, but the evidence suggests that every alternative gravitates back to the old parental model. The Israeli kibbutz movement, which never severed the connection between parent and child though it did attenuate it, has tended with time and experience to restore the parent-child relationship. Parents found they wanted to enjoy the specialness of that relationship. But, more importantly, it was discovered that if the bonds between parents and children are weakened the children form equally powerful but usually less benign attachments—in their case peer-group attachments. The kibbutz children, even with enormous social investment in their well-being, did not develop into the autonomous individuals that their society expected to produce. As Brigitte and Peter Berger have put it,

> These [children] are individuals who find it extraordinarily difficult to stand up against their group, who find it difficult to develop an inner life outside the sphere of collective activity, and who very often find it hard to exist in any less collectivist situation (such as the rest of Israeli society, outside the kibbutzim).[37]

Other communal experiments with child-rearing have in general been very much less successful than families generally are. Many of the 1970s experiments were consciously in rebellion against 'the family', though they sometimes borrowed its rhetoric, but very few have survived and demonstrated their viability. Even fewer can be counted as clear successes. The reasons for this failure are not obscure: child-rearing is very time-consuming and sometimes tedious, and few adults will persist with it conscientiously unless they enjoy close and reciprocal emotional bonds with the children, of the kind taken for granted in the average family.

The same problem arises in state-supervised substitute care for children who have lost or been rejected by their parents. In general, the state has found it preferable to relocate such children in other families than to create alternative childcare institutions. The best alternative institutions may be

37 Berger, *The War Over the Family*, 172.

moderately successful, but they are so by mimicking the family. They serve as surrogate families, not as alternatives to the family. And (to keep the extent of state supervision in perspective) only about one child in every three hundred requires state-supervised care, whether through adoption, foster parenting or institutional care; the other 299 are with their parents or one of their parents. Of these 15,000 children about one third were in institutional care and one half were with foster parents.[38]

The universality of the family makes it and the work it does almost invisible. We notice it only when it is missing. If there were other ways of doing that work we would certainly know about them, for the family has had more than its share of enemies. But there are no alternatives, because the family does the job vastly better than anyone else. No matter how much we might argue about any number of its many apparent defects, the family seems to continue to hold the field without any serious challenger. If we want to sustain our social world then, it would seem, we should be prepared to recognise the organisation which preserves the continuity of that world.

We return to the original question: Should those who do not have children be required to help those who do? The case for denying any such obligation is usually put as follows: The decision to have or not have children is just like any other consumer choice. Those who make the decision or who take the risk of becoming pregnant are fully aware of what they are letting themselves in for, or if they are not they should be. Children who really add to the general good of society are few and far between: the majority are just extra members of society, and are on the whole neither desirable nor undesirable additions to the common stock of humanity. Some are unquestionably a burden on the rest of the population. Even if the newcomers were on the whole beneficial, their being added to the population entails no obligations upon those who never sought them in the first place.

Any adequate response to this kind of objection will need to engage in the wider debate about the nature and value of the institution of the family, a debate well described in the Bergers' *The War Over the Family*. The Bergers do not discuss family finances, but we know that (in Australia at least) finance appears to be a critical difficulty for many families. But, as the above objections show, the question of financial support for families cannot be considered in isolation from the larger debate. Assistance schemes which are optional, or which do not involve those who never have children of their own, are difficult to design and achieve. Any family assistance scheme must, therefore, be acceptable to those who do not benefit directly from it.

The issue here is not simply one of fairness, because many who will not benefit directly may be happy to waive their own claims in favour of promoting what they perceive as conducive to a more harmonious and

38 See ABS Cat. 4119.0, 50-52.

constructive society. This is, arguably, what we already do—or aim to do—when we accept programs which tend to equalise incomes between rich and poor. Jordan's analysis of incomes provides strong evidence that at present much of the contrast between rich and poor is a contrast between those with dependent children and those who never have children. Shifting our welfare system towards a family assistance system may be a way of putting that equalising intention more effectively into practice. It would also, as we saw, tend to make families more effectively self-supporting over the whole life cycle.

The case for family assistance would be more impressive if there were good evidence that financial aid would improve the social performance of families. Ideally, a two-fold campaign is needed which both assists families financially and reinforces their status, authority and stability in a manner that tends to reduce the socially-destructive anomie arising from family failure so evident at present. Part of the case for believing that this can be done is made out in *The War Over the Family*. The authors (both distinguished sociologists with a strong interest in child development) contend that the empirical consequences of the pressures upon families today include 'juvenile delinquency and (increasingly) serious crime, drugs and alcoholism, suicide, a frenetic preoccupation with sexuality, mental disorders, and the appeal of fanatical cults'.[39] Their book is a defence of what they call the 'bourgeois family', a unit characterised by two adult parents providing children with the stability, authority and love required for the development of a secure identity, capable of resisting disintegrative forces at work in the larger society, and often enough within the family itself. ('Bourgeois' here is more a cultural than a sociological term; the authors believe that the 'bourgeois' family is now more likely to be working class than wealthy middle class.)

The Bergers' claims are to some degree sociologically testable. In Australia, however, research on such matters is either non-existent or somewhat primitive.[40] At present the questions have to be considered in the

---

39 *The War Over the Family*, 175.

40 Paul Amato's *Children in Australian Families* concluded that 'a low level of [family] income is bound up with an unsupportive and fragmented family life'. Among young boys low family income 'was associated with low support from mothers, low support from fathers, and low family cohesion'. These negative family features were strongest when income was very low. Unfortunately, however, these correlations do not indicate in which direction the causation (if any) is running. It may be that 'an unsupportive and fragmented family life' is a cause of low income, not an effect of it. Amato remarks that 'Although governments can do little in the short-term to change parents' educational attainment, they *can* initiate policies to distribute more income towards families in poverty' (219). The case for doing this would be very much stronger if we had a causal story which suggests that raising family incomes will improve family relationships which might in turn improve children's educational and occupational achievements.

subjunctive. The case for family assistance rests in part on the Berger hypothesis that such a scheme could play an important part in preventing the further formation of a violent, aimless, self-destructive and costly underclass. We have good reason to doubt that existing welfare policy is arresting this process, and good reason to believe that it may be promoting it. Subsidising families who take their social responsibilities seriously may even be a more cost-effective approach than that presently employed. If it is true that the Bergers' 'bourgeois family' produces 'responsible and autonomous individuals' more successfully than any other social arrangement, then a society which wanted to produce such individuals would have good reason to assist that kind of family, and the value of this assistance might well be apparent to those who do not have children of their own.[41] If it were possible to support only the kind of family which produces those individuals then social policy might seek to give selective assistance. At present a selective approach is indeed being adopted, but it is for the most part selective in favour of a family model which does not generally meet the Bergers' criteria of family success. It may not be possible or desirable to *reverse* this selectivity but there is no obvious reason why assistance to the Bergers' 'bourgeois family' might not be equalised with that to the level enjoyed by single-parent families and non-custodial parents.

Not all those who would oppose such a family assistance scheme would do so for self-interested, short-sighted or sophistical reasons. In areas as controversial as this a variety of intelligent viewpoints may be held. Some may believe quite sincerely that families with children neither need nor deserve social assistance. However, we cannot know what public opinion will be on this matter until it is tested in the political marketplace. One reason for thinking that it might be politically acceptable is that it has been commonly assumed that families with dependent children do benefit from government; the discovery that they do not is recent and not yet widely appreciated. Increased assistance to families may only put into practice what has been assumed, falsely, to exist already. But in politics it is impossible to please everyone, and even when the case has been made as well as it can be, there will still be those who, even with good reason, may oppose such a policy. How significant such opposition is has to be decided by politicians, by public debate and by the electorate.

Of course family assistance is not just assistance to parents. Those who never have children benefit when they themselves are children. Another consideration is that we presently subsidise immigration to this country, which suggests that we do set a positive value upon new members of our society, even if not upon new members produced by the present membership. Further, it may not be necessary to assist families throughout the whole of their children's childhood. It may be sufficient to provide generous family allowances up until the child turns (say) ten. Although the recurrent costs of children (food, clothing, etc.) increase with age, the

41 *The War Over the Family*, 182.

capital costs, particularly housing, are also greatest in the early stage of the child's life. The constraints on parents' ability to work are greatest during the early childhood years. Another reason for weighting assistance to the early years is that at present families are assisted to a small degree in the later, secondary school years, whereas in the early pre-school years governments take more than they give.

Whatever the decision on the appropriate age criteria for recipients, any scheme which seeks to have a significant impact must be by present standards very generous—say something in the order of $50 per week for the first child, $40 for the second, $35 for the third and $30 for all subsequent children. Such a scheme could be assets-tested just as the age pension is assets-tested, perhaps even on the same financial basis. The total cost of a scheme restricted to under-ten year olds would be about $6 billion, or about $3 billion net allowing for present expenditure on Family Allowance, Family Allowance Supplement, and other forms of family expenditure. (That is, roughly equivalent to what we now spend on keeping unemployed people—or keeping people unemployed.[42])

Family support of this magnitude would represent a very large change in social policy. The Social Security Review laboured mountainously in this area and, in the end, seems to have brought forth only the squeaking mouse of Family Allowance indexation. The Review's failure even to debate the relevant considerations should not be taken as proof that there is no case to consider. What is needed is rational debate about such a proposal by both economists and the public at large. The argument presented in this chapter should be read more as presenting the case for such a debate rather than as presenting the case for any particular conclusion, but it should at least be evident that there is a case for family assistance which needs to be considered.

Broadly speaking, the proposal being advanced in this chapter for a system of assistance for families with dependent children is similar to the existing system of age pensions, and raises much the same issues of justification and design. Both systems may entail some economic loss. That loss needs to be justified in terms of social benefit. Both must be designed to strike a fair balance between contributions and needs. One way of justifying such a scheme for children is to compare the standard of living enjoyed by dependent children and their parents under the present regime with that enjoyed by age pensioners. If it turned out that the elderly were markedly better off than the young then considerations of parity would suggest some action to equalise their situations. No such careful comparison seems to have been carried out in the Australian welfare literature. Some of the material for such an analysis is now available through the ABS household

42 In 1984, Chapman and Gruen (*Unemployment, the Background to the Problem*) estimated the total economic cost of unemployment at $4 billion. Since then the unemployment rate has fallen but, with inflation, the cost is not likely to be less than $3 billion.

expenditure survey and the subsequent fiscal incidence study, and in Jordan's *Common Treasury*, but we are still far from having a good picture of the comparison. One complexity which needs to be taken into account is the existence of assets, for many elderly will be asset-rich even if income-poor, while young families may be asset-poor even if income-rich. It is also important to remember that any prudent person has a longer time-span in which to prepare for the costs of old age than he or she has to prepare for the costs of the child-rearing phase. These questions will be reconsidered in Chapter Eleven; they are mentioned here only as a suggestion for future research by others qualified to undertake it.

6 Children and taxes

The case for family assistance presented in the previous chapter may or may not be successful. The crucial arguments are admittedly somewhat speculative, and fly in the face of much informed opinion in this area, but at the least they seem to merit academic analysis and public discussion. If they stand up to criticism then it would become a long-term social goal to move towards a family assistance policy. But there is another, more compelling argument for alleviating the burdens borne by families that needs to be heard and considered. The main source of difficulty for those who have favoured greater family assistance has been whether it should be implemented through the taxation or the welfare systems. Majority opinion has favoured the welfare approach, but the problems that have emerged make that a much less attractive option than it once appeared. This chapter will consider the merits of the taxation approach, but it will rest its central argument on criteria intrinsic to tax policy, and not on welfare assistance considerations.

In the past fifteen years the Australian taxation system has been analysed and assessed from almost every possible angle. Almost, but not quite. Remarkably, very little has been said in this debate about children. Are children taxpayers? The question seems an obvious one, yet it has not been squarely faced. The obvious fact that children do not file an income tax return does not settle the matter; economists are accustomed to dealing with income flows other than those in which actual dollars and cents change hands, and there is also no doubt that the burden of a tax can effectively fall on quite other people than those on whom the law formally imposes it. We can phrase the question differently: should adult taxpayers be taxed on their actual incomes or on their equivalent incomes? The case for equivalent income taxation is argued by Alan Jordan in *The Common*

Treasury, and will be restated here, though in a modified form. This chapter will argue that children are taxpayers, and that the standard criteria of horizontal equity require that they not be taxed at higher rates than other taxpayers on comparable incomes. As Jordan puts it, the basic intention 'is not to provide assistance for families in consideration of the costs of raising children, or in recognition of the value of children to the community, but to tax both parents and children on the same basis as other people'.[1]

The argument in favour of equivalent-income taxation—known as *quotient familial* taxation in its French version, but to be referred to here as 'family-based' or 'family unit' taxation—will be presented, and objections to it answered. But, whatever the abstract merits of such a proposal, changes in the tax system must also be realistic from a variety of viewpoints. After a general defence of family unit taxation, it will be argued that family-based taxation has a number of extrinsic virtues, two of which are particularly important. It would significantly alleviate poverty traps which are at present caused by the interaction between the welfare system and the taxation system; and it might also alleviate what is perhaps the most glaring inequity in the present taxation system, that between PAYE and self-employed taxpaying families.

It is not quite true to say that children have been ignored in the tax debate, for much has been written about the appropriate income unit for taxation purposes. Should we tax individual incomes or joint family incomes? The present argument favours the latter but it differs from the usual case for family unit taxation. Past discussion of family-based taxation has usually involved some form of income-splitting between spouses. Though no doubt well motivated, this proposal misguidedly makes the married couple the primary taxation unit. Opponents of this proposal have objected that it would disadvantage secondary earners by raising their marginal tax rates. Both sides have discussed the question as if it turned on the distinction between single people and couples. But the main issue should be not marriage but children. It is argued here that having a spouse at home should in itself offer no tax advantage; if anything, in fact, the reverse. What should count is the spouse's social role in caring for children and other dependants; at present we give only token recognition to this role. But more importantly, what should be valued is children themselves and the work which both parents contribute—whether at work or in the home—towards their well-being.

The argument turns on the notion of horizontal equity. Jordan quotes Martin Feldstein's standard definition: 'in tax design ... individuals who would be equally well off in the absence of the tax should be equally well off with the tax. The tax system should preserve the utility order of individuals'.[2] All tax regimes acknowledge this principle but they vary greatly in their treatment of children. The variation follows from the

1 *Common Treasury*, 2, 217.

2 *Ibid.* 234; Feldstein, 'On the Theory of Tax Reform'.

question of whether children are 'individuals' for the purpose of taxation. Systems which do not acknowledge children as taxpayers in their own right tend to treat them as consumption choices of their parents, as alternatives to a new car or a holiday abroad. On this assumption the costs of children are reckoned to be either matters of indifference for the purposes of income taxation or matters subject to tax imposts on a consumption tax basis. However, this is usually thought to be too harsh and punitive to be carried through completely, so some *ad hoc* mitigation in the form of child rebates or family allowances is introduced as a tax equity measure. The *ad hoc* nature of the resulting compromises leaves the justice of any particular solution hopelessly confused.

The Australian taxation system is unusual in two respects: it is one of the purest individual unit systems in the world; and it relies very heavily upon personal income taxation and recoups relatively little from indirect taxes. Both points require discussion.

First, our individualism. It is sometimes pointed out that the trend in OECD countries in recent years has been away from family-based and towards individual unit taxation. But it is also true that by the standards of some OECD countries Australia provides a low level of support for families, in the tax system or otherwise. After 1945, three decades of prosperity, with close to full employment, low inflation, low taxes, and low interest rates, kept family finances buoyant. During this period living standards rose for everyone, though—as we saw in the previous chapter when examining the changes in tax rates—the standard for those without dependants rose faster than for those bringing up children. This disparity became visible after the 1974 economic downturn, though its full significance is only slowly being appreciated.

The present personal income tax regime includes no allowance at all that is directed to families or children as such and universally. There is a $200 rebate for first children in families with a dependent spouse, but not all spouses are dependent; and there is a $1000 Spouse Rebate which goes to many couples who do not have dependent children and only to some of those who do. The Family Allowance may be seen as a tax equity measure —but it too is no longer universal. Taxation on the basis of equivalent income would dispense with the need for both the Family Allowance and the Spouse Rebate/Additional Rebate as tax equity measures for families.

The second unusual feature of the Australian tax system is its heavy reliance on direct taxation, especially personal income tax. Other OECD countries collect much greater proportions of their revenue from indirect taxes. The direct/indirect tax mix has been much discussed from the point of view of economic efficiency. There are many reasons for a shift to indirect taxation. If this involved increased taxes on necessities it might be detrimental to family interests in the short run, but it should not be ruled out for that reason alone. Compensation for families can be provided by adjustment of the income tax and/or welfare systems. Practically speaking, however, this compensation might be difficult to arrange, and politically speaking it might be difficult to guarantee. This proved to be one of the sticking points for the Option C consumption tax at the 1985 Tax Summit. The steady erosion of family interests in the past two decades has been in part a reflection of the fact that families are, for reasons discussed in Chapter One, one of the most poorly-represented interest groups in our society, and have been unable to compete with the many other more formidable—though less representative—interest groups clamouring for government support.

The fact that consumption taxes impact more heavily on families than on individuals might be regarded as fair because all individuals in every family benefit from public goods such as law and order and defence, but not all pay income tax. It will be assumed, somewhat arbitrarily, that the present tax mix reflects that greater benefit and is thus not unfair to families in that respect. The case for reform will concern personal income taxation only. (Nevertheless, people concerned about family interests should look at the other structural inefficiencies which hurt families, most particularly the very regressive impact of industry protection.)

It will be taken for granted that one purpose of the tax system is to redistribute income in some degree from rich to poor through a progressive adjustment of the tax scales. The underlying assumption here is that wealthier income units have a greater capacity to pay than the less affluent, on the grounds that the last dollar earned by the former makes up a smaller proportion of his or her total income than does the last dollar earned by the latter. It is sometimes added that the wealthy are likely to make more use than the poor of government services and benefits, but the best evidence we have suggests this is not the case. The ABS fiscal incidence study indicates that all household income deciles get roughly equal benefits from government, with most going to the second and third deciles.[3]

The same study gives some indication of the amount of taxes paid on average by each household income decile. These figures, however, do not tell us whether the total tax system is progressive, regressive or proportionate. Research by Neil Warren would indicate that (perhaps contrary to common belief) the present tax regime, taken as a whole (Federal, state and local, direct and indirect) and measuring its impact on households (not individuals), is progressive only between the second (28 per cent), third (29 per cent) and fourth (36 per cent) deciles (see figure 6.1 overleaf). All other deciles, from the fourth onwards, pay between 36 per cent and 40 per cent of their income in tax. The first decile also pays 36 per cent. Warren's analysis is based on 1984–85 statistics. Top income tax rates have been lowered from 60 per cent to 48 per cent since then. At first sight this suggests that the heaviest burden is now borne by the middle deciles, but there is now worldwide evidence showing that lowering very high marginal tax rates tends to increase rather than reduce the tax take from the top

3 See Figure 2.1 above.

deciles.[4] Nevertheless, the lack of progressivity in the overall tax system would be even more striking if we could measure tax avoidance and evasion and the receipt of non-taxable income such as fringe benefits and capital gains, things of which the upper deciles are best placed to take advantage. As Warren observes, 'The net result would be very much like an inverted "U" tax incidence pattern across household income deciles'.[5]

Figure 6.1: Tax Incidence by Household Income Decile

(as per cent of gross money income. ◆ 1975–76 ◇ 1984–85)

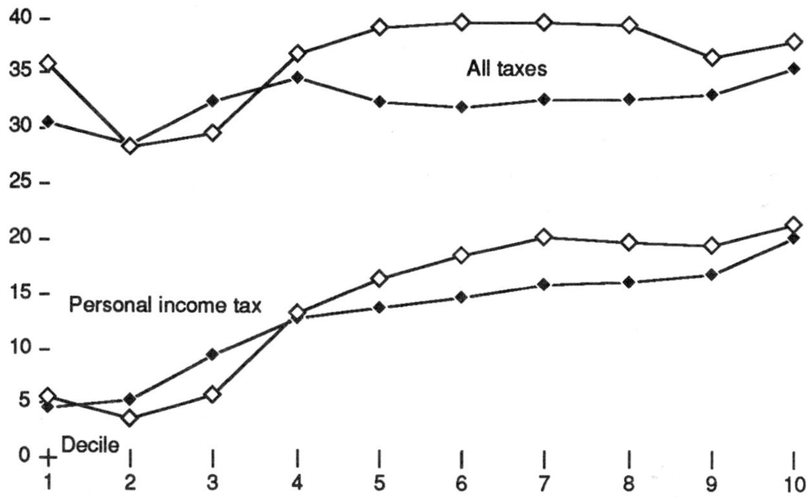

Source: Tables 4 & 5 in N. Warren, 'Changes in Australian Tax Incidence between 1975–76 and 1984–85', in N. Warren, Papers on Taxation and Tax Incidence, U. NSW Centre for Applied Economic Research, 1988.

Failure to index the income tax scales for inflation has resulted in the average wage earner now paying the top marginal rate, and this may explain much of the tax bulge in the middle ranges (compare Figure 6.1's curves for 1975–76 and 1984–85). The most powerful reason for maintaining a progressive personal income tax is therefore to ensure that the overall tax take is not regressive. If we wish to make the entire tax system moderately progressive from bottom to top, personal income tax alone would have to be substantially more progressive than it is now. (We should also identify the most regressive other taxes and eliminate or minimise them.) Increases in marginal rates for top income earners appear to be ruled out by the counterproductive 'Laffer curve' effects that have prompted reductions in top marginal rates in most developed countries. So the only practical way to make the system more progressive is to reduce the average tax rates

4 See e.g. *Taxes and Growth: the London Conference.*

5 Warren, *Papers on Taxation and Tax Incidence*, 30 and Figure 4.

on low and middle incomes. A family unit tax system could be designed to do this.

Family unit taxation can nevertheless be revenue-neutral: the scales can be arranged so as neither to lose revenue or increase the total tax burden. (The trend in the near future in OECD countries seems likely to be towards lower taxation as some of the extravagances of government expenditure are wound back; and major tax reforms are always easier if the total grab is simultaneously reduced.) Other things being equal, reduction of taxes for families will of course entail a tax increase for persons without dependants. But other things are not necessarily equal, and part of the cost can be met from reductions in public spending. There are many ways to reduce the overall tax burden[6]; and taxpayers without the responsibilities of dependants are those in the best position to fight to reduce that burden.

One way of working towards the long-term objective of fairness for families is, for the time being, to pass on such tax reductions as are possible to families only. This would mean postponing tax cuts for individuals until the more urgent needs of families had been met. In the May 1989 Economic Statement this was done to some extent, though barely enough to compensate for bracket creep in the few previous years. The proposal here is that this process should be taken very much further.

Designing a Tax Regime

There are a number of ways of implementing family unit taxation. We shall sketch four—and the subsequent discussion will reveal some of the difficulties and complications involved in any attempt to achieve an equitable tax system that yields the revenue demanded by the modern state.

The key factor in defining a 'family unit' should be, as argued above, dependency. The basic idea is that income should be taxed according to how many people it supports; or, taxable income should correspond to equivalent income.

(1) Aggregate and divide

If we accept Jordan's estimate of equivalent income as real income divided by the square root of the number (N) of people in the unit, we get: taxable income (TI) equals aggregate income (AI) divided by root N:

$$TI = \frac{AI}{\sqrt{N}}$$

A single person with an income of, say $40,000 would pay tax (on a progressive scale not unlike today's) on the whole amount (less expenses

6 See Freebairn, Porter & Walsh, *Spending and Taxing* and *Spending and Taxing II*, and Cole, 'A Tax System for the 'Nineties'.

and deductions much like today's). With the same (aggregate) income, a married couple with no dependants, a single parent with one child, or a single person supporting an aged relative would pay tax as if their income was $28,280 (with no dependent spouse rebate). And so on: a four-person family would pay tax on $20,000, and a seven-person family would pay tax on $15,120. (Jordan's square root formula may be inexact, and better measures may be devised, but here its role is only illustrative.)

This simple approach leaves significant inequities. A $40,000 earner and dependent spouse would have the same after-tax income as a couple earning $20,000 each. But although each couple has the same cash income, the second has spent perhaps twice as many hours earning it. The other side of this coin is that the first has much more time available for 'domestic production'—housework, gardening, home improvements, etc.—and for leisure. By any reasonable measure this should make it better off. To overcome this inequity, taxable income would have to be adjusted by imputing a value to the opportunity for domestic production and/or leisure. The simplest way would be to add a notional amount to the taxable income of the single-income family. (Alternatively, and more palatably, a corresponding amount could be deducted from the taxable income of two-income families; but this would complicate matters elsewhere.) The details of this calculation will be discussed below in the section on domestic production.

(2) Factoring Thresholds

The approach here is to aggregate the income, but also to increase the thresholds at which the various rates in the progressive tax scale cut in in accordance with household composition.

For example suppose the basic tax scale began with a 25 per cent rate on incomes over $5000, increasing to 50 per cent over $10,000 (figures chosen merely for convenience). Single persons would be taxed on the basic scale. A second full-time income-earner would benefit from the same thresholds as the first: two full-time earners would pay 25 per cent on joint earnings over $10,000 (5000 x 2), and 50 per cent on earnings over $20,000. A dependent spouse, however, would bring only partial (say one half) thresholds, for the reasons of leisure and domestic production discussed above. Thus a single-income couple would pay tax at 25 per cent on earnings over $7500, and at 50 per cent over $15,000. A sliding scale would be necessary, as before, to allow for part-time workers.

Children too would bring partial thresholds. In the previous scheme, gross income was divided by a factor based on family size; here, the tax thresholds would be multiplied by a factor.

(3) Rebates or credits

The basic feature here would be an income tax rebate or credit for each dependant. In a single-income household, a 'gross' amount of tax would be calculated by applying the tax scales to taxable income; the 'net' tax—the amount actually payable—would be gross tax minus the sum of the rebates or credits.

The difference between rebates and credits counts at the bottom of the income scale. With a system of rebates, if the sum of the rebates exceeds the household's gross tax figure the result is simply that no tax is payable. With a system of credits, if the sum of credits exceeds the gross tax, then the difference is paid from the revenue to the household. Tax credits can thus be made to take the place of Family Allowance and Family Allowance Supplement.

Where there is more than one income-earner in the family, several approaches are possible: (a) the two incomes would be taxed separately as at present except that the rebates or credits could be divided between the two earners; (b) the incomes would be aggregated, with a suitable rebate (or extra threshold) for the second earner, before gross tax is calculated; (c) both the incomes and the rebates or credits could be split between the earners.

(4) Modified splitting

The simplest tax reform to assist families would be to let couples with dependent children, but no others, split their incomes for tax purposes. This would be most help to the single-income families who, we have seen, most need assistance. The benefits would not be especially well targeted, but as far as horizontal equity goes it would at least be an improvement on the present system.

Comparison

Clearly, methods (1), (2) or (3) are preferable to (4) because less *ad hoc*. The main difficulty with (2) is to find some way of setting appropriate threshold levels. We would need to design 'equivalent' thresholds, thresholds which are a function of family size. It may also be objected that high thresholds for families with children are inefficient because they benefit middle and high income families at the price of raising their top marginal tax rates.

Method (1) appears more promising: by building in the equivalent income concept it allows us to arrive at a calculation of taxable income, based on an apparently objective measure of capacity to pay. The most obvious difficulty with (1) is that it seems to favour high-income families. A high-income family with only one child, say one earning $50,000, would get greater benefit than a low-income ($20,000) family with four children. Thus, solving the horizontal equity problem seems to lead to 'vertical' inequities. This is puzzling—both vertical equity and horizontal equity are attempts to respect and measure 'capacity to pay'. How can they conflict?

We might contend that there is no conflict here. Alan Jordan takes this view when he claims that 'The possible objection that greater benefit would accrue to families on higher incomes is groundless because, under whatever progressive scale was found necessary, all members of those families would be taxed more heavily than people on lower incomes.'[7] No net gain accrues to those richer families who get more tax relief than poorer ones, because they pay for that relief out of their taxes at other stages in their life.

Nevertheless, it can still seem unjust to allow greater reduction for one child and less for another. There is a strong intuition that all children are to be thought of as equally valuable, or at least that their value bears no necessary relation to their parents' income. On this view the tax system should be designed so that, as far as possible, each child counts for the same. In other words, the system would represent something like a universal tax allowance for children. The preference to be adopted here is for this approach, number 3 of the list above.

One very important advantage is that it would permit tax credits for large, low-income working families, a possibility not catered for under Jordan's arrangement. As we shall see, this solution will help us to eliminate poverty traps. However, in doing this we need not abandon Jordan's central notion, the equivalent income. The function of this notion in this modified version of equivalent income taxation would be to set the benchmark for comparing average families with average individuals without dependants. It would be from this test that the tax value to be imputed to all other children could be derived. These are of course only the most general guidelines for a tax scheme. Exactly how the whole tax formula is to be calculated is a matter for expertise, and would require considerable and complex analysis. But difficult though it would be, there is no apparent reason why it cannot be done.

It should be emphasised that family unit taxation, though it takes family size into account, does not 'equalise' after-tax incomes of those with and those without families. It merely adjusts the taxable income and thus the amount of tax paid by those two classes of taxpayer. The standard of living enjoyed by a single earner will still be considerably better than that of families, at the same level of gross income. Income equivalence could be achieved only if wages and salaries were determined by family size.

Poverty Traps

The most important extrinsic advantage of family unit taxation is that it provides a way of removing or reducing poverty traps, and to some extent also employment traps. Welfare disincentives come in two kinds. One kind arises at the point of transition from benefits to work, the other at the

---

7 Jordan, *Common Treasury*, **2**, 217.

transition from part-time or low-paid work to full-time or better-paid work. The first is an employment trap, the second a poverty trap, though they both concern the movement out of poverty and into employment.

In the Australian tax/welfare system, poverty traps are most severe in three situations: for families on Unemployment Benefit; for families on Sole Parents Benefit; and for families on Family Allowance Supplement (FAS). As this indicates, poverty traps are a form of disincentive which affects families more than people without children. The reason for this is that, because families have high needs, assistance to families must approximate more closely to potential earnings than it does for individuals. All kinds of assistance may increase effective marginal tax rates (EMTRs). EMTRs are a measure of the combined effect of taxes and welfare assistance withdrawals on each extra dollar of earnings. Thus, an EMTR of 80 per cent represents a loss of 80 cents in tax and assistance for an extra dollar of earnings. Persons facing such high rates, as many welfare and social security recipients do, have little incentive to work their way out of poverty. The range of factors that can create high EMTR barriers is great. As tax economist Terry Dwyer puts it, 'EMTRs depend upon ordinary personal income tax rates, exemptions, rebates, thresholds, the Medicare levy, social security and other income tests, indirect taxes, income-tested subsidies [childcare] and pensioner concessions'. Dwyer adds that 'because of other factors (e.g. costs of working or childcare) EMTRs of 50 or 60 per cent may mean that social security recipients have virtually no incentive to achieve additional earnings'.

We have seen in the previous chapter how tax increases in the past twenty-odd years have been levied disproportionately on families with children. Something similar can be said regarding EMTRs. Comparing EMTRs in 1968 with those in 1986, Dwyer observes that

> The most striking change has been in the pattern of EMTRs faced by taxpayers with dependants. The move from deductions through rebates and universal cash payments for dependants combined with the increase in tax rates generally has resulted in such taxpayers facing higher standard [marginal tax rates] at lower levels of income than formerly. In addition, the introduction of income-tested, non-taxable FIS/FAS has meant that such taxpayers may face EMTRs as high as 110 per cent over large income ranges near median and sometimes average full-time earnings.[8]

Figure 6.2 illustrates the extent of these disincentives for two representative families.

The severity of poverty traps is a function of three factors: the income tax rate; the level of welfare and family assistance payments; and the rate at which those payments are tapered off with increased earnings. High levels of payment with rapid tapering rates produces the sharpest form of

8 EPAC, *Working Papers to Council Paper 35*, 23, 32.

Figure 6.2: Equivalent Marginal Tax Rates

(a) for a one-income couple with two children

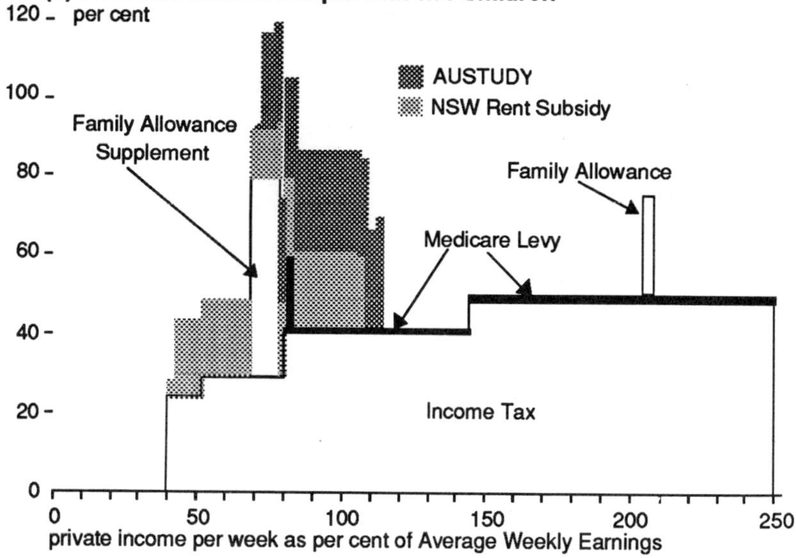

(b) for a single mother with two children

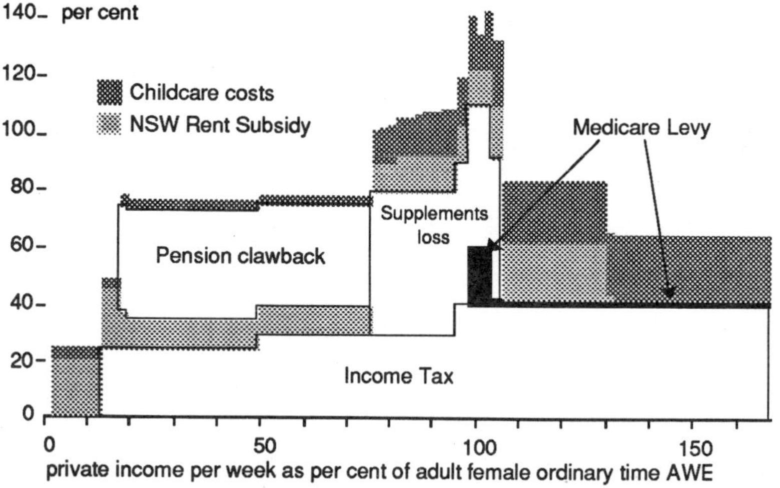

Notes: Calculated as at 31 December 1987. Both families in NSW public housing. Children in (a) are assumed to be 10 and 16 years old; those in (b) are assumed to be both under 13. Adult male full-time average weekly earnings were about $518, and adult female ordinary time a.w.e. were about $392.
Source: Based on charts 3.1 and 3.4 in EPAC Council Paper No. 35. Data supplied by EPAC.

trap. Slower tapering rates will reduce the EMTRs by spreading them across a wider range of earnings, but it is not at all clear that this spreading will reduce the net disincentive effect on behaviour. Some analysts favour high but narrow EMTR 'walls'; others prefer relatively low but widely spread disincentives.

Dwyer ranks different kinds of family assistance according to their effects on EMTRs as follows:

- means-tested cash payments will create higher EMTRs;
- universal payments will not directly affect EMTRs;
- tax rebates will reduce MTRs by extending the tax-free threshold higher up the income scale;
- additional thresholds or deductions will reduce EMTRs by shifting all tax brackets up the income scale.[9]

The EPAC paper on *Income Support Policies, Taxation and Incentives* (of which Dwyer was a co-author) lists five possible strategies for reducing these EMTRs:

- Taxation changes—tax thresholds could be increased or social security payments (such as family allowances) which are paid to large numbers of taxpayers could be converted to tax allowances.
- Social security income test changes—involving adjustments to the free areas and the tapers, especially for certain types of recipient.
- Administrative measures (such as waiting periods for benefit, the treatment of temporary incomes and reviews of the continuing eligibility of recipients for payment)—these can influence the number facing high EMTRs.
- Ambitious schemes for the integration of taxation and social security (e.g. that proposed by the [Henderson] Commission of Inquiry into Poverty).
- Equally ambitious schemes for the separation of taxation and social security—ensuring that no persons simultaneously receive benefit and pay tax.[10]

The paper briefly discusses each of these. It concludes that the second option, the selective easing of income and means tests, as recommended by the Social Security Review, deserves tentative approval, but rejects the others as being unproven, too drastic and not likely to be cost-effective. However, what is 'cost-effective' depends very much on how we estimate the cost of the problem as well as the cost of the solution. Otherwise intractable problems may require drastic measures. The EPAC paper has set out the issues very clearly but it has not weighed them correctly. The disincentive effects are more serious than it allows, and far more serious than is admitted by the Social Security Review. And correspondingly, the solution is likely to require a re-arrangement of our basic priorities, rather than a mere readjustment of present policies. It is because those policies have for a long time been moving in the direction of making welfare subsistence more bearable, and ordinary (two-parent) family life more difficult

9 *Ibid.* 34.
10 EPAC Council Paper 35, 65f.

that we have created a barrier between the two. Removal of that barrier requires a change in basic direction, towards easing the tax burden on working families and making welfare subsistence less like a possible permanent way of life. This needs to be done for reasons both of fairness and efficiency; and it can be done if we remain clear about the basic direction. But before presenting a possible strategy for achieving that goal, the magnitude of the problem, which is usually underestimated, must be fully appreciated.

One cause of this underestimation is the artificially sharp distinction between poverty traps and employment traps which the EPAC paper rests much of its argument on. It treats the first as a relatively minor force, but regards the second as relatively powerful. The relation between the two is important, and it seems implausible to divorce them as this paper does. Both have the same general disincentive tendency. Both affect much the same population, those in the border area between economic hardship and economic self-sufficiency. And the argument used to distinguish between them is not persuasive.

The paper contends that, if they could get a job, most of the unemployed would be likely to earn incomes considerably above the level of unemployment benefit payments, and it concludes from this that those payments are unlikely to serve as a disincentive to job-seeking.[11] This presumes that the unemployed, many of whom have been out of work for a year or more, are capable of winning and holding down something approaching an average-income job. This assumption is at odds with Bettina Cass's demonstration that 'The burden of unemployment in terms of both rates and durations has fallen most heavily on people with a lower level of educational attainment and job skills....'[12] In the past fifteen years the median duration of unemployment has risen dramatically. Replacement rate estimates which fail to take this into account (such as those in the EPAC paper and the accompanying working paper) are obviously out of touch with reality. If Cass is right then we have little reason to believe that the long-term unemployed are capable of stepping 'over the wall' of high EMTRs, into a median income job.

Recent research by the Brotherhood of St Lawrence provides direct evidence that families find unemployment benefits preferable to low-paid work. A study by Jenny Trethewey reports that 'Twenty-four adults (38 per cent of all adults interviewed) said they were concerned that if they returned to work they would lose eligibility for government concessions'.[13] The sample is small, but the result may be significant. These were families who would have received the Family Allowance Supplement if they took a job but who still thought the advantages of unemployment outweighed the

11 *Ibid.* 36; *Working Papers*, 17–22.

12 Cass, *Income Support for the Unemployed in Australia: Towards a More Active System*, 57ff.

13 Trethewey, 'What Do Our Futures Hold?', 10.

losses. If 38 per cent were prepared to say that they would work were it not for the loss of fringe benefits then presumably there were others who thought the same but would not say so.

If the distinction between poverty traps and employment traps is an artificial one, and if both present severe disincentives, then tax/welfare policy seems to require more than the probably ineffective 'fine tuning' advocated by both EPAC and the Social Security Review. Two questions must be asked which are not commonly asked: Are welfare payments too high in relation to ordinary wages for a working family? Are taxes too high and allowances too low for that same family? Reducing welfare payments, lowering taxes on families and increasing family allowances will all tend to ease poverty and employment traps. The introduction of the Family Income Supplement (later the Family Allowance Supplement) was implicitly a recognition that, in 1983 at the time of introduction, welfare payments were too high in relation to low-level wages. Since that time poverty trap disincentives have come to be seen as not less, but much more serious than was previously thought.

In Chapter Eight of this book it will be argued that the present level of payments to the great majority of sole parents can be safely lowered quite considerably (down to a level which equalises the position between broken and intact families) without consigning those families to destitution. Such a lowering would eliminate the poverty trap in that situation. If, however, we are going to continue with the present system of payments to sole parents, then modifying the taper rate by relaxing the means test is unlikely to lower the general level of work disincentives. It will lower the level over one range of incomes merely by spreading it across a greater range of incomes. Many sole parents, unlike most of the unemployed, are capable of winning average income jobs, but their childcare responsibilities predispose them (like married mothers) to seek part-time work.

It might also be contended that, in the buoyant labour market such as has existed in the past five years, unemployment benefits could also be lowered or durations restricted. Plausible as this claim is, in a highly regulated labour market it is difficult to know whether all those presently unemployed could find work when benefits cut out. This may be a limitation on this method of abolishing poverty traps. Further, these solutions may not be politically acceptable. Governments certainly would prefer an easier way out of the present impasse. The most obvious, and probably the most popular solution is a system of family unit taxation.

Family unit taxation removes or reduces the income tax component of the poverty trap. The proportion of the high EMTRs which is income tax varies from situation to situation. In the standard cases presented in the EPAC paper income tax constitutes between one third and two thirds of the poverty trap barrier. (See Figure 6.2 above.) In these cases the family is taxed to provide revenue which is then returned to the family in the form of pensions, benefits, allowances and rent subsidies. Part-time work in particular is heavily discouraged. A family tax regime which required families with two or more children to pay tax only as their income approached average weekly earnings would reduce the poverty trap disincentive by at least a third and often by much more. Such a regime is thus both required by the principle of tax justice for children and desirable on welfare efficiency grounds.

It will be presumed here that, in general, tax reductions are preferable to universal allowances for children. There are two preliminary reasons for this assumption. Allowances, like appearances, are deceptive; they look bigger than they actually are. If one half of taxpayers—those with dependent children—receive allowances and the same half pay one half of total personal income taxation, then one half of their allowances will have come out of their own pockets. (This is roughly true of the present Family Allowance.) Politicians might prefer allowances as a means of making themselves seem more 'generous'. As Thomas Sowell has remarked, 'Ninety per cent of the political art consists of ostentatious giving and surreptitious taking'.[14] With allowances, the taking is real enough, but the giving is partly fake.

This 'churning' means that family allowances raise marginal tax rates in order to give the money back to the taxpayer. Raising marginal tax rates reduces work incentives which leads to a 'deadweight' loss of both efficiency and equity. As a tax equity measure for families, allowances should be used only if the desired result can not be achieved by tax reductions.

Intra-family Equity

One common argument for preferring family allowances to tax reductions is that, because they are paid to the mother, they tend to bring about a better balance of income and power within the family. Two matters arise here: should the state play a part in determining the distribution of incomes within the family? and if it should, is there any evidence that family incomes are at present unfairly distributed?

It has been the general position of this book that only extremes of injustice within the family fall within the state's domain. The basic reason for this is that the family is a voluntary association which can be presumed competent to manage its own internal affairs. The opposite assumption requires us to believe that legislators and administrators are in a better position to determine those affairs than are family members, an improbable assumption and one which should be adopted only on very strong evidence. As Jordan observes, 'Stable relationships of dependency entered into privately must be assumed reciprocal, and any disappointed expectation creates, as such, no public obligation'.[15]

14 *Pink and Brown People*, 59.
15 Jordan, *Common Treasury*, 223.

No doubt there are some cases of extreme injustice within families, but how prevalent they are is a matter of dispute. According to one survey, 'The vast majority of both men and women saw household income as "ours", to be spent in ways mutually agreed on'. Peter Whiteford, on the other hand, confidently asserts that 'Evidence on income-sharing within the family is scant ... but there is general agreement that resources are often very unequally shared'.[16] What is the basis for this 'general agreement', and how often is 'often'? Whiteford refers only to a 1980 survey of fifty families in Queanbeyan by Meredith Edwards, which argues for the view that considerable injustice may occur within families.

Apart from its very small sample, Edwards's survey is of doubtful validity. She found considerable diversity in the control and management of family finances, but in the majority of cases there was joint control, with management by the wife. When comparing men's and women's personal spending she concludes that 'in only one family was the wife's personal spending money a higher proportion of family income than that of her husband', but she seems to include petrol and lunch costs in men's personal spending when they might be better considered as work-related. In the most extreme cases of apparent unfairness the wife, as Edwards notes, explicitly accepted her husband's greater spending power. 'Most wives and husbands considered the expenditure of their partners on pastimes to be reasonable', she remarks.[17] A considered reading of Edwards's survey suggests that, contrary to the common interpretation given of it, there is rather little injustice in family income allocation. Whiteford's 'often' is unfounded, and the traditional assumption of income pooling should be allowed to stand.

Edwards has argued that her survey shows that 'tax cuts or concessions provided to the husband as taxpayer but designed to benefit all members of his family may not in fact do so. Tax concessions may well cause some redistribution of income within the family in favour of the husband'.[18] However, her own survey contradicts this conclusion. When asked how they would spend an extra $20 a week, only one in five men said they would spend it on themselves, compared with two out of five women.[19] The rest of the men favoured spending it on more generally beneficial objects. All in all there is no evidence that intra-family income distribution is so badly skewed as to require corrective policy action.

It is curious that in discussing this topic no-one seems to ask whether expenditure is skewed in favour of or, more importantly, against children, who are far more vulnerable than spouses. Jane O'Donohue claims that

---

16 Burns, 'Why Do Women Continue to Marry?', 226; Whiteford, *Issues in Assistance for Families*, 41.

17 Edwards, *The Income Unit in the Australian Tax and Social Security Systems*, 136f, 139.

18 Edwards, 'The Australian Taxation Unit: An Evaluation'.

19 *The Income Unit...*, 139.

'income splitting is likely to be a less effective means of providing assistance to children than direct assistance to the primary carer of children', and cites Edwards' study as 'evidence that family income is frequently not pooled and shared'.[20] Apart from the fact that Edwards has not demonstrated anything to warrant the term 'frequently', her survey also does not support the conclusion that direct assistance to the mother is more effective than tax cuts for children. About five out of eight women spent the present Family Allowance primarily on the children. Whether or not this ratio would improve if it was directed through tax cuts the evidence does not permit us to say. Surprisingly, Edwards found that 'the majority of women [three out of five] said they would not mind if family allowances were paid to their husbands'.[21] This proposal was opposed most by women in high income families where the women were not in paid work and the husband controlled family expenditures.

The goal of assisting homemakers, while it is only one element of family assistance, is to be taken seriously, as the *Women in the Home* survey showed. However, a basic decision has to be made about whether that goal stands on its own or is a by-product of family assistance. The view to be taken here is that whether a family has one or two income earners is an internal family decision. It is to be regarded as a form of specialisation in which both partners are working equally for the general family good whether they are in the home or in the workforce. Assistance to homemakers is then part of family assistance, along with assistance to children. The assumption will be made that (there being no good evidence to the contrary) income is pooled, and benefits to the family in general benefit all the members of the family. How that assistance should be allocated they are competent to decide.

Despite the fact that there is no good evidence that family incomes are unfairly allocated in more than an indetectable proportion of cases, we need not assume that family assistance should be directed through the primary breadwinner. One way of giving tax assistance to all family members is to require that any tax refunds on a jointly-filed return be paid into a joint family account. Being optional, no injustice would be done by this arrangement. In families with two earners such a solution is the obvious arrangement. In single income families where both partners recognise the importance of each other's contribution there is also no conflict. In those few cases where the parties are at odds this arrangement might gently impose some redistribution.

20 O'Donohue, *An Examination of Taxation Arrangements for Couples with Children*, 25.
21 Edwards, *The Income Unit...*, 147, Table 7.9, and 149.

Women's Labour Force Participation

Family-based taxation schemes are often suspected by feminists of having the effect, or even the intention, of driving women out of the workforce and back into the home. Their argument comes in two versions, one to do with equity, the other to do with efficiency. Both hinge on the claim that family unit taxation raises effective marginal tax rates (EMTRs) for secondary earners, and thus constitutes a work disincentive for married women. The equity version contends that this is both unjust in itself and a setback for women's aspirations towards equality with men in the public domain. The assumptions are that work in the home is mostly done by women; that women are just beginning to break free from the shackles of housework and childcare; that this process is at a vulnerable stage, and that any incentives offered women to remain at home will be all too effective.

This objection is unfounded: family unit taxation does not discriminate against women. For one thing, the reasoning employed could just as easily be used to show that the opponents of family-based taxation intend to force women to remain in the workforce. Secondly, it does not follow automatically that the spouse who stays at home, if one does, will be the woman. Experience shows that it will be mostly women, but some will be men. Family unit taxation offers this freedom to men as well as to women. Thirdly, the feminist objector presumes to be a better judge of each family's arrangements than are those families themselves. This is both illiberal and irrational. No arguments are offered to show how the critic gets into this superior position. Fourthly, feminists are themselves at odds on this issue. The 'Wages for Housework' movement must surely approve any move to reward the work of those who look after children. And in this they will be reflecting the feelings of many ordinary women and men, both feminist and anti-feminist.

The efficiency argument is more reasonable. The issue is the effect of family unit taxation on the marginal tax rates of secondary earners. The objection is that joint taxation lifts the secondary earner's marginal tax rate up to that of the primary earner, and thus discourages him or her from working. Most secondary earners are women, and women generally have greater elasticity of labour supply than men, so high marginal tax rates affect them more than they do men. Taxation and economic efficiency requires that those with high elasticities should be given lower marginal tax rates.

It is not necessary to contest this objection. The objection holds against the jointness of family taxation, but it is not essential that family taxation (unlike marriage-based income splitting) be joint taxation. The only essential feature of family taxation is that it takes account of children. The system could perfectly well be set up so that a couple with children could arrange their tax so that they submit separate tax statements, dividing the child component between them (or assigning all of it to the secondary earner, if that was thought preferable).[22]

Domestic Production

It is sometimes claimed that families get considerable benefit from having one spouse available for housework, home improvements, and the like, and that these benefits should be measured and included in the taxable income of the household. Certainly, as we have seen, inequities arise if we tax cash income while taking no account of the number of people who put their time into earning it. And if family size and consequent needs are to be taken into consideration because they lower family living standards then it seems only fair that whatever raises family living standards must also be counted in the tax equation.

Domestic production is difficult to measure not just for practical reasons but conceptually. It is tempting to treat homemaking as an average job and to settle upon a figure around the average earnings of female workers. But this fails to distinguish between work done for children and work done for their parents. It makes a very great difference whether or not the time, money and effort parents put into children is regarded as a form of production. The amount of domestic production achievable for the benefit of the parents by a homemaker with children, especially small children, is really rather limited. Should domestic production include the time and cost of raising children? There are a number of arguments against this view. It implies children are a purely private good, a form of investment in one's future security perhaps. In our society children are not such an investment. We cater for our financial needs in old age through the taxation and superannuation systems. If we think of the family as a welfare institution, as this book has advocated, then the costs of children will be seen as neutral in the tax equation.

Further, the leisure of family life, such as there is, is a rather different thing from other leisure. It is an essential condition of family life. Much of that leisure is socially productive. Is it leisure to read a story-book to a child? If it is then why do we deem it virtually compulsory for children to attend public buildings five days a week to have the same activity performed—perhaps less well—by a stranger who is paid a salary out of the taxes of the child's parents? But if reading to children is not leisure, is talking with them? We know that conversation between children and their parents is crucial to the child's development. But if this is not leisure is it leisure to provide a setting where children can play safely and happily? As Montaigne observed long ago, 'Children's playings are not sports and

22 This point answers the main objection to income splitting raised by Patricia Apps and Elizabeth Savage in a number of papers.

should be deemed their most important actions'. Spontaneous interaction with adults, especially within their family, is the main way they become civilised.

In any case, as most parents will attest, there is not much leisure left at the end of a normal day of looking after small children. And there is no obvious reason why we should count only the work performed by parents during normal working hours. There is much still to be done by parents for their children at the end of the day, and much carries through into the remainder of the week. Of course, it is difficult to distinguish here between work and leisure, and it is characteristic of parenthood that this distinction is not made. It is a labour of love, sometimes more love than labour, and sometimes the reverse. The outcome of this discussion seems to be that imputed income from domestic production is in principle quite properly included in the calculation of taxable income if a distinction is drawn between the production performed for the parents' benefit and that performed for the children; but that when the effort expended by parents on their children is excluded from the total calculation of domestic production the remaining imputed income will probably be small. In fact, inclusion of the imputed value of domestic production in taxable income would affect single-earner couples without children far more than it would families with children.

To be consistent, we have to allow for part-time workers by scaling the imputed value appropriately. It would not be very difficult to include a statement of hours worked on group certificates. Alternatively, and very crudely, the second worker's income could be used as a surrogate for hours worked, as in a sense occurs at present when one partner's dependent spouse rebate is reduced in line with the other partner's income when this is too small to be taxable in its own right.

Horizontal Equity

A second extrinsic virtue of family unit taxation (apart from alleviating poverty traps) is that it tends to reduce one of the most obvious inequities in the present personal income taxation system, that between PAYE taxpaying families and non-PAYE self-employed couples. As O'Donohue observes, 'Currently married couples may seek to use a business partnership as a way of minimising tax by splitting the income of the household head among family members in a partnership formed to conduct the family business...'.[23] The parties may share the income of the partnership without both being income-earning active members of it. Curiously little is said about this discrepancy either in public debate or in the technical tax literature, as if it were a natural and permanent feature of the taxation landscape. The case is all the more surprising given that PAYE voters far outnumber self-employed voters. No political party seems to regard the issue as

23 *An Examination of Taxation Arrangements for Couples with Children*, 24.

requiring corrrective action. The discrepancy may perhaps be ironed out by more stringent Tax Office scrutiny. Whether this can be done is partly a technical and partly a political question. If it can not then the inequity provides another reason for supporting family unit taxation.

One point to note here is that the inequity cannot be removed by a system of child rebates, even if those rebates are equivalent monetarily to the effect of full family unit taxation. Rebates would be available to self-employed tax minimisers as much as to PAYE taxpayers.

Conclusion

The sad fact seems to be that in the past fifteen years the debate about family assistance has only gone around in a circle. When in 1976 family tax rebates were converted to Family Allowances the rationale was two-fold: to help low-income families who paid little tax anyway, and to help improve the economic position of women within the family. Much the same rationale applied to the introduction of benefits for single mothers. Now it appears that in doing this we merely abolished the economic advantages of being self-supporting and created poverty traps instead. To begin to remedy this we will need a radical, but fair, family tax system, one which goes back beyond 1976 to the sort of tax advantages for families, particularly low-income families, which existed thirty years ago. This will not disadvantage women, for many of them now work and many are sole parents who could work. Feminists now sometimes recognise that the Family Allowance Supplement does provide a work disincentive for second income-earners. It is equally obvious that the single-parent poverty trap discourages women who would otherwise take a job.

Estimating the net economic effect of family unit taxation is a matter of balancing the efficiency losses of the necessarily higher tax rates on individuals without dependants against the efficiency gains which would flow from removing the poverty traps affecting low-income families. This estimation cannot be attempted here. But if it turns out that family unit taxation is not economically less efficient than the present system then the equity merits of the argument are the crucial determinant. The equity case requires a debate about whether or not children are taxpayers, a debate which has never been undertaken, at least not in Australia.

In the previous chapter it was suggested that an assistance scheme for families with children is both justifiable in itself, because of the financial strain experienced by (particularly low-income) families, and also—a point to be developed in Chapter Eight—the best way to produce an equitable relation between two-parent and single-parent families. In this chapter it has been contended that the application in the tax system of the generally-accepted principle of horizontal equity to children is both a requirement of justice and also necessary to eliminate or alleviate the adverse effects of poverty traps, economically inefficient and socially undesirable disincentives operating on families in the welfare system. If the argument of this chapter is correct then, merely because they are children, over four million Australians are annually denied elementary taxation justice, without a murmur of objection from the rest of us. We now need to see how the arguments in these two chapters are related. There are four goals here: financial assistance for two-parent families; equalisation of assistance for all family types; taxation justice for children and their parents; and the elimination of poverty traps. All four seem reasonable in themselves and consistent with each other; all four involve greater assistance to ordinary two-parent working families. All the arguments that favour general family allowance-type welfare assistance for families with children carry through to the case for tax assistance, but tax relief must take priority over welfare assistance if we are to avoid counter-productive 'churning' and reduce poverty traps.

Whether such support would help to reduce family breakdown is a separate question, about which little is known. At least we can say that it might be helpful in this way. But the general topic is one which now requires an extended examination.

7 Understanding family breakdown

Interpreting the divorce revolution

'All happy families are alike, but an unhappy family is unhappy after its own fashion'. These opening words of Tolstoy's *Anna Karenina* turn up not infrequently in the Australian literature on family breakdown, most recently in the chapter on single-parent families in Jean McCaughey's *A Bit of a Struggle*.[1] Yet it is a puzzling proposition. Why should happiness be less complex and diverse than unhappiness? Are the forms of family unhappiness endlessly various? Novelists naturally have an interest in the complexity of social relations and in the varied and unexpected forms of social and personal failure. Social researchers are, or should be, similarly interested in failure, but they cannot operate on the assumption that each instance of failure requires for its adequate description the richness and subtlety of a novel. Their task is to seek patterns in a body of data which is somewhat removed from the world as experienced by its participants—though they must also try to translate their findings into terms, motives and intentions recognisable to the people whose lives they are trying to describe. This chapter will aim to find such patterns in the evidence concerning family breakdown.

As the notion of 'family breakdown' is a contentious one, something needs to be said at the outset about its usage. The notion implies something more than the ordinary unhappiness experienced in many families much of the time. Such unhappiness usually comes mixed up with elements of hopefulness, cheerfulness and humour, and most people regard it as part of the normal course of events which they have to struggle with or endure. It is not by itself a threat to family relations. A family can only be said to

1 *A Bit of a Struggle*, 48.

have 'broken down' when this unhappiness becomes dominating and irresolvable. Sometimes this breakdown ends in divorce; sometimes the family is not formally broken up but continues, though with lasting alienation and disaffection or perpetual arguments.

'Family breakdown' is, then, a description applicable to both chronically unhappy continuing families and families that end in dissolution. The term itself does not presume that one outcome is better than the other. Nevertheless, it does presume that long-term separations and divorces are themselves unhappily broken relationships. As the evidence will show, few marriages end amicably and by mutual agreement. Equally importantly, almost all marriages still aspire to permanence, amongst other ideals. From the point of view of these aspirations divorce is certainly to be counted as failure. Of course, few (if any) marriages fully live up to their initial ideals, but there are degrees of lack of success. Divorce is almost invariably a 'solution' to family problems premissed upon the assumption, made by at least one of the parties, that there can no longer be even a modest fulfilment of those initial ideals.

The most obvious indicator of family breakdown is the divorce rate—usually measured as the number of divorces per year per 1000 married couples. The very conspicuousness of this figure can be misleading, for it cannot by itself serve as an index of marital or family unhappiness. It is of course impossible to obtain any direct measure of human happiness or unhappiness, but the task of trying to measure the quality of family life is not one which should be abandoned merely for that reason. We do not abstain from studying the state of the economy simply because the evidence is complex and partly intangible. The divorce rate needs to be examined and interpreted in conjunction with many other indicators. No doubt the results will never be conclusive, but they may give us reasons to re-appraise our practices and policies, as well as our personal assumptions. Without such research we are all at the mercy of our own intuitions and experiences, and the subject is of course a deeply emotional one about which it is difficult to be detached.

It has been a general theme of this book that to devise any welfare policy we need some theory about the basic causes in operation and some account of the basic values we want to promote. Unfortunately, fundamental studies of the causes of family breakdown and its incidence in relation to all the standard social indicators—class, employment and occupation, education, religious and other beliefs, political preference, ethnic background, geographic location—have not been done in this country. Researchers, it seems, have taken Tolstoy's maxim about the variety of family unhappiness all too literally, as if the enterprise of interpreting and understanding data of this kind is doomed before it starts. And yet the subject—decline in family stability, if not of family success—represents a major social change, and it is hard to believe that any change of this magnitude could possibly pass by without careful analysis and examination.

It is not quite true that there has been no serious research on this subject. A considerable amount of work has been done on the process of divorce and separation, most notably in the Australian Institute of Family Studies project on *The Economic Consequences of Marriage Breakdown in Australia*.[2] What we lack is work on the causes of divorce and separation and on the causes of enduring and successful male/female relationships. The best contributions to our understanding of these topics have been made by Bettina Arndt, Ailsa Burns, Ronald Conway and Peter Jordan. The strategy in this chapter will be to see whether a common pattern or picture emerges from their research, and how well it corresponds with the limited body of data that we have available from the work of the Australian Bureau of Statistics and the Australian Institute of Family Studies.

Rapidly rising divorce rates in the 1970s—the 'divorce epidemic' as it is sometimes described—were an international phenomenon, affecting all the major Western industrialised countries. Although the general pattern is similar throughout the West, by comparison with these countries Australia ranks as having a fairly high divorce rate, much lower than that of the United States, much higher than that of France and West Germany, on a par with that of the United Kingdom. Any account of the Australian experience will need to be compatible with the general trend in these other countries. It cannot rest too heavily on factors peculiar to Australian life and character.

An analysis of the raw divorce rate figures might not seem a very revealing place to begin, but in fact a good deal can be gleaned from them. The first question that must be tackled is the relation between legal and social change. Between 1959 and 1975 marriage and divorce in Australia was governed by the *Matrimonial Causes Act 1959*, which replaced a patchwork of state laws with a uniform federal law. The Act permitted divorce on fourteen different grounds of 'fault', including brutality, mental cruelty, adultery by either party, habitual drunkenness, and desertion for three years. It allowed a divorce without proof of fault if the parties had been separated for five years. In 1976 the *Family Law Act 1975* abolished the notion of fault and all the fourteen categories of fault, and permitted divorce after 'irretrievable breakdown' of the marriage as evidenced by twelve months' separation. Consent by both parties was not a requirement.

Before 1976 the system was often legally complex, formalised, expensive, publicly visible, embarrassing, and conducted in traditional moral categories. After 1976 the procedure aimed to be simple, informal, cheap, out of the public eye, business-like and morally neutral. As legal changes go, this was a radical reversal. Whether the new Family Courts have achieved these aims, and whether they are appropriate aims, has been the subject of much public discussion since 1976, but these topics will not be

2 McDonald, *The Economic Consequences of Marriage Breakdown in Australia.*

considered at the moment. The issue here is whether these changes in the law can be seen as a major cause of the changing divorce rate.

Figure 7.1: Divorce Rates

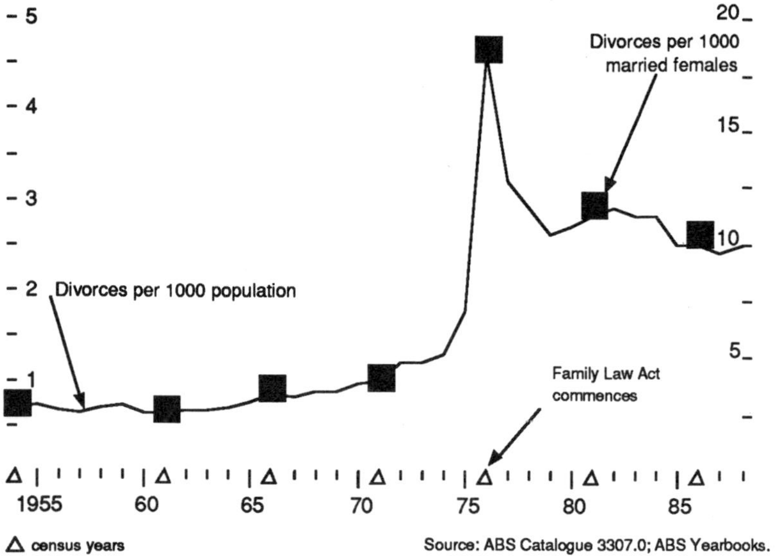

Source: ABS Catalogue 3307.0; ABS Yearbooks.

Two things emerge from a study of figure 7.1, which plots the divorce rate. The most striking is the sky-rocketing of the rate in 1976 with the introduction of the new law. At first sight this would seem to support the view that the 1975 Act played a great part in changing social behaviour. But a second and closer scrutiny suggests the opposite conclusion. If the data for the years 1976–1978 are removed from consideration, what emerges is something like a natural curve, beginning around 1970 and levelling off in 1983. This curve appears to represent a social trend operating relatively independently of the state of the law. The divorce rate began to rise in the early 1970s even under the much harsher 1959 Act, and after 1978 it rather rapidly came back to the shape suggested by that early rise. If the legal change produced social change, then we would expect a more abrupt contrast between the 1975 trend and the 1976 result, we would expect a less abrupt drop in 1977–78, and we would not expect an increase between 1978 and 1983. The divorce rate suggests that the legal change was as much a response to a social change as it was a cause of social change.

A further conclusion emerges when we add to the divorce rate the available figures on the median duration of marriages that ended in divorce in this period. What this comparison shows is that the social change at work here was not a long-standing trend, but really began to take effect only in the late 1960s and early 1970s. In 1969 the median duration (from marriage to divorce) was thirteen years. In 1982 it was 10.4 years, and it has remained around that figure since then.[3] If the liberalisation of divorce in 1976 was a response to a long-term trend, we would expect the introduction of the Act to be followed by a sudden rise in the median duration of marriages ending in divorce. In other words, there would be a 'backlog effect' as many unhappily married couples who had stayed together for ten or twenty years largely because of the difficulty in obtaining a divorce would at this time take advantage of the easier legal solution. The sudden rise in the rate in 1976 certainly looks like such an effect, but the median duration figures contradict this conclusion. The median duration in 1976 and 1977 was only eleven years. Between 1969 and 1982 the median actually fell steadily every year. The new law caused not the slightest increase.

This is surprising. It suggests that the rising divorce rate of the 1970s cannot be explained as the result of removing the 'repressive' or 'punitive' 1959 Act and thereby freeing many couples from unhappy marriages contracted under that legislation. Rather, it suggests that on the whole marriages were happier in the 1950s and 1960s than they were in the 1970s. It suggests that the rising divorce rate indicates not merely increased ease of divorce operating upon an unchanging level of desire to obtain a divorce, but a decline in the general quality of married relationships. This interpretation is reinforced by the fact that the rate did not drop off once the supposed backlog had had time to work its way through the system.

It would be rash to jump to the conclusion that the divorce rate exactly reflects the state of marriage, but it now appears that those who would deny any connection between them have some explaining to do. As a matter of fact, most discussions of this subject do tend to assume that there has been a decline in the quality of marriage. Ailsa Burns, for instance, poses the question: 'why then has this increase [in the divorce rate] occurred at a time when women have been gaining more rights?' And elsewhere: 'why are so many younger women less satisfied than their mothers' generation?'.[4] The answer to the first question, she says, 'lies in the weakening of the social, economic and legal constraints against divorce'. But this rests too much on external factors which are themselves responses to internal changes. Some commentators, including Ailsa Burns, argue that what has changed is that people, and especially women, expect much more from marriage than did the previous generation. This view does not accept the decline thesis; its claims will be examined later on.

---

3 See ABS *Social Indicators*, Table 2.6. and ABS Cat. 3307.0. The 1988 figure was 10.1 years.

4 'Why Do Women Continue to Marry?', 231, 226.

Let us assume for the moment that the object to be explained is a decline in the quality of marriages as indicated by a rise in the divorce rate. It is possible that this decline is the result of many different factors working together, and some discussions of the subject break down those factors into many different components. This approach risks missing something central. Marriage, like any other social relationship, is always at risk in many ways. The multi-factorial approach may forget to explain why those factors have conspired at this time in this way to produce such a striking social change. It may be just happenstance that the divorce rate has risen so markedly in so many countries at much the same time, and that the trend will vanish just as quickly and mysteriously as it has arisen; but it is more likely that this change is linked to some other large-scale changes. Successfully to explain this phenomenon, we must keep the overall shape of these changes in view.

Looking at the general shape of the divorce rate, a Martian observer would perhaps conclude that there has been a slump in the marriage market parallel to the decline in the economic situation. Indeed, some human observers have hypothesised that economic slowdown has caused marital decline. One version of this thesis holds that inflation and taxation have forced married women to enter the workforce to preserve family living standards. The economic power that women then acquire reduces men's comparative advantage as providers of the family income, and thus destabilises the balance which previously existed between men and women. This thesis conflicts with the common claim that families tend to stick together more strongly in times of economic adversity. Another line of argument reverses the relation between economics and marriage. It points out that marital breakdown is frequently not a result of economic decline but a cause of it, especially for women and children. After divorce, it is observed, men's standards of living tend to rise and women's to fall.

These arguments, though no doubt contestable, warn us that there may be some connection between the general slowdown of Western economies and the general decline of marriage, but because there are tendencies running in opposite directions any more exact account of it will not be easy to formulate. Furthermore, there are other theorists who hold that *rising* living standards mean that the two sexes need each other less than they did in the past. This argument would predict higher divorce rates with increasing affluence—for those who are increasingly affluent.

Our general lack of research on the causes of family breakdown makes it almost impossible to confirm or refute any of these conflicting claims. The one piece of economic information that we do have seems to be neutral on the matter. Alan Jordan's study of incomes in Australia, *The Common Treasury*, found that broken families have no economic distinguishing features which might account for their failure. As Jordan puts it, 'sole parents are not a natural group, and therefore sole parenthood in general has no natural history, the histories of different sole parents depending on the characteristics of the groups from which they have originated'.[5] This suggests that it would be fruitless to look in great detail at economic circumstances to explain family breakdown.

A large number of factors suggest that marriages should have been stronger in the 1970s than previously. Ronald Conway lists six predictors for marital success, based on American life insurance research:

1 As people grow older their chances of making a successful marriage increase. Chances of marriage breakup increase almost logarithmically to the degree to which the age of the older partner falls below 21.
2 Length of acquaintance and courtship increase the chances of a successful marriage choice. On the average, the shorter the acquaintanceship, the less successful the marriage.
3 Despite the evident success of many second marriages in recent years and the removal of the stigma once attached to divorce, marriages in which one party has already been divorced are likely to be less successful than one in which neither party has had a previous spouse.
4 Shared religious faith or strong code of religious values makes for more successful marriage than is the case with partners who have no such beliefs.
5 Intelligence and a good education possessed by at least one party in the marriage is a better augury than if neither partner possesses these advantages.
6 If the couple's parents are happily married the odds that a new young marriage will succeed are far more favourable. This is one of the most important predictors of marital success.[6]

Conway adds that 'In the decade or so since these six predictors were formulated little has happened in the way of research to unseat them'. But he does not note how remarkably inadequate these six are in accounting for the rise of the divorce rate in the 1970s. The only factor clearly correlated with divorce is (4), the decline in religious values. Factor (3), the relative failure of remarriages, may play a small part, but a high rate of remarriage presupposes a high first divorce rate, and so cannot explain that rate. What we can expect from this factor is a 'snowball effect'—rising first divorce rates and a high rate of remarriage will accelerate the overall divorce rate.

All the other indicators suggest that marriages in the 1970s should have been stronger than previously. Factor (6), the parent model, is a little ambiguous. If marital success means marital permanence then the low divorce rate of the 1950s will have tended to produce a low divorce rate in the 1970s. If success is defined in some other way then the parental model will at least be neutral, for it predicts that each generation will be just as successful as the preceding generation.

The tendency of the 1970s was towards later marriage, longer premarital acquaintanceship, and more education. (At least more formal education—real educational standards may well have declined in this period.) We are forced to the conclusion that either these are not good

5 *Common Treasury* 2, 98.
6 Conway, *The End of Stupor?*, 83.

predictors of marital success, or there was some other factor at work which powerfully over-rode their influence. There may be some evidence that later marriage is not a good predictor. While teenage marriages are certainly the least stable of all first marriages (and the reduction in teenage marriages must have tended to reduce the overall divorce rate), first marriages where the wife is between 20 and 24 achieve better than the median rate of success.[7] In other words, marital success does not improve in proportion to age at marriage. Nor is it at all clear that couples who live together before marriage—and thus maximise their premarital acquaintanceship—tend to develop better marriages.[8]

It appears that something has been missed by the American life insurance companies, and by Ronald Conway, a usually astute observer of these matters. Yet there are a number of other factors which also suggest that divorce rates should have declined in the 1970s. Living standards rose steadily between the 1950s and the 1970s, taking economic pressure off families. Feminism must have boosted women's confidence, and their increasing involvement in public life has greatly expanded their opportunities. Fewer children per family should have made domestic life less strenuous. Reliable information and advice about sexuality is now more readily available. Homosexuals are less likely to be trapped in marriages for which they are entirely unsuited. Young people no longer rush blindly into marriage. According to Peter McDonald, 'Teenage marriage is now at its lowest level in Australian history'[9], and this dramatic decline, which began in 1971, should have lowered the divorce rate significantly. The tendency to postpone parenthood until the marriage has become well established must have relieved some of the pressures felt in the early stages of marriage. And most importantly of all, the overall rate of first marriage has itself steadily dropped since the mid-1970s. This must have had the effect of 'screening out' many who felt themselves unsuited to marriage.[10]

Other hypotheses

All in all, the evidence suggests that the divorce rate indicates not a lesser, but a considerably greater social change than the figures themselves would show. At this point we have almost exhausted what can be discovered from the broad and crude statistics about marriage and divorce. We need to turn to more specialised, though possibly less representative, studies and con-

7 See ABS *Social Indicators*, 1984, Chart 2.5.

8 Peter McDonald suggests that perhaps 40–50 per cent of couples marrying for the first time in 1984 had lived together before marriage: 'Families in the Future', 41.

9 *Ibid.*

10 This shift should make us somewhat wary of figures that measure the divorce rate as the number of divorces per 1000 people. The number of divorces per 1000 married couples is a preferable measure.

jectures. So what has happened? Perhaps the 'divorce epidemic' has been the by-product of an outbreak of the traditionally accepted causes of family breakdown? Has there been a corresponding increase in domestic violence, drunkenness, mental cruelty, male desertion, adultery, etc? Reliable comparative information on the incidence of these phenomena is, in the nature of the case, difficult to come by. The most recent Australian study of domestic violence, *Beyond These Walls*, estimates that chronic domestic violence afflicts about three to four per cent of women in domestic relationships, so even if violence has increased it is still not at a level to account for more than a small part of the divorce rate.[11] It is also well known that couples in such a violent relationship very often stay together for many years. The report cites the American research of Straus and Gelles, which suggests that the level of such violence may have declined between 1975 and 1985 by about 26 per cent.[12]

At least this much can be said here, that few who write seriously about marriage and divorce claim that the divorce rate reflects rising levels of the traditional grounds for divorce as laid down in the 1959 *Matrimonial Causes Act*. The most likely candidate here, adultery, being the fugitive thing that it is, is not easily quantified; but it is a curious case in another way. Conway reports on a 1981 nationwide survey conducted by the Melbourne *Age* showing that '63 per cent of the men agreed that it was wrong for a married person to have sex outside marriage and 70 per cent of the women felt the same way'.[13] It may be that more liberal attitudes of this kind make adultery less of a threat to marriages than previously, though of course people's actual reactions to the real thing may bear little relation to their professed opinions.

Ailsa Burns attempts to relate women's decisions to separate to another traditional ground for divorce, failure of the husband to provide economic support. 'In many cases income has been erratic during the course of the marriage, and a smaller, but reliable income is considered preferable. In addition, a significant minority [of women] have been the major bread-winner during the course of the marriage/relationship (due to the partner's unemployment/physical or mental illness/absence/failure to support), so that the move into sole parenthood improves financial status'.[14] No doubt these causes are at work (as they always have been) and they are of course important for those who have to deal with them, but there is little reason to think that they help us to understand the overall divorce phenomenon. As Alan Jordan's evidence shows, family breakdown has been occurring fairly evenly across all levels of income and status.

Bettina Arndt provides a different angle on the subject, reporting on a 1985 study of 168 recently-separated men by a Brisbane Family Court

11 *Beyond These Walls*, 45.

12 *Ibid.* 48. See Straus & Gelles, 'Societal Change and Family Violence'.

13 Conway, *The End of Stupor?*, 21.

14 Burns, 'Mother-Headed Households', 11.

counsellor, Peter Jordan. First, Arndt notes, male desertion of women is no longer the central issue. 'In Australia it is women rather than men who are making the decision to end the marriage. In 65 per cent of cases studied, the wife made the decision to separate (the husband's decision accounted for 19 per cent of divorces...)'.[15] This finding is broadly confirmed by the Australian Institute of Family Studies in their *Economic Consequences of Marriage Breakdown in Australia*; from their analysis of 825 cases they estimate that more than two out of three unilateral separations are instigated by women, whereas Jordan's finding was more than three out of four.[16] Second, separation does not seem to be an amicable parting of ways—only 16 per cent of cases involve mutual agreement (18 per cent according to the AIFS study). Third, 'Upon separation most men experience emotional and physical symptoms normally associated with extreme grief and stress'. Women tend to have decided that the marriage is heading for failure at least a year before separation, and have usually done their grieving before they leave.

When she attempts to generalise about what went wrong in these relationships, Arndt places the emphasis on the emotional imbalances between the partners. She quotes an English study of marriage in which one-third of the women complained that 'their partners were inept as companions and ineffectual as confidants'. Arndt's general view is that 'Along with the shift in economic balance in the family, women are now beginning to resent their continuing emotional support of men and are expecting men to supply the same emotional input into relationships as they do'. Even after separation, men (26 per cent of them, in Jordan's estimate) say that they do not understand what went wrong, and it is usually the man who attempts reconciliation after the event.

Conflict over power and decision-making in the family does not seem to be the central issue. A 1982 Australian Institute of Family Studies report by Helen Glezer concludes that 29 per cent of men and 16 per cent of women felt that important family decisions should be made by the husband.[17] This suggests that in only 13 per cent of families is there disagreement about decision-making processes. (It is possible that in up to 71 per cent of cases the man thought decisions should be mutual and the woman thought they should be hers, but this appears unlikely.) This seems surprising: it suggests that the familiar feminist portrait of marriage as downtrodden women being ruled over by domineering men is wide of the mark. But such a conclusion would not surprise Ronald Conway, who in his writings has mustered a large body of evidence to show that (like their American counterparts) Australian families are generally mother-dominated.

15 Arndt, *Private Lives*, 53–56; Jordan, *Effects of Marital Separation on Men.*

16 McDonald, *The Economic Consequences of Marriage Breakdown in Australia: A Summary.*

17 Reported in *Private Lives*, 49.

Helen Glezer's research reports disagreement over roles in the home—battles over the kitchen sink—as a major cause of conflict; other work seems to show that this is not the primary problem and indicates that men today are very much more likely to do their share of housework and child care. As we noted in Chapter Four, only 6 per cent of homemakers surveyed by *Women in the Home* thought that their partners failed to appreciate their contribution to the family; and the ABS *Time Use Pilot Survey* showed that in general men and women contribute equally to the overall workload of society.[18] Even Glezer's own study showed that young married men (those under 34) differ very little from their partners in their attitudes to these things.[19] Yet it is this group of men who are experiencing the full force of the divorce revolution. Perhaps it is best to conclude that the home front becomes a major battle-ground only when the more basic emotional imbalances between the couple are not sorted out. Ailsa Burns describes the case of a woman breaking away from traditional sex roles who complained that 'the real source of her dissatisfaction was her husband's failure to communicate with her ("he never listens")—that is, it was her disappointment in the relationship rather than the unjust division of labour and authority in the marriage that had changed her attitudes'.[20]

Burns describes well how difficult it is to work out a fair division of labour between home and work. She speaks of an

> exchange rate confusion that occurs in traditional marriages, because of the fact that transactions are made in different coinage. (How much child-rearing and homemaking equals how much providing?) An exchange rate between the two currencies has to be struck, which is necessarily arbitrary in the absence of any measurable criteria; and under such conditions it is relatively easy for the more powerful group to mystify the weaker into accepting the legitimacy of a rate struck by itself.[21]

Whether or not this mystification is common, conflict between couples can easily be aggravated by these exchange rate difficulties, and it is plausible to think that they will loom even larger in the process of transition from one system of well-known roles to a new and relatively untried arrangement.

Conflict over child-rearing is, apparently, also not crucial. There is very little evidence that women who divorce feel that men, for all their emotional limitations, are inadequate as fathers of their children. Since 1974 the proportion of divorces in families with children to total divorces has fallen from 68 per cent to 60 per cent. In Arndt's account, many of the men were reported to be too absorbed in their work to provide their wives with the companionship they sought, which suggests they were also not closely involved in their children's lives. But after separation had occurred,

18 See page 88 above.

19 Reported in *Private Lives*, 48.

20 'Why do Women continue to Marry?', 223, based on Williams, *Open Cut*.

21 *Ibid.*

ninety-eight per cent of them 'claimed strong feelings for their children and 91 per cent did not want to be separated from them'.[22] It would be very presumptuous to assume that these feelings are not genuine. (In the divorce debate men commonly find themselves being blamed for lacking emotion and then being expected to show none when they lose their family.)

One element in this situation that has perhaps not been given full weight is the age distribution of the divorce figures. Arndt remarks in one place that 'most divorces are taking place not towards the end nor at the beginning but somewhere in the restless middle of her marriage rather than his'. But elsewhere she observes that 'In Australia, divorces are happening earlier—the peak age group is the twenty-four to twenty-nine-year olds....'[23] It is difficult to see how a twenty-seven year old can be described as 'in the restless middle of her marriage'.

There is good evidence that a marriage that survives the first ten or so years is likely to survive most other contingencies. The median duration of failed first marriages between the date of marriage and final separation is around seven years.[24] Any general account of these issues has to keep this in mind. This fact suggests not that the difficulties between men and women are irreconcilable but that many of us enter marriage very unprepared for the responsibilities it entails. This is all the more surprising in that few now enter marriage without having had some experience of life with the opposite sex.

Clearly, for most couples at the earlier stage of family formation, money is not a crucial difficulty (unless they have put themselves deeply into debt with mortgage repayments). Typically, they have both been in the workforce for at least five years and have not had dependants to consider. For this group the issues have more to do with morale and education, with an understanding of what marriage and family life require, than with dollars and cents. (Nevertheless, marriage guidance counsellors do emphasise the role of financial stress in family breakdown, and the family assistance policies argued for in earlier chapters might alleviate some of this.)

The crucial age group here—say, twenty-four to thirty-four—is also the peak child-bearing period. A twenty-seven year old woman is very likely to have a two-year-old child and a baby. The stresses of first children at this time seem to be compounded by the strain women feel in moving (if they do move) from the workforce to the home, with all the attendant loss of status and (sometimes) sense of purpose. Further, many young Australian men take longer to 'settle down' than women; they go through a phase in which drinking, sport, sex and danger are the main interests; and some never manage to make the transition to becoming stable sources of

22 Arndt, *Private Lives*, 61.
23 *Ibid.* 60, 71.
24 See *Social Indicators*, Table 2.6, 'Divorces: Duration of Marriage'. The ten year median duration figure given earlier is a measure of the period between date of marriage and the date of decree made absolute.

support for their family.[25] It would seem from this evidence that we are on the whole—both women and men—poorly prepared and educated for this transition period. That it should so often result in divorce, leaving a woman on her own to cope with young children, seems both tragic and unnecessary. We know that the effects of divorce on young children are often traumatic. That women in this situation should be choosing to leave their main source of economic, if not emotional, support is even more puzzling. And if emotional support is their main objective it is difficult to see how they might obtain this at all on their own with small children. Arndt's portrait of an emotionally strong woman leaving an emotionally inadequate man, though plausible in some respects, seems out of kilter with this aspect of the picture.

One theory which has had some acceptance is demographic. The rising divorce rate of the 1970s corresponds roughly with the entry onto the marriage market of the 'baby boom' generation. This sudden growth in numbers looking for marriage partners does not by itself make a difference, but it might in conjunction with another well-attested feature of marriage—the fact that men tend to marry women about two years younger than themselves (or, if you prefer, women marry men two years older than themselves). This age difference—the so-called 'marriage gradient'—is very constant, and can be observed since at least 1920.[26] In a rapidly rising population men's choice of partners will expand and women's will contract. (The reverse will hold in twenty years time when the present declining birth rate produces a decline in those seeking marriage partners.) The result (as Bettina Arndt observes) was that in the early 1970s, 'For every 100 women aged twenty-three to twenty-five, there were 94 males two years older'.[27]

How does this affect the divorce rate? The original proponents of this theory, Marcia Guttentag and Paul F. Secord, postulated that population growth causes a two-stage liberalisation of personal values. Ailsa Burns presents their argument as follows:

> In the first stage the men come to realise that they have more appealing options than tying themselves to the role of breadwinner, and to a single woman. In the second stage the women come to realise that, given the shortage of men and the development of libertarian male attitudes, investing too much in marriage is a recipe for disappointment. They too become more cautious about marriage. The marriage age rises, women involve themselves in careers and leisure involvements, and short-term relationships, cohabitation and divorce all increase.[28]

---

25 Ronald Conway's *Being Male: A Guide for Masculinity in a Time of Change* is a useful attempt to understand some of these phenomena.

26 See *Social Indicators*, Chart 2.3, 'Median Age at First Marriage'.

27 *Private Lives*, 67.

28 Burns, 'Mother-Headed Households', 387–400. See also Guttentag & Secord, *Too Many Women?*

Burns shows that this thesis does not match the Swedish experience, and she therefore doubts its applicability to Australia. But there are even stronger grounds for doubting the theory. If women stand to lose more than men from divorce, then women will be less likely than men to initiate separation, even if men are more 'libertarian'. But, as we have seen, women are far more likely than men to end a marriage: the reasons which lead the argument to postulate a relaxed male attitude to marriage must lead to the opposite attitude in women, and this does not seem to be the case. Whatever the plausibility of the demographic argument in explaining changes in general attitudes, it does not explain the divorce rate. In fact, if the theory has any plausibility at all, then, because it predicts results so contrary to the actual case, it requires us to find a real cause powerful enough to countervail the demographic forces.

One common hypothesis about divorce is that nuclear family breakdown is a function of extended family breakdown. But the matter is far from straightforward, for at least five reasons. The evidence of the breakdown of the extended family is far less certain than the evidence of breakdown in the nuclear family. The Anglo-Saxon tradition has always been one of a 'modified' nuclear family, not of the European co-resident extended family.[29] If extended family relationships are dissolving this is likely to be a long and slow process, and therefore not a fact well adapted to explain a sudden rise in the divorce rate. The fact of increased mobility cannot be taken as direct evidence of extended family disintegration: what the family car has done to separate people, it and the telephone can also do to keep them in touch with each other. And if the breakdown of the extended family is associated with the breakdown of the nuclear family, might it not be that there is some underlying factor which is causing both kinds of breakdown, and not that one kind of breakdown is causing the other? For all these reasons we are still only guessing when we make claims about the relation between the two forms of the family.

Another common hypothesis relates divorce to sexual ethics. Undoubtedly, attitudes to sexual morality have changed greatly in the past two decades. The present combination of increased early sexual knowledge and decreased marital stability is unlikely to surprise any traditional moralist, from (perhaps) the author of *Genesis* onwards. In a philosophically articulate defence of traditional sexual morality Roger Scruton contends that sexual desire can only be integrated into a satisfying life through the contrasts required by the notions of modesty, shame and innocence. Scruton observes in passing that 'Nabokov's Lolita, who passes with such rapidity from childish provocativeness to a knowing interest in the sexual act, finds, in the end, a marriage devoid of passion, and dies without knowledge of desire'.[30] Whether a Lolita-like loss of innocence has been a general ten-

29 For a brief summary of research on this topic see Mount, *The Subversive Family*, Chapter 4.

30 Scruton, *Sexual Desire: A Philosophical Investigation*, 343.

dency is difficult to say, but we know that teenage marriages tend to be unstable and it may be that teenage sexual experience tends to inhibit the forming and maintenance of fulfilling adult relationships. Countries with the highest divorce rates—notably Sweden and the USA—appear to be countries with early pair-bonding, though little is really known about this subject.[31]

Perhaps, more generally, sexual permissiveness, made possible by improved contraception, has led to a devaluation of marriage. But this thesis suffers from a similar defect to that of Guttentag and Secord's demographic theory. It is a central dictum of the older folklore about courtship that 'a man pursues a woman until she catches him'. Men, in other words, are at first more interested in the pleasures of marriage, women in the permanence required for stable child-rearing. On this hypothesis, if a desire for sexual freedom is a major cause of marital breakdown, then we would expect men to seek divorce more often than women, which is contrary to fact. If on the other hand the folklore was once accurate but now is false then the issue to be explained is how and why such a change in attitude has occurred.

Changing expectations

So far, then, only two patterns have emerged: marital breakdown is mainly about emotional imbalances, and it tends to show up early in married life. We are now in a position to consider the 'higher expectations' thesis mentioned earlier on. Brigitte and Peter Berger put this viewpoint very strongly. They maintain that

> the high divorce rates indicate the opposite of what conventional wisdom holds: People divorce in such numbers *not* because they are turned off marriage, but, rather, because their expectations of marriage are so high that they will not settle for unsatisfactory approximations. In other words, divorce is mainly a back-handed compliment to the ideal of modern marriage, as well as a testimony to its difficulties.

This interpretation is supported by the very high levels of remarriage by both men and women. Modern marriage, according to the Bergers, 'is designed to provide a "haven" of stable identity and meaning where these are very scarce commodities'.[32] If this were so we would expect people to cling desperately to the identity and security that marriage provides, and perhaps they do.

It needs to be remarked, however, that Christian and Jewish teaching has always fostered high expectations of marriage—the commitment entailed has been represented as total, mutual, lifelong and exclusive.

31 See David Popenoe, *Disturbing the Nest*, 298.
32 *The War over the Family*, 181.

Amongst the purposes of marriage, companionship and mutual emotional support have always ranked highly. It can be easily argued that these expectations are humanly far too high. This objection is well put by Jonathan Raban:

> One of the oddest features of western Christianised culture is its ready acceptance of the myth of the stable family and the happy marriage. We have been taught to accept the myth not as an heroic ideal, something good, brave, and nearly impossible to fulfil, but as the very fibre of normal life. Given most families and most marriages, the belief seems admirable but foolhardy.... Out of the family, it is often hard not to feel like the astigmatic child who had been left behind after the teams have been picked. Inside the family, one is made insistently aware of the widening gulf between the squally here-and-now and the bright arc of the myth as it sails, oppressively yet unattainably, over one's head.[33]

However, Raban's formulation obscures the fact that lifelong monogamy has always been the preferred mode of life for the vast majority of European people (excluding the aristocracies and those subject to the most grinding poverty), whether or not they accepted an overlay of Christian ideals. He exhibits just that tendency to overstate the ideals that he deplores in those he is criticising. Perhaps Judith Wallerstein has summed up the question of expectations best: 'today we expect more from marriage than previous generations did, and we respect it less'.[34]

Raban and the Bergers illustrate the difficulty inherent in determining what are and are not realistic expectations about marriage and family life, and it may be that many people today are similarly confused about this issue. But this difficulty does not explain why there should be a sudden upsurge of marital conflict at any one time. High expectations do not by themselves lead to conflict; only divergent expectations will have this effect. A distinction has to be drawn between high expectations of mutual fulfilment and high expectations of self-fulfilment. It may be that in many cases what seems like high expectations for marriage are actually high expectations for each person considered separately from the marriage partner. Finally, any account of the divorce revolution as a revolution of rising expectations cannot easily be gender-neutral. Some account needs to be given of the already-mentioned fact that separation is so often instigated by women.

The fact that women initiate separation and divorcevery much more often than men suggests that feminism, or the social changes to which feminism is in part a response, is a significant force in the divorce revolution. Yet there are strong reasons for doubting this. For schematic convenience we can consider feminism as having three main components: a relative devaluation of the importance of motherhood and child-rearing in women's lives; a strong emphasis on participation in public life and especially in the workforce; and a tendency to denigrate conventional married life. None of

33 *For Love and Money*, 220f.

34 Wallerstein and Blakeslee, *Second Chances*, 16.

these three is very strongly correlated with the phenomenon of sole parenthood.

Changing attitudes to motherhood are well documented. As Arndt puts it, 'Women no longer regard motherhood as their most important role. In 1971, 78 per cent rated motherhood as their *raison d'être*; by 1982, only 46 per cent gave it such a high priority'.[35] Questions couched in terms of 'primary function' are unpleasantly reminiscent of Napoleon's description of women as 'nothing but machines for producing children'; and the fact that someone comes to see *X* as more important than *Y* does not show that they no longer regard *Y* as important. Nevertheless, not even feminism's best friends could claim that the movement has always striven to preserve the highest ideals of motherhood. Indeed, many of its leading protagonists now think that the movement failed badly in this central regard. Mica Nava, to take but one of many possible instances, observes that 'The interests of children, their dependency and vulnerability, have never really been explored within feminist theory'. She adds that feminists were short-sighted in neglecting 'the insistence of many women (outside the movement) that family life and motherhood can be both rewarding and a source of authority'.[36] The early attitude of the movement is epitomised in the perhaps apocryphal comment of one of its founders that 'Bringing up children is not a real occupation because children come up just the same, brought up or not'. Fortunately, propositions like this are now admired merely for their period flavour. Few parents would be so silly as to attempt to put this attitude into practice, but it may be that the underestimation of the requirements of parenthood that it signifies has been influential.

However, there is evidence which suggests that this is not an important factor. We know that after separation sole mothers are far more likely than fathers to seek and accept the primary custody of their children. By international standards Australia has a high rate of sole fathers caring for children after divorce or separation—about 15 per cent as compared with the international average of ten per cent. But the fact that 85 per cent of sole parents are mothers is not suggestive of a very strong tendency by women to abandon their children. This is not what might be expected if a relative decline in the perceived importance of motherhood is a major factor in the increase in the divorce rate.

Much the same can be said about workforce participation. The international increase in workforce participation by women needs no documentation here. What is striking is that sole mothers are *less* likely than married women to be in the workforce. Although they are more likely than married mothers to be in full-time employment, they are very much less likely to be working part-time (this is discussed in the next chapter). This is not what

35 *Private Lives*, 48. A 1988 *Adelaide Advertiser* survey—admittedly a self-selected sample—found that only two per cent of women now see motherhood as their primary function.

36 Nava, 'From Utopian to Scientific Feminism?'.

we would expect if female employment is a major factor in family breakdown. Some of the anomaly may be explained by the effects of the poverty trap, but the evidence is still inconsistent with the familiar feminist picture of women for whom paid work is a psychological necessity. On this evidence it would appear that divorce and separation are more likely than marriage to 'relegate' women to the traditional roles of child-carer and homemaker.

Nor is this all. It is difficult to avoid the conclusion that much of feminism has been hostile to conventional marriage and family life. Instead of affirming the value and importance of both public *and* private life, the movement was strongly inclined to promote the former partly by devaluing the latter. Least of all was it interested in finding ways of sustaining and enriching long-term relationships between men and women. Whether feminism and its emphasis on the pursuit of public goals at the expense of private achievements and satisfactions have played—and continue to play—a large part in the divorce upsurge cannot be demonstrated directly from the available evidence. However, the indirect evidence does not indicate any very strong or lasting hostility to marriage. Most women who divorce remarry (or at least re-partner), often within a few years of the first break-up. Some remarry more than once. If we emphasise this evidence we seem forced to conclude that we have no good explanation of family breakdown which links the phenomenon to feminist *or* anti-feminist themes.

Figure 7.2: Women receiving Supporting Parents Benefit

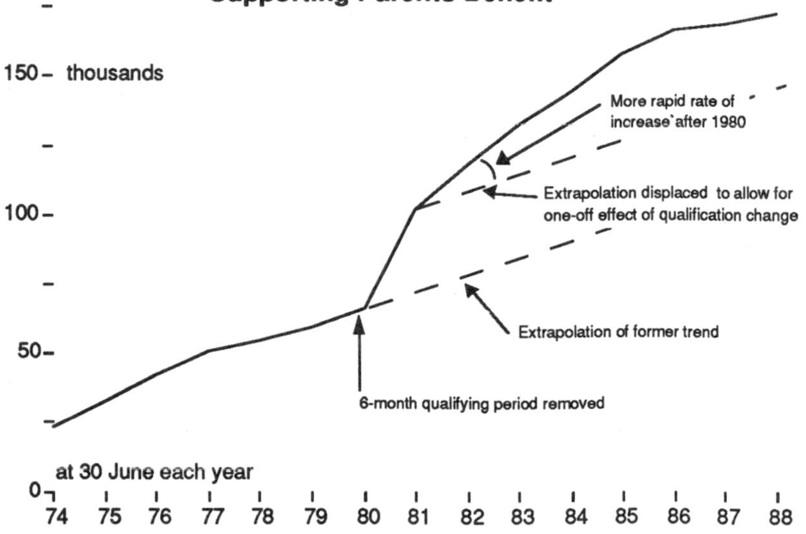

Source: ABS Yearbooks.

As we observed earlier, there is no immediately obvious reason why increased workforce participation should have weakened marriages. Bettina Arndt, as we saw, connects workforce participation with a redressing of emotional imbalances: 'Along with the shift in economic balance in the family, women are now beginning to resent their continuing emotional support of men and are expecting men to supply the same emotional input into relationships as they do'.[37] This suggests that work has given women the confidence to stand up for their rights to care and consideration within marriage. Whether this is so depends partly on whether we accept Arndt's and Conway's picture of men as emotionally inarticulate. But even if we accept this—and it is difficult to gainsay—we need not accept all of Arndt's account. An alternative view would be that the focus on work and public life has now made women as emotionally limited and brittle as it previously made men. This interpretation seems just as consistent with the evidence as Arndt's more widely accepted picture. Arndt's account is gender-based. The alternative is based on the distinction between public and private life.

The welfare role

Perhaps the welfare state has played a large role in the divorce revolution? The case for claiming that the welfare system has been a major cause of family breakdown has been argued by economists Peter Swan and Mikhail Bernstam, who have also conducted a detailed study of the American evidence on this question. The conclusion of their comparison between the two countries is that:

> There can be no doubt that Australians have taken to welfare benefits like junkies to a fix. The doubling of the number of female teenage recipients and quintupling of overall SPB [Supporting Parents Benefit] recipients in just over ten years is an almost unparalleled 'accomplishment'. By contrast, in the United States the number of recipients of Aid to Families with Dependent Children (AFDC) rose only five-fold over the much longer period 1950–1980. For Australia, in just over ten years the proportion of families with children dependent on sole parent benefits has increased from about 5 to 12 per cent.[38]

As evidence of the direct responsiveness of behaviour to the welfare system, Swan and Bernstam note that the numbers of women in receipt of SPB took a sudden and permanent upturn after 1980, just when the six-month qualifying period for benefits was removed (see Figure 7.2). On the basis of their US data they also contend that sole parent dependency is

37 *Private Lives*, 53.

38 Swan & Bernstam, 'Brides of the State'. See also Bernstam and Swan, 'The State as Marriage Partner of Last Resort'; Swan & Bernstam, 'Support for Single Parents'; and Swan & Bernstam, *Malthus and the Evolution of the Welfare State*.

responsive to labour market changes. Young unskilled workers, unable to find work, cease to be able to support a family and are replaced by the social security system.

Swan and Bernstam's claims are mainly about welfare dependency, not divorce and separation as such, but it seems probable that there would be considerable overlap between the two. Further, we saw in Chapter Five that the general growth of the Australian welfare state in the past few decades has been very disproportionately financed by taxes on families with children, and thus this growth represents the rise of one kind of welfare system at the expense of another. Australian family policy consists mainly in supporting broken families and taxing intact families. Given this evidence, most economists would predict a large shift from one family form to another.

There are two grounds for doubting this analysis. First, even when the evidence that behaviour is highly responsive to even small monetary incentives is strong (as in Figure 7.2), it seems hard to believe that highly charged emotional decisions are being governed to a large extent by such changes. The argument entails that if those monetary incentives were not operating the divorce rate would be very much lower than it is; but the divorce rate is no lower among people not eligible for welfare assistance. Second, the picture is complicated by the fact that in only a small proportion of cases does separation or divorce bring any financial advantage to women, who are the main initiators. In general, separation and divorce leave women financially worse off. Without doubt it is now economically very much easier than ever before for women to support themselves outside marriage. Some of this independence will have come from greater workforce participation, although if we emphasise this aspect it becomes difficult to account for the welfare dependence of sole mothers. Greater economic independence must be seen as a catalyst speeding up a reaction which was disposed to occur for other reasons. But this still leaves us unclear about the primary forces at work, especially if (as was claimed at the beginning of this chapter) there is no good evidence that marriage before the divorce revolution was as stressful as it has since become.

If the account in this chapter has any validity then we may be left with a three-fold phenomenon: traditional male emotional immaturity; the stresses of women's growing public independence, combined with a possible loss of understanding about private life; and the intervention of the welfare system, in a way which was (and is) biased against two-parent families. These may be enough to explain the divorce explosion, and why it occurred when it did. They may help to explain the two other important questions that arise here: why it is that women instigate separations; and why these tend to happen so early in marriage. But in general the available evidence is both scanty and poor in quality, the conclusions reached are obviously very conjectural, and it is easy to marshal evidence which runs counter to those hypotheses. None of the arguments accommodates the fact that—as this discussion has emphasised—there are strong reasons for expecting marriages to have improved in this period.

Although the Australian Institute of Family Studies was established (as its journal, *Family Matters*, proclaims on the back of each copy) 'in order to promote the identification and understanding of factors affecting family and marital stability in Australia', it has contributed almost nothing to this central task. We seem forced to accept that we know remarkably little about the Australian manifestations of a phenomenon which has closely affected the lives of almost everyone in Western societies in the past two decades. Such a conclusion would be in line with overseas work, or lack of work, on the subject. An English study entitled *Who Divorces?* ends with the observation that 'Research into the causes of marital dissolution, both in this country and in the USA, has so far not enabled the firm identification of any one, or even several, dominant variables'. An American account entitled *Family Breakup* comments that 'Virtually no research has focused on the *processes* by which family bonds shift and deteriorate'. Another American writer claims that 'Except for the work of a few scholars, marriage and divorce, as a subject of study, has only been pecked at and not studied in its totality'. One major study which comes close to integrating the sociological evidence with an understanding of the personal dynamics—Wallerstein and Blakeslee's *Second Chances*—emphasises the deep-seated and long-lasting adverse after-effects of divorce trauma, but it has no general theory about causation.[39] Maybe the divorce revolution should be thought of not as a function of other social changes but as *sui generis*.

Perhaps Tolstoy was right after all: family unhappiness is more mysterious than family success. The fact that we find the questions perplexing, and seem to lack even a useful common vocabulary in which to discuss them, is probably unsurprising. This theoretical confusion may simply mirror the confusion which exists at the level of practice. In matters of this kind we seem to be inept and primitive. This would not matter if the subject was purely a speculative one, but, as the next chapter will indicate, we do know enough to be clear that the divorce trend often has damaging consequences for children. For this reason, if for no other, thoughtful research of a kind we have not even begun to contemplate is urgently needed both on the causes of family breakdown and on appropriate social policies to minimise the damage caused by family breakdown.

---

39 Thornes & Collard, *Who Divorces?*, 132; Little, *Family Breakup*, x; Arnold, 'Marriage, Divorce and Property Rights: A Natural Rights Perspective', 195; Wallerstein and Blakeslee, *Second Chances*. See also Popenoe, *Disturbing the Nest*, for a wide-ranging sociological analysis of these questions. In 'Theorizing about the Quality and Stability of Marriage', Lewis and Spanier provide a useful formal schema for considering these complex questions, but they offer no particular hypotheses to account for the known evidence.

8 Repairing the damage

If it is true that little research has been done on the causes of family breakdown in Australia, it is equally true that there has been little serious effort to analyse the interaction between family breakdown and that part of the welfare system designed to repair some of the damage done by family breakdown. Even to speak of 'repairing family breakdown' as one of the goals of the system is risky, because the relevant aims are rarely, if ever, articulated. It makes a world of difference, for instance, whether the goal is to 'repair family breakdown' or merely to 'alleviate the consequences of family breakdown', yet this distinction is barely acknowledged. The notion of 'repair' here may be unpleasantly suggestive of social engineering, but the case to be argued will attempt to maximise personal liberties, while contending that it has been other kinds of social engineering that have played a significant part in causing breakdown in the family.

Before going any further we need to summarise the results of the last chapter, for—in the absence of any better description—it is to the situation as described there that public policy has to respond. Marriage is still a popular institution, and most people who marry do so with high expectations of forming a lifelong and happy companionship. There are many reasons why the period since the mid-1970s should have been a period of strong and happy marriages. There is no reason to believe that the traditionally accepted reasons for marital failure are any more prevalent now than in the past. Family breakdown does not appear to have strong economic causes. It does have to do with emotional imbalances between men and women. It tends to show up early in marriage, usually in the first ten years. That it happens so early suggests that it may be in some way a function of personal immaturity. It seems to have something to do with women's increased commitment to public life and the paid workforce, but after separation women are no more likely to be in the workforce than before. It has been aggravated by the hostility of feminism to marriage and family life, but the feminist emphasis on marriage as a power struggle between men and women does not seem to describe even a majority of marriages that fail. Conflict over children and child-rearing is not a central feature of marital failure, and conflict over the division of domestic labour seems to be a secondary problem. The great majority of separations are initiated unilaterally by women. Women's attitudes to the process of divorce have not been well documented, but we have good evidence that the results are usually painful to men. Women leave marriages in part because they seek both companionship and independence, but they subsequently lead social lives restricted by their care for children. After separation many women and children tend to suffer from low incomes and most fall into dependence on state welfare. Both men and women frequently remarry or re-partner not long after divorce, but these second relationships are often no more stable than the first. Marital failure seems to be transmitted between generations, which suggests that the present divorce rate will be passed on to the next generation.

The whole phenomenon has become a burden on the average taxpayer, including those who also have a family to support and who work hard to keep their marriages together. As we noted in Chapter One, more of the Federal family assistance budget is now spent on the consequences of family breakdown than is devoted to assisting all two-parent families, though the latter outnumber the former by about seven to one. The social and personal costs also take the form of work absenteeism, lower productivity, legal aid and court costs, ill-health, depression, violence and suicide.

Most important of all for social policy purposes, children find divorce traumatic, and in many cases they become separated from and lose touch with their fathers, a loss which can lead to adolescent anger and delinquency. A survey of primary school children by the Australian Institute of Family Studies indicates that more than half of all eight and nine year olds today fear the divorce of their parents.[1]

The most generally accredited work on the effects of divorce on children is the American research of Judith Wallerstein and Joan Kelly, who distinguish between immediate and long-term effects. There is now little doubt that the immediate effects of parental separation are usually very painful for children. In a great many cases, it appears, the separation comes as a surprise to the children who have little understanding of the depths of hostility that exists between their parents. Wallerstein and Kelly describe the effect of this surprise as a period of 'reactive depression'. What distinguishes their research, however, is that they have supplied

1 See Amato, *Children in Australian Families*, 65f. Another but much smaller study found that 71 per cent of non-custodial parents kept 'regular' contact, and only 7 per cent had no contact at all (Smiley, *et al.*, *Implications of Marital Separation for Young Children*, 7).

some of the first reliable evidence on long-term effects. They found that five years after divorce about one third of the children showed no adverse consequences, another third were undergoing 'appropriate developmental progress' though with some lingering resentment and unhappiness, and the remaining third were significantly worse off than before, suffering from moderate to severe depression manifesting itself in delinquency, poor learning, drug abuse and apathy. The crucial determinant was whether the absent parent had kept in touch with the children. They summarise their position in this way:

> [I]f the divorce is undertaken primarily as a unilateral decision which humiliates, angers or grieves the other partner and these feelings continue to dominate the post-divorce relationship of the divorced partners; if the divorce fails to bring relief from marital stress or to improve the quality of life for the divorcing adults; if the children are poorly supported and poorly informed or co-opted as allies or fought over in the continuing battle and viewed as extensions of the adults; if the relationship with one or both parents is impoverished or disrupted; if the stresses and deprivation are no less than those of the failed marriage—then the most likely outcome for the children is developmental interference and depression.[2]

We know that most divorces in Australia are unilateral and that they involve bitterness and recrimination. We know also that relationships with at least one parent do become impoverished or disrupted: Paul Amato found that after divorce 26 per cent of children never see their fathers, and no doubt a much higher percentage lose close contact.[3]

Australian research on these questions has been meagre but what there is does not contradict Wallerstein and Kelly. The most careful Australian study, Rosemary Dunlop and Ailsa Burns's *'Don't Feel the World is Caving In': Adolescents in Divorcing Families*, is of limited general relevance because it is focused on teenagers. Almost all of the families they studied involved couples who had been together for at least 13 years. Their children had enjoyed considerably more stability and joint parental investment than is the case for most children of divorce; and, being adolescents, they presumably had acquired some of the skills and emotional maturity to cope with the process of parental separation. It is therefore not very surprising

---

2 Wallerstein & Kelly, *Surviving the Break-up*, 316f. Wallerstein's 15-year study of divorced Californian families (the longest longitudinal study anywhere) has concluded that there is considerable unpredictability in the long term effects: 'One cannot predict long-term effects of divorce on children from how they react at the outset' (Wallerstein & Blakeslee, *Second Chances*, 15; see also 24ff and 56ff). Since it can be objected reasonably that Wallerstein's sample (sixty relatively well-off families) is too small to support any large conclusions it needs to be noted that other studies have reached similar results. See e.g. Hetherington *et al.*, 'The Aftermath of Divorce'; Mitchell, *Children in the Middle*; and Morgan, 'For the Sake of the Children?'.

3 *Children in Australian Families*, 113.

that, as Dunlop and Burns found, they differed little from the control group of teenagers in intact families. Even so, when asked how they reacted to the separation commonly the responses were those of sadness, shock, and disbelief. These are not findings which Dunlop and Burns choose to highlight, though they do acknowledge that many adolescents 'had gone through a period of confusion, anger and distress when the family crisis was at its height'.[4] We may presume that these effects are more acute for younger children. Another study focused on children who were six to eight years old at the time of breakup, and found that 'many children retain negative feelings about parental separation even though their life adjustment was satisfactory'. When asked to express their wishes, 40–45 per cent of the separated children wanted family changes, compared with only 7 per cent of children from intact families.[5]

One response to Wallerstein and Kelly's results has been to conclude that since divorce is not universally harmful to children, it is not necessarily harmful to children, and therefore the effects of divorce on children should be regarded as a private and not a social issue. This response is analogous to concluding from the fact that children sometimes run across the road safely without looking, that they need not be taught to look. Five years is a very large part of childhood, and the one-third of children who suffer for that length of time are likely to have great difficulty making the transition to emotionally secure and competent adulthood. Even those who suffer 'only' lingering resentment and unhappiness are entitled to our concern and respect. Children are resilient—they survive wars, natural disasters and personal tragedies—but this is never a justification for causing suffering.

If Wallerstein and Kelly's results are reliable and transposable to the Australian situation, then the divorce epidemic has to be viewed as, in general, comparable to an epidemic of child abuse. The abuse in this case is certainly not intentional, but it may be regarded as negligent. (The fact that a child's general competence may be unimpaired despite family crisis is not grounds for ignoring the effects of divorce - we do not argue that child abuse is acceptable if it does not impair competence.) The standard reply to comparisons of this kind has been that making divorce more difficult will only shift the location of this suffering back into 'intact' but unsuccessful families. This reply misses the essential point that it is their attachment to both of their parents which matters most to children, and it is this which should be jeopardised as little as possible. That family breakdown leads all too often to social disintegration will be argued in the last part of this chapter.

The picture of the divorce phenomenon presented in the previous chapter is a composite formed from a diverse body of statistics, reportage and informed comment. It is derived from external evidence, and it may

4 *'Don't Feel the World is Caving In'*, 65, 105.

5 Smiley *et al.*, *Implications of Marital Separation for Young Children*, 26, 24.

not match up very well with particular cases. Furthermore, it is not a coherent picture in the sense that it does not reveal any pattern or purpose capable of explaining at any basic level why marital breakdown has become so prevalent. Taking this external evidence alone, it would be difficult to avoid the conclusion that marriage today is a source of very great confusion, both personally and as a subject for thought and discussion. Viewed sociologically in this way, marriage failure appears to have little to recommend it. The evidence indicates that in the majority of cases it leaves the woman worse off economically and socially; it leaves the man and perhaps also the woman badly hurt emotionally; and—if we can add the evidence of Wallerstein and Kelly—it disadvantages children emotionally, economically and (sometimes) educationally.[6]

This conclusion will emerge more clearly if we distinguish sharply between family breakdown as it appears from the above description and divorce as it is quite commonly conceived to occur. One familiar picture is that of a woman who after years of struggle finally decides to leave a man who is drunken, violent, tyrannical and mean, or some combination of these, taking her children with her. Such men do exist, and such women still go through the same agony, but they do not account for the majority of cases. Another picture is that of a couple who, after perhaps fifteen or twenty years together, having raised their children to an age and stage where they can understand what is happening and why it seems necessary, finally decide to separate. As John Milton put it in the seventeenth century, 'it is less breach of wedlock to part with wise and quiet consent betimes, than still to fail and profane that mystery of joy and union with a polluting sadness and perpetual distemper: for it is not the outward continuing of marriage that keeps whole that covenant, but whatsoever does most according to peace and love, whether in marriage or in divorce'. Certainly, parting with wise and quiet consent has been facilitated by the liberalisation of divorce, but it too does not account for the majority of cases. Both of these stereotypes involve a median duration of marriage far in excess of the actual case. The second differs from the common pattern in being a mutual decision. The first case is a unilateral decision, but the justification of the decision is readily apparent. Further, if the divorce epidemic is a temporary and transitional phenomenon, as optimists prefer to believe, there is little evidence that it is likely to abate. It is true that the divorce rate has levelled off in the last few years, but that can be accounted for partly by the declining marriage rate. Judith Wallerstein has observed of the American situation: 'Having worked with more than two thousand troubled families since 1980, I have to say that things are not getting better and divorce is not getting easier. If anything, it is getting worse'.[7] It would be difficult to show that this is not true also of Australia.

6 The educational evidence will be discussed in Chapter Ten.
7 Wallerstein & Blakeslee, *Second Chances*, xixf.

Although marital breakdown has become such a common feature of our lives no-one has managed to show how divorce of the kind described above might be seen as beneficial. Feminism, which has dominated discussions of 'sexual politics', has had surprisingly little to say about the advantages of divorce for men, children or even women, and tends to fall back on the well-worn stereotypes rather than tackling the situation that really exists. Liberalism, which shapes so much of our thought about moral matters, avoids the subject, apparently on the grounds that ethics should not prescribe how we conduct our private lives. Christianity and the mainstream churches, the traditional guardians of personal morality and the ethics of marriage, appear afraid of seeming illiberal and antediluvian. Nor can it be said that conservatism has provided any notable insight into the questions at issue, partly because the questions are without historical precedent, and partly because the ethics of marriage have been for so long articulated within a Christian framework which can no longer be assumed. The combined forces of strident feminism and complacent liberalism seem to have silenced any more reasonable voices.[8]

What is most immediately visible about the current ethics of marriage is the considerable gap between profession and practice. The marriage ceremony in either its traditional form or in the forms commonly used by civil celebrants seems to bear little relation to the outcome of many marriages. The couple swear to care for each other through thick and thin and for as long as they both shall live, but in a great many cases they do not manage to clear even the first hurdle down the track. This may be because the ceremony itself no longer expresses our aspirations and firm intentions or it may be because we now find those intentions too difficult to fulfil. Neither explanation seems very plausible. The hurdles are no higher than they have ever been—they may well be lower than ever before—and people's express ambitions are no lower than in past times.

That about a third of all marriages now end in divorce is a fact which everyone intending to marry should be required to understand; it is also a fact which bears strongly upon the way in which we as a society think about the institution of marriage. Marriage as it exists today is (to vary the metaphor) an institution with its head in the clouds and its feet on the edge of quicksand. The fault lies not in the institution itself but in our failure to think realistically about its capacities and purposes. And to think realistically about this involves re-thinking the legal and social welfare frameworks within which marriage and divorce function. The strategy of this chapter will be to discuss first the law of marriage and divorce, then to consider the system of welfare benefits and pensions, and lastly to look at the response of welfare services to family breakdown.

---

8 In Australia almost the only honourable exception to this dismal rule is Ronald Conway, who has consistently attempted to keep alive intelligent public discussion of the subject.

The role of the law

We get married in churches or in some other public ceremony, and we divorce in court. Yet perhaps we choose these locations badly. Marriage, it might be argued, should take place in court and divorce in church or in public. Such a reversal might inject some salutary realism into the first act, and impose a degree of equally-desirable mutuality and respect upon the second. We need not take this suggestion entirely seriously to see that it makes a serious point.

Part of the argument in the previous chapter was that the 1976 *Family Law Act* should not be seen as in itself a major cause of family breakdown: the causes are social, not legal. But it would be question-begging to infer from this that the Act as it stands is appropriate to the social situation. Even very bad laws need not themselves be causes of publicly-visible distress. The main victims of the present divorce trend are children, whose opinion in these matters is not consulted. Nor does it follow that because there is at present no great public pressure to change the law, there is no need for intelligent discussion about what an appropriate legal system might be. So the first questions here are legal.

The most powerful justification for no-fault divorce is that the state is in no good position to effectively determine the rights and wrongs of marriage disputes; only the couple themselves are in a position to do this. This is an extension of the generally-accepted principle that the state should stay out of internal family matters. This principle is, we have argued, one which should be breached only in extremes: the question is therefore whether divorce is such an extreme? Clearly it is not in the case where a couple without children agree to separate. But the matter is less clear where the interests of the children are likely to be affected by divorce. In placing limits on domestic violence, for instance, the state recognises that not everything that happens between spouses can be regarded with indifference by society, and it might be argued that a unilateral decision to break up a relationship is comparable to an act of violence against children. The state might decide that in some instances the interests of children who are innocent third parties may come before the interests of the parents who seek separation. At least, the general liberal principle of non-interference will not by itself show that the state has no role in protecting those interests.

The family is a society within a society, and the act of marriage is the act of forming a new society. This act is essentially a private act—the role of the state at a marriage ceremony is merely to register the existence of the new society (and to see that the relationship is not bigamous). Indeed, marriage is so much a private agreement that even this registration is not essential to the formation of a family, a fact which we and the law recognise in speaking of long-term sexual and communal partnerships as *de facto* 'marriages'. The primary purpose of state registration is not to regulate the conduct of a marriage but to take note that children of that partnership belong to the married couple and to be on hand to supervise the deregistration and dissolution of the partnership if and when it occurs. The essential point here is that the ending of a marriage cannot easily occur without some form of independent arbitration, though it need not be arbitration by state agencies. The main thing required here is someone of mature intelligence whose judgement can be respected by both parties. There is no reason why any person with the capacity to win such respect should not be able to set up in business as a private arbitrator (the equivalent for divorce of a marriage civil celebrant). But in the last resort there is an inescapable role for the state in the ending of a marriage because the terms of the dissolution will sometimes require enforcement, if only to protect the interests of children. This can only occur if those terms are known to the state, so all private arbitrations would need to be registered with a state office.

One primary reason why divorce is difficult, messy and so frequently unjust is that the parties themselves have never articulated the terms by which they understand their relationship to have been conducted during the lifetime of the marriage. In general these terms have to be derived by the courts from the common assumptions of the community and from the traditions of the law, and neither of these is very helpful when the community is divided about basic tenets and the law itself has failed to adapt to the complexities of the issues. In attempting to untangle these knots there are two methods possible. One is to stipulate by legislation some general conception of the purpose and nature of marriage. The other is to require the parties themselves to stipulate the terms of their own relationship (allowing them to renegotiate the terms as they find necessary).

The first approach is attractive largely because there is a framework available which seems to cover our most basic intuitions about the institution. Marriage, we commonly think, is a partnership between equals. Unfortunately, this assumption is not readily reconciled with the no-fault doctrine. People's contributions to a relationship are not always easily comparable, and inequality in fact can be the main reason why a marriage is ending. To insist that two parties are to be treated equally even when they are radically unequal in what they have contributed seems plainly unjust.

This conflict is unwittingly demonstrated in a recent book which argues from a liberal feminist standpoint for the equal partnership position in relation to property settlements. In their conclusion to *For Richer, For Poorer: Money, Marriage and Property Rights*, Jocelynne Scutt and Di Graham seek to clinch their argument that 'Under a system of equal rights to marital assets, all women would be better off because all would receive 50 per cent of all assets' by describing two 1984 High Court cases.[9] In one, a successful businessman's wife was awarded 34 per cent of their combined assets. In the other the hard-working wife of an apparently irresponsible man was awarded 70 per cent of their assets. In a system of

9 *For Richer, For Poorer*, 133.

judicial discretion much depends on the details of these cases and different judges will reach different conclusions. Under an equal partnership arrangement both wives would get half of the assets, which would advantage the first but disadvantage the second. Scutt and Graham contend that both wives have suffered injustice but they do not observe that their own preferred solution would rectify one of these injustices at the same time as it would aggravate the other. Earlier in the book they take the view that in a marriage where one of the parties believes the other is not pulling his or her weight they should either decide to leave and cut their losses at a fifty:fifty settlement or they should be prepared to put up with their partner's faults. All of this is a logical deduction from the two starting principles: equal partnership and no-fault settlements. But whether it is the best way to deal with divorce disagreements is still debatable because of the apparent injustice which even Scutt and Graham feel has been suffered by the wife in the second of the above two cases.

There is no need to take a general position here on the issue of property settlements. Property is important whether we are well-off or not, but to most of us children are even more important. If property settlements are difficult on the equal partnership assumption, custody settlements are almost impossible. Assets at least are divisible; children, on the whole, are not. There are only three ways of 'dividing up' children: joint custody; alternating custody; and in families with more than one child, the division of the children between the parents. Joint custody presupposes that the parents are willing and able to cooperate, which is likely to be rare when, as we have seen, the great majority of divorces are not mutually agreed. The law seems not to favour alternating custody arrangements, though there would appear to be something to be said in their favour. Perhaps the objection is that switching between parents would unsettle the children, though it is not clear why this should be more of a problem than with joint custody. The division of children between the parents has the drawback of separating siblings from each other at a time when they no doubt need each other's company, but it may be workable in some cases. All three solutions are painful to both parents and children. And apart from these three options there is no arrangement which comes even close to embodying the notion of equal partnership. So much of the bitterness of divorce arises from the fact that most disputed custody settlements require what will seem to the loser a 'winner take all' result. The bitterness is compounded by the fact that the loser usually has to pay maintenance for the children he or she has lost.

The weaknesses of the equal partnership interpretation as a device for settling divorce disputes are apparent: it can disadvantage partners of poor contributors to a marriage, and it is little help in achieving equitable solutions to custody conflicts. Is there any better answer? The alternative to a general judicially-imposed principle of equality in the interpretation of the marriage contract seems to be to require the parties themselves to specify more clearly the terms they wish their contract to bear. This approach satisfies the intuitively strong assumption that marriage is an association of equals, for both partners will have an equal say in writing the contract. But its main advantage is that it would relieve some of the enormous burden of interpretation borne at present by the courts. It would give the judges some guidelines about how each particular couple understood the terms of their relationship. Most importantly, it could provide guidance about how the ending of the relationship is to be conducted.

The Christian assumption of lifelong marriage and the romantic belief in endless connubial bliss—two otherwise very different views of the world—have conditioned us to evade responsibility for these problems, but even the mildest realism now requires a change of outlook. Individualised contracts can easily be parodied: will they specify who is to wash and who to dry the dishes? But there is no need to descend to this level of absurdity. The main points which require clarification in marriage are: Should the marriage end by mutual consent only or can the decision be unilateral? After what period of time is breakdown to be considered 'irretrievable'? By what criteria should custody disputes be settled? Should all property be divided fifty:fifty? These are matters which do vary from couple to couple and it is too much to expect the courts to be able to discover each couples' preferences.

One major advantage of individualised contracts is that, unlike the present Act, they do not require the fiction that fault has no causal role in family breakdown. As Patrick Tennison has remarked, 'In working from the concept that neither party is to be blamed for the marriage breakdown, the [Family] Court can completely ignore blame where it demonstrably exists. In doing this it has rewarded the blameworthy and penalised the blameless in times and ways which have been a disgrace to any legal jurisdiction.' Ronald Conway adds that 'Tennison's criticism is incontestable when one realises that the desertion of a spouse and children without grave reason is a breach of marriage, yet it is not regarded as such by the Family Court.'[10] Desertion, without grave reason, which involves taking the children and then managing to get custody of them through the Family Court because the Court does not want to disturb the children's status quo seems even more reprehensible, being something akin to child theft, even though legalised by the courts.

It is of course true that in many marital failures the causes of and responsibilities for failure are complex. Nevertheless, in some cases the responsibility is relatively clear-cut, and in others the issue is not who is at fault but what constitutes a fault for this particular couple. A system torn between appealing to general but vague 'community standards', and privately specific but publicly unspecified marital preferences, is attempting to reconcile irreconcilables. It is a vital principle of jurisprudence that

10 Tennison, *Family Court: The Legal Jungle*, 10f; Conway, *The End of Stupor?*, 98.

the law must be as certain as it can be. The only way to restore some certainty is to return the onus of definition back to the marriage parties themselves. Until this is done both marriage and the law will suffer.

Any discussion proposing a reintroduction of fault is open to the charge that it will restore all the evils of the old Act. Gordon Goldberg, a lawyer who has argued the case for individualised contracts, answers this objection in this way:

> The great fault under the *Matrimonial Causes Act* was that it prevented people from regulating their own affairs, so that divorce could be achieved only on certain restricted and often quite silly grounds. The virtue of the Act was that it let people fight over the issues that really concerned them, that it made a person's rights dependent upon the fulfilment of his obligations and that it protected a person who had developed just expectations from a promise freely given in return for a promise which he or she had given. The fault of the current Act is that it talks about rights with no question of duty and its virtue is that it lets people regulate their own affairs so that they can dissolve a marriage when they both want to. The virtue, which each Act has and had, is that which it shares with the general law of contract; the vice which each Act has and had is the distinction between it and the general law of contracts.... Because the *Matrimonial Causes Act* was too far on one side and the *Family Law Act* too far on the other, what we should be looking for is a compromise and the obvious compromise is a contract; marriage should be treated as a contract just like any other relationship between two sensible human beings.[11]

Goldberg envisages three kinds of marriage: one, dissoluble only by mutual consent; two, a partnership dissoluble by either party giving notice to the other (he favours a two-year notice period, but this term might be set by the parties themselves); and thirdly, marriage dissoluble by death, by mutual consent or for just cause where just cause consists of either of two sorts of breach, 'one which develops through nobody's fault which a contract lawyer would call frustration ... and one which develops through fault or default'.

Goldberg would also like marriage contracts to specify provisions for custody. It is his opinion (or it was in 1981) that 'the results of many custody cases are a lottery', and he emphasises the importance of having certainty in the law. But it might be thought inappropriate to have about-to-be-married couples discussing the post-divorce care of children they do not yet have. (Many may not even have discussed whether they intend to have children.) Even if we think this, Goldberg's clarification of the different kinds of marriage would seem to ease the difficulty of custody problems. In marriage dissoluble only by mutual consent, the parties would not part unless they had agreed on a custody settlement. In the third kind of marriage there might be a term or a presumption that custody goes to the party not responsible for a breach by fault or default. In cases of breach by frustration difficulties would remain. The second kind of marriage,

11 Goldberg, 'Law and Family', 71ff.

dissoluble unilaterally (as at present), would not remove custody conflicts, but assuming that only a minority of couples chose it, such conflicts would be reduced.

One obvious objection to individualised contracts is that an about-to-be-married couple are in no frame of mind to think clearly about such painful matters. But the terms of the contract could be re-negotiated at later intervals in accordance with the progress or regress of the relationship. In any case, to require such couples to face the realities of the present situation from the start may well be salutary. Divorce now has a large measure of community acceptance yet the causes and effects of divorce and breakdown have hardly begun to penetrate our common consciousness. It seems probable that one important cause of divorce is the fact that both parties enter marriage quite unprepared for difficulties. Anything which promotes awareness that there are hurdles to be faced at one time or another can only help to strengthen marriage.

Marriage, it seems, is an institution which corresponds to many of our most basic desires and aims. But some of those desires are unrealistic; and sometimes our aims change. In many circumstances we can alter our behaviour to suit ourselves, but in marriage there are other persons—most importantly children—whose wishes and needs also have to be taken into account. A legal framework which allows people to modify their relationships according to those changes is desirable, and contracts are one way of doing this. It is, however, an important observation that the notion of contract sounds alien to the description of family life. Family relations are essentially or ideally permanent relations, and their imprint remains (genetically, for instance) even when they become fractured. It would certainly be better to fight the divorce epidemic by reinforcing the importance of this permanence, but that is a cultural task and cannot be achieved by public policy. What public policy can do is fight the epidemic with its own weapons. If marriage is to be treated as a contract then let it be a real contract, and not a mere instrument of one person's will.

Marriage is not endlessly modifiable at the wish of one party only. Karl Marx once observed that 'Nobody is forced to enter into a marriage, but everybody must be forced to make up his mind that he will obey the laws of marriage when he enters into it. A person entering into marriage does not *make* or *invent* it, just as a swimmer does not invent nature and the laws of water and gravity'.[12] About the first of these propositions Marx was right; about the second he was wrong. A person—or more correctly, a couple—may in entering marriage 'invent' some of its terms. But once they enter marriage those terms will then be as morally binding upon them as the laws of water are upon the swimmer. And what holds here for marriage holds also for divorce. To rethink the nature of marriage in this way is to attempt a basic change to a fundamental social institution, but such a change would be no more radical than the changes which have already

12 Marx, 'On a Proposed Divorce Law', 140.

occurred, and which have necessitated such rethinking. Almost all present discussion of family law starts from the two assumptions that have been challenged here: that it is the job of the state to standardise the terms of marriage; and that it is never the job of an arbiter to sort out the rights and wrongs of marriage dissolution in families with children. At the least we should be prepared to question these assumptions.

Welfare assistance

As we have seen, the basic causes of family breakdown are mainly personal, cultural and ideological, not economic or legal. But it remains the case that governments can seriously exacerbate the effects of those basic causes. The first line of public policy is legal, and we have argued that the law relating to marriage and divorce is seriously defective, leaving many families in crisis in a worse state than they were before they took their problems into the public arena. The second line of public policy is in the welfare domain, and it will be argued that the policies we presently have here are equally inappropriate to the situation they attempt to deal with.

The 1976 *Family Law Act*, the divorce revolution and the upsurge in welfare spending on benefits and pensions for sole parents are, of course, all different manifestations of a single phenomenon, family breakdown. To devise an appropriate welfare policy for dealing with this phenomenon requires some account of that phenomenon and its causes, but government policy in this area has attempted to be studiously neutral about the nature and causes of family breakdown. There has, for instance, never been a government inquiry into the subject, though the changes in the past twenty years have been massive, and governments delight in inquiries into almost every other aspect of social life. The closest that government has come to considering the matter is in the recent Social Security Review Issues Paper *Bringing Up Children Alone: Policies for Sole Parents* by Judy Raymond, a paper which makes an intelligent contribution to our understanding of many matters related to sole parenthood but which fails essentially because its account of family breakdown is very inadequate.

The objectives of welfare policy for sole parents are not often articulated. One attempt at such a statement was proposed by Alan Jordan in a 1982 Department of Social Security paper entitled *Sole Parents on Pensions*. In his view there are six aims to be kept in mind:

> (1) to maintain a level of income sufficient for parents and children to survive without undue hardship, and without undue detriment to the future prospects of the children, and (2) to raise this minimum as permitted by the prosperity of the community, while (3) not discouraging the parent's efforts to improve on the minimum and (4) minimising long-run costs to the community. Two formal or procedural objectives may be added to these substantive objectives: in administration of the provisions (5) to maintain equity between members of the population of sole parents, and between that population, other families and other

individuals, and (6) at the least possible cost, to maintain a high degree of accuracy in determination of entitlements and making of payments.[13]

Jordan makes no mention of preventing family breakdown as a reasonable policy goal, though he does observe that there is a need to ensure equity between sole parent families and two-parent families. Discussion in recent times has focussed on (3) and (4), not discouraging the parent's efforts to improve on the minimum and minimising long-run costs to the community. Before taking up a position on the economics of sole parenthood we need to tackle the questions of ethics and equity.

Public opinion on policies concerning sole parenthood is deeply divided, and feelings run high when the subject is discussed. In matters which raise such passions it is often the case that there is powerful and plausible imagery at work on both sides. The dominant stereotypes are of just the sort required to arouse such passions. One is the maltreated or deserted wife who fights to protect and preserve the integrity of her family against a violent or negligent husband. The other is the woman who breaks up her family for personal reasons, taking her children with her and leaving their father in the position of having access to them for brief periods every second weekend. Both of these stereotypes contain enough plausibility to get a grip on public discussion. The difficulty they present is that any policy designed to help the woman in the first case is likely to assist the woman in the second and thus further injure the man in the second. And vice versa: any policy designed to help the man in the second case is likely to hurt the woman in the first. Two questions follow here: One, are these accurate ways of characterising the situation? Two, if they are, can we help those who need help without hurting others who also need it?

To consider the first question we need to return to the composite picture of family breakdown. The relevant points are these: Sole parents are not *by origin* an especially disadvantaged section of society. Most are women who have instigated separations unilaterally; most have done so for reasons to do with emotional imbalances in their marriages; relatively few are the victims of violence or other forms of extreme maltreatment; many have separated within the first ten years of the marriage; most have taken with them young dependent children, and have managed to obtain custody of them. There will be, of course, many exceptions to this picture, and some of them will be cases of deserted or maltreated women, but social policy needs to keep some account of the overall situation with which it is dealing.

It may seem as if the pictures at issue are somewhat melodramatic, with fully-fledged heroes or heroines and villains or villainesses. This need not be so. The interaction between marriage partners is notoriously complex, and it is foolish to assume that in any marriage breakup one party is innocent and the other wholly to blame. People who commit acts of

13 *Sole Parents on Pensions*, 121.

violence against their spouse or who break up their family may well deserve some form of social assistance. But they will deserve these as persons, and not for what they have done. It is only the act of violence or desertion which public policy has a role in preventing or restraining, most especially because these are known to adversely affect children. A society which takes a definite stand against these acts is not lapsing into a primitive moralism; it is merely recognising that marriage does entail some obligations and that it is not a licence to inflict pain and suffering on one another, or, more importantly still, upon children.

Policy in this area need not seek to disadvantage single parents, and it would be unwise if it were to do so, for some of them are greatly to be admired and fully deserve social support. The aim of such a policy must be to be, as far as possible, neutral about the general phenomenon. A neutral policy would be one which gave single-parent families exactly the same support that it gave to two-parent families. At present, as we have seen, two-parent families in Australia get little or no support from the rest of society. Under the present system a policy of neutrality would give most single-parent families merely a Family Allowance for each child, with Family Allowance Supplement for families with incomes low enough to be eligible. This book has argued that this level of support is a wholly inadequate form of recognition for the work that families do. Neutrality would recognise that two-parent families do exactly the same work as that done by single-parent families and have exactly the same needs that they have, and it would assist both equally. Such a policy would meet Jordan's fifth objective, that of maintaining equity between sole parent families and other families.

Jordan's first policy objective was 'to maintain a level of income sufficient for parents and children to survive without undue hardship, and without undue detriment to the future prospects of the children'. It is of course commonly believed that sole parents have greater needs than other families, and much has been said and written about the poverty suffered by single-parent families. The prevention of child poverty is one of the official objectives of the present Government, and (if we can trust the standard 'poverty line' criteria, which is very doubtful) most child poverty is single-parent poverty. There appears to be an insoluble conflict between preventing child poverty and not rewarding single parenthood, at least within the constraints imposed by the present legal framework. This tension is apparent in Jordan's paper when he notes that: 'On the one hand, sole parents are favoured. They are the only category with substantial earning capacity entitled to income security payments free of work test. If actually in the labour force, they are entitled to supplementation of comparatively substantial earnings.... On the other hand, the depressed economic status of sole parents as a group could be and often is taken as evidence that they are victims of inequity'.[14] However, it is now clear that the poverty of sole

14 *Sole Parents on Pensions*, 124.

parents is not caused by pre-existing inequalities, but by the fact that they have become sole parents.

Here we need to distinguish between being income poor and being resource poor. Sole parents may well be income poor, but they are not generally resource poor, as can be seen from their educational qualifications. Family breakdown is today clearly the main cause of what is called 'child poverty', but most child poverty is 'income poverty', not 'resources or assets poverty'. Jordan's *Common Treasury* found that the educational differences between married and sole mothers were very slight:

> The differences in educational status are unremarkable overall, a slightly higher proportion of sole mothers having no formal qualification. Looked at more closely, that small difference turns out to be interesting. Of sole mothers with children under five, and themselves presumably younger rather than older, 47 per cent left school before age 16, as compared with 35 per cent of married mothers with children under five. And, that disaggregation being performed, sole mothers whose youngest children are older than five resemble married mothers more closely. We have here another indication ... that the population [of sole mothers] contains a small, fairly distinct group of educationally disadvantaged young single mothers with young children....[15]

As Jordan has observed, 'The main apparent reason for sole mothers being so much worse off than other women is not that they suffer from particular disadvantages or that they choose not to work, but that they have no husbands'.[16] They are only victims of injustice if they suffered injustice in becoming a single parent, and this is a moral and legal question rather than an economic one. To discuss and to deal with the causes of child poverty we need to consider the phenomenon of family breakdown.[17] But we also need to distinguish between income poverty and resource poverty.

But if sole parents are not victims of economic inequity, are they a favoured category entitled to income security payments free of work test? The answer to this question is not quite straightforward, because, as this book has argued, the work of caring for children may be seen as an important contribution to society. Thus, although sole parents are not required to be available for work in the paid workforce, they are assumed to be working in the unpaid workforce. A society might choose to make caring for children in the family an occupation deserving of social support, but if we were to do this equity would require us to do it for all who performed this work, irrespective of whether they were single or married. It follows that payments to single parents for their work as parents are justified only if the same payments are made to anyone who does the same work. Without equity of this sort, as at present, they do have to be regarded

15 Jordan, *Common Treasury*, **1**, 94f.

16 *Ibid.* 97.

17 The point seems trite, yet curiously the most recent discussion of this subject, Edgar *et al.*'s *Child Poverty* barely mentions family breakdown and divorce as a cause of childpoverty.

as a favoured category. Until we are prepared to provide such general support for parents at home with children, sole parents should be expected to be at least partly self-supporting. The general position has to be that society will support the children of sole parents at the level it supports all children.

Although there has been no very clear rationale for welfare assistance to sole parent families, one reason for its introduction was the absence of any effective enforcement of maintenance payments by non-custodial parents. The failure by many non-custodial parents to provide for their children made state income support appear a necessity. But these two wrongs do not cancel each other out: the failures of the maintenance system should not have been remedied by conscripting assistance from intact families. Society cannot and should not prevent couples from divorcing if they agree that separation is the best course of action for all concerned, but it can and must insist that the end of a marriage is not the end of a person's responsibility for their children. That principle is now widely accepted and is embodied in the Child Support Scheme introduced in 1988. The 'fundamental precept' behind the Scheme is that 'During the children's financial dependency they should share in [their] parents' financial circumstances just as they would if they were growing up with both parents'.[18] To put the same point differently, parents' financial responsibilities to their children do not change when the parents cease to be married or to live together. This precept needs now to be applied to the custodial as well as to the non-custodial parent.

While the details of the new scheme are debatable, the assumption that society is entitled to enforce support, even by use of the taxation system as a collector of payments, is not in doubt. The scheme cannot hope to catch all defaulters, for not all non-custodial parents can be found or identified. In such cases welfare payments will be needed at a level higher than that given to other families. But the general rule should be to treat 'broken' families no differently from intact families. Society should require both parents to contribute fairly to the joint enterprise of child-rearing, regardless of whether the parents choose to live together. Some sole parent families do suffer from both income poverty and resource poverty, but so also do some two-parent families; the state should treat them each alike.

A policy of equalisation of assistance for all family forms, it will be objected, will only plunge sole-parent families even deeper into poverty, and thus harm thousands of innocent children. But this does not follow. There are a number of ways by which it is possible for single parents to support themselves. Many manage to combine parenthood with full-time or part-time work, just as many married mothers manage this combination. This solution has all the attendant stresses of maternal employment, but it can improve the mother's self-confidence at the same time as it raises the family standard of living. To what degree this solution actually makes the

18 *Child Support Formula for Australia*, 7.

family genuinely self-supporting depends on whether there are less-than-obvious state subsidies in the provision of childcare.

Having the care of children is both a barrier to workforce participation and a reason for being at home to care for the children, particularly when they are young. But it is possible for a parent to stay at home with the children when they are young and still be self-supporting. Parents who want to do this can be given loans (over and above their entitlements to general family assistance) to cover the costs incurred at this stage of their lives. Such loans could be interest-free (but indexed for inflation) and repayable in instalments when the parent is able to return to the workforce. Loans of this kind would allow single parents to raise their living standards above the levels permitted by present social security payments. Most single parents remarry or re-partner within about five years of divorce, and will thus share in a regular source of income from which to make repayments. And those who do not will still be likely to spend fifteen or twenty years in the paid workforce after the children reach school-age or leave home. This solution seems the only morally neutral resolution of the conflict between the equity claims of single and two-parent families, and it is thus in keeping with the moral neutrality required by the *Family Law Act*. It is also a legitimate extension of the feminist assumption that women should be independent self-supporting members of society. The argument is not that there should be no assistance to single-parent families, only that they should get exactly the same assistance as that given to two-parent families. (Actually, interest-free loans constitute a subsidy, but a small one.) This goal can be achieved either by lowering assistance to single parents or raising assistance to dual parents or by a combination of both.

Welfare policy has generally assumed that if a person is 'poor' they therefore need public assistance. This argument is valid for children but not for adults. For adults we need to know how they came to be poor and whether they can support themselves before we have a good argument for assistance. Many sole parents can support themselves at least partly while they are sole parents, and almost all will earn enough at other times to be able to pay for their needs when they have children. Some sole parents had poverty thrust upon them, but most seem to have chosen it for reasons which remain obscure from the publicly-discoverable data. Most have come from economically-adequate backgrounds. Voluntary poverty is thought to be a contradiction in terms by those few people still wedded to a naive economism, but it should not surprise anyone who lived through the 1960s and 1970s. It is easy to think that because someone suffered a large drop in income when they left their spouse, they must have had, or believed they had, some very compelling reason for doing so. This reasoning is plausible enough, as far as it goes. But it ignores the fact that in most cases their spouse did not believe there was a good reason for the breakup. Welfare policy does not need to take sides in this domestic dispute, which from an outsider's viewpoint is just one person's word against another's.

But to take a person's act of becoming poor as proof that they had no choice is hardly better than taking their word that they had no choice.

It will be objected that this interpretation of the plight of sole parents is mean-spirited and inhumane. This objection fails to understand both the role of the state and the nature of generosity. It is the state's first task to see that justice is done. Misplaced generosity is dangerous just because it may exacerbate injustice. The present system of support for sole parents does this, because it tends to facilitate family breakdown and to thus bring about unnecessary suffering to children, and because it penalises two-parent families financially. Those who want a more generous society should look around for better objects to support. Within the welfare field they might advocate special support for couples caught in the cycle of chronic domestic violence, or for widowed sole parents, whose situation is by definition involuntary and whose needs might well be better catered for than those of the other categories. Or they might choose to advocate the cause of foster parents, who care for children from broken and unhappy families but receive minimal remuneration for this important and difficult task.

What makes divorce and separation clearly different from most other events for which we provide welfare assistance is that it is a voluntary act and not an accident. It is not necessary here to claim that the relationship breakdown which usually precedes divorce or separation is wholly subject to avoidable voluntary decisions. What is clear is that voluntariness enters into the question more than in any other welfare matter. It is obviously unjust to require couples who stay together to pay for the actions of other couples who, in the same circumstances, choose to separate. We can reasonably presume that all marriages are, at one time or another, subject to the sort of pressures which presently cause break-ups. (If we had a strong causal account of family breakdown we might not make this assumption, but as we do not the assumption should stand.) It follows that the only fair form of family assistance is one which assists all families, those which separate and those which do not.

It is sometimes argued that we need special support for sole parents on the grounds that divorce 'could happen to anyone'. Since the divorce phenomenon is widespread and unpredictable this has some plausibility, but it is not a reason for supporting *only* families which break up. We should support all families equally because all relationships suffer occasional crises, because staying together is socially important and valuable, and because those who stay together should not be penalised. General family support through the financially difficult child-rearing years helps even families which eventually break up, by improving their home-buying chances for instance. It may also help couples to stay together. On the other hand, a system which assists families only if they break up must, in a matter which is so significantly voluntary, distort behaviour.

Full 'minimum' incomes for sole parents, it has been argued, are both unnecessary (because sole parents are capable of being partially self-supporting) and unjust (if they go to one-parent families only, and not to all families with children). It is sometimes said that, on standard liberal grounds, the state should be neutral about the form and structure of families, just as it should be neutral about how people raise their children or how many children they choose to have, etc. In other words, the state should not step in to prop up the two-parent family, if the general trend of people's preferences is away from that form of family. This claim may be reasonable enough but it misconstrues the real situation. At present, as we have seen in previous chapters, the state supports single-parent families but not two-parent families. There is no proof that single-parent families, as such, have greater needs than the traditional family. Their special needs arise only from the failure of the state in the past to see that non-custodial parents contribute fairly to the costs of their children. All parenting can be stressful and difficult—and those who manage to keep their families together may do so only by means of much effort and self-sacrifice. To say this is not to say that those who succeed in keeping their family together are better people than those who do not, only that what they have succeeded in doing is important and valuable, and that fairness or 'neutrality' requires some recognition of this. Society, though it does have a role in supporting all families, has no obligation to subsidise family breakdown.

Workforce participation

We are now in a position to move from ethical and equity questions to economic matters, and to consider the more frequently-discussed of Jordan's objectives, 'not discouraging sole parents' efforts to improve on the minimum level of benefit payments' and 'minimising long-run costs to the community'. Both of these objectives are met more effectively by the policy proposed to deal with the equity question than by any other solution which has yet been put forward. The strategy will be even more effective if sole parent families are included in a system of family-based taxation, as they would be.

There is some good evidence that the present system of payments to sole parents does discourage their workforce participation. Judy Raymond reports that 'the proportion of female sole parents in the labour force has declined from 45.1 per cent in 1974 and 47.9 per cent in 1975 to 40.8 per cent in 1985, while the proportion of male sole parents has declined from from 94.7 per cent to 79.0 per cent over the same period'. This decline might be regarded as a consequence of a declining labour market were it not for the fact that in the same period married mothers have been steadily increasing their labour force participation rate—'from 40.7 per cent in 1974 to 50.5 per cent in 1985', according to Raymond.[19] Any theory of sole parent work effort must explain this simultaneous downward trend for

19 *Bringing Up Children Alone*, 65.

one population and upward trend for the other, where the two groups appear similar in every way except in their differing access to social security benefits.

These contrasting trends are today not as striking as they were in 1985. Since then, part-time work by sole mothers has increased rapidly, so that now about 50 per cent of them are in the labour force, a figure close to that for married mothers. However, this does not invalidate the claim that sole mothers are less disposed to seek paid work than married mothers. Undoubtedly, the biggest workforce 'barrier' for all mothers is children. In this regard sole mothers have considerably less to 'overcome' than married mothers. According to Jordan's research, whereas 30 per cent of married mothers have only one child, the figure for sole mothers is as high as 54 per cent. According to ABS figures, sole-parent families have on average 1.7 children, and two-parent families 2.2 children.[20] The chances that a sole mother will have all her children at school for most of the day are therefore much higher—perhaps twice as high—as for married mothers. This fact makes the actual work patterns even less explicable than is commonly assumed. These differences between married and other mothers is confirmed by the ABS *Time Use Pilot Survey* which shows that married mothers spend about 20 per cent more time per day on all labour force, domestic and child-minding activities than do sole mothers, despite having fewer children on average.[21]

On the face of it part-time work would seem to be the best way to combine childcare and income supplementation, as many married mothers have decided. And as Jordan has remarked, sole mothers in the work force 'are entitled to supplementation of comparatively substantial earnings'.[22] The most obvious explanation of the fact that relatively few sole parents seek part-time work is, then, that many find they can live quite adequately on a full pension. The most obvious policy requirement if we believe that they should become more self-supporting is to lower the level of full benefits and pensions, while reinforcing maintenance payment requirements. The present system of welfare payments is both inefficient—because it discourages sole parents from working when they would otherwise willingly do so—and inequitable—because it favours one kind of family over another. Removing this inequity would solve the efficiency problem, because it would remove the greatest barrier to sole parents' workforce participation, social security payments.

Whatever the justice of this argument, the conclusion is so contrary to current practice and ideology that it could not be implemented without considerable public argument. For practical purposes policy need not be as rigid as strict justice would require. A compromise position might allow welfare payments of the present scale for a limited duration—say for the

---

20 *Common Treasury*, **1**, 94; ABS Cat. 2506.0, Figure 1.3.

21 ABS Cat. 4111.1, Table 1.6.

22 *Sole Parents on Pensions*, 124.

first few months after separation. However, some reform is also required at the point of first receiving payments. At present it is possible for a person to obtain payments simply by presenting themselves at the counter of an office of the Department of Social Security and claiming to be separated from their spouse. The breakup of a family, which this act signifies, is not to be treated as merely a switch from one source of income to another. We need an arrangement here which gives some weight to the symbolic and social importance of this step. The most obvious such arrangement would be to require couples facing separation in which one partner is applying for welfare assistance to seek low-cost marriage guidance counselling aimed at reconciling their difficulties.

Prevention and guidance

So far it has not been argued that benefits and pensions cause family breakdown. The argument has been about establishing an equitable relationship between single-parent and two-parent families, and about whether we should expect single parents to be partly self-supporting. It was not claimed that pensions and benefits cause breakdown, because in only a small proportion of cases is there any financial advantage created by separation. Nor has it been claimed that sole-parent families are necessarily worse as families than two-parent families, though it has been suggested that the predominant reasons for divorce are not morally or socially acceptable reasons where children are involved. Nevertheless, there is reason for concern both about benefits and pensions as causes of breakdown and about the quality of family life which results from a significant proportion of breakdowns. Most important of all here is the effects on children, of the kind documented by Wallerstein and Kelly.

One response to this evidence is to promote joint custody arrangements. This seems the best way to keep both parents involved after divorce in the future of their children. But exactly the same reasons would lead us to do all we reasonably can to promote marital stability, even if that makes divorce less readily available. So far joint custody arrangements have not proven to be very durable, mainly because the divorce and separation were painful and unilateral. As these painful, unilateral separations appear to be the norm rather than the exception, there seems little likelihood of joint custody becoming a common solution to the needs of children in failing families.

Exactly the same arguments that lead us to favour joint custody whenever possible lead also to promotion of marriage guidance counselling facilities. At present Australia spends at least $2000 million annually on caring for broken families and just over $8 million on marriage guidance to help keep families together. The twin facts that most people who divorce marry again and that second marriages fail even more often than first ones suggest that very many people want marital success but do not know how to achieve it, whatever the qualities of their partner. Marital failure appears to be in large part a failure of understanding, but it can also be aggravated by impatience and haste. A recent British survey of 667 divorcees found that a quarter of the women and half the men felt that the divorce had been a mistake. They found that, once having filed for divorce, the parties did not want to admit to the other that they might be wrong after all, and they felt impelled to carry on with the process despite doubts and misgivings.[23]

One way to integrate counselling into the process is to require couples seeking a divorce to register their intention at the beginning of the mandatory (though often disregarded) twelve months' separation and to offer them the possibility of counselling at that point. They might be required to attend a panel which would explain to them their legal situation and outline for them the range of advisory services available.

By comparison with the success rate of other kinds of welfare assistance, marriage;guidance counselling appears to have a good track record, yet it remains the unwanted orphan of the welfare world. One staunch advocate of marriage guidance counselling as a means of alleviating or preventing family breakdown is the Executive Director of the Western Australian Marriage Guidance Council, Jim Crawley. He maintains that

> As the rate of marital and family breakdown has increased, and as the consequences of such breakdown have become clearer, the one thing we have studiously avoided doing is to give a clear and unequivocal commitment to prevention. Yet nothing could be more clearly in our social and economic interests, or more clearly in keeping with the espoused values and aspirations of a large majority of the population than to espouse such a policy.... Marriage counselling is a service whose effectiveness has been clearly established by numerous research studies, and it is a service which without doubt returns ten or twenty-fold every dollar of government funding invested in it. Yet the network of services in Australia is fragmented and under-developed. There are frequently long—and therefore disastrous—waiting lists for counselling, and services in country areas are sparse or non-existent.[24]

A report on marriage guidance counselling organisations conducted by the Australian Institute of Family Studies estimates, conservatively, that every dollar spent on marriage counselling services by the Commonwealth government results in a saving of seven dollars in other government expenditure, principally in social security benefits and legal expenses.[25]

Crawley, however, also supplies some reason for scepticism about the counselling 'solution'. He is as critical of the failings of the family therapy profession as he is of the wider society which refuses to take family breakdown seriously. Family therapy, he contends, has frequently ignored the social, economic and moral predicaments faced by those families it

23 Davis & Murch, *Grounds for Divorce*, 53f.
24 Jim Crawley, 'Preventing Marital and Family Breakdown', 18, 25.
25 See Edgar, 'Family Problems: The Cost-benefits of Prevention', 43f.

seeks to help; and when it does attempt to come to terms with those predicaments it has tended to adopt extremist versions of feminism which do not reflect 'the issues of concern about family life of the ordinary Australian'. Family therapy tends to 'rush lemming-like after the newest fad'. It is dominated by 'gurus', each 'with their own unique approach, packaged for the market-place', not by those 'who have done the hard work of trying to develop a flexible and eclectic repertoire of theoretical insights, interventive skills and—above all—clinical wisdom'.[26]

Fortunately, as Moira Eastman has shown, academic psychological research on the healthy functioning of families is moving towards a consensus which can supersede the exoticism and faddishness preferred by some family therapists. The work of (amongst others) Jerry M. Lewis and J.G. Looney, Burton L. White, Salvador Minuchin, Virginia Satir, R. Blum, R.M. Blakar and Urie Bronfenbrenner, summarised in Eastman's *Family: The Vital Factor*, adds up to a new 'science' of the family, one free from the limitations of behaviourism and the arbitrariness of psychotherapy and anti-psychiatry.[27] One pleasantly surprising discovery—surprising to the researchers themselves—is that healthy families do exist and can be recognised. Some of the new work began from the jaundiced anti-family premisses of R.D. Laing and David Cooper but found these assumptions untenable under scrutiny. Eastman observes that 'many, or even most, mental health professionals were raised in mid-range or severely dysfunctional families and, since they spend their time treating the products of such families, are rarely exposed to optimal health in family functioning'.[28] It was also found that professionals and lay people reached very similar conclusions about the criteria and evidence of family success. On this evidence it appears that family therapy need not be in any way an esoteric form of treatment, but one whose principles are accessible to the patient and to the general public. This proposition is not necessarily at odds with the conclusion of the previous chapter, that the general social causes of family breakdown are little understood. There are different levels here: the lack of good sociological hypotheses does not show that there cannot be what Crawley calls 'clinical wisdom', just as in the medical field good general practitioners need not know anything about epidemiology. And the best potential reservoir of such wisdom is likely to be found in mature men and women who have themselves sustained families and marriages of their own over many years.

If it is true that, despite these hopeful signs, some forms of family therapy remain radically out of touch with the wishes and concerns of those who could most benefit from sensitive and appropriate counselling then it may be asking the impossible to expect government funding processes to distinguish between the genuine and the counterfeit. What is

26 Crawley, 'Family Therapy's Coming of Age'.
27 For one such example see Lewis, *How's Your Family?*
28 *Family: The Vital Factor*, 63.

needed is a way of both providing funding and making counselling responsive to the reality of client's lives. If such funding depended upon success as measured by the client, and if failure to satisfy client's wishes carried a financial penalty, then, gradually, effective family therapy would prosper and irrelevant therapy would be put out of business.

The objective must be to make marriage guidance counselling both accountable to the taxpayer and responsive to the needs and wishes of the consumer. Even those who dispute the track record of marriage counselling could have little grounds for objection if marriage guidance agencies could be expanded at no cost at all to the taxpayer. Suppose that the average duration of sole parents on benefits and pensions is three years and the average cost to the taxpayer of each such case is $30,000. Marriage guidance agencies could tender for responsibility for a randomly-selected number of these families. Such an agency would provide the advice and support needed to bring back together a higher proportion of families than is presently the case. An agency which had responsibility for 1000 families would both make a profit for itself and reduce the cost to the taxpayer if it could meet those families' needs (including their income support costs if they do separate) for less than $30 million. Very obviously, an agency would need to be remarkably incompetent if it could not do better than this. If it was thought objectionable to make a profit out of helping people in marital distress the use of such profit could be regulated so that a proportion of it was used towards counselling for the prevention of marital breakdown. If it was thought that these agencies would be successful but would not provide an adequate return to the taxpayer then they could be regulated so that a proportion of their profit went directly back into government revenues.

In any case it should be obvious that much rests on our ability to encourage and support the marriage guidance profession. Family breakdown is unlikely to go away, and it will not become easier or more benign. The health of families is at least as important as the health of our bodies, though it has been seriously neglected by government policy for some long time.

Poverty and social breakdown

This chapter has argued that the fact that marriages are breaking down earlier requires us to think of the issue as a failure of family formation. Couples frequently do not manage to get over the first hurdles in a marriage, most of which coincide with the arrival of first children. But though now common, this is not the only kind of formation failure. The real complexities arise in the formation of families where the men and possibly also the women are out of work, where they may never have had a stable job, and where they may never have seen any point in making a permanent commitment to each other. In this situation pregnancy, especially teenage pregnancy, is a passport to semi-permanent welfare dependency. At this end of the income scale it has to be said that supporting parent's benefit is easier, more secure and financially preferable to most of the jobs available to an unskilled teenage girl. Swan and Bernstam point out that in Australia in 1985, sixty-eight per cent of all children born to teenagers were born out of wedlock, a figure not far behind the 89 per cent for all babies born to black teenagers in the US, and a radical increase on the 36 per cent in Australia in 1973.[29] Eighty-three per cent of all sole parents are dependent on welfare payments, so probably an even higher percentage of teenage sole parents are welfare-dependent. Teenage motherhood is generally thought to be a main source of lasting dependency, permanently affecting a person's chances of pursuing a satisfying work career, and passing on tendencies towards dependency in the next generation.

The question of sole parent benefits for the sub-population of genuinely disadvantaged recipients identified by Jordan in his analysis of incomes needs to be considered quite separately from the general policy question. As McCaughey suggests, this minority comes from families with a history of low educational achievement, welfare dependency, unemployment, alcohol abuse and violence.[30] Marriages in this section of society tend to be fragile and de facto, with a high proportion of teenage and illegitimate births. The population includes a high proportion of Aborigines.

No-one can doubt that many families in this sub-population are chronically poor in both income and resources, and that they provide a less than optimal setting for the raising of children. However it is far from obvious that simply providing higher levels of income support will help to return them to the mainstream of society or help to increase family success and stability. Even more important than income support is family structural support, and any income support which is destructive of family systems will be counter-productive. Social policy here has to face the classical dilemma of seeking both to minimise the disadvantages suffered by such families and to prevent that category of family from expanding to take advantage of the welfare assistance on offer. It was the severity of this dilemma that caused Charles Murray to conclude that the best solution was to abolish all income transfers to this population, and that caused Lawrence Mead to argue that welfare transfers must be tied to basic 'civic obligations' which promote family stability and social responsibility. Alan Jordan skates over this dilemma when he contends that 'Redistribution in favour of young lower-status couples with young children ... would automatically relieve and prevent a deal of poverty'.[31] Relieving and preventing poverty are two very different objectives, and there is no *a priori* guarantee that they can be reconciled. Action to achieve one objective may very well militate against the other equally important goal.

---

29 Swan & Bernstam, 'Brides of the State'.

30 *A Bit of a Struggle*, Chapter Two.

31 *Common Treasury*, 2, 209.

Indeed there are good grounds for believing that existing policy action has already done much to aggravate the problem of family poverty in the last fifteen years.

The question of youth homelessness, which has been given great public exposure recently, gives us one window into the larger social changes which are taking place. Young people have always run away from home, but the evidence is clear that this phenomenon is now more widespread than at any time in the past. Most discussion of the issue has been more symptomatic than diagnostic. The root of the problem clearly is that the traditional causes of family stress—alcoholism, violence, child abuse and parent/teenager conflict—have been aggravated very greatly by an upsurge of separation, divorce, sole parenthood and strained step-parental relationships. The evidence for this claim is clear in the Burdekin Report, *Our Homeless Children*. One submission to the report from a Perth group asserted that 'about three-quarters of the young people coming into Home Sharers [a refuge] were from single-parent or blended families'. A Mildura submission held that family breakdown (meaning separation and divorce) 'is present in the history of 99 per cent of the young people using our service'. Evidence from Darwin and Queensland corroborated these high estimates, and none contradicted them. An independent analysis by I. O'Connor concluded that of 100 homeless youth '40 per cent were members of reconstituted or step-families and another 26 per cent were from single parent families', a ratio about three times that to be found in the general population. Other submissions to the report described backgrounds of family violence and alcoholism.[32]

Clearly (although the Burdekin Report makes little of this point), one basic objective of welfare policy must be to foster stable and successful family relationships and to make those families capable of being self-supporting in the workforce. What other ultimate objective could there be? The American example, in which 70 per cent of all black children are born out of wedlock—in many areas the percentage is much higher than this—and 50 per cent are raised in single-parent households, is one which we should study carefully in this country. The earlier part of this chapter has dealt with the larger legal and welfare framework; here we are concerned with the work of the welfare agencies. But how welfare agencies might achieve the above goal is a large subject, worthy of a book in itself. (A general survey of the multitude of small welfare operations scattered around the country, comparing methods and rates of success, could be a very useful contribution to policy debate.) In what follows the emphasis will be on basic aims and assumptions. The nature of any would-be solution must be dictated by the nature of the problem. Welfare agencies

32 Burdekin Report, 88ff. These figures are certainly more reliable than the Report's highly-publicised but extremely dubious figure of 25,000 homeless youths in Australia.

cannot replace families—family acceptance and care are irreplaceable, which is why reconciliation must be a primary goal of welfare policy.

To understand something of how family breakdown produces social breakdown, consider Chris's story, as told by him with great insight in John Embling's *Fragmented Lives*.[33] Chris's parents separated when he was ten, and he never saw his father or his family home again. His mother joined the sub-culture of single mothers and Chris was left free to wander the streets. Without parental attachment his greatest fear, he says, 'was of being ignored and rejected by all the other kids around the flats. So I learned to put up with violence towards me from kids and adults.... If you have no one to care about you, you lose interest and don't bother about yourself.... When nobody takes any interest in you, it's like being starved'. He became inured to violence: 'you see a bloke stab someone with a knife and the blood spurts out, and next time you're handling a knife in your own flat it feels strong and warm'. At school Chris was continually in desperate trouble, yet he says he and his fellow-troublemakers would have respected any teachers who were prepared to understand 'how hurt and desperate he is for his mum and dad or someone like them to take him seriously'.

When Chris joined John Embling's Footscray household he transferred all his anger and 'mounting, directionless violence' onto Embling and the Foundation. A safe and caring environment was not enough to settle him down. As Embling discovered, 'Here was a boy I'd spent a considerable time with who was threatening to stick a knife into my body'. In such cases, Embling learned, it is 'a matter of throwing away the books, the clichés, the ideologies.... It was necessary to get a grip on Chris's reality, so that he could feel the strength and power of another person's life and love'. At the inevitable showdown Embling could do this only by offering Chris the chance to carry out his knife threat, so calling the bluff around which Chris's self-made street-toughened life had been built. Embling's gamble worked, and Chris became a vital member of the Foundation's team. Looking back on this crisis Embling remarks: 'Sometimes I feel we sell our children short, even the more desperate, defiant ones, by not giving them the true, honest force of our anger and feelings at what they are doing'.

Chris's story is only one of many thousands, each following what may well be a standard pattern. Very few have such successful outcomes. As Embling observes,

> Isn't it about time that people stopped and thought about the young male delinquent—the person our system is producing in ever-increasing numbers? There's nothing more conservative than your standard delinquent. He's male, racist, sexist, mostly fascist, and totally materialistic. He's exploitative, out for something for nothing, and a quick buck. He's no conservationist or ecologist; he takes what he wants because he wants to. In other words, he's the worst kind of capitalist, not an honourable, benign one, he wants easy money and plea-

33 *Fragmented Lives*, 77–89.

> sure.... He doesn't fit into the open society of individuality and choice.... He's a person of action, not of inner reflection or sensibility, a right-wing activist often frustrated to the point of anarchy.[34]

He is, in other words, someone we could do without. It seems a reasonable social policy objective to want to avoid producing such people, as far as possible.

But nothing can be achieved unless we understand the lessons learned by Chris and Embling. There are two sorts of lessons, about cure and about prevention. Cases like Chris will never be cured by impersonal or purely social means. Even in the friendly environment of the Foundation he remained just as violent as before. Only the discovery that another person thought him worth risking life for was enough to break through his second nature of pseudo-toughness. Only people like John Embling prepared to take such risks will succeed in making changes for the better. All the available welfare resources should be devoted to finding, supporting and rewarding such people. In this area everything else is a waste of time and money. Such work will not be done by the public service, which should see its role as fostering the (sometimes erratic) efforts and talents of others outside the conventional framework of career paths and committee meetings. But, as Embling warns, such workers risk 'over-identifying, over-compensating and, sometimes, over-indulging themselves in the turmoil of the lives of the people they deal with'.[35] This can be avoided only if we grasp the nature of the emotional hungers which result from family failure.

Chris's real troubles began when his family broke up. Before then his life may have been difficult; afterwards it was impossible; and the difference between the impossible and the difficult is all the difference in the world. Once Chris gave up hope he came to take pride in his own capacity for self-destructive behaviour. The prevention of this downward spiral has to begin with the prevention of family breakdown. The relevant lesson here is that having two bad parents is better than having one bad parent, and vastly better than having what is effectively no parent at all. To say this is not to roundly condemn all single parents. Rather, as John Embling puts this point,

> a strong, caring mother is capable of raising their child to become a fully functioning and loving human being, but there also need to be uncle and aunt figures just around the corner to provide another aspect of the necessary, daily, humanising contact with other people. Even the strongest, most capable, single parent finds it difficult to give his or her child all that is needed to make a human being.[36]

34 *Fragmented Lives*, 48f.

35 *Ibid*, 21.

36 *Ibid*. 51.

Relatively few single parents are strong and capable, and few of the families that need them most have aunts and uncles who are so readily available. Boys without fathers or father figures very often do not learn to master the art of combining strength and gentleness, a skill which they might learn from observing a father who himself may not be good at doing that. Boys need pride, and Chris took pride in his perverse behaviour because he had no-one to show him anything else to take pride in.

Parenthood, this book has argued, is about transmitting to the next generation self-confidence, competence and respect for others. Parents do this by showing affection, by providing guidance and by exercising authority. Chris missed out on all three and he failed to acquire the three corresponding attributes. Affection without authority is as bad as authority without affection, and both need guidance to give life direction. Chris's central problem was not poverty. None of the things he lacked can be made up for with money alone, and exactly the same syndrome can be found at all levels of society. Had his mother been given more 'adequate' social security payments her family's condition would have been no better. It may have been better if she had been required to work to supplement the family income. Nor would Chris have benefited from greater social expenditure on his education. His problem at school was to find someone who would take him seriously.

John McLeod, a former school psychologist and friend of the Foundation, summed up his years of experience with the observation that 'generally when a child was in deep trouble in his or her behaviour, he or she would go out of their way to take on the strongest, most visible adults available'.[37] The only thing useful to Chris and the thousands like him is adults capable of reading this message and responding with both authority and affection. To assume that because Chris acts tough he is to be treated like a fully-formed adult is to fall for one of the oldest tricks in the book. To treat his difficulties as economic is to fall for an only slightly more sophisticated version of the same trick. Rather than blaming 'society' for destroying the lives of Chris and his kind, we should be not be afraid to give them 'the true, honest force of our anger and feelings at what they are doing' when they try to destroy themselves and others. Only then will they know that they are being taken seriously as potential adults. And if 'society' is to be blamed then it is for not taking seriously the importance of marriage and family life rather than for any alleged economic injustices it may have perpetrated.

Having for so long neglected family needs and taken lightly family responsibilities we are now having to deal with the social destructiveness which is a natural consequence of this indifference. We know that in the most severe cases of family failure both the criminal justice system and the conventional welfare approaches are of very little help. (Providing the equivalent of adult unemployment benefit to homeless youth, as the

37 *Fragmented Lives*, 50.

Burdekin Report recommended, is likely merely to multiply the homeless population, which undoubtedly contains some who prefer the excitement of life on the streets to the boredom, restrictions and tension of life at home.) The most eloquent and hopeful testimony given to the ABC television program on youth homelessness, *Nobody's Children*, came from a former young criminal. Speaking of the army-style Wilderness Work Camp in the Northern Territory, he said:

> When I first came here I had a bad attitude. I was an arsehole. I wouldn't do what I was told. I hated the world and the world hated me. Do a little while here and then you realise how good it is for you. Not just in your head, deep down you know, deep down it really changes you. You start caring for things. You start respecting people. You're not the only person in the world. There are a lot of other people, you meet them half-way.

Welfare programs which can produce testimony like this are surely worthy of public assistance. Not all need follow an army-style approach, but approaches which offer only sympathy seem unlikely to get to the heart of the matter. In this case the camp provided the direction and authority and pride which had been missing from the family background. The cost of such programs needs to be weighed against the cost of long-term welfare dependence and social disruptiveness.[38]

The worst possible approach to this issue is one which assigns the task of providing authority and direction to one kind of agency—the police and the courts—and the task of giving assistance and sympathy to another, the welfare system, with the two kinds of agency either distant from or even hostile to each other. This approach, though common, fails to provide the coherent combination of love and discipline more or less characteristic of most families, and leads only to further confusion and alienation.

The destructiveness discussed here is more a male than a female phenomenon, though not exclusively so. Severe family breakdown, apart from releasing such destructiveness, also tends to perpetuate itself in the next generation through failures of family formation. This is not an invariable rule—some victims respond by fighting fiercely to achieve the stability which they themselves missed out on when young—but it contains enough truth to warrant thought about appropriate policy responses. Discussions about whether girls do or do not get pregnant in order to get Supporting Parents Benefit easily bog down in debate about the complexities of human motivation. A 1985 *Los Angeles Times* survey found that 51 per cent of the general population did not believe that 'poor young women have babies so they can collect welfare'; but when they surveyed people in poor neighbourhoods 70 per cent of poor women thought that this is 'almost always' or 'often' true.[39] It would be interesting to see a similar study in this country. Nor is the international evidence here merely

38 For an American example, see Adams, *Path of Honor*.

39 *A Community of Self-Reliance*, 31.

anecdotal. In advanced societies non-marital fertility is very low in those countries which have low levels of child allowances (Japan, Italy, Spain, Israel) or which do not give special subsidies to unmarried parents (Switzerland, West Germany, Belgium, the Netherlands), whereas those which do give such subsidies have high levels of non-marital fertility.[40]

It does not need to be claimed here that girls get pregnant simply in order to get a guaranteed minimum income. But there is ample anecdotal evidence that desire for a secure income and the desire for emotional security can and do reinforce each other. Ronald Conway observes: 'Many times I have heard young single mothers state that "I wanted to have a baby so that there would be someone to love me", with little thought in their minds that a child's reason for existence should represent something more than satisfaction of the needs of a lonely, unhappy and immature parent....' He adds that 'Out of such fostered and discarded child debris come the criminals, mercenaries and public enemies of the future'.[41] Many welfare workers would agree with this general assessment. Jeff Collman's study of outback Aboriginal life notes that, as a result of welfare policy, Aboriginal families are tending to become matricentric and to 'socially repress the significance of fathers altogether'. He concludes that 'Because women have privileged access to welfare resources, they have more secure domestic livelihoods than men, and men often depend upon them for their more basic requirements. The conditions under which women acquire welfare benefits, however, encourage them to minimise their relationships with men'.[42]

While it is understandable that a young mother may not wish to commit herself to a male as destructive and futureless as many now are, when the state will provide a more stable alternative, this strategy deprives the child of the essential close contact with one half of the human race. Income support for sole parents, while it helps the custodial parent to look after the children, facilitates the phenomenon of the vanishing father. It does appear that we are creating whole suburban areas in which single women struggle to bring up children without the assistance of men, and that this rarely provides those children with the balance they need to become successful working and loving adults.[43] John Embling asks the anguished question:

> Where have all the fathers gone? Over a ten year period I have worked with hundreds of children and their families. I spend most of my life with children, young adults, mothers—but where are the fathers? Where have they gone? I have only known four or five fathers-as-parents, as providers, as role models, over those ten years.... I often look around for the fathers of 'our' children. I

40 Bernstam & Swan, *Malthus and the evolution of the Welfare State*, Part 1, 35.

41 *The End of Stupor?*, 27.

42 Collman, *Fringe-Dwellers and Welfare*, 121, 105.

43 The NSW Director of Education has noted that in some of his schools 80 per cent of children are from single parent families (Pollard, 'The Family and the Economy', 15.

> feel a sense of profound loss, of defeat, of inhumanity, as I see men devoid of personal contact with their children. Their loss, the loss of something central to the human process, is also our loss. Something is being crippled, and all the money, technology, bureaucracy, professionalism, ideology in the world won't make it right again.[44]

The obvious conjecture is that the men are living somewhere else, quite likely on unemployment benefits. If we really wish to prevent this 'loss of something central to the human process' then we will have to take seriously the question of paternity. DNA labelling makes it now possible to trace paternity. There may be ways of making welfare benefits conditional upon an agreement to support rather than neglect the recipient's children. We could also make Supporting Parents Benefit conditional upon some effort to establish the father of the children, and then make any benefits to the father conditional upon some commitment to those children and their mother.

These questions are at once both moral and economic. It is the combination of poverty with demoralisation which has such a devastating impact in reinforcing cycles of deprivation, but we can not expect to break such cycles merely by injecting money. It may be more effective to take seriously the moral side of the issue, or it may be that any policy which overlooks the moral side will not succeed. On this moral issue Germaine Greer, in *Sex and Destiny*, quotes Stevie Smith:

> Oh these illegitimate babies!
> Oh girls, girls,
> Silly little valuable things,
> You should have said, No, I am valuable,
> And again, It is because I am valuable
> I say, No.
>
> Nobody teaches anybody they are valuable nowadays.[45]

Teaching teenagers that they are valuable also involves teaching them to say No. Both of these are art forms we have failed to cultivate adequately in the past two decades. Once again we face the problem of exercising authority. At the same time we need to teach that children are valuable, and that every new child deserves better than to be brought into the world single-handedly by one of Conway's 'lonely, unhappy and immature parents'.

All this is, of course, easier said than done. A state welfare system which does not promote irresponsibility is part of the answer. But such a system needs to be supplemented by small-scale agencies which, at their best, will provide emergency aid, financial and domestic advice (some parents are incapable even of cooking a hot meal), marital and parental counselling, employment assistance, and a community centre for self-help

---

44 Embling, *Fragmented Lives*, 51f.
45 Greer, *Sex and Destiny*, 80.

groups. Some of the private agencies do perform most of these diverse functions. Many also encourage an ethos which promotes responsibility and maturity. To do this they need to be small and local, so that they can be accepted and respected as part of a community and so that they can know the people they are helping. Organisations of this kind cost far less than the impersonal bureaucracies which dispense money without genuine assistance. The first priority of state welfare policy here should be to identify and promote such organisations. If the state continues to promote ethical irresponsibility then we can expect to have the social problems that we do have. But if it were to support the ethical beliefs and status rewards which presently operate in ordinary working-class communities then we can hope to turn around the disintegration now so obvious.

9 Caring for children

Should the state subsidise childcare? This question appears to be a special case of the more general question, Should the state help to support children and their families? This book has argued that the state might reasonably assist families with children. If we were to establish such an assistance scheme—or, better still, a tax system which had the same net effect—then there would seem to be nothing more to be said about childcare. Simply by assisting families with children the state would be assisting families wanting childcare, just as it would be assisting families wanting play equipment, or children's books, or to be able to afford holidays together. Obviously it is better for each particular family to decide which of these forms of expenditure best meets its circumstances—governments have no special insight into matters of that kind. Looked at from this angle, it seems no more necessary to have a public policy about childcare than it is to have one about any of the other many important decisions that families make.

If we are to have a policy that subsidises childcare directly rather than through general assistance to families, then a special case needs to be made out that distinguishes childcare from the many other ways of helping children and families. Further, the rationale for such a policy must be something more than the special pleading of a particular interest group. It needs to be grounded in reasons which anyone can recognise as valid. Is the present system of childcare subsidies grounded in such reasons?

The aims of Commonwealth government funding of childcare, known as the Children's Services Program, are:

1 to facilitate workforce participation by women;
2 to ensure access to appropriate childcare for special-need groups, including Aboriginal, migrant and disabled children and the children of sole parents attempting to re-enter the workforce;

3 to provide occasional care for children of parents at home;
4 to ensure that childcare is affordable for low and moderate income families;
5 to ensure a good standard of quality in childcare services;
6 to ensure that childcare is delivered in a cost-effective manner.

However, a set of objectives of this kind is not at all the same as a clear rationale for a policy. None of the stated objectives, except perhaps (6), is self-evidently desirable. The statement of objectives does not by itself tell us why childcare should be specially subsidised. To pursue this question we need to turn elsewhere. A recent paper from the ANU Centre for Economic Policy Research on *Government Spending on Work-Related Child Care: Some Economic Issues* is an attempt to provide at least part of such a rationale.[1] Although the paper was commissioned by the Department of Community Services and Health, it is not a government policy document. It is, however, presented as a partial defence of the existing system of subsidies, and it seems to be the clearest discussion document available on the subject. The authors are careful not to claim that the present system is the only way or the best way to achieve the objectives which they see as the fundamental rationale for the existing system.

The authors distinguish between two broad justifications for childcare subsidies: an efficiency argument and an equity argument. Roughly speaking these correspond to objectives 1 (facilitating women's workforce participation) and 2 (helping groups with special needs) in the above list. Objective 4, making childcare affordable to lower income groups, is also presumably an equity objective. We can discuss the other objectives after the equity and efficiency arguments have been considered. Equity and efficiency are basic social goals; the only question at issue is whether equity and efficiency require special subsidies for childcare.

On the efficiency question, the paper argues not on the basis of benefits to society through benefits to children, but on the basis of benefits to society through benefits to women, particularly women's participation in the workforce. 'Many of the gains that would flow from investing in an increasingly well educated female workforce may be dissipated by the depreciation of human capital that occurs when workers withdraw from the labour force for long periods of time', it contends.[2] This assumes that the capital invested in a woman's education does not benefit her children, and thus society, through her contribution to their education when she cares for them in the home. It also fails to weigh up the value of the skills required in being a full-time parent against the value of those required in the workforce. It may be that a woman's workforce skills deteriorate when she leaves the workforce but it seems equally true that she acquires other useful skills. Increased workforce participation by mothers who might

1 Gregory *et al.*, *Government Spending on Work-Related Child Care.*
2 *Ibid.* 11.

otherwise be at home with children will show up as an increase in gross domestic product, for the obvious reason that GDP measures only formal economic activity. But this increase is not at all the same as an increase in economic activity. For all that we can really know it might amount to a net decrease in economic activity. The figures are distortions because they fail to measure economic activity that takes the form of domestic production.

Another consequence of the argument presented is that childcare subsidies should be proportional to the level of capital invested. The efficiency argument requires that subsidies should be greatest to women with tertiary qualifications. Less highly qualified mothers would be less eligible for assistance. A further consequence is that women or men who would be more efficiently 'deployed' at home with their children should be subsidised to stay at home.

There is something peculiar in the claim that those who have benefited most from public investment in their higher education should be given even more subsidies to help them reap further benefits from their education. The subsidy is a subsidy from poorer families to richer families, often from poor single-income families to rich double-income families, and often from families with several children to families with few children. Highly educated women are already rewarded in the salaries they command. Any further subsidy to them is middle-class welfare of the most obvious and objectionable kind. Anyone concerned with the well-being of low-income families should want the highly educated to repay to society the costs of their educational subsidies, not to devise new forms of subsidy.

It will be said that the working mother in the public economy is taxed and the mother at home is not. This is misleading. If, as Chapter Six contended, caring for children is not a form of production for private ends but is rather to be thought of as a welfare activity, then there is no reason why childcare in the home should be taxed. Equally there is no reason why commercial childcare organisations should be taxed. But they are not: mothers who use such facilities are not taxed for using them. Employees who work in childcare are taxed on their income, but so are other equally important workers such as nurses.

In Chapter Six it was argued that a tax system based on equivalent income should take some account of domestic production. If this is all that is at issue then the objection has been met, and there is no need for special tax deductions for those who use childcare services. Allowing for domestic production in the calculation of personal income tax will suffice to remove any economic distortions which may occur. At present the mother at home is taxed on her share of the total family income. The only tax concession she gets is the spouse rebate. By parity the working woman is entitled to the same sort of tax deduction. This could be secured by an equivalent income system whereby mutual dependency within the family is recognised and not simnply the dependency of the wife at home.

On the equity issues, *Government Spending on Work-Related Child Care* argues that funded childcare 'offsets some or all of the biases in the [tax/welfare] system that encourage women not to participate in the paid labour force'.[3] This brings us to the second objective of the Children's Services Program, assistance to groups with special needs. The arguments for childcare assistance to Aboriginal, migrant and disabled children involve questions about the particular characteristics of these groups which cannot be entered into here, but we can consider the claim that sole parents need special childcare assistance.

About 80 per cent of those sole parents with children under five who are in the labour force use funded childcare (compared with 26 per cent of working married women), but only 50 per cent of all sole parents are in the labour force. On this evidence the potential savings from encouraging sole parents to be more self-supporting would seem to be considerable. The argument would be that funding childcare will provide equity for a disadvantaged group but more efficiently and at a lesser cost than that of the social security approach.

This reasoning does have a certain logic but it is the logic of a latter-day *Alice in Welfareland.* The position is this: Alice, a sole parent, having reached a point where she feels ready to return to the workforce, finds that it is only financially worthwhile to do so if much of the cost of her childcare is paid for by the state. In stepping in to provide that subsidy, government is in effect providing assistance to help her need less assistance. The logic in this rests upon a premiss which disguises Alice's actual situation. If Alice is ready to be self-supporting then clearly she no longer needs social assistance. She therefore does not need assistance to help her need less assistance. Alice is ready and willing to work. All she 'needs' is the removal of the main 'barriers' to working, her benefit or pension. Since she no longer needs those payments no injustice is done in ending them.

Of course if Alice is able but not willing to become self-supporting, the situation is slightly more complex. At present the state merely waits patiently for her to declare herself willing, but justice does not require such patience. Alice may be somewhat lazy or she may have only an intermittently active conscience about receiving payments which she no longer needs. (Few of us are very vigilant about such matters.) The question of when a person is ready to be self-supporting is a question for government to determine, not the recipient. All that public policy requires is a fixed term for beneficiaries. In Chapter Eight it was contended that there is no equity argument to show that sole parents require assistance not available to intact families. If this general argument is correct then the same applies to childcare funding.

Government Spending on Work-Related Child Care is a model of how not to discuss these questions. The paper moves from an efficiency argument to an equity argument as if the first props up the second, when they

3 *Government Spending on Work-Related Child Care*, 14.

are clearly quite separate issues. (The first would support cheap childcare for tertiary graduates only, and it would do so only by raising taxes on the less well-off.) It proceeeds as if the new economics of the family does not exist. By not counting work in the home, the paper confuses measured GDP with total economic activity, yet it wants to count home production as imputed taxable income. It fails to see that caring for children at home is as real a contribution to the whole well-being of society as any other. It does not establish its claim that taxpayer-funded childcare adds real jobs to the labour market.

Objective (5) of present government childcare policy is 'to ensure a good standard of quality in childcare services'. The question of quality is as paradoxical as the previous issues. Quality is often judged by adult/child ratios and by the frequency and closeness of interactions between adult and child. By these standards the family home must rate as by far the best of all childcare environments. The classic modern parable about childcare is that told by Linda Burton. After researching, inspecting and interviewing all the available options, seeking someone who would 'encourage my children's creativity, take them on interesting outings, answer all their little questions, and rock them to sleep', she came to see that the only person who met her own specifications for the job was—herself. 'I had been desperately trying to hire me', she concluded.[4] If objective (5) is about giving children these advantages then it entails support for mothers at home with children.

That there are substantial advantages in very young children being at home with their mother, father or other close relative is now commonly recognised by child psychologists. Both Penelope Leach and Dr Benjamin Spock endorse this claim. Perhaps educational psychologist Burton White, director of the Harvard Preschool Project, can be taken as sufficient authority on the subject. White's emphatic advice to parents is this:

> Unless you have very good reason, I urge you not to delegate the primary child-rearing task to anyone else during your child's first three years of life... Babies form their first human attachment only once. Babies begin to learn language only once... The outcomes of these processes play a major role in shaping the future of each new child.[5]

At the very least it has to be said that there is no developmental reason for governments to favour childcare out of the home over childcare in the home, or to tax families who care for their children at home to pay for the childcare of those who do not. This argument is not a conclusive case against funding for formal childcare institutions: Burton White may be wrong; some parents may be able to compensate for the deficiencies of the available out-of-home childcare; older preschool children may benefit from some formal childcare attendance; and some childcare centres may be warm and friendly places. But if there is a case for subsidising *any* form of

4 Zinsmeister, 'Brave New World', *Quadrant*, July 1989, 26.
5 *Ibid.* 25.

childcare, this is a conclusive argument in favour of funding *all* forms, including childcare at home. Objective (3) of current policy, 'to provide occasional care for children of parents at home', does give some recognition of the needs of mothers at home, but in practice it is little more than words in a document. In 1986–87, Commonwealth government expenditure on occasional care amounted to less than three per cent of all childcare funding.[6]

One of the many absurdities in 'the childcare debate' is its exclusive pre-occupation with *formal* work-related childcare. The fact that only about 30 per cent of all work-related childcare takes place in the formal sector is almost never mentioned. (Sixteen per cent in pre-schools, ten per cent in childcare centres, and three per cent in family day care.) The remaining 70 per cent is carried out by other family members or by informal private arrangements.[7] Yet it seems obvious that children whose parents must both work are often best cared for by grandparents, other relatives or friends, in homes where they feel at home and known personally, possibly with cousins as playmates. (With the general ageing of the population there are now more retired grandparents available than ever before.) All the arguments for supporting children in their own homes carry across to support for children in informal childcare arrangements. Yet at present informal care is given no support at all, nor is it discussed in public debate, which is dominated by the voices of the formal childcare sector. Exactly which form of childcare best suits the needs of each particular family at any particular time is a matter about which governments are necessarily quite ignorant. This is a choice that only parents can make. Public policy should be rigorously neutral in its allocation of funding, and leave the decision to the families themselves.

The main theme of this chapter is that the case for childcare subsidies rests on the general case for family assistance. The point is a simple one, but it seems to escape the notice even of otherwise sharp thinkers. A fairly typical specimen of the confusion which bedevils this issue is provided by Padraic P. McGuinness, writing in defence of the Liberal Party's 1989 commitment to providing an $800 million childcare rebate, which he acknowledges 'will clearly benefit relatively well-off double income families without benefitting the genuinely poor at all'. According to McGuinness,

> Genuine equality of opportunity for women must mean that they are not penalised for having children. A high-income working woman has to incur childcare costs to earn her income, and there is a strong case for arguing that this cost ought to be fully tax-deductible at whatever is her marginal rate of taxation. We cannot and should not try to push women out of the workforce; and we have to recognise that if we want our population to reproduce itself, equality and equity between the sexes demand that women be compensated for carrying that responsibility. This is an issue which has little to do with the distribution of

6 Department of Community Services Annual Report, 1986–87, Table 5.
7 ABS Cat. 4119.0, Table 5.3.

> income. Where is the sense in compensating poor or single unemployed women for having children while placing a negative value on the children of intelligent and educated women who play a valuable role in the workforce?[8]

Four reasons are being given here. One, childcare subsidies will help to maintain our population. But the fair way to do that is to help anyone who chooses to have children. Two, women should not be pushed out of the workforce. But women should not be 'pushed' anywhere, out of or into the workforce. On this reasoning we should assist all mothers and let them decide where they want to go. Three, equality and equity between the sexes demands that women be compensated for carrying the responsibility of child-bearing. But this applies equally to all mothers. Four, we should support not just poor and single mothers but also intelligent, educated mothers who play a valuable role in the workforce. But then we should support all mothers who play a valuable role in society, whether in the workforce or in the home. Only in this way can we ensure that women have a free and fair choice about how they manage the relation between work and home.

Childcare subsidisation is not at present a large item in the Commonwealth budget—a 'mere' few hundred million dollars—but there are plenty of signs that it may become one. It has been argued here that the case for childcare subsidies rests on the general case for family assistance. A rational feminism would argue the general case. The particular case looks like nothing more that the special pleading of a sectional interest group, not a group which has at heart the interests of all women, or all children. Those who defend the particular case (including the leaders of both major parties) have an obligation to show how, in taking from the family childcare system and giving to the public childcare system, state subsidies differ from organised expropriation.

---

8 *The Australian*, 20 October 1989.

10 Education and the family

The education debate

Education is a bewildering business. In the past twenty years Australian schools appear to have improved in many ways. Student/teacher ratios have fallen markedly. Buildings are less crowded and better appointed. The curriculum is more diverse and more attractively presented. High quality teaching materials and resources have been developed in every subject area and are freely available to teachers and students. Specialist assistance in art, music, sport and drama is now common in primary as well as secondary schools. Remedial courses for disabled or disadvantaged children exist that were not available before. Retention rates in secondary school have improved. Most young children begin school with some pre-primary or kindergarten experience behind them. Libraries and laboratories are very much better endowed and equipped. Computers and video facilities are becoming widely available at both primary and secondary levels. Counselling facilities have expanded and much effort is made to improve students' self-esteem. Excursions to take part in community activities are now relatively frequent. Teachers are less authoritarian and more responsive to student rights, interests and sensitivities. Teachers are now more highly qualified (at least formally) than ever before. In-service and professional development courses to improve teacher performance are readily available. Teacher contact hours have been reduced and preparation time during working hours has increased. Administrative assistance exists at regional and head offices. In short, almost everything that money can provide has been provided. And yet, at the end of this long process of expansion and improvement, a community-wide controversy exists about whether the education system is now more or less successful than when the process began.

Some accounts attempt to talk down the importance and seriousness of this controversy, but it should not be so lightly dismissed. Those who would so dismiss it tend to measure the success of the system by the quality and quantity of the inputs and not by the quality of its products, which is like judging a sporting team by the quantity of seating in its stands or the colour of its jumpers rather than by success on the field. Yet even when this simple fallacy is exposed another often goes unnoticed. The debate has been about whether educational standards have or have not declined. The fact that this is what is being debated would seem to be itself an indictment of the education system. In effect this question asks whether the massive increase in resources has or has not only just managed to prevent a decline in educational standards! Expenditure per primary and secondary school pupil (at constant 1987 prices) has increased from $1248 in 1967 to $2799 in 1985, an increase of 125 per cent.[1] The relevant question should be whether educational achievement has improved in proportion to the increases in input. And, as resources have doubled, then (all other things being equal) we should expect something like a doubling in achievement. There are very few wholehearted defenders of the schools, and not even the most positive and optimistic believes that they have been this successful.

Much of the public debate on school achievement has focused on the basic skills of literacy and numeracy, for the obvious reason that a school which fails to equip its pupils to read, write and compute well has not provided them with the grounding necessary for the acquisition of other skills. Yet it might also be questioned whether the schools have done well in those other areas—in science or social studies, for instance. Many of Australia's most distinguished thinkers, writers and social critics believe that our education system is failing to produce literate, intelligent, self-critical, responsible future citizens. Most of the critics are, however, outside the educational establishment, having made their mark in a wide variety of traditional disciplines and professions. Although our universities and colleges of advanced education contain dozens of educational theorists, no substantial reply to the criticisms of the education system has ever been made.

Professor Peter Karmel, who chaired the 1973 *Schools in Australia* report which led to rapid expansion of Commonwealth educational activity and the setting up of the Schools Commission, accepts that one reason why there is much public scepticism about schools is that 'the large increase in resources devoted to education had not produced any obviously visible

1 Freebairn *et al.*, *Spending and Taxing: Australian Reform Options*, 94. Peter Karmel ('Quality and Equality in Education', 279f) calculates that 'the real volume of resources devoted to education in Australia had, over a 20-year period [from 1958 to 1978], increased almost fivefold'.

outcome'. Karmel himself believes that 'The education process is a long one and it would be absurd to expect immediate results from additional inputs', but he gives no reason for preferring a long-term perspective to a short-term one. Karmel also notes that expenditure on schools has not been curbed by public criticism. 'Notwithstanding the chilly atmosphere in which educational institutions have been operating,... in the school sector resources devoted to education for current operations have continued to expand. Over the last decade, recurrent expenditure per pupil in real terms has increased by between 4 and 5 per cent per annum in both government and non-government schools'.[2]

Nevertheless, governments are coming to share many of the doubts about educational spending being voiced in the community. This has never been more forcefully put than by the then Commonwealth Minister for Education, Susan Ryan, speaking in 1985:

> I want to make it clear that the Commonwealth is deadly serious about its increasing concentration on outcomes; that is, with what comes out of the education system, not just how many billions we pour into it. It is clear that the community wants quality education, and it is to this demand that the Government will respond. The Commonwealth Government is no longer prepared to pour buckets of money into the education system in an indiscriminate manner.[3]

Michael Hogan has observed that 'Despite massive grants and very expensive capital works programs it is questionable whether the quality of schooling in the poorer areas of the main Australian cities has approached much closer to a socially acceptable standard in the 1980s than was the case in the 1960s'. He adds that 'It is time that the use of such funds should be directed beyond the traditional targets of capital expenditure on school buildings and recurrent expenditure for teachers' salaries into a concerted attempt to redesign what happens in the schools themselves and to attack the culture of alienation, apathy and despair which can permeate a whole school from senior teachers to junior pupils'.[4]

What is required from educational policy discussion, then, is a search for the missing ingredients in current practice: educational success, and its principal determinants. This cannot be carried out directly because the teachers' unions will not permit any such investigations, and if testing could be performed it would take time before an adequate body of data could be built up. Rather, we have to work from other indications, wherever they may be found. The particular theme of this book is the place of the family in social policy, and there is certainly much to be said about the place of families in education, but before proceeding to that subject we need at least a rough sketch of what leads to educational achievement.

---

2 'Quality and Equality in Education', 281f.
3 Quoted in *ibid.*, 283.
4 Hogan, *Public versus Private Schools*, 13, 16.

Educational achievement

A recent film, *Stand and Deliver*, is one possible starting point. The film tells the story of Garfield High, a predominantly Hispanic slum school in East Los Angeles, plagued by drug-taking, vandalism, gang warfare and economic depression of a kind not totally unfamiliar to Australian teachers. The hero is a middle-aged Bolivian-born electronics expert, Jaime Escalante, who in 1982 chose to return to teaching in this unlikely setting. (Escalante is played with conviction by Edward James Olmos who himself grew up in East Los Angeles.) Unable to teach computing because the school had no computers, and unwilling to teach the low-level maths program which the school had designated as suitable for slum teenagers, Escalante decided to badger and cajole his pupils into aiming for the highest possible target: the advanced calculus exam set by the Educational Testing Service of Princeton.

The most interesting aspect of the film is what it shows of Escalante at work in the classroom. His methods are at once both unorthodox and highly conventional. He does not attempt to get students to like him—he aims to have them take pride in themselves. He has a sense of humour and an affection for his class but those who seek to distract or destroy the teaching process he simply excludes from the class until they are willing to return on his terms. He employs a little showmanship, but its main purpose is to lighten a great deal of hard slog. Much of his instruction is simply rote repetition, but he has a talent for getting students to see the deeper patterns and beauty of mathematics. He stirs up their pride in themselves as (mostly) Hispanics, but he avoids cheap political answers and does not permit them to blame 'society' or anyone else for their plight. He dares the students to risk failure, persuading them that the only alternative is the kind of automatic failure to which their surroundings will condemn them anyway. Self-pity has no place in his scheme and even sympathy is for the most part withheld, but his generosity with his time and knowledge is unlimited. The key concept in his approach is 'ganas', desire.

Escalante's methods worked. At the end of the year all but one of his original students sat the exam which only two per cent of American students attempt, and all eighteen of the Garfield High team passed it easily, six of them with perfect scores. The authorities were so surprised at the result that the pupils were required to sit the exam again under official supervision, and the process engendered a crisis about whether 'the system' is stacked against any such unlikely successes. By now their determination to succeed and their affection for Escalante was enough to get them through the crisis, and they demonstrated once again their ability.

The most unexpected thing about this story is that it is true. Had it been only cinematic fiction it would certainly not have produced the suspension of disbelief that fiction requires. As it happened Hollywood showed no interest in backing such an improbable story, despite its truth to reality.

Furthermore, Escalante's success was not a once-off event—since 1982 the school has increased its calculus success rate every year, with 87 passes in 1987. *Stand and Deliver*, though it made no great impact in Australia, deserves to be what *Summerhill* was for the progressive educationalists of the 1960s, and Jaime Escalante should become as familiar a name as A.S. Neill's. One simple and cheap method of improving Australian education would be to show the film every year to all senior school students and teachers.

Stand and Deliver cuts across educational orthodoxies. It shows, as progressives have long insisted, that schools need not neglect as hopeless failures those at the bottom end of the social spectrum. It shows, as progressives have also believed, that in the right circumstances learning can occur at an astonishing speed, and that it can be tremendously exciting. It suggests that the conservatives' insistence on a return to basics is too modest a goal. But, equally, it implies that the progressives' insistence on relevance also lacks ambition. It indicates that we all have a capacity to appreciate the beauty of abstract thought and structured reasoning. It endorses the use of simple rote learning as a means of mastering those structures. It accepts the challenge of examinations as a means of demonstrating achievement. And it shows that real achievements are the secret of genuine self-esteem.

In the past twenty years there have been endless debates about curriculum design and content. Much of this has been a search for something magical, as if it is possible for a curriculum by itself to solve the problems of the classroom. The importance of all this has been much overrated. Some of it has hoped to tap directly into the interests of the students and to lead on from there to larger interests. This approach overlooks the fact that many students find it perfectly possible to cultivate a state of mind which has no interests at all which are even remotely educational. Teachers are then forced into the position of having to lower themselves to the lowest common denominator and thus to neglect those who do not need such condescension. As a matter of fact, neither do those who act as if they do need it. Almost all of these students are perfectly intelligent young people. They are merely using their intelligence in ways which are counterproductive for themselves, for their classmates and for their teachers. Lowering the level of classroom teaching does them no favours at all. Escalante's principle here is that 'Students will rise to the level of expectations' held by their teachers and their society. This principle is also, as *Stand and Deliver* shows, the key to the discipline problem.

The main complaint that many older students have about school is that it is too childish for them at a time when they want to be able to show that they are adults. Reducing the level of the curriculum does nothing towards raising these students' estimate of the value of schooling; it only confirms their suspicion that—as they see it—this is an artificial environment in which people play compulsory but pointless middle-class word games. It was partly because calculus is untainted by this infantility that it proved acceptable to the students of Garfield High. What appealed to them was the adultness and toughness of the subject. Calculus is not impossibly difficult, and they did not find it so. The difficulty of calculus is not much greater than the complexity of the social world which bored teenagers construct for themselves.

The example shows also that students do not need to be taught about what goes on in the world immediately around them. They already know as much as they want to know about *that* world. Why sit in the classroom hearing about the world that they have already explored for themselves and become bored with? Instead of narrowing students' horizons, education should take people to worlds which are beyond their everyday social environment. Far better to teach them Egyptology or classical Indian dance or the evolution of the flowering plants—but not as a form of entertainment. Calculus was not a diversion in *Stand and Deliver*. Given a choice between all the subjects best calculated to hold the interest of such a class, it would rank well down the list, along with English grammar, trigonometry, religious studies, Latin and classical music. Escalante persuades his students that 'Maths is the great equaliser'. The point might be generalised: knowledge itself is the greatest social leveller. In this it differs essentially from fashion and *savoir faire*, much of which is designed to reinforce arbitrary privilege and social status.

In most schools most of the time the most basic classroom problem is behavioural rather than educational. It is just pathetically easy for a few students who do not want to learn what schools have to teach to monopolise all of a teacher's time, attention and nervous energy. Few teachers are cut out for this war of attrition, while many teenagers thrive on it because it gives them a sense of their own importance which they have not found elsewhere. For those students this is a war which they cannot lose, for if they make the teacher irate they have scored a victory and if they get their way against the teacher's wishes then they have also won. Or at least, they will win all the battles, but eventually they lose the war. Education is a long-term process, and long-term goals are difficult to pursue against those whose whole minds are geared to short-term advantages. It takes a special kind of person to continually shrug off the lack of respect and affection which many teachers experience through no fault of their own. Looked at in this way the wonder is not that we have so many second-rate teachers in the system but that so many good ones remain there.

Jaime Escalante's intuitive grasp of the requirements of educational success is not freakish. Many others have come to the same conclusions, though often only through painful experience. There is nothing in his approach which would have seemed unusual to a good teacher forty years ago.[5] In the United States, this teaching philosophy has acquired a name

5 See e.g. Highet, *The Art of Teaching* (1950), or Brogan, *The Educational Revolution* (1954).

and some institutional momentum as the 'effective schools movement'. Don Edgar has summarised its main tenets as follows.

> First and foremost, an effective school has a strong principal with a vision of what his/her school can achieve, willing to buck the system and militantly committed to academic achievement. The teachers at such a school are also mavericks, willing to innovate, to tutor pupils outside school hours, to work *with* parents, and above all, holding high expectations for their pupils.
>
> The spirit of such a school is a united thrust to help children learn, where principal, teachers, parents and students have the same vision of breaking through the poverty barrier. Such schools, however, are not sops to an idealised 'democratic togetherness'. Instead, there are:
>
> - clearly stated and promptly enforced school rules and penalties
> - daily visits by the principal to classrooms and rigorous supervision of staff
> - meaningful parent participation in the school program (not just lunch stalls and endless meetings)
> - close monitoring of students' progress
> - criterion-referenced tests to determine reading groups
> - an end to the practice of social promotion from grade to grade and the creation of 'promotional gates' at grades 4 and 7, with special reduced-sized remedial classes for those children who were held over because of failure to achieve the basic competency level
> - teaching assignments determined by expertise, not teacher preference
> - highly-structured, self-contained classrooms modified by *some* team-teaching and tempered with affection and consideration
> - using effective teaching materials (not necessarily those 'approved' by the authorities), especially in phonics, maths, word problems, and ethnic (Black) history, culture and literature
> - teachers who routinely dispense homework and literary assignments and who devote time to discussing problems with their students and encouraging the interest of parents.[6]

Edgar goes on to comment that 'all of these characteristics have one theme in common: that with consistent effort, *all* children can strive for and achieve excellence and that striving for standards is *not* an elitist attack on notions of "equity" and "access" but the only sensible goal if these notions are to mean anything at all'. Edgar also adds that there should be clear limits to school intervention in family life. 'Teachers are neither social workers nor surrogate parents other than by default, and ... the teacher's role should be more specific, less affectively involved, more rational, more intentional and more concerned with the whole group than a parent can or needs to be'. On the other hand, 'All the research known on this topic shows how strongly every parent feels about the importance of schooling.... [P]arents will help if they are made feel competent to help'.[7]

---

6 Poverty and its Impact on Educational Life-Chances, 8f, summarised from Social Policy **15** (1984).

7 *Ibid.* 11f.

It is an obvious truth that education at school is continuous with and very much affected by the educational and emotional processes which take place in the child's home—yet it is an oddly neglected truth. It is of course a truth which cuts in two directions. Family indifference or stress may cause a perfectly capable child to be unteachable even by the best of schools. And conversely, students may progress rapidly in a mediocre school if they enjoy a stimulating home environment. It is also a truth which undermines the emphasis placed upon material factors by some popular educational theories and by much standard educational practice. There is by now much evidence to suggest that the crucial determinants of children's development are intangible factors such as parental interest.

The best known analysis of this question was conducted by James Coleman in the United States as long ago as 1966. Coleman's *Equality of Educational Opportunity Report* concluded that 'differences between schools account for only a small fraction of the differences in pupil achievement'.[8] Subsequent American research has confirmed this finding. According to American child psychologist Jerome Kagan,

> During the first half-year [of life], the infant born to parents who have not attended college is not very different from the one born to parents who graduated from college. Yet, by age six, the differences between the two youngsters are dramatic. Something has happened in the intervening years to produce the divergent psychological profiles; it is likely that the reasons for the difference at age six lie with family experiences.[9]

Kagan's observation applies to pre-school development, but much the same continues to hold throughout the schooling years. Australian educational sociologists R.J.R. King and R.E. Young also note that 'The positive association between parental encouragement and adolescent academic attainment has been repeatedly substantiated' (though they add that 'the ways in which parents convey these attitudes vary across families').[10]

Moira Eastman says of this that

> the implications of this research have been poorly comprehended. Educational research and practice has continued as if the findings were the reverse of what they actually are: as if children's learning in school were primarily related to school policies and programs—curriculum, books, buildings, teacher training programs and so on—and only very marginally affected by family factors.

She adds that

> we now have a much clearer picture of what are the factors which distinguish those families who create competence, spontaneity, self-esteem, confidence, energy, intelligence and cooperation from the families where self-doubt, depression, hostility, aggression and failure prevail. The key lies, not in the

---

8 Quoted in Eastman, *Family: The Vital Factor*, 12.

9 Kagan, *The Nature of the Child*, 276. Kagan, however, regards the claim that family influences are crucial as unproven.

10 King & Young, *A Systematic Sociology of Australian Education*, 158.

family's material resources, helpful as these may be. The distinguishing variable or variables reside in the way family members relate to one another.[11]

Family factors are not the same as socio-economic status. The fact that educational potential is relatively independent of income is not difficult to show. Basic education is, for the most part, not expensive. Most people own a television set which (although the general standard is poor) does put out some quality programs which will expand a child's world, if parents seek them out. Books are often reasonably affordable even new, and are cheap if bought second-hand. Public library services are free and their resources are very great, in poor as well as wealthy areas. Reading regularly with children requires only a commitment of time. Talking intelligently, in a manner which encourages children to question and reason objectively, is even less costly. Even poor parents can cultivate these practices, and many do so far better than some well-to-do families who take their success and privileges for granted. The essential ingredient here is Escalante's 'ganas'. The largest barrier to educational success for poor families is lack of access to good schools, and—as the later part of this chapter will attempt to argue—this barrier is created by public policy, not by lack of family income.

We do not need to take these connections between family factors and educational success as rigid and invariable. Schools can succeed even against a background of parental indifference or hostility. Escalante's students came from economically deprived backgrounds; their families also showed little interest in their schooling (and in some cases opposed the efforts of the school). But this does not invalidate the main tendency of the research. In any case, Escalante's success involved a shrewd combination of authority and affection, a combination which elsewhere in this book has been taken as the central strategy of all effective parenting. Escalante did not become a substitute parent, but he did provide his students with both the confidence for risk-taking and the criticism by means of which they could measure and regulate their attempts at improving their lot.

These findings on the importance of family factors appear deceptively commonplace, which may be one reason why they have been so much ignored. Another probable reason for overlooking them is that it may seem that not much can be done about them by policy-makers. Certainly it will take some time before they can be properly digested and policy planning

11 Eastman, *Family: The Vital Factor*, 20, 48. In Part 2 Eastman documents the evidence on 'creative family processes' in a way which avoids the tautological thesis that successful families produce successful children. See also Jencks *et. al.*, *Inequality: A Reassessment of the Effect of Family and Schooling in America*. Jencks observes categorically that 'school resources do not appear to influence students' educational attainments at all' (159). Other research has tended to show that educational success has little to do with teacher/pupil ratios (Hanushek, 'Throwing Money at Schools' and 'The Economics of Schooling: Production efficiency and government schools').

can begin to incorporate them. The immediate response should be to promote public awareness of their importance. In the longer view educational planning will need to aim at bringing together schools and homes, at building cooperatively upon the strengths which both possess. There are some simple but effective ways in which this can be done. Teachers can encourage parents to be seen in the classroom and to take part in class activities; they can set homework and reading which requires parent participation. Many teachers and parents appreciate the importance of these practices, and there is no shortage of academic research to support their more intuitive preferences.

However, if this is the right general direction to pursue then perhaps we need to go much further than is presently envisaged. Perhaps we should deem it to be part of their professional duty that teachers visit regularly the homes of each of their students, particularly at the primary school level. The present sharp separation between home and school is, after all, one of the more bizarre features of our society. Most children would be delighted to observe, on their own home territory, some interaction between the most significant adults in their life. Teachers could learn a lot about the particular circumstances of each child. They could discover more of the expectations that parents have for their children. Their role would be not that of an amateur social worker but to establish a sense of connection and to pass on some simple skills. Parents could be reminded—if they need reminding—that they have an important part to play in the educational process. Teaching might well become easier if visits led to an improvement in support from families.

A home visiting scheme of this broad kind, the La Trobe Parents and Reading Project, has been conducted and described by Derek Toomey. Toomey observed that programs which encourage parents to participate in the school, because they tend to attract only a minority of parents who are already well-motivated to help their children, are 'likely to do little to reduce educational inequality and may well increase it'.[12] The La Trobe project sought to overcome this barrier by having teachers and aides visit the child's home. In a pilot test involving a number of disadvantaged preschools the result of this approach was that almost all of even the poorest families actively encouraged their children's reading, and rapid improvements in reading performance followed. According to Toomey, 'At the heart of the success with these families is the loving, caring attitude of the parent toward the child, the child's enthusiasm for reading, motivated by the school and/or other factors, and the child's responsiveness to the parent'.[13]

---

12 Toomey, *Home–School Relations and Inequality in Education*, 5, and *Children's Reading and Parental Involvement*.

13 *Home-School Relations*, 12.

When, however, the project attempted to achieve the same results with older primary school children the results were less impressive. There were three reasons for this failure: the home visits were conducted by a specially-appointed aide, not by the teacher; the visits were few and infrequent; and the aide preferred to visit families already enthusiastic about the program. We may doubt that special aides are the appropriate response here. Parents do not want to meet intermediaries, they want to get to know their child's teacher. This may be particularly true of those who do not normally participate in activities at the school because they lack the social confidence required to do so. Toomey also observes that, when non-specific extra funding is made available to schools, teachers use it mainly to hire aides to lighten their workloads, not to improve home/school relations. Clearly, to make a program like this succeed educational policy needs to be specific about how the program will operate and who will do the visiting.

Interestingly, Toomey is sceptical about the value of parent participation in school management and policy-formation. He comments that 'A recent review by Hawley *et al.* ... cited five studies finding no relationship between parents' participating in decision-making processes and student achievement'.[14] He believes that this strategy for improving home-school relationships is least likely to succeed in disadvantaged areas. He notes also that the Victorian government 'has set up a special school Council Support Unit and in each region a school Council liaison worker to support parental participation on school Councils, but has devoted no resources to supporting parents as educators of their own children'. In his view, 'We need to get to parents through television and radio, the community language press, the churches, the workplace, the social club, the library and the local video loan club'. He concludes that 'Above all we have to avoid the tunnel vision which sees only schools as the site of legitimate school learning and we need to target available resources to supporting the families' efforts of those who need it most—students of below average ability whose parents do not feel confident in assisting their learning at home'.[15]

To pursue the theme of home/school interactions we need to consider those family factors that might hinder educational objectives, and that might help explain why high educational expenditure apparently has led to little or no improvement in performance. The three most obvious changes in children's lives in recent times are that their mothers are more likely to be in the paid workforce, their parents are more likely to be divorced (and perhaps re-married), and they themselves are more likely to spend much of their spare time watching television. The first of these changes may be less

14 *Ibid.* 7; Hawley *et al.*, 'Good schools: What Research Says About Improving Educational Achievement'.

15 *Home-School Relations*, 30f.

significant than it at first appears. Most mothers of young children who work do so part-time, and to some extent their paid work only replaces work in the home. It is the second and third changes that need to be discussed here.

Television

Australian children up to age eleven spend on average 1 hour 40 minutes per day, or twelve hours per week, watching television, compared with about 20 minutes reading, 25 minutes on outdoor activities and (for the 5–11 age group) 17 minutes on homework and study.[16] One simple way to lift children's interest in education, and to revitalise family relationships, might be to get rid of the television set. This need not be for a very long period—twelve months would be quite adequate but a shorter period would do—and at the end of this time an evaluation of the results could be conducted. Nor need it be painful. One common finding is that children miss television very little; many seem relieved to lose it. Few suffer from any serious 'cold turkey' symptoms, and those who do are perhaps those most in need of 'drying out'. At present few families give themselves the chance to weigh the pros and cons of the matter experimentally and objectively.[17]

The central issue at stake here is the child's confidence in his or her individual capacity for play, invention, fantasy and wonder—in other words, those things which make childhood so fresh and distinctive and which form the basis of adult creativity. Whether television does or does not dampen this self-confidence can be debated academically, but the matter is not essentially an academic one. The point is for families to try the experiment with an open mind, to discuss it themselves, and to reach their own conclusions.

Children, like all young mammals, are born curious. Language makes their capacity for questioning and investigating even more potent than that of animals. Television brings the world to the living room in vivid colour. We would therefore expect the combination of children's curiosity and television's wide-ranging imagery to be a lively interaction, yet very often —even when the programs seem interesting to adult eyes—television

16 ABS Cat. 4111.1, 1987, Table 1.7. These figures are based on a Sydney survey; they may not be universally valid.

17 In *The Plug-In Drug*, Marie Winn argues the case for most of the claims here sketched very briefly. And see also Postman's *Amusing Ourselves to Death*. The research evidence is summarised in Hodge & Tripp, *Children and Television: a Semiotic Approach*. They conclude that although children who do poorly in school watch more television than those who do well, there is no evidence of a direct causal relation between the two. They may be right, but if we think of television as playing a role in wider family patterns, we would expect some complex causal relationships here.

seems to act more as a sedative than as a stimulant. Children usually appear mesmerised; they rarely talk about what they have seen; they rarely go away determined to find out more about the subject.

As an educational instrument television has turned out to be roughly on a par with the dullest of old-style schoolmasters or the most vapid of progressive educationalists. Much of the time it manages to combine the spuriousness of the second with the tedium of the former. Its real genius is of course as a baby-sitter, in which capacity it performs the dual role of pacifying the restless natives while persuading their tribal elders that the programs fulfil the missionary task of civilising and educating them. There is no evidence that its missionary gospel is good news. At the very least, after three decades of TV, we would expect children's knowledge of world geography—the ins and outs of the global village—to be vastly greater that that of their pre-TV predecessors, yet this is far from being the case. Without some grasp of geography it is of course impossible to take an intelligent interest in world affairs. If geographical understanding has not been improved by television, what has? The question is not easily answered.

Television-watching skills—'media awareness'—cannot replace reading skills, simply because the culture of the book is immensely richer and more powerful than that of the screen. Many more children will read Roald Dahl or C.S. Lewis or *Asterix* or *Alice* than will encounter them on television; and the performance itself should be regarded as only a prelude to the original. Those who never acquire the reading skills to enjoy the original have been deprived of something special. Similarly, television can introduce a child to the phenomena of the natural world far more excitingly than can a textbook, but it does not usually teach the principles which will give the child a chance to become a competent biologist.

Tele-addiction has one possible side-effect which is not often discussed: it may tend to cause parents to lose confidence in their own capacity as teachers. Children learn far more at home than they do at school, not in the formal sense, but in what they pick up incidentally from conversation and as a by-product of other family activities. But some parental 'teaching' is more direct than this. When a child asks why cars have gears the usefulness of the answer will depend less on the parent's knowledge of the subject than on his or her willingness to explore the question. This willingness has to be cultivated—it requires practice and skill in the interaction between the limited but nimble mind of the child and the broader but duller mind of the adult, and such skill takes time to acquire. It requires a capacity to hear what exactly it is that the child needs to know. It is not a skill well cultivated by years of silent communing with the flickering screen. And the less it is practised the less children will see their parents as people interested in their questions. If, in addition, they come to feel that asking too many questions will disrupt the routine of instruction at school then their curiosity will lack connection with the adult world.

Education and divorce

The era of child-centred education turned out to be the era of high levels of divorce, a conjunction which raises questions about the interaction between the two. The most complete research on this issue, Paul Amato's *Children in Australian Families*, argues against a 'simple deficit model' which assumes that children from disrupted families will do worse educationally than children in intact families. His research for the Australian Institute of Family Studies concluded that children from one-parent families appear to be equivalent to children from intact two-parent families in a variety of measures of general competence—reading ability, practical life skills, self-esteem, social competence, self-control and independence. However, children from step-families did somewhat less well than either of the first two family types. Amato suggests that 'gaining a new parent can be more debilitating than losing an old one'. As Amato acknowledges, these results are likely to appear surprising to teachers, who tend to expect less from children of sole parents than from other children.[18] In his view the educational disruption caused by divorce is likely to be short-term only. It is to be seen as an emotional crisis rather than as a lasting educational setback.

However, Amato also acknowledges that there is something to be explained in these results. It is a basic assumption of his book that for a child to lose contact with a parent, whether through death or divorce, is tantamount to losing 'a major source of nurturing, information and material support'. Both his relatively good results from children of one-parent families and the lesser results from children of step-families seem to defy this basic assumption. Amato also argues that 'lack of attention from fathers was related to low self-esteem, low self-control, low life-skills, and low social competence among sons and daughters of primary school age'. He adds that 'these findings indicate that the importance of the father-child bond should not be underestimated by practitioners working with problem children'. If attention from fathers is so crucial we would expect its absence to be even more apparent in the lives of children disrupted by divorce than in intact families where the father is unresponsive, remote or work-obsessed. Fathers not living with their children are not likely to have more time with them than fathers in either intact or step-families. While it is possible that in some cases non-custodial fathers will maintain close relationships with their children the evidence is that they tend not to do so. Amato reports on research showing that after divorce 'contact between most non-custodial fathers and their children declines rapidly'; and his own work concluded that twenty-six per cent of such children never see their fathers.[19]

18 Amato, *Children in Australian Families*, 142-48, 153.

19 *Ibid.* 15, 99, 106, 113.

We have, then, a paradox: support from fathers is crucial to the growth of competence, but children who lose close contact with their fathers through divorce are unaffected by the loss. Amato tries to resolve this paradox by suggesting that intact families may exhibit levels of 'father absence' not markedly different from that in separated families. He contends that 'For many children, the actual loss of support from fathers after separation and divorce is probably minimal'. He bases this surprising claim on his finding that between one third and one half of all children, whether in intact families or not, would like to spend more time with their fathers. However, his own evidence will not bear the weight of interpretation that he places upon it. In his survey about three-quarters of the children responded that their fathers talked to them 'a lot' and two-thirds said that their fathers were 'very interested' in them; only 13 per cent said their fathers did not talk to them very much and 11 per cent said their fathers were not very interested in them.[20] To establish Amato's claim that separation and divorce do not reduce children's support from their fathers we must suppose that most separations and divorces come from that small section of the population of families in which fathers play only a minor role, and this is a supposition for which no independent support is given. (These figures include responses from children in one-parent families but are weighted to be representative of the general population. Therefore some of those children who did not get father support would have been children in one-parent families, a fact which further reduces the plausibility of Amato's hypothesis.) If there were a well-established theory showing that families exhibiting 'father absence' are likely to end in divorce then Amato's account would be moderately plausible, but the review of this subject in Chapter Seven found no evidence to support this claim, so on those grounds Amato's position is not particularly plausible.

Obviously there is much here that we do not understand, and more work is required. Moira Eastman cites an American longitudinal study which did find significant educational as well as emotional disruption after divorce.[21] And, as Amato notices, many teachers are convinced that they have to patch up the after-effects, both educational and emotional, of the divorce revolution. Others have observed that divorce tends to make children 'grow up' very rapidly. This enforced emotional development is contrary to the body of educational theory which speaks of children learning and maturing 'at their own pace'. It is possible that Amato's step-children often react against their new step-families or against their schools because they have exhausted their emotional reserves in coping with the first transition to a one-parent family. Amato's own insistence on the general importance of fathers is enough to make us wary of claims that divorce and separation do not disrupt a child's normal growth to competence. Beyond that the research evidence will permit no strong assertions. Common sense will

20 *Ibid.* 124, 31f.

21 *Family: The Vital Factor*, 18f.

have its own views on the matter, but common sense is not a recognised court of appeal in disputes of this kind.

Parents, knowledge and discipline

The psychological findings about the educational importance of family practices have implications for policy and planning on the larger scale also. Before discussing these it will help to turn to look in some detail at the most important Australian analysis of relations between school and home.

The general theme of *Making the Difference*, a study of the lives and beliefs of a hundred high school students, published in 1982 and written by R.W. Connell, D.J. Ashenden, S. Kessler and G.W. Dowsett, is indicated by its subtitle, schools, *Families and Social Division*. Half the hundred pupils were sons and daughters of tradesmen, factory workers, truck drivers and shop workers; the other half were the children of managers, owners of businesses, lawyers and doctors. This suggests that a comparison is to be made between two distinct populations but the reality is a little more complex. The authors have two kinds of 'difference' in mind: first, the difference between school achievement levels of children from professional and managerial families and children from families of skilled, semi-skilled and unskilled workers; and second, the differences in school achievement levels of children from independent, Catholic, and state school systems. They produce figures to suggest that 'higher status' children are nearly twice as likely to complete secondary school as 'lower status' children; and that independent school children are twice as likely to complete secondary school as Catholic school children, who are in turn fifty per cent more likely than state school children to reach that level. Because they interviewed only two groups, higher-status/private-school families and lower-status/state-school families, their study was constructed in such a way as to tend to conflate the status distinction with the private-school/state-school distinction. Quite different conclusions might have been reached if they had compared lower-status/*private*-school families with higher-status/ *state*-school families.

The authors reject explanations of these results that rest on differences of ability—'It is emphatically not the case that some groups are less educable than others'[22]—or differences of family interest. They reject the first claim without any discussion, but in passing we can note that *Stand and Deliver* can be seen as supporting their preference here: Escalante's students demonstrated quite unexpected abilities. They did so without any help at all from their families. How families help their children towards educational success is a main theme of *Making the Difference*.

In Chapter Five of the present book we interpreted Alan Jordan's analysis of incomes as showing that Australian society exhibits shades of

22 Connell *et al.*, *Making the Difference*, 110.

class difference but no clear-cut class divisions. *Making the Difference*, like many other works in the sociology of education, interprets the educational evidence as showing that Australia is a class society. However, the general fact that children's educational performance in some way mirrors their parents' status is not obviously a cause for surprise. The home is a 'learning environment' quite as much as is the school, and children spend far more of their lives at home than they do in the classroom. If most education takes place at home then naturally children will tend to follow the career paths of their parents. Parents who understand the mysteries of computer programming or automotive electronics or horticulture will tend to pass them on to their offspring. Those who do not pass on their skills are depriving their children of a crucial legacy, and schools have a role in correcting such deprivation; but there is no obvious reason to assume that working-class parents are less likely than middle-class parents to pass on their skills. It is also implausible to expect that schools would ever be able radically to counteract family influences, for the Marxian reason that the educator himself needs to be educated. Education does not stand outside society and family life; it will itself exhibit the limitations of the society and of the families from which it is derived.

Making the Difference contends that the long attempt to provide equality of opportunity for working-class students has failed. It has failed, the authors maintain, because equality of opportunity entails a school system 'which divides the working class, undermines its self-confidence, [and] attaches part of its energy and talent to a process of competition'.[23] The study tells a story of working-class exclusion from educational policy-making:

> With the sole exception of the diffuse demand for *more* education, it is difficult to think of any major change in state schools postwar that has actually stemmed from demands articulated by their working class clientele. Changes have been imposed upon the working class.... Whether liked or not, they are things that have *happened to* these families, rather than things that they and their friends and relations and acquaintances and people like them have caused to happen.[24]

To overcome this, a strategy of 'making working-class schools organic to their class' is necessary. What does this mean? Three things, at least:

> a closer connection with the knowledge and resources of working-class people, most notably parents; an opening of the school's policy-making to their influence and the kids', and (for that matter) the teachers'; [and] sufficient independence from Departmental control to allow this to happen, though close enough connection with the rest of the education system to be able to draw on resources that aren't available locally.[25]

---

23 *Ibid.* 197.
24 *Ibid.* 139.
25 *Ibid.* 201f.

The argument is clarified in an unexpected way. The authors contend that although their proposed future for working class schools is only sketchy, 'ruling class schools' do provide a 'working model ... in very good order' from which it is possible to learn.

> The ruling-class schools studied in this project are organic to their class in exactly the sense we are talking about here. They help to organise it as a social force; they help to give it its sense of identity and purpose; they form an integral part of its networks; they express common purposes and an agreed (for the most part) division of labour between teachers and parents. As we have seen, they are far from being conflict-free; and as we have also seen, they are far from being the direct and immediate agents of the parents' wishes. Being organic to the class in this case means having a reasonable degree of independence, that makes possible the invention of new strategies and the management of conflicting interests'.[26]

This insistence on the necessity of connectedness between working-class life and schooling arises partly from the difficulties encountered in teaching the traditional academic curriculum, but it has other roots in the body of the book. *Making the Difference* documents graphically the conflict between the values of working-class parents and the style and content of the schooling which their children presently receive in the state secondary schools. On this, however, the authors seem to be critical of the parents rather than of the schools. They observe that:

> Eighty years into 'the century of the child', none of the working-class parents we interviewed held recognizably child-centred views of education. Most of them clearly supported firm discipline, teacher-centred pedagogy, and job-oriented curricula.... Education is still defined as the transmission of an accepted body of knowledge, in every context they know about.... Education is also 'socialisation', in the old, full sense of making the asocial infant a fully social being. This means, among other things, learning to do what you're told, hold yourself in check, accept the necessity to do things you don't want to do. It means accepting legitimate authority, deferring to those who are older and wiser than you are, keeping in your proper place.[27]

Obviously, it is crucial for the assessment of the argument to decide whether this approach to schooling is to be counted as an aspect of 'making working-class schools organic to their class'. There are two issues here, discipline and knowledge. The two are of course related: 'the attempt to get most [working-class state school] kids to swallow academic knowledge produces insurmountable problems of motivation and control. Not only because of the abstractness of the content, but also as a consequence of the formal authority relations of its teaching'.[28]

On the question of working-class attitudes to knowledge the authors remark that 'What seems to us to be missing from most accounts of the

26 *Making the Difference*, 202.
27 *Ibid.* 60.
28 *Ibid.* 199.

matter is the widespread, non-instrumental, respect for education that is ... present among working-class families. The teachers who see working-class suburbs as cultural deserts are entirely wrong in this sense'.[29] Making working-class schools 'organic to their class' must incorporate this understanding if it incorporates anything at all. The authors' recommendations for achieving this are very sketchy, but that may be more a consequence of long years of neglect than a failure of the authors themselves.

Making the Difference advocates that the curriculum in working-class state schools should give the students 'access to formal knowledge via learning which begins with their experience and the circumstances which shape it, but does not stop there'. The authors reject the progressive educationalists' search for a more 'relevant and meaningful' curriculum on the grounds that its content 'is often a matter of personal preference, reflecting the kids' immediate world rather than expanding or explaining it'.[30] Their own strategy is intended to overcome the present resistance to academic learning. The study says nothing about how this can be done without a mastery of the basic skills of literacy and numeracy. (Calculus is perhaps not likely to rate highly in any such redesigned curriculum.)

On the question of discipline the authors reject the parents' position. In their view, 'A shift to heavier-handed discipline is a recipe for more conflict, not stabler authority, in the schools'.[31] They do not underestimate the importance of the question, and they note that many parents

> see kids answering back to teachers, classes in uproar, apparently unplanned curricula, no measurable learning; and they are worried. Some see it reacting back on the family and creating discipline problems there. If this is what new ideas in education mean, they could do with less of them.[32]

Elsewhere in the book there is evidence that this is a central problem in many schools (both independent and state, though much more acute in the state system), and that both teachers and some students are as worried about it as the parents. Teachers get tired of 'the unending guerrilla-war aspect of classroom life' in working-class schools. As a result they adopt a 'keep your distance' strategy and concentrate on surviving from day to day. The authors also observe, though without giving it much weight, that students accept and even like 'discipline' if it is fair and purposeful, showing that the class is going somewhere. Students universally dislike slack teachers; they like those who feel 'there is something to be got out of school'. On this evidence it is difficult to see who is being served by schools which are incapable of establishing their own authority.[33]

---

29 *Ibid.* 62.
30 *Ibid.* 199.
31 *Ibid.* 61.
32 *Ibid.*
33 *Ibid.* 102f.

The question of discipline needs to be taken further. Sheer authority needs to be used as sparingly as possible; its effectiveness suffers from the law of diminishing returns. What is needed more than authority or affection is a sense of purpose and a vision of what schooling aims to achieve. It is the loss of this sense of purpose which is at the bottom of the problem. This takes us back to John McLeod's observation noted in Chapter Eight that

> generally when a child was in deep trouble in his or her behaviour, he or she would go out of their way to take on the strongest, most visible adults available. Sometimes they would run up against an unwilling person or crash through the defences of the nearest adult. Often they would find the response they sought and needed, regardless of the authoritarian or progressive style of the teacher.[34]

Compliant, bland, agreeable teachers present no challenge; tough, idiosyncratic, straight-talking teachers they can learn from. And similarly, a bland, unchallenging, 'relevant' curriculum is equally unlikely to command respect. Without high expectations schools head into a downward spiral of aimlessness and authoritarianism. The raising of expectations both requires and justifies the imposition of limits on disruption in the classroom.

Teachers do have authority by virtue of their position but it needs to be made credible by the authority of their superior knowledge and wisdom. High expectations can only be generated by teachers who expect a lot of themselves, and who set a high value on knowledge and understanding. A profession which recognised this would not hesitate to have its members' knowledge of their subject matter tested periodically. It would reward those who demonstrate high levels of intellectual competence and the ability to pass on those skills to others. This must involve both a system of pupil assessment and the salary system. A profession concerned to show what it can achieve would be keen to design and employ fair tests of student progress.[35] It would provide recognition and rewards for teacher performance and productivity, particularly for those who (like Escalante) find ways, however unorthodox, to raise the levels and morale of the more backward pupils. A lockstep salary system, like lockstep pupil promotion, conveys to teachers and students the message that education is a routine matter in which advancement requires no special effort and has no particular purpose.

Education vouchers

Thus far in this chapter three theses have been put forward. The first is that teachers who have high expectations of their students will generate high

34 Embling, *Fragmented Lives*, 50.

35 Pupil testing appears now to be back on the agenda. In 1991 New South Wales will test every Year 3 and Year 7 student. In other states the question is probably not 'whether?' but 'when?'.

levels of performance and high self-esteem, whereas teachers who hope to generate self-esteem by lowering expectations will achieve neither results nor self-confidence. Secondly, the literature on parents and schools suggests that progress in education requires close interaction between the home and the school. Thirdly, *Making the Difference* has shown that what many parents want from their schools is more knowledge and a greater sense of purpose. All three bear upon the way in which educational funding is organised and allocated.

Making the Difference indicates some deeper structural reasons for the relative success of independent schools and the relative failure of working-class state schools. The authors note that 'The private school is much less secure in its very existence than the state school.... [T]he vulnerability of such schools, and the uncoerced nature of attendance there, is crucial for the way they operate and for the role they play in class relations'. These schools are in the main 'much more open to parents' approaches'. The parents 'find it easier to include the kids' schooling as an integral part of the families' collective practices'. Independent schools have higher expectations of their teachers. In the state schools 'There is no principal breathing down [the teachers'] necks for 100 per cent pass rates at Matriculation; who in their right mind would expect anything like that?'.[36]

The reader would expect *Making the Difference* to advocate structural changes which will enable working-class students to enjoy similar advantages to those that make private schools 'working models in very good order', but at this point the authors draw back from what appears to be the logic of their position. They will allow that 'Since Departmental control does produce a bruising experience of bureaucracy for many parents, the "freedom to choose" represented by "voucher" schemes and "private enterprise" in schooling may temporarily appear attractive'. But, they say,

> it's not a hard calculation to recognize that for the working class this would mean a thinner spreading of already inadequate resources, a futile multiplication of efforts, and, above all, not the organization and empowering of the working class but its greater vulnerability and deeper internal division. Under any conceivable conditions, an educational market will advantage the rich, and no-one else.[37]

Considering the importance of the question for the logic of their case this is a very peremptory dismissal, and it forces the reader to do the authors' thinking for them. There are three objections being put forward here—inadequate resources, futile multiplications, and divisiveness.

Are working class state schools at present inadequately resourced? *Making the Difference* does not elsewhere suggest that this is a reason why they do not succeed. Rather, it speaks of a school system which for twenty-five years 'expanded at a tremendous pace'. It talks about 'educators who

---

36 *Making the Difference*, 81, 54, 89f.
37 *Ibid.* 202.

had come to rely on continuing growth almost as a natural law'. It does express concern at the 'running-down of a range of programs concerned to enliven and support public schooling, such as the Disadvantaged Schools Program, and the abolition of others, such as the Schools Commission's Innovations Program and the Education Research and Development Committee', but none of this is central to the theme of the book.[38] In any case it is difficult for anyone to deny the accuracy of Susan Ryan's remark quoted above about government having for a long time poured buckets of money into the education system in an indiscriminate manner. What makes *Making the Difference* an interesting exploration is that it does not fall back on the hackneyed plea of 'more money for education'.

Would a voucher system entail a 'futile multiplication of efforts'? It would certainly generate a multiplicity of educational experiments, but why should this be thought of as futile? Is it not centralised bureaucratic thinking to imagine that there is only one correct answer to the problem of education? The authors themselves speak critically of the tendency towards 'standardisation of curricula and tighter central control of schools'.[39] Do the independent schools exhibit the 'futility' being objected to? The whole tenor of the book suggests that they achieve their goals with considerable efficiency: they give their students a 'sense of purpose and identity', they equip them with social and intellectual skills, they help to organise their class as a social force, and so on. Surely this is what the authors want working class schools to do? The role of government in education should be to govern the ends of education, not the means. As American educator Chester Finn has observed, 'The ends of education should be universal, and should be determined by policy makers, and should be inviolable by schools, and should be achieved for all students in all schools... The practice of regulating the processes of education and the means of education and then leaving people to their own choices about the ends is exactly backwards. We should regulate the ends, the outcomes, but leave people highly flexible with respect to the means'.[40]

Would a voucher system produce 'greater vulnerability and deeper internal division' in the working class? *Making the Difference* gives no reason for believing that it would. Much of the book indicates that working class people are fairly clear and united about what they want from an education system, and that they generally believe they are not getting it from the present system. What they want, the book shows, is more knowledge and more discipline. Only a system which takes seriously this desire can be counted as 'organic to the working class'. The book shows that working-class wishes are systematically thwarted by the present system, for both ideological and structural reasons. A more flexible structure would be more responsive to the actual wishes of real people.

38 *Making the Difference*, 25, 203.

39 *Ibid.* 205.

40 Chester Finn on 'Education Now' interview, ABC Radio, June 1989.

Perhaps the underlying objection to freedom of choice is that it would result in competition rather than cooperation between working-class people? Middle-class families, it seems to be suggested, are inherently competitive, and working-class families inherently cooperative. This is a tendentious claim but let us suppose it has some general resemblance to reality. In that case, working-class schools set up under a voucher system will reflect that truth, and thus exhibit a cooperativeness which is 'organic to the working class'. The assumption that giving freedom of educational choice to working class families will cause them to make decisions which are class-divisive implies that their class cohesion is caused by the absence of freedom, a claim which is both paradoxical and improbable. In places *Making the Difference* seems to regret the demise of the old technical schools, which, it says, 'for 40 years had been the educational pride of the labour movement'. If, as it also insists, the replacement of these schools by 'a particular form of comprehensive schooling has done great damage to working-class kids and working-class interests' then an obvious case exists for restoring that pride by returning to a system over which working-class people have a measure of control.[41]

Elsewhere it is contended that 'Public education should be defended precisely because it is a public service, our only chance of asserting the common good as the highest principle of educational policy, in the face of rampant private interest'.[42] This claim is somewhat confused. Education is mostly a private good—the benefits are enjoyed by the recipient—just as is food or exercise or housing. Teaching may in some cases be undertaken as a form of service to the poor, but if so it primarily serves the private interests of disadvantaged people, not the common good of society. There is no reason at all why teachers might not devote themselves to helping the poor within the framework of a voucher system, even in a voucher system which abolished all state schools—which is in any case a most unlikely eventuality. Within such a system good teachers, following the Escalante example perhaps, could set up their own schools in poor areas and attract students by the quality of their performance, thus putting second-rate state schools out of business. Of course a fair-minded society would want a system framed so that the poor are given an adequate share of resources, and it would also want to prevent exploitation by 'rampant private interests', but those are different points.

No Australian educational research has made a more powerful case for a voucher system than that made unintentionally by *Making the Difference*. But to pursue the matter further we need to examine the literature explicitly on this subject. George Fane, who in 1984 prepared a major study for the Economic Planning Advisory Council entitled *Educational Policy in Australia*, has argued that 'the present funding policies only manage to target the schooling subsidies towards the poorer families because the govern-

41 *Making the Difference*, 20, 198.
42 *Ibid.*, 207.

ment schools fail to deliver the kind of education most parents want'. Fane's conclusions were based partly on 1981 statistics from the Commonwealth Schools Commission showing not only that (as is well-known) state schools spend more per child than Catholic schools but also, and surprisingly, that government schools have higher recurrent expenditure per child than the non-Catholic non-government schools.

> Measured by expenditure per child the government schools are, on average, the most affluent and if they could use their resources as efficiently as the private schools they would have driven the private schools out of business long ago.... Everyone is eligible to go to the government schools and they spend the most—so how come the private schools can survive? The obvious answer in my opinion is that the incentives, or rather, disincentives, within the government schools have greatly reduced their ability to produce what parents want.[43]

According to Fane, 'Present policy, which provides free places at government schools and smaller government contributions for children at private schools amounts to a voucher, equal to the expenditure on education per child in government schools, combined with hidden taxes on those who send their children to private schools'.

More recent statistics, from the Department of Employment, Education and Training, modify Fane's premises but do not alter his basic case.[44] They show that the Catholic secondary schools are still behind the state schools but the other independents are now clearly ahead of the state. However, if we take the aggregate figures for the non-government sector, it turns out that the state secondary schools are still being subsidised by on average $1400 per pupil. The state system still outspends the private by $3720 – 3561 = $159, though not by the massive advantage apparent in the 1982 CSC figures. (In primary schools, the subsidy is about $950 per pupil and the expenditure difference is about $317 per pupil in favour of government schools.) It remains very much the case that, as Fane put it, 'the present taxes on private educational spending shelter the government schools from competition with private schools'.[45]

Tom Brennan has aptly likened this situation to the old practice of employers paying their workers not with cash but with credits for goods to be purchased in the employer's shops at the employer's prices. He remarks that 'If we really think in a particular case—like education, for example—that we know what people want or need better than they do, let us say so and why. Let us not tell them that they need our help to enable them to choose what we happen to have to sell'.[46] Until some clear justification for this favouritism is provided or the favouritism is abolished, educational

43 Fane, 'Education and Society', 25. Fane argues his position more fully in *Education Policy in Australia*.

44 Department of Employment, Education and Training, *Schooling in Australia: Statistical Profile No. 2*. See Appendix to this chapter.

45 Fane, Education *Policy in Australia*, 45.

46 Brennan, 'Commentary', in Henderson (ed.), *The Welfare Stakes*, 41.

policy will remain irrational. If, as *Making the Difference* indicates, most working-class parents are not getting the kind of education they want for their children, then the question of fair choice becomes a matter of social justice.

But to think clearly about education policy it is necessary to have a picture of the larger framework of government spending and taxing. The actual situation here seems to be contrary to some common assumptions. In Australia, the net effect of all government spending and taxing is progressive.[47] But it is more difficult to discover the actual impact of educational expenditure. How should the incidence of educational expenditure be determined? Any educational policy will perforce contain at least an implicit answer to this question. We can be clearer about the aims of education only if we are explicit about the question of allocation. Perhaps the most commonly accepted and intuitively plausible answer to the question is that educational expenditure should be allocated equally to each child. This leaves difficulties with expenditure on optional, higher education and with expenditure on private school pupils, for clearly at present neither of these cases conforms to a policy of equal allocation. It is also likely to come under attack from those who think the net effect of a proportional tax system and an equal allocation of educational resources is not a sufficiently progressive form of redistribution. (They may even deny that this is progressive at all, but in this they would be mistaken. The fallacy here is to assume that because only equal amounts of expenditure are being allocated to each child such expenditure does not have an equalising effect. It does, because most of the money is being taken from the better-off families.) A further line of objection is that educational expenditure should favour specially disadvantaged groups—the disabled, the mentally handicapped, racially disadvantaged groups—to give them an equal chance of success.

The central difficulty in public provision of services which might have been provided (at least in part) by the recipient for herself, or by her family for her, is that it is impossible to tell whether the value to the recipient of the services is equal to the per capita amount of the expenditure. In the absence of a market for the services there can be no price indicators to guide government providers. It may be that the voting mechanism does duty for the market mechanism with some degree of success as a device for rationing public expenditure, but one can only vote for an entire policy package which is unlikely to contain the policies one would prefer for every area of government activity.

The difference between funding for state and funding for independent schools amounts to a form of taxation for the purpose of redistributing income. As such it may be perfectly justifiable, but to be justifiable it must meet the standard requirements of taxation fairness. This is where it fails. It may be that in general those who choose private schools are wealthier than those who choose state schools, but as a generalisation this is only a crude

47 See Figures 2.1 and 5.1 above.

approximation to reality. No tax system should be permitted this degree of inexactitude. As a form of taxation the present system fails to meet the elementary requirements of horizontal equity. It taxes heavily poorer families who send their children to independent schools, and the tax deters other such poorer families who would like to send their children to independent schools. It also fails to tax those wealthier families who send their children to state schools, though their capacity to pay such a tax is exactly the same as that of the many families who do use the private schools. The only way to eliminate such inequities is to allocate educational expenditure according to family means, and not according to family choice. About all such choices government has an obligation to remain neutral. It is not in a position to determine what is best for each or any family.

The central difficulty in all voucher schemes concerns not equity or efficiency, by which criteria vouchers are clearly preferable to the present system, but at what level to set the value of the voucher. If the voucher is to be set at the present average cost of a place in a state school—say \$3600 in 1987 dollars—then taxes will have to be raised to pay for the increased assistance to private school pupils. If the level is set at the average cost per pupil of present state subsidies to private education—say \$2000 in 1987 dollars—then the net effect is no different from the present system and the voucher's advantages of efficiency and equity are lost. This second option is no option at all. Any solution will need to move some way towards the first proposal. But how far? And how to do it without raising taxes?

It is certainly not inevitable that a voucher scheme would in the long run increase total educational expenditure. The efficiency gains should ensure a long-run reduction in expenditure. And those efficiency gains could make a voucher scheme self-financing. Consider a voucher set at the mid-point between the average state school subsidy and the average private school subsidy, \$2800 in 1987 dollars. If there is no net movement from state to private schools then such a scheme will cost \$800 times the number of private school pupils. But if an exodus from the state schools caused the number of private school pupils to double the scheme would cost nothing (leaving aside capital costs for the moment). The increase in one kind of subsidy would be balanced by the reduction in the other kind.

Whichever view we take of vouchers, a very large question remains: How can it be that in twenty years educational expenditure per child has doubled in real terms without, apparently, any demonstrable improvement in educational performance? Working out new directions and strategies in education will in part require retrospective analysis aimed at answering that question. Some sketchy suggestions have been made in this chapter, but almost everything remains to be done.

Appendix: School Expenditure, $ per Pupil, 1987

	Primary	Secondary
Government schools	**2483**	**3720**
Catholic schools		
Commonwealth grants	1045	1581
State grants	505	807
Contributed services	102	113
Other private inputs	463	921
Total	**2115**	**3422**
Other non-government schools		
Commonwealth grants	858	1151
State grants	480	747
Contributed services	194	46
Other private inputs	1262	2667
Total	**2794**	**4611**
All non-government schools		
Commonwealth grants	1031	1531
State grants	503	800
Contributed services	109	105
Other private inputs	523	1125
Total	**2166**	**3561**

Note: These figures do not include government grants for capital works, which may be slanted towards expenditure on state school buildings and grounds. They also exclude expenditure on superannuation and long service leave for state school teachers.
Source: Department of Employment, Education and Training, *Schooling in Australia: Statistical Profile No. 2*, Canberra: AGPS, 1989, Tables 4.6 and 4.8.

11 Greypower, childpower and taxpayers

The age policy debate

Families are mainly focused upon the care and raising of children, but the network of relationships which surrounds this central task usually forms a stable community which also serves other purposes. The most obvious of these is the care of the elderly, particularly the frail and dependent elderly. At present this caring role is shared with the state. Even after two or three decades of massive growth in public expenditure on nursing homes, two-thirds of all severely handicapped elderly people live in private households. Public policy in this area needs to find the optimal balance between public and family assistance for the aged. Much thought has been given to this question in recent years but, for many reasons, the right balance is not easy to achieve. This chapter will attempt to review these questions, particularly in the light of the family policy issues already discussed in this book. The general theme of the chapter will be that the debate about aged policy, though wide-ranging, has been unnecessarily restricted, and that there are still some fundamental questions which have not been asked. In part those questions concern the balance between support for families with children and support for the elderly; in part they concern the justification of support for the elderly, quite independent of the question of support for children. The chapter does not answer the questions it asks, but it does point to a few considerations which seem to have been overlooked so far.

Most of the Australian debate about financial assistance in old age has been about coping with the imminent 'greying' of the population. The demographic 'crisis' has three dimensions: an increased proportion of the elderly population requiring high levels of medical and nursing support, an increased ratio of elderly to young when the 'baby boom' retires, and a decrease in fertility—the 'baby bust'—amongst those of child-bearing age.

The first 'crisis' may be quite as severe as the second, and its impact is being felt before the first has begun to take effect. It is a product of increased longevity amongst the over-eighty age group. Daryl Dixon has calculated that this group will increase by 120 per cent between 1985 and 2000. Hal Kendig, after noting that Commonwealth outlays on aged care programs grew at a compound rate of 20 per cent in the decade 1975–1985, remarks that 'There seems little prospect that this situation can be easily changed'. Peter Saunders contends that 'if the recent growth in expenditure on community services and institutional care for the aged continue[s], it will exceed the age pensions bill before 2021'. These are significant claims. If we add to this the second crisis, the 'baby boom' retirement, which by about 2030 may have doubled the ratio of the aged to the working aged population from its current level of 17 per cent, then clearly some hard thinking is required about how to accommodate these changes in the existing framework of pensions and services.[1] It is obviously essential that the twin questions of income support and aged services be considered together if we are to keep track of the overall costs of present policies and if our aim is to achieve a proper balance between the legitimate claims of both the elderly and the young.

But there may be even more basic questions which need to be considered. Why do we have a system of social security for the aged? Do they particularly need such assistance? Do they need it more than do families with dependent children? Does social security for the elderly seriously reduce savings, and thus lower economic standards? Does it reduce informal, personal assistance from the working generation to the elderly, and thus weaken extended family networks? Or does it strengthen those networks by endowing the elderly with financial surpluses which they can transfer privately to their children and grandchildren? Has social security generated perverse incentives comparable to those that distort the lives of the unemployed and sole parents—leading to medical over-servicing, unnecessarily early retirement and discouragement of part-time work for those who would otherwise prefer it? How can we encourage those elderly who are well off to be more self-supporting without penalising the poorer elderly? Has the post-war Welfare State merely created a single 'welfare generation' which enjoyed low taxes during its working life and high benefit levels in its retirement—leaving little behind for its successors in more stringent times? Should we think of these issues in terms of 'intergenerational justice'? What moral obligations exist between the elderly and their adult children? Has public provision created a system which provides the elderly with a form of comfortable loneliness, isolation and powerless-

1 Dixon, 'A Broader Perspective on Aged Care Services and Financing', 3; Foster *et al.*, 'National Perspectives', 46; Saunders, 'Overview', 406; Dixon & Foster, 'Overview', 343.

ness? Or do they prefer to lead markedly separate lives from those of their children? Is the rise of 'greypower' merely the addition of one more narrow interest group to a political system already over-burdened with such groups?

These are all questions which are both difficult and yet inescapable. They are made all the more difficult when taken in combination with the demographic changes. And so far little progress has been made with them. At the conclusion of a seminar entitled *Who Pays? Financing Services for Older People*, Peter Saunders in his 'Overview' was forced to observe that 'there was relatively little discussion of the question of who pays, important though this undoubtedly is. Most participants were more concerned with the question of who benefits, and the form that provision of services should take rather than their finance as such'.[2] Even *Spending and Taxing*, which tackled many of the thorniest Australian public policy issues, drew back from the basic question of aged policy on the grounds that

> A very important (implicit) contract exists, whereby the working generation pays taxes to support the elderly, in expectation that the subsequent generation will do the same for them. Thus any changes to the nature of pension arrangements must be applied with great sensitivity and recognition of the lengthy phase-in period which is required. Support for the aged is not a candidate for ad hoc, cost-saving measures.[3]

This presumes, rather questionably, that we know the terms of this implicit 'contract', and that present policies are adhering to those terms. That 'great sensitivity' is required in these issues is undeniable, but without analysis we cannot know whose interests are being most affected by the system as it stands.

Thus far in this book, four points have been made that are relevant to the subject of this chapter. First, we have seen that old age is the only phase of the normal life-cycle which is supported financially by the state.[4] All other phases either pay their own way or are net contributors to the well-being of the elderly. Throughout this book it has been questioned whether this is a well-balanced welfare policy. If the proposal in Chapter Six for a horizontally equitable taxation system were adopted that apparent imbalance would be redressed to some degree.

Second, as we saw in Chapter Five, the elderly can be expected to be the wealthiest section of society, at least at retirement age and presumably for some time after that, because there has been more time for them to save and for the interest on their savings to compound (or for the value of their bought-long-ago houses to increase). The decile around retirement age may command about thirty per cent of the total wealth of the society. Alan Jordan's analysis of incomes supports the view that equivalent incomes are

---

2 Saunders, 'Overview', *op. cit.*, 405.
3 Freebairn *et al.*, *Spending and Taxing*, 134.
4 See Figure 5.1 above.

at or near their highest at retirement.[5] These considerations raise a very fundamental question about why we choose to direct all our life cycle assistance to such a fortunate group. There would seem to a much better case for assisting families with children, who have not yet had the opportunity to build up their assets. Or we might conclude that the elderly should be assisted only after their assets have fallen to something below the community average.

Third, a distinction needs to be drawn between the independent and the dependent elderly. The dependent elderly need basic care from someone. Some—about two thirds—obtain that care within the family network, usually from a spouse or daughter. Those who do so are in a comparable position to children, and taxation policy should treat them as family members just as it should treat children as family members. Horizontal equity requires that their presence in the family be taken into account in the calculation of family income tax, just as the presence of children should be taken into account. One general theme of this book is that the state tends to favour its own social programs, at the expense of family-initiated welfare practices. The fact that our taxation system gives only token recognition to care of the elderly within the family is consistent with this theme.

Fourth, in discussing family breakdown, we have touched upon the thesis that the extended family has also suffered some sort of 'breakdown' which is (according to some accounts) prior to and causative of breakdown at the nuclear level. The claim that there has been widespread extended family breakdown has been treated in this book as 'not proven'. The available sociological evidence suggests that people both young and old—particularly those of Anglo-Saxon derivation—generally prefer what is now referred to as the 'modified extended family' and that extended family relationships describable as 'intimacy at a distance' are generally alive and usually well.[6] Most elderly people seem to want to live not with but near their families. As demographers have observed, this is the first time in history that the average married couple has more parents than children. Children today are likely to grow up knowing most of their grandparents and some of their great-grandparents.

Whether we can expect to see in the near future a reverse form of causal relationship, nuclear family breakdown causing damage to extended family networks, is perhaps a more urgent question. Most people do form new families after divorce, though some of these also turn out to be unstable. But some do not, and the prospects in old age for non-custodial parents who have lost touch with their children may well be bleak. At present those who never marry and who become handicapped in old age are far more likely to be in institutional care than married persons; the same may apply to the divorced when the 'divorce revolution' generation reaches the frailty of advanced old age. Divorce also tends to cut off grandparents from their

5 Nurick, *Wealth and Power*, 28f; Jordan, *The Common Treasury*, 1, 127.
6 Don T. Rowland, 'Family Structure', 27ff.

grandchildren, to the detriment of both. Whatever the causes, there does seem to be considerable anecdotal evidence of acute loneliness in old age for some, particularly those who get lost and forgotten in public institutions.

Some of these issues concern aged care and some are matters of income support. It might be convenient to draw a sharp distinction between the two but in practice this is more difficult than it first appears. Aged care costs money, and policies on income support affect the social relations of the elderly. Generous forms of income support may limit the availability of care for those who need it. Assisting family networks to care for their dependents will involve a loss of tax revenue.

Together, these four points and the complex questions raised in the international debate suggest that we may be far from achieving the best possible balance of policies. Yet some things should be said on the credit side of the ledger. The most striking is the fact that poverty amongst the elderly seems to have been almost eradicated in the past two decades. This is an international phenomenon. According to the editors of a recent study, 'The historical reduction of old-age poverty is one of the great successes of modern welfare society'.[7] They allow that in some countries there is still some residual poverty, but the evidence suggests that Australia is one of the success stories. In 1985–86 only 5.5 per cent of the over-65 age group were estimated to be below the poverty line after housing costs are taken into account.[8] In general, the trend during the period of expanding welfare expenditure was for aged poverty to decline and family poverty to increase. These conflicting trends may result, at least in part, from the fact that welfare systems create adverse incentives for the able-bodied but not for the elderly, who are generally thought to have moved into a different stage of life. (It is confirmed by the fact that age pension and superannuation schemes have created very substantial adverse incentives for those *approaching* retirement age, incentives quite as severe as the poverty and employment traps distorting the behaviour of younger workers.) Since the elimination of aged poverty is an unqualified good, the main aim of aged policy should be to find ways of making that achievement sustainable, consistent with other social aims of equity and efficiency.

Privatisation

Broadly speaking, government policy on age pensions and aged services has in recent years followed a single strategy, that of encouraging private alternatives—superannuation and care in the home—to the traditional public system of support. This strategy is generally agreed to be the correct one, because it offers more choice than before, because it it capable of

7 Johnson *et al.*, *Workers versus Pensioners*, 1.
8 EPAC Council Paper 35, Table 2.2.

promoting efficiency and because it should lower income tax levels. The main objection to the strategy is that, as far as it has yet been taken, it is probably far less cost-efficient than it seems to be or than it ought to be. No good proof has yet been given that the superannuation or the private care approaches as they presently stand are in fact saving money for the taxpayer or that they are likely to save money in the future.

Whether and to what extent taxation incentives for superannuation will encourage self-provision and reduce the ultimate cost to the taxpayer is a technical question which has been much debated, and need not be discussed here. All that needs to be said here is that the savings are unlikely to be dramatic. It seems to be agreed by experts in the field that current-year expenditure on concessions does not represent a saving, and that real savings will only take place if the preservation age (the minimum age at which one may draw from one's superannuation fund) is raised, the higher the better. According to Treasury, 'Tax concessions to occupational superannuation cost the government an estimated $3.1 billion in forgone revenue in 1985–86, with these concessions favouring higher income groups, given their higher coverage rates'. David Knox's model estimated the current value of the existing concessions to be 'in the vicinity of $2.0 billion, approximately $1 billion less than the Treasury's estimate'.[9]

Something similar can be said about the present privatisation of aged care. The Home and Community Care program (HACC) provides at-home help with nursing, housekeeping, shopping and meals; home maintenance and home modifications; day care centres for the disabled; respite care to relieve primary carers; and paramedical aid such as physiotherapy. All these make it substantially easier for elderly people to remain in their own homes or to be cared for within their wider families. HACC should reduce the demand for costly beds in nursing homes and hostels, which will be used only by those who are severely dependent or who have no family support. Entry to hostels and nursing homes is now being determined not on a 'first come first served' basis but according to need, as determined by a Geriatric Assessment Team. As recently as 1986 a study by Minichiello reported that 'Factors other than health accounted for three quarters of all reasons cited by patients for moving into a nursing home'. When asked how they felt about this move the most common terms used by his respondents were 'helplessness, abandonment, horrified and resentful'.[10] Some of this anguish is now preventable.

Most of the users of HACC services are married couples, one of whom is caring for a disabled spouse; some live alone; and some (about 15 per cent) live with other family members. The main criticism of HACC seems to have been that it transfers the burden of care from the state to the family, and particularly to wives and daughters. Hal Kendig has spoken of 'a

---

9 See Freebairn *et al.*, *Spending and Taxing*, 133f; and Knox, *Taxation Support of Superannuation in Australia*, 45.

10 M. Victor Minichiello, 'Social Processes in Entering Nursing Homes', 167.

massive but hidden set of social inequalities, with the consequences falling most heavily on women'.[11] It cannot be doubted that caring for a disabled family member is often an extremely trying business, even with the best assistance of HACC. There is also a question of equity here. Why should those families who care for their disabled or frail elderly in their homes have to subsidise those who do not? On this basis there is a case for a carer's pension which, together with the cost of whatever HACC services are used, amounts to the equivalent of whatever would have been spent by the state to keep that disabled or frail person in a nursing home or hostel. Such a pension would ensure that the decision of where the care takes place is made not for extrinsic, and often inappropriate, financial reasons, but according to the desires of the family and the patient. (Conflict between the desires of family and patient will still arise to some extent, but it might be alleviated.) It is highly unlikely that carer's pensions at present measure up to the level required by this criterion. Obviously, we do not do things this way because it is felt, plausibly enough, that the cost is prohibitive. In other words, even with HACC in operation, we still prefer to skew the kind of assistance we provide in favour of the state and against the family. Yet carer's pensions of this kind are the logical complement to the HACC approach. To pursue this line of argument we are forced to look again at the general picture of the financing of old age.

Who pays?

Though there is agreement about the general direction aged policy should take, the crucial question 'Who pays?' is as yet unanswered. It may be that even once the privatisation program is complete old age will remain at once the most naturally wealthy phase of the life cycle and the most heavily subsidised. Or at least, it will remain so until the demographic forces compel a re-evaluation of what can be afforded, in which case the 'single welfare generation' prophecy will still be fulfilled. Privatisation will have taken us no nearer to solving the basic issue of a sustainable and balanced distribution of income between the generations.

In a brief but incisive discussion of the question 'But why is there social security?' Denis Kessler maintains that 'The creation of social security schemes and the development of pension schemes in most developed countries, just before and after the Second World War, is still a puzzling phenomenon'.[12] Kessler tries out four hypotheses to explain this phenomenon. Since the issues he raises are not peculiar to social security arrangements, but expand to cover the larger question of public financial assistance to the elderly, we can use his hypotheses to reconsider the general question of 'who pays?'.

11 Kendig, 'Ageing, Families and Social Change', 184.
12 Denis Kessler, 'But Why is There Social Security?'.

Kessler's first candidate is the myopia hypothesis: individuals work within a limited time horizon, and do not plan for their retirement. Such individuals will eventually need public assistance, if they are to avoid poverty. But, as Kessler points out, 'In a myopic world, one can suppose that the government will also be myopic. Why should the government be far-sighted if most or all individuals are myopic?' Social security schemes can force people to save, but the fact that democratic governments enforce this saving suggests that most people would save anyway. (We can for the time being ignore the distinction between funded and pay-as-you-go government pension schemes. The difference becomes noticeable to the recipient or prospective recipient when the system begins to break down.)

A second candidate is the life cycle hypothesis: individuals are not myopic but forward-looking and rational. They arrange their income to meet their various life cycle needs. But of course 'in a world full of people behaving as in the simple life cycle model ... there is no a priori need for social and pension schemes'. Only uncertainty about the duration of one's life or imperfect capital markets would compel the need for such schemes.[13] But this seems to be a rationale only for a residual pension scheme, to help people through unforeseeable circumstances, not one which guarantees a tax-funded income they would otherwise provide for themselves.

The life cycle model assumes that individuals think only about their own lives, and do not plan to leave bequests. The third model, the intergenerational transfer hypothesis, assumes that they do want to leave bequests and that they are sufficiently farsighted to do so. The model derives from the observation that bequests usually go to the succeeding generation. There is, in this view, a reciprocal altruism in which the younger generation help the elderly through old age, and after death become the beneficiaries in the relationship. But if this is the model then there is no need for public social security schemes—the family can function as such a scheme. Kessler suggests that disruption to families as a result of war and migration may have prompted the switch to public social security schemes in the first half of this century, but if that is so then there is no comparable need for them now.

A fourth theory is that it is labour market factors that dictated the formation of public social security schemes. Most people retire when they are still able to work. Why choose to have so much leisure then, and relatively little earlier in life? But predictable semi-compulsory retirement and public social security go along with industrialisation. Social security 'has been a useful tool for reducing the aggregate rate of unemployment'. It permits firms to offload workers who have ceased to be productive.

13 The argument presented in Chapter Five for family assistance assumed an imperfect capital market. If capital markets were perfect, individuals could borrow in the private sector against their future earnings to help them through the child-rearing stage.

'Pensions act as severance pay.... [T]hey are deferred wages'. Their introduction was a response to the unemployment of the 1930s and to new intensive methods of production which required long-term employer-employee relationships.

If Kessler's analysis is plausible then he is surely right to say that both the formation and the durability of public social security schemes should be thought of as rather puzzling. None of the theories advanced seems very compelling. But if this is so then why is there social security? And why keep it? It seems that we do not know. All that can be said is that social security seems to reduce poverty amongst the elderly. But poverty-reduction may be achievable more simply and efficiently. All this would not matter greatly if there were nothing to be said against social security schemes, but in fact there is a case to be made against them. They may be more than merely unnecessary. Through their effects on marginal tax rates they may substantially reduce our general living standards.

Whether today people are as chronically myopic as to require the pension system that we have we perhaps do not know, because the system makes far-sightedness unnecessary. Whether the elderly today are generally as wealthy as they naturally could be (given a lifetime in which to save and invest) we also do not know, because little research appears to have been done on the subject. However, there are a few relevant indicators. One is that most old people own their own homes. Ian Manning found that 80 per cent of elderly (head over 65) married couples were owners, seven per cent purchasers, nine per cent renters and three per cent lived rent-free. Of single persons over 65, 60 per cent were owners, four per cent purchasers, 14 per cent renters, 13 per cent rent-free, and 10 per cent lived with their landlord, probably a family member.[14] Most purchasers would have very low mortgages; some renters receive state subsidies. In general then, the great majority of the elderly today appear to be comfortably accommodated.

Second, private monetary transfers within the family appear generally to flow from old to young. Manning has remarked that 'It is generally believed that few elderly people in Australia depend on their children for cash help....'[15] The evidence that money tends to flow the other way is perhaps only anecdotal. Research on the subject would be of some interest. If it is the case that substantial amounts of money now flow from old to young then Kessler's second 'intergenerational' rationale for social security—the young support the old through their taxes—would seem to have outlived its usefulness.

Third, the elderly do not commonly run down their assets. According to Manning, 'elderly households have, on average, positive savings ratios'. This claim is confirmed by the EPAC study, *Economic Effects of an Aging Population*, which reports on ABS figures showing that the over-65 group

14 Manning, 'Private Savings and Retirement', 175.
15 *Ibid.* 178.

has the highest saving ratio of all age groups.[16] This fact is inexplicable on the common view that the elderly are generally not well off. (To make sense of the figures within that assumption we need to postulate that the elderly have radically different attitudes to savings and consumption from their juniors—and the onus of proof is on those who take this view to defend it.) From this evidence we might conclude that the main function of the old age pension is to serve not as an income maintenance device but as an asset maintenance mechanism. Since the elderly are likely to be asset-rich, discussions about the 'adequacy' of pension incomes may be largely irrelevant.

One piece of evidence which suggests that the elderly are not asset-rich is cited by Chris Foster in his Social Security Review paper, *Towards a National Retirement Incomes Policy.* According to Foster's research, approximately 72 per cent of single pensioners and 69 per cent of married pensioners report financial assets of less than $10,000. He concludes that 'Notwithstanding problems of valuing the assets of pensioners and the probability of under-reporting, the picture which emerges is not one of a particularly wealthy population'.[17] However, this calculation measured only liquid assets (bank and building society accounts, bonds, shares and debentures), not fixed assets; and self-reported assets are notoriously likely to be underestimates.

Equally basically, Foster fails to compare the welfare of the elderly population with the position of any other population segment. Since all Australian life-cycle assistance is directed to the elderly and none at all to the average family with children we need to ask whether the elderly are wealthier than the average family, and if they are, why do we support one group but not the other? Suppose we use the equivalent income concept to compare the living standards of young families and old couples or individuals. A single pensioner on maximum pension will be receiving about $6,000 per annum, giving him or her an equivalent income of 6,000. By the square root rule pensioner married couples are better off than single pensioners. Their equivalent income is over 7000 (10,000 divided by 1.414). With fringe benefits (on public transport, electricity bills, motor vehicle registrations, drivers' licences, property rates, health expenditures, etc.) worth at least $20 per week this increases to an equivalent income of 7,000 for the single pensioner and perhaps 8,500 for the married couple. An average family of two children and two adults on an above-average income of $30,000 per annum has, by the square root rule, an equivalent income of 15,000. So far it would seem that the family enjoys a standard of living nearly twice as high as that of the pensioner.

16 *Ibid.*, 169; EPAC Council Paper 29, 34.

17 Foster, *Towards a National Retirement Incomes Policy*, Table 17. On page 44 Foster writes '77 per cent' for the first figure, but his Table 17 shows 72 per cent to be correct.

However, this is to leave out the effects of income tax and housing considerations. Real living standards depend on net income after taxation. Equivalent income comparisons also fail to correct for the lifetime accumulation of assets. What is needed here is not the limited notion of equivalent income but a notion of equivalent wealth. On a modest home worth $100,000 a typical family of two adults and two children might have a mortgage of $50,000, with repayments at $7,000 per annum. On an income of $30,000 this family will be paying about $7,000 in income tax. Their disposable income after housing costs is thus $16,000, and by the square root rule their equivalent disposable income is 8,000. The possibility of some income in the 'free zone', and the absence of an assets test for pensioners over 70 tips the comparison further in favour of the elderly. By this (admittedly very crude) reckoning the married pensioner is better off and the single pensioner a little worse off than the family under consideration. By extension the average pensioner seems to be better off than families with two or more children earning less than $30,000 annually and better off than many families with three or more children earning more than $30,000.

The figures here for both family income and mortgage repayments may be well below the median. The Real Estate Institute of Australia claims that in 1989 the median family income was $44,000 and the average annual mortgage repayment was 41 per cent of gross income, or $18,000.[18] Taxation on such an income is likely to be about $12,000. If these figures are accurate then, by the process of calculation used above, even families with incomes as high as this—1.75 times average weekly earnings—are no better off than couples on the age pension.[19] If this sort of comparison is at all plausible then it is difficult then to see why taxation on families with dependent children should be increased to provide additional income for age pensioners. The position would be somewhat different if we had a horizontally equitable personal income tax system of the kind argued for in Chapter Six. However, such a system would increase the tax burden on individuals without dependants, and thus make them a less eligible source of tax support for the elderly.

This brings us back to the question of demographic ageing. The basic strategic question is whether the costs of demographic ageing are to be borne by the working population or by the elderly. This may look like a false dichotomy because of course workers retire and grow old; but the contrast is a real one, because the decision will have significant economic effects, and also because it is important that different stages of the life-cycle should each bear as much of the burden of dependency as they

18 Real Estate Institute of Australia, reported in *The Australian*, 24 July 1989.

19 Further support for this line of argument comes from a paper prepared for the WA Community Services Board, which, as John Nurick has shown, while arguing that social security benefits were inadequate, unintentionally showed that they provided living standards close to those of families on 80 per cent of average weekly earnings. See Nurick, 'The Future of the Welfare State'.

reasonably can. Discussion of this decision has tended to take it for granted that the burden will have to be borne by those of workforce age, and the question has been seen as a matter of how heavy that burden will be relative to such matters as female workforce participation, immigration levels, economic performance, and superannuation policy. While no doubt all these are important it may be that this approach is starting at the wrong end of the stick. We should at least ask seriously whether the great majority of age pensioners are not capable of being rather more self-supporting than they are at present required to be.

Policy possibilities

Daryl Dixon has listed four obvious changes which need to be made if the elderly are to become more self-supporting:

- remove lump sum superannuation benefits;
- enforce the preservation of superannuation benefits until age 65 (presently it is age 55);
- tighten the assets test, possibly to include the family home;
- institute compulsory savings schemes for those without superannuation.[20]

Dixon also advocates a Retirement Savings Credit which substitutes for the tax threshold and 'provides a strong financial incentive for saving during working life to provide a retirement income'. Each of these is so obviously necessary as hardly to require discussion. Dixon notes that 'Australia is the only country offering superannuation tax concessions that permit benefits to be taken in lump-sum form'. This is a classic instance of a 'welfare generation' program which is simply unsustainable. Anyone who wants to enjoy a big spend-up when they reach retirement should find some way of financing it that does not involve taxation monies.

Similarly, voluntary early retirement is a classic instance of adverse welfare incentive effects. The labour force participation rate of men aged 60–64 dropped from 76.1 percent in 1974 to 47.7 percent in 1982. Observing this trend, Henry J. Aaron commented that 'The plain fact is that the early retiree receives nearly as large a pension as the late retiree and, of course, receives assistance for a much longer period. In this fashion the Australian system encourages early retirement'. He also spoke of unemployment benefits for older workers as a 'de facto early retirement pension'. And he noted that pensions for couples without children rose by 42 per cent in real terms between 1970 and 1980.[21]

Measures such as the above are urgently needed, but they may not go far enough. They do not tackle the basic questions of whether we need, and whether we can afford, age pensions and superannuation concessions of the

20 Dixon, 'How Mr Hawke Has Cut Welfare Dependency'.
21 Aaron, 'Social Welfare in Australia', 371.

form and scale that we presently have. Demographic change in coming decades will require either that the proportion of gross domestic product spent on pensions be greatly increased, or that pensions be made less generous or harder to qualify for. At present superannuation has to be heavily tax-supported in order to make it more attractive than the pension. (Dixon has contended that 'Labor's superannuation changes may have weakened the incentives for superannuation saving, especially for lower income Australians.'[22]) Similarly, if the cost of helping people in their own homes through the Home And Community Care program approaches that of keeping them in hostels or nursing homes then the gain in this area will have been a social but not a financial one.

Kessler's question, 'But why do we have social security?' has still not been answered. One possible answer is that pension monies and superannuation concessions are matters of right, based on a lifetime of taxation payments, and therefore cannot be tampered with. But the likelihood is that the actuarial entitlement of pensioners is considerably less than what is now reckoned to be a minimally adequate retirement income. All present recipients lived through a low-tax era and benefited from the start-up phase of the Australian post-War expansion of age pensions, when end-of-life benefits far exceed lifetime contributions. (In 1950 only 40 per cent of persons of age pension age relied on the pension; in 1980 about 80 per cent were so reliant. Subsequent tightening of eligibility criteria by the Hawke government means there are now some 300,000 fewer recipients of the age pension than would otherwise have been the case.[23]) The entitlement argument might lead to a drastic reduction in pension payments.

The present position is made urgent by three factors: the Australian economy is weak; we have just reached the full maturity phase of our social security system, and are beginning to see how costly it is; and we are about to be hit by the twofold demographic crisis, ageing and baby boom retirement. In these circumstances something has to give. The evidence that today's elderly are a 'welfare generation' is not conclusive but it is sufficient to be thought-provoking.[24] Kessler overlooks one fairly obvious 'rationale' for social security, a socio-political one. The present generation of elderly lived through the Depression of the 1930s and at least one World War. The shock of these events, combined with the rapid post-War economic recovery and the fact that social security schemes are much easier to start than to maintain, perhaps led to a desire for absolute security

---

22 Dixon, 'How Mr Hawke Has Cut Welfare Dependency'; see also Dixon & Martin, *The New Super Made Easy*.

23 See Goodin & Le Grand, 'Creeping Universalism in the Australian Welfare State', Figure 6.1; Dixon, 'How Mr Hawke Has Cut Welfare Dependency'.

24 The 'welfare generation' thesis is argued by David Thompson, 'The Welfare State and Generation Conflict: Winners and Losers', and *Selfish Generations: The Ageing of the Welfare State*. See also Daniels, 'Justice and Transfers between Generations'.

and for a maximum of generosity. If this is the real rationale then there is no imperative reason to maintain the system when this generation has passed.[25]

But even if there were substantial economic and social gains in phasing out some of the present system—lower effective marginal tax rates and less financial pressure on families with children—is it politically feasible to do so when the phenomenon of 'greypower' is becoming a political force to be reckoned with? Is there a relatively painless solution to the problem? Perhaps there is. The Australian system of tax-free private housing serves as a de facto superannuation scheme with almost universal coverage and a high level of pay out benefits. What distinguishes it from more conventional superannuation schemes is only that its benefits are paid out not in incomes but as assets. In Australia home ownership is undoubtedly the most significant form of private saving, yet it is rarely used to finance consumption after retirement. However, there is no obvious reason why it should not be so used. According to Gruen's EPAC paper on housing, the total cost of tax concessions to home buyers on the rental value of their homes (i.e. the cost of not imputing the rental value of the house as taxable income) could be as high as $3 billion per annum—or roughly the equivalent of tax concessions on superannuation.[26] A system of reverse annuity mortgages;[27] would convert the family home into an important source of retirement income, thereby raising or at least maintaining the present high living standards of the elderly without adding to the tax burden on the young. This strategy also looks like the best available method of coping with the ageing crisis.

Of course if relatively few pensioners owned their own homes this approach might be less justifiable. Only 55 per cent of persons fully reliant on the pension are home owners or purchasers, but this figure is not the whole story. Seventy-four per cent of pensioners for whom the pension amounts to over 90 per cent of their income are owners or near-owners, and 84 per cent for those who get over 50 per cent of their income from the pension.[28] As we have seen, by Manning's calculations only nine per cent of elderly couples and 14 per cent of single elderly persons are renters.

---

25 Goodin & Le Grand list four equally plausible but less reputable reasons for age pension expansion: see footnote 27 in Chapter Five above.

26 Gruen, *Housing Australians.*

27 Reverse annuity mortgages are one of a number of financial arrangements, novel in Australia but well-established in countries such as France and Canada, that let home-owners in effect sell some or all of the equity in their property without having to move out. The buyer gains possession on the death of the seller or when the seller moves to an old people's home. Payment may take the form of a lump sum or a regular income. Numerous variations in detail are possible (for instance, which party takes the risk of a 70-year-old seller failing to die on time and occupying the property for 20 or 30 years instead of the expected dozen years or fewer).

28 Foster, *Towards a National Retirement Incomes Policy*, Table 8.

Politically speaking, it may be necessary to do little more than to refuse to push pension payments any higher as a proportion of average weekly earnings than they presently are. This at least would be contrary to the Hawke government's (presumably meaningless) talk of eventually raising pensions to 30 per cent of AWE. On this way of reckoning the matter there is no basic retirement incomes crisis, nor will there be one in the next few decades. The elderly are a relatively well off section of society; most of them are benefiting from a pensions system which pays out far more than they contributed to it in their taxes; many of them can, and may even wish to, work longer than they do. All that we need to do is to make these facts well understood, and to establish and gain acceptance for ways, such as reverse annuity mortgages, in which elderly people can conveniently convert illiquid assets into income.

But can all this be done without increasing poverty among the elderly? The relatively assetless poor need not suffer from controls on pension and aged care expenditure. The assetless elderly are mostly over 75, and mainly women. It would be quite feasible to have a more generous pension for this age group, or one which is phased in as assets and health decline. If the assumptions made above about wealth are roughly right then the age pension system might be designed so that: no-one receives the pension before age 65; between 65 and 70 the pension is set at half its present rate (say 12 per cent of average weekly earnings) and simply supplements income from assets, savings and superannuation; between 70 and 75 it stands at four-fifths the present rate (20 per cent of AWE); and after 75 it rises to something over the present rate (say 30 per cent of AWE). In this way the pension would correspond more closely to needs. Assets and superannuation would be used to provide income. The effective marginal tax rate barriers to continued work for those who desire it would dissolve. The tax burden on families with children could be lowered. And the health care needs of the frail elderly could be effectively met, and their at-home carers could be adequately remunerated.

But of course, in the real political world where narrow interest groups seem to enjoy selective competitive advantages, all this is impossible. At most we can only debate the merits of such a proposal. Nevertheless, the issue will not go away. The urgency of the present situation, and the necessity of at least enforcing Dixon's recommendations, can be made clearer still. The windfall gains of the 'welfare generation' have their obverse side—the windfall losses of the unlucky generation whose job it has been to fund the welfare generation, but who in future are likely to get little benefit from what will remain of the system they funded. The longer we postpone ending the welfare generation the worse the present working generation will fare when it comes to their turn to 'benefit'. If families were perfectly altruistic and everyone was integrated into a family network then government pension policy would make no very great difference to people's actual well-being, apart from the general loss due to churning. But we know that families are only imperfectly and relatively altruistic, and not everyone has strong family ties, so government policy does matter.

The main intra-family effect of a tighter assets policy is to lower the level of gifts and bequests from old to young, which we have suggested may at present be quite substantial. Yet this may be no bad thing. At present family members may do nothing to help their elderly except pay their share of pension and health care taxes, yet they often stand to benefit considerably when the old person dies. Those who do nothing for elderly family members stand to gain most. If assets were run down, however, the heirs would lose potential bequests. This would be a spur to care within the family. This point complements Kendig's objection to the equity disadvantage suffered at present by families who do care for their elderly.

Since almost all the crucial propositions in the argument of this chapter are speculative and contrary to common assumptions the reader is free to be sceptical about the conclusions drawn from them. All that need be claimed here is that those conclusions are at least as plausible as any other. Our ignorance about the basic rationale for and remote consequences of social security schemes is quite as great as it is with other welfare programs.

12 Conclusion

Human attachments and affections are generally arranged as it were concentrically, first to family, then to friends, to work, to community and to the state, roughly in descending order of perceived importance. A welfare system which makes the state the first line of support in time of difficulty can expect to suffer from the alienation and anomie which accompany such a divorce between natural attachments and artificial obligations. Such a system can be made to work moderately well, but it goes against the grain and requires special effort, such as a bureaucratic investigative and policing mechanism. The difficulties are only compounded if—as we have done—we try to pretend that they do not exist. They are doubly compounded in a time in which, for relatively independent reasons, family status and morale is low and the family as an institution is subject to much unbalanced criticism.

Unfortunately, we understand very little about why family status and morale have fallen so dramatically. At the heart of this book there is a blank: in Chapter Seven it is argued that we have no good explanation of the increase in family breakdown in the past fifteen years. All the hypotheses presently in the field are found to be either deficient or else tend to suggest that family stability should have improved in that period. Most discussions do not seem to notice that there is something to be explained here. The Social Security Review, which set out to consider the financial position of families and appropriate family support policies, and which included the 'increase in the formation of sole parent families' as one of the main determinants of the present situation, has devoted barely a single paragraph to the causes of family breakdown.[1] Some better grasp of the issues here seems urgent, for without it our collective self-understanding of

1 Cass, *The Case for a Review...*, synopsis.

family matters will continue to flounder. Even mere curiosity should prompt us to want to make sense of such a massive phenomenon. The distinguished historian Lawrence Stone, a specialist in family demography, has said of the international situation that 'The scale of marital breakdown in the West since 1960 has no historical precedent and seems unique. There has been nothing like it for the last 2000 years, and probably much longer'.[2]

On the question of causes Stone believes that we have no good general theory. At the end of the most comprehensive recent analysis, that by Roderick Phillips in *Putting Asunder: A History of Divorce in Western Society*, we are 'left hanging, faced with choosing between contradictory reflections of individual spouses, vague statistical correlations of sociological probabilities, broad socioeconomic models based on urbanisation and industrialisation, and the influence of cultural forces like individualism, secularisation, and sexual liberation'. Of these, Stone suggests (following Phillips), the most important of all was 'rising expectations of emotional, sexual, and economic fulfilment in marriage, hopes that were inevitably disappointed when faced with the rough reality of married life, with its critical in-laws, cranky children, disabling sickness, and the frustrating day-to-day grind of intimate cohabitation'.[3]

Is the divorce phenomenon to be thought of as an epidemic or as a form of liberation? Stone goes on to remark that 'Divorce in the 1980s is ... often a liberation from an often agonising relationship for both husband and wife. But it also often ends up as a financial bonanza for men, a financial and personal catastrophe for women, and a psychological disaster for the children'. Why so many relationships have turned out to be agonising in this way we do not understand. Stone speaks of spouses 'being traded in almost as cheaply and easily as used cars'. He underestimates the 'personal catastrophe' which men suffer after divorce, but he is surely broadly right about the 'psychological disaster' for children. In response to this disaster Stone maintains that we need to think again about 'no-fault' divorce. He believes that 'An argument could ... be made that the divorce laws and divorce practice in the 1950s and early 1960s had the virtue of being free enough to liberate the desperately unhappy, but restrictive enough to make both spouses think long and hard before smashing up a marriage'.[4]

Another distinguished commentator, David Popenoe, concludes his *Disturbing the Nest: Family Change and Decline in Modern Societies*, a comprehensive and intelligent survey of the international trends, with a 'Personal Appraisal'. Popenoe sees the family today as a 'perishable social institution that is being quietly corroded by some of the social and cultural currents of our time'. In his view the opposite to the natural ethos of family life is an individualism in which 'self-fulfilment has become one of the

2 Stone, 'The Road to Polygamy'.
3 Phillips, *Putting Asunder*; Stone, *op. cit.*, 15.
4 *Ibid.*, 14f.

paramount cultural values'.[5] The most important recent shift has been away from a child-centred view of family life and towards an emphasis on the emotional needs of the adults. In Popenoe's judgment, 'The trends of our time that are improperly labelled "revolutions", each of which has advanced in its own way the value of self-fulfilment—the sexual revolution, the feminist revolution, the therapeutic revolution, the welfare revolution, the consumer revolution—have probably all played a role in the weakening of this main human relationship', the parent-child bond.

> It has become clear that adults no longer need children in their lives, at least not economically. The problem is that children, as much as they ever did, still need adults. They need not just adults, however, but parents who are motivated to provide them with, in the words of Urie Bronfenbrenner, 'enduring, irrational emotional involvement'. Just any adults cannot ordinarily provide that environment, only parents (at least one, but preferably two).... What is still required, and has no substitute in the technological realm, is an abundance of time, patience, and love on the part of caring parents. In short, children need strong families.[6]

Popenoe expresses the hope that 'today's children of divorce, in view of what they have been through, will as adults take the lead in bringing about a more child-centered, familistic society'.[7]

He also notes that in most modern societies, as divorce has been gradually made a private matter (though subject still to controls over the division of property, custody and maintenance), children have been given no legal protection against psychological injury. 'With regard to the continuation of the parental bond, children are regarded as having virtually no rights at all'. The oddity of this fact in an age preoccupied by personal rights and welfare provisions is certainly striking, yet it is almost never discussed. Popenoe adds that 'in virtually every welfare state the growth of benefits for the elderly has exceeded that for children. If children were involved in formulating welfare-state policies, I have little doubt the situation would be different'. He concludes that although the state cannot and should not try to force parents to stay together, 'there is much to be said for making divorce more difficult for the parents of children and for the state signalling in various ways that family stability *is* extremely important to children and therefore to society as a whole'.[8]

Neither Stone nor Popenoe claim to explain the trends in family life, but they agree that the tendency has been generally retrograde for children's interests. Fortunately, it does seem that we can devise appropriate social policies for families without any very good theory about the causes of family breakdown. The policies argued for in this book are based not on a speculative diagnosis of the causes of family breakdown but primarily on

---

5 Popenoe, *Disturbing the Nest*, 329f.
6 *Ibid.* 330.
7 *Ibid.* 332.
8 *Ibid.* 335f.

the requirements of justice between different family forms and between families with dependants and individuals without dependants. Whether a fairer social welfare and taxation system of this sort would help to reduce family breakdown we do not know, though we may suspect that it would, and we have no reason to think that it would have detrimental effects on family stability and success.

The basic message of this book is simple and twofold: Do not subsidise family breakdown. Do support families which care for their children by staying together. The book's basic claim is that at present we do subsidise family breakdown, and we do not support families which stay together. The book's main policy proposal is that the state should treat separated and divorced families exactly the same as it treats intact families. It is also argued that a taxation system committed to horizontal equity would eliminate many of the main perverse incentives in the welfare system. More generally it has been argued that the welfare state in Australia (and probably elsewhere) has been unbalanced in three ways: against families with children (and more generally against people with dependants), and in favour of independent individuals; against intact families, and in favour of families which break up; and (probably but not yet provably) against the young, and in favour of the elderly.

The contention that we subsidise family breakdown is of course controversial, so it is necessary here to restate in outline the argument for it. The argument takes two forms. One form rests on the claim that *in general* (though not always in particular) two-parent families are preferable to sole-parent families. Sole parent families tend to give children less support; and they are commonly formed by a separation and divorce process which children usually find emotionally traumatic, sometimes with severe and lasting after-effects. These are not tendencies we have any reason to promote. The appropriate social policy response must surely be to assist families to avoid these consequences, which would involve supporting two-parent families at the same level as we support sole parent families.

However, the evidence for these claims is (like so much social research) somewhat sketchy, and some observers take Paul Amato's view that the divorce revolution has done no lasting harm to children's 'growth to competence'. Even if that is so, the contention that we are subsidising family breakdown can be recast as a horizontal equity argument. No good reason has ever been given in the Australian literature why, for every dollar spend supporting children in two-parent families, we should spend about ten dollars on children in sole parent families. The common assumption that the needs of the two family forms are radically different is quite implausible. Families which split up are just an ordinary cross-section of the whole population of families, and they have the same social resources, educational achievements, occupational qualifications and child-rearing commitments as do families which stay together. Since the two forms are so similar in essentials there is no obvious justification for treating them as differently as we do.

In a time such as Stone and Popenoe describe, political leaders might seek to restore the self-confidence of families with children, and might sponsor policies which give families real status in society. At the least, responsible politicians should seek to do no harm to families. This book has argued that harmful policies are presently in operation in the Australian system; it has tried to show how they might be corrected; but it does recognise that to repair the damage will require considerable courage and wisdom.

The Hawke Labor Government has four achievements to its credit in the welfare and social security field. During its tenure of office unemployment has fallen from ten to six per cent; it established the Child Support Scheme; it built up the Family Allowance Supplement; and it shifted the emphasis in support of the elderly away from reliance on the pension and nursing homes and towards superannuation and assistance in the home. All these are significant improvements upon what went before. However, they go only halfway towards the generally accepted goals of equity and efficiency.

Unemployment has been halved by two strategies, by controlling wage demands and by enforcing stringent benefits criteria. (Rapid growth in the money supply has also aided job creation, though with seriously detrimental effects for inflation and the current account deficit.) In both cases marginal members of the labour force have been protected not by giving them more generous assistance but by protecting them from unscrupulous wage and benefit claimants. The success in this area suggests that pursuit of the same tactics could continue to eliminate the evil of involuntary unemployment. There is no obvious reason why the goal should not be to cut unemployment back to two per cent, as it was for thirty years after 1945.

The Child Support Scheme is important because it recognises the basic moral principle that obligations to one's children do not end with separation and divorce. Enforcement of fair maintenance payments can be viewed as a form of 'protecting the vulnerable', though again this is not a matter of more generous payments. This book has argued that the basic principle here requires the elimination of all payments to broken families which are not also given to intact families. The argument is an argument for justice. Families which stay together should not be penalised for meeting their obligations to their children, as they are at present.

The Family Allowance Supplement (originally a Fraser government initiative), which assists working families and reduces the incentives to welfare dependency, has done much to alleviate the hardship faced by low-income families. But it too goes only half way. In reducing poverty it has created poverty traps. This book has argued that poverty traps are in large part a by-product of an inequitable tax system which fails to recognise the necessity of horizontal equity between families with children and individuals without dependents. To really protect vulnerable low-income families it is first necessary to establish a fair taxation system.

By encouraging superannuation, the Hawke Government has gone part of the way towards preparing for the demographic changes of the next few decades. But it is by no means clear that superannuation as presently structured will on balance significantly relieve the burden of the retirment income system on the taxpayer. Nor has there been any public discussion of the extent to which the elderly need an income-support system—whether pensions or superannuation—on the present scale. The Home And Community Care program has partly corrected the imbalance between the family and the state in aged care, but the carer's pension remains little more than a token.

At various points this book has touched on economic questions. The comments made at those points have made no pretence of economic expertise. Economists can make their own evaluations of the policies here argued for on equity grounds. All that has been presumed here is that a policy of justice for families would not be economically imprudent. It is assumed here that we do have available to us many purely economic strategies to improve Australia's competitiveness and thus to maintain our high living standards. Some of these have already been implemented, but our failure to pursue the obvious remaining strategies is more a failure of nerve than a failure of insight and argument.[9] Broadly, it seems best to proceed simultaneously towards both fairness for families and economic efficiency. There is no glaringly obvious conflict between the two, but if to some degree fairness does detract from efficiency then we should simply try harder to achieve both at once.

Both economic criteria and equity require an efficient welfare system—a system with stringently designed eligibility tests, willing to eliminate welfare cheating, and with the primary objective of making recipients self-supporting as soon as possible. Some progress has been made in this direction by the present government but there is still a long way to go. If fairness for families is felt to be 'too costly' then much could be saved in the social security and welfare area. Reducing unemployment to two per cent, eliminating lump sums to people contemplating retirement and tightening the assets test on pensioners would all be moves in the right direction. At present, if this book is right, it is families with children which are carrying the costs of these inefficient and inequitable practices.

Families, friends, community and the state are all, to some degree, welfare systems. The fact that there is more than one natural welfare system makes it difficult to evaluate the performance of any one system. We now put the emphasis on the state system, but no proof exists to show that this is the optimal approach. For all we know we might all be better off if we

---

9 See e.g. Kasper *et al.*, *Australia at the Crossroads* (1980); Nurick (ed.), *Mandate to Govern* (1987); Marsh, *Australia Can Compete* (1988); Freebairn *et al.*, *Savings and Productivity* (1989); and the Garnaut Report (1989).

abolished the welfare state. This, however, has not been the main theme of this book. All that has been argued for here is a better balanced welfare state. We have a state welfare system partly because we have been living in a period in which the state has been powerful and has therefore tended to absorb functions previously regarded as outside its ambit. If, as we become disillusioned with its general performance, the power of the state is beginning to wane, so will its welfare functions tend to decline. This tendency is not at odds with this book's theme of the need for welfare balance. We can still insist that state welfare should decline in a balanced way.

In passing, the argument of this book has involved a deconstruction of the standard feminist 'critique' of the family. That critique turns out to be tendentious, over-stated or plainly false insofar as it is distinctive, and to be commonplace and commonsensical when it is not. Liberal feminist thinking about public policy—about taxation and childcare, for instance—is little more than the special pleading of a narrow interest group, of a kind all too familiar in democratic politics. Fortunately, however, there is no need to construe the issues as a battle for and against the true spirit of feminism. At various points my argument has borrowed from the work of lively and intelligent women thinkers and social critics, some of whom have or have had at least one foot in the 'feminist' camp. But the term is obsolescent, if not yet quite obsolete. 'Feminism' so-called never did manage to speak for women in general; its portrait of men was rarely better than a caricature; it had no feeling at all for the interests of children; and it failed to see that families often embody the cooperative, communal ideals which it espoused more often than it practiced. It will not be missed. The obsolescence of 'feminism' is matched by a similar irrelevance in the traditional 'Left/Right' dichotomy. It is as pointless to categorise the political arguments borrowed in this book as 'Left' or 'Right' as it is to categorise the claims about personal life as 'feminist' or 'anti-feminist'. Debate about 'the family', which so often descends into name-calling, is far more fluid—and interesting—than those committed to rigid, partisan positions would like us to believe, but then partisan rigidity has always been the main enemy of free thought.

The power of the state has always had a tendency to mesmerise. Welfarism is in part a phenomenon of this kind. State power also tends to entrench special interest groups who enjoy selective incentives to act as what Olson calls 'distributional coalitions'. These are the forces which must be resisted if we are to achieve a balanced and functional welfare state. In democratic theory at least, the majority should have no difficulty in controlling such minorities, but in practice the matter is not straightforward. We may doubt that, on welfare matters, the majority opinion is being put and heard. This book has been an attempt to articulate majority opinion on family policy, but whether it has succeeded in this can not be known in advance. If it has not it may still have succeeded in expressing an alternative to the ruling but disintegrating orthodoxies in the field.

Bibliography

—, *A Community of Self-Reliance: the New Consensus on Family and Welfare*, Report of the Working Seminar on the Family and American Welfare Policy (Chairman: Michael Novak), Washington: American Enterprise Institute, 1987.

—, *Beyond these Walls*, Report of the Queensland Domestic Violence Task Force, Brisbane, 1988.

—, *Child Support Formula for Australia*, Canberra: Department of Social Security, 1988.

—, *Taxes and Growth: the London Conference*, Critical Issues No. 10, Perth: Australian Institute for Public Policy, 1987.

—, *Targetting Welfare Expenditure on the Poor*, papers presented at meeting on Welfare Services for the Needy, Sydney: New South Wales Council of Social Services, 1985.

Aaron, Henry J., 'Social Welfare in Australia' in Richard E. Caves & Lawrence B. Krause (eds), *The Australian Economy: A View from the North*, Sydney: Allen & Unwin, 1984.

ABS (Australian Bureau of Statistics), Catalogue No 2506.0, *Census 86: Australian Families and Households*, Canberra, 1989.

ABS, Catalogue No. 3307.0, *Divorces Australia*, annual.

ABS, Catalogue No. 4101.0, *Social Indicators*, 4, Canberra, 1984.

ABS, Catalogue No. 4111.1, *Time Use Pilot Survey*, Sydney, 1987.

ABS, Catalogue No. 4119.0, *Australia's Children 1989: A Statistical Profile*, Canberra, 1990.

ABS, Catalogue No. 6227.0, *Transition from Education to Work: Australia*, May 1989.

ABS, Catalogue No. 6537.0, *The Effects of Government Benefits and Taxes on Household Income*, Household Expenditure Survey, Canberra, 1990.

Adams, Dennis, *Path of Honor: The Story of Vision Quest*, Tucson: Blue Horse, 1987.

Adler, Dan L., 'Matriduxy in the Australian Family', in A.F. Davies & S. Encel (eds), *Australian Society: A Sociological Introduction*, Melbourne: Cheshire, 1965.

Amato, Paul R., *Children in Australian Families: The Growth in Competence*, Melbourne: Australian Institute of Family Studies & Sydney: Prentice-Hall, 1987.

Anderson, Digby, June Lait & David Marsland, *Breaking the Spell of the Welfare State: Strategies for Reducing Public Expenditure*, London: Social Affairs Unit, 1981.

Anstie, R., R.G. Gregory, S. Dowrick & J.J. Pincus, *Government Spending on Work-Related Child Care: Some Economic Issues*, Discussion Paper No 191, Canberra: ANU Centre for Economic Policy Research, 1988.

Apter, Terri, *Why Women Don't Have Wives: Professional Success and Motherhood*, London: Macmillan, 1985.

Arndt, Bettina, *Private Lives*, Ringwood: Penguin, 1986.

Arnold, Roger A., 'Marriage, Divorce and Property Rights', in Peden & Glahe, *The American Family and the State*, 195–228.

Baier, Annette, 'Hume—the Women's Moral Theorist?', in Eva Feder Kittay & Diana T. Meyers (eds), *Women and Moral Theory*, Totowa: Rowman & Allenheld, 1987.

Barrett, Michele & Mary MacIntosh, *The Anti-Social Family*, London: Verso, 1982.

Beck, Jean, 'Wounded Men: The Hidden Face of Violence' in Crawley (ed.), *Counselling and Domestic Violence*.

Becker, Gary S. & Kevin M. Murphy, 'The Family and the State', *Journal of Law and Economics* **31** (1988), 1–18.

Becker, Gary S., *A Treatise on the Family*, Cambridge Mass.: Harvard University Press, 1981.

Beggs John J., & Bruce J. Chapman, *The Forgone Earnings from Child-Rearing in Australia*, Discussion Paper 190, Canberra: ANU Centre for Economic Policy Research, 1988.

Berger, Brigitte & Peter Berger, *The War Over the Family: Capturing the Middle Ground*, Harmondsworth: Penguin, 1984.

Bernheim, B. Douglas & Kyle Bagwell, 'Is Everything Neutral?', *Journal of Political Economy* **96** (1988), 308–337.

Bernstam, Mikhail S. & Peter L. Swan, 'The State as Marriage Partner of Last Resort: a labour market approach to illegitimacy in the United States, 1960–1980', Kensington: Australian Graduate School of Management Working Paper 86-029, 1986.

Bernstam, Mikhail S. & Peter L. Swan, *Malthus and the Evolution of the Welfare State: An Essay on the Second Invisible Hand*, Working Paper 89-012, Kensington: Australian Graduate School of Management, 1989.

Blaug, Mark, *The Methodology of Economics, or How Economists Explain*, Cambridge: Cambridge University Press, 1983.

Brogan, Colm, *The Educational Revolution*, London: Frederick Muller, 1954.

Burdekin Report: Report of the National Inquiry into Homeless Children, *Our Homeless Children*, Canberra: AGPS, 1989.

Burns, Ailsa, 'Mother-headed households: what is the future?', *The Australian Quarterly*, 1987, 387–400.

Burns, Ailsa, 'Why Do Women Continue to Marry?' in Grieve & Burns, *Australian Women: New Feminist Perspectives*, 210–232.

Butler, Stuart, & Anna Kondratas, *Out of the Poverty Trap: A Conservative Strategy for Welfare Reform*, New York & London: Free Press, 1987.

Butlin, N.G., A. Barnard & J.J. Pincus, *Government and Capitalism: Public and Private Choice in Twentieth Century Australia*, Sydney: Allen & Unwin, 1982.

Canovan, Margaret, *G.K. Chesterton: Radical Populist*, New York: Harcourt Brace Jovanovich, 1977.

Cardozo, Arlene Rossen, *Sequencing: Having it all but not all at once*, New York: Atheneum, 1986.

Cass, Bettina, *The Case for a Review of Aspects of the Australian Social Security System*, Social Security Review, Canberra: AGPS, 1986.

Cass, Bettina, *Income Support for Families with Children*, Social Security Review, Canberra: AGPS, 1986.
Cass, Bettina, *Income Support for the Unemployed in Australia: Towards a More Active System*, Social Security Review, Canberra: AGPS, 1988.
Castles, Frank G., 'Thirty Wasted Years: Australian Social Security Development 1950–80 in Comparative Perspective', *Canberra Bulletin of Public Administration*, May 1987, 41–46.
Castles, Ian, 'Government Welfare Outlays: Who Benefits? Who Pays?', *Canberra Bulletin of Public Administration*, May 1987, 47–57.
Chambers, Trevor, 'Psychosomatic Suicide', unpublished paper, Carlton: Care & Communications Concern, n.d.
Chapman, Bruce J., & Fred H. Gruen, *Unemployment, the Background to the Problem*, Discussion Paper 90, Canberra: ANU Centre for Economic Policy Research, 1984.
Clark, Wendy, 'Home Thoughts from not so far Away: a personal look at family' in Segal, *What is to be done about the Family?*, 168–189.
Cole, Bill, 'A Tax System for the 'Nineties', *Economic Witness* **38** (13 September 1989).
Collman, Jeff, *Fringe-Dwellers and Welfare: The Aboriginal Response to Welfare*, St Lucia: University of Queensland Press, 1989.
Connell, R.W., D.J. Ashenden, S. Kessler & G.W. Dowsett, *Making the Difference: Schools, Families and Social Division*, Sydney: Allen & Unwin, 1982.
Conway, Ronald, *Being Male: A Guide for Masculinity in a Time of Change*, Melbourne: Sun Books, 1985.
Conway, Ronald, *The End of Stupor? Australia Towards the Third Millenium*, Melbourne: Sun, 1984.
Conway, Ronald, *The Great Australian Stupor: An Interpretation of the Australian Way of Life*, revised edn, Melbourne: Sun, 1985.
Cosell, Hilary, *Woman on a Seesaw: The Ups and Downs of Making It*, New York: Pocket Books, 1985.
Crawley, Jim (ed.), *Counselling and Domestic Violence*, West Perth: Marriage Guidance Council of Western Australia, 1988.
Crawley, Jim, 'Family Therapy's Coming of Age: Less Haste, More Speed', *Australian and New Zealand Journal of Family Therapy* **7**, 13–18.
Crawley, Jim, 'Preventing Marital and Family Breakdown', Public Lecture for 1988 National Marriage and Family Week, Perth: Marriage Guidance Council of WA, 1988.
Curthoys, Ann, *For and Against Feminism: A Personal Journey into Feminist Theory and History*, Sydney: Allen & Unwin, 1988.
Daniels, Norman, 'Justice and Transfers between Generations', in Johnson *et al.*, *Workers versus Pensioners*, 57–79.
Danziger, Sheldon H. & Daniel H. Weinberg (eds), *Fighting Poverty: what works and what doesn't*, Cambridge: Harvard Univerity Press, 1986.
Davis, Gwynn & Mervyn Murch, *Grounds for Divorce*, Oxford: Clarendon Press, 1988.
Department of Employment, Education & Training, *Schooling in Australia: Statistical Profile No. 2*, Canberra: AGPS, 1989.
Dixon, Daryl, 'A Broader Perspective on Aged Care Services and Financing', unpublished address to the Fifth National Congress of Australian Nursing Homes, 1986.
Dixon, Daryl, 'How Mr Hawke Has Cut Welfare Dependency ... and how he must cut it further', *IPA Review*, March–May 1989, 5.
Dixon, Daryl & Chris Foster, 'Overview' in Mendelsohn (ed.), *Finance of Old Age*.
Dixon Daryl, & Barry Martyn, *The New Super Made Easy*, Melbourne: Australian Investment Library, 1989.

Dixson, Miriam, 'Gender, Class, and the Women's Movement in Australia, 1890–1980', in Grieve & Burns, *Australian Women: New Feminist Perspectives*, 14–26.

Dunlop, Rosemary & Ailsa Burns, *'Don't Feel the World is Caving In': Adolescents in Divorcing Families*, Monograph No. 6, Melbourne: Australian Institute of Family Studies, 1988.

Dworkin, Ronald, 'What is Equality?', *Philosophy and Public Affairs* **10** (1981), 185–246, 283–345.

Eastman, Moira, *Family: The Vital Factor*, Melbourne: Collins Dove, 1989.

Edgar, Don, *Poverty and its Impact on Educational Life-Chances: Family-Produced or System-Produced Disadvantage?*, Melbourne: Australian Institute of Family Studies, 1985.

Edgar, Don, 'Family Disruption and Violence', *Family Matters* **22** (1988).

Edgar, Don, 'Volunteerism and the Changing Pattern of Women's Lives', *St Mark's Review*, March 1988.

Edgar, Don, 'Family Problems: The Cost-benefits of Prevention', *Family Matters* **25** (December 1989).

Edgar, Don, David Keane & Peter McDonald (eds), *Child Poverty*, Sydney: Allen & Unwin, 1989.

Edwards, Meredith, *The Income Unit in the Australian Tax and Social Security Systems*, Melbourne: Australian Institute of Family Studies, 1984.

Edwards, Meredith, 'The Australian Taxation Unit: An Evaluation', in John G. Head (ed.), *Changing the Tax Mix*, Sydney: Australian Tax Research Foundation, 1986, 325–340.

Elshtain, Jean Bethke, *Public Man, Private Woman: Women in Social and Political Thought*, Princeton: Princeton University Press, 1981.

Embling, John, *Fragmented Lives: A Darker Side of Australian Life*, Ringwood: Penguin, 1986.

EPAC (Economic Planning and Advisory Council), *Aspects of the Social Wage: A Review of Social Expenditures and Redistribution*, Council Paper 27, Canberra: AGPS, 1987.

EPAC, *Economic Effects of an Aging Population*, Council Paper 29, Canberra: AGPS, 1988.

EPAC, *Income Support Policies, Taxation and Incentives*, Council Paper 35, Canberra: AGPS, 1988.

EPAC, *Working Papers to Council Paper No. 35*, Canberra, 1988.

Erikson, Erik H., *Childhood and Society*, London: Imago, 1950.

Espenshade, Thomas J., 'The Price of Children and Socioeconomic Theories of Fertility', *Population Studies* **25** (1972), 207–222.

Espenshade, Thomas J., *Investing in Children: new estimates of parental expenditure*, Washington: Urban Institute, 1984.

Ewin, R.E., *Liberty, Community and Justice*, Totowa: Rowman & Allenheld, 1987.

Fane, George, 'Education and Society', in *Family, Youth and Work*, fourth national seminar, Australian Family Association, Canberra, 1985, 21–27.

Fane, George, *Education Policy in Australia*, Economic Planning Advisory Council Discussion Paper, Canberra: AGPS, 1984.

Feldstein, Martin, 'On the Theory of Tax Reform', *Journal of Public Economics* **6** (1976), 77-104.

Foster, Chris, Hal L. Kendig & Verdon Staines, 'National Perspectives', in Foster & Kendig (eds), *Who Pays? Financing Services for Older People*, Canberra: Commonwealth Policy Co-ordination Unit & ANU Ageing and the Family Project, 1987, 11–58.

Foster, Chris, *Towards a National Retirement Incomes Policy*, Social Security Review, Canberra: AGPS, 1988.

Freebairn, John, Michael Porter & Cliff Walsh (eds), *Spending and Taxing: Australian Reform Options*, Sydney: Allen & Unwin, 1987.
Freebairn, John, Michael Porter & Cliff Walsh (eds), *Spending and Taxing II: Taking Stock*, Sydney: Allen & Unwin, 1988.
Freebairn, John, Michael Porter & Cliff Walsh (eds), *Savings and Productivity: Incentives for the 1990s*, Sydney: Allen & Unwin, 1988.
Freeman, M.D.A., *The Rights and Wrongs of Children*, London: Frances Pinter, 1983.
Garnaut Report: Garnaut, Ross, *Australia and the Northeast Asian Ascendancy*, Report to the Prime Minister and the Minister for Foreign Affairs and Trade, Canberra: AGPS, 1989.
Gilbert, Neil, *Capitalism and the Welfare State: Dilemmas of Social Benevolence*, New Haven: Yale University Press, 1983.
Goldberg, Gordon, 'Law and Family', National Seminar on the Family, Melbourne: Australian Family Association, 1980, 68–76.
Goodin, Robert E. & Julian LeGrand, 'Creeping Universalism in the Australian Welfare State', in Goodin & LeGrand, *Not Only the Poor: The Middle Classes and the Welfare State*, London: Allen & Unwin, 1987.
Gough, Ian, *The Political Economy of the Welfare State*, London: Macmillan, 1979.
Green, David G., *Social Welfare: The Changing Debate*, St Leonards: Centre for Independent Studies, 1988.
Greer, Germaine, *Sex and Destiny: The politics of human fertility*, London: Secker & Warburg, 1984.
Gregory, R.G., R. Anstie, J.J. Pincus & S. Dowrick, *Government Spending on Work-Related Child Care: Some Economic Issues*, Discussion Paper 191, Canberra: ANU Centre for Economic Policy Research, 1988.
Grieve, Norma & Ailsa Burns (eds), *Australian Women: New Feminist Perspectives*, Melbourne: Oxford University Press, 1986.
Grimshaw, Patricia, & Lynne Strahan (eds), *The Half Open Door*, , Sydney: Hale & Iremonger, 1982.
Gruen, Fred, *Housing Australians: Puzzles, Policies, but No 'Solutions'*, Discussion Paper No. 175, Canberra: ANU Center for Economic Policy Research, 1987.
Guttentag, Marcia & Paul F. Secord, *Too Many Women?*, New York: Sage, 1983.
Hanushek, Eric A., 'Throwing Money at Schools', *Journal of Policy Analysis and Management* **1** (1981), 19–42.
Hanushek, Eric A., 'The Economics of Schooling: Production efficiency and government schools', *Journal of Economic Literature* **24** (1986), 1141–1177.
Harding, Ann, *Assistance for Families with Children and the Social Security Review*, Social Security Review, Canberra: AGPS, 1986.
Hawley, W.D., S.J. Rosenholz, H. Goodstein & T. Hasselbring, 'Good Schools: What Research Says About Improving Educational Achievement', *Peabody Journal of Education*, 1984, 117–124
Henderson, R.F. (ed.), *The Welfare Stakes: Strategies for Australian Social Policy*, Melbourne: Institute of Applied Economic & Social Research, University of Melbourne, 1981.
Henderson Report: Commission of Inquiry into Poverty, *Poverty in Australia*, Canberra: AGPS, 1975
Hendrie, Delia & Michael G. Porter, 'The Capture of the Welfare State', *Canberra Bulletin of Public Administration*, May 1987.
Hetherington, E.M., M. Cox & R. Cox, 'The Aftermath of Divorce', in J.H. Stevens & M. Matthews (eds), *Mother-Child, Father-Child Relations*, NAEYC, 1977.
Hewlett, Sylvia Ann, *A Lesser Life: The Myth of Women's Liberation in America* New York: Morrow, 1986.
Highet, Gilbert, *The Art of Teaching*, New York: Knopf, 1950.

Hodge, Robert & David Tripp, *Children and Television: a Semiotic Approach*, Cambridge: Polity Press, 1986.
Hogan, Michael, *Public versus Private Schools: Funding and Directions in Australia*, Ringwood: Penguin, 1984.
Hyde, John, *Deregulate or Decay: the lesson of the 1930s for the 1990s*, Policy Paper No. 14, Perth: Australian Institute for Public Policy, 1989.
James, Michael (ed.), *Restraining Leviathan: Small Government in Practice*, St Leonards: Centre for Independent Studies, 1987.
James, Michael (ed.), *The Welfare State: Foundations and Alternatives*, St Leonards: Centre for Independent Studies, 1989.
Jamrozik, Adam, 'Social Policy: Are there Alternatives to the Welfare State?', in Jamrozik (ed.), *Income Distribution, Taxation and Social Security: Issues of Current Concern*, Social Welfare Research Centre Reports & Proceedings No. 55, Kensington NSW, 1986.
Jamrozik, Adam, 'Social Security and the Social Wage', in Jamrozik (ed.), *Social Security and Family Welfare: Directions and Options Ahead*, Social Welfare Research Centre Reports & Proceedings No. 61, Kensington NSW, 1986.
Jencks, Christopher, *et al.*, *Inequality: A Reassessment of the Effect of Family and Schooling in America*, New York: Basic Books, 1972.
Johnson, Paul, Christoph Conrad & David Thompson (eds), *Workers versus Pensioners: Intergenerational Justice in an Ageing World*, Manchester: Manchester University Press, 1989.
Jordan, Alan, *Sole Parents on Pensions*, Canberra: Department of Social Security, 1982.
Jordan, Alan, *The Common Treasury: The Distribution of Income to Families and Households*, Social Security Review, Canberra: AGPS, 1987.
Jordan, Peter, *The Effects of Marital Separation on Men*, Research Report No 6, Brisbane: Family Court of Australia Principal Registry, 1985.
Kagan, Jerome, *The Nature of the Child*, New York: Basic Books, 1984.
Karmel, Peter, 'Quality and Equality in Education', *Australian Journal of Education* **29** (1985), 279f.
Kasper, Wolfgang, *et al.*, *Australia at the Crossroads: Our choices to the year 2000*, Sydney: Harcourt Brace Jovanovich, 1980.
Kasper, Wolfgang, *Accelerated Industrial Evolution in East Asia: Some Lessons*, Economics & Management Discussion Paper 1/89, Canberra: Australian Defence Academy, 1989.
Kasper, Wolfgang, comment in Michael James (ed.), *Restraining Leviathan: Small Government in Practice*, St Leonards: Centre for Independent Studies, 1987.
Kendig, Hal L. (ed.), *Ageing and Families: A Support Networks Perspective*, Sydney: Allen & Unwin, 1986.
Kendig, Hal L. 'Ageing, Families and Social Change' in Kendig (ed.), *Ageing and Families*.
Kessler, Denis, 'But Why is There Social Security?', in Johnson *et al.*, *Workers versus Pensioners*, 80–90.
King, R.J.R., & R.E. Young, *A Systematic Sociology of Australian Education*, Sydney: Allen & Unwin, 1986.
Knox, David M., *Taxation Support of Superannuation in Australia: Its Costs, Equity and Efficacy*, Research Study No. 7, Sydney: Australian Tax Research Foundation, 1987.
Lasch, Christopher, *Haven in a Heartless World: The Family Besieged*, New York: Basic Books, 1977.
Lasch, Christopher, *The Culture of Narcissism: American Life in the Age of Diminishing Expectations*, New York: Norton, 1978.
Lewis, Jerry M., *How's your Family?*, New York: Brunner/Mazel, 1979.

Lewis, Robert A. & Graham B. Spanier, 'Theorizing about the Quality and Stability of Marriage' in Wesley R. Burr *et al.* (eds), *Contemporary Theories About the Family*, New York: The Free Press, 1979, **1**, 268–294.

Little, Marilyn, *Family Breakup*, San Francisco: Jossey-Bass, 1982/1983.

Lovejoy, C. Owen, 'The Origin of Man', *Science* **211** (23 January 1981), 341–350.

Macdonald, Ian, 'The Cyclic Pattern of Abusive Relationships' in Crawley (ed.), *Counselling and Domestic Violence.*

Mack, Joanna, & Stewart Lansley, *Poor Britain*, London: Allen & Unwin, 1985.

Manning, Ian, 'Private Savings and Retirement', in Mendelsohn (ed.), *Finance of Old Age.*

Marsh, Ian C., *Australia Can Compete: Towards a flexible, adaptable society*, Melbourne: Longman Cheshire, 1988.

Marx, Karl, 'Private Property and Communism', in T.B. Bottomore (ed.), *Karl Marx: Early Writings*, London: Watts, 1963.

Marx, Karl, 'On a Proposed Divorce Law', in Loyd D. Easton & Kurt H. Guddat (eds), *Writings of the Young Marx on Philosophy and Society*, Garden City, NY: Anchor Books, 1967.

McCaughey, Jean, *A Bit of a Struggle: Coping with Family Life in Australia*, Ringwood: McPhee Gribble/Penguin, 1987.

McDonald, Peter (ed.), *Settling Up: Property and Income Distribution on Divorce in Australia*, Sydney: Australian Institute of Family Studies & Prentice-Hall, 1986.

McDonald, Peter, *The Economic Consequences of Marriage Breakdown in Australia: a Summary*, Melbourne: Australian Institute of Family Studies, 1985.

McDonald, Peter, 'Families in the Future: The Pursuit of Personal Autonomy', *Family Matters* **22** (December 1988).

McGuinness, Padraic P., contribution in *Conference Discussion Relating to the Paper 'Social Welfare in Australia' by Henry J. Aaron*, Discussion Paper B8, Canberra: ANU Centre for Economic Policy Research, 1985.

McLanahan, Sara S., 'Family Structure and the Reproduction of Poverty', *American Journal of Sociology* **90** (1985), 873–901.

Mead, Lawrence M., *Beyond Entitlement: The Social Obligations of Citizenship*, New York: Free Press, 1986.

Mendelsohn, Ronald (ed.), *Finance of Old Age*, Canberra: Centre for Research on Federal Financial Relations, 1986.

Mendelsohn, Ronald, 'A Sharing, Caring Community', in Henderson (ed.), *The Welfare Stakes.*

Midgley, Mary & Judith Hughes, *Women's Choices: Philosophical Problems Facing Feminism*, London: Weidenfeld & Nicolson, 1983.

Midgley, Mary, 'Sex and Personal Identity: The Western Individualistic Tradition', *Encounter* **63** (June 1984), 50–55.

Minichiello, M. Victor, 'Social Processes in Entering Nursing Homes', in Kendig, *Ageing and Families*, 149-168.

Mitchell, Ann, *Children in the Middle: Living through Divorce*, London: Tavistock Publications, 1985.

Morgan, Patricia, 'For the Sake of the Children?' in Digby Anderson (ed.), *Full Circle: Bringing up Children in the Post-Permissive Society*, London: Social Affairs Unit, 1988.

Mount, Ferdinand, *The Subversive Family: An Alternative History of Love and Marriage*, London: Unwin Paperbacks, 1982.

Moynihan, Daniel P., *Family and Nation*, San Diego: Harcourt Brace Jovanovich, 1986.

Murray, Charles, *Losing Ground: American Social Policy 1950–1980*, New York: Basic Books, 1984.

Murray, Les, *The Peasant Mandarin: Prose Pieces*, St Lucia: University of Queensland Press, 1978.

Nava, Mica, 'From Utopian to Scientific Feminism? Early feminist critiques of the family' in Segal (ed.), *What is to be Done about the Family?*, 65–105.

Nozick, Robert, *Anarchy, State and Utopia*, New York: Basic Books, 1974.

Nurick, John, 'The Future of the Welfare State' in Nurick *et al.*, *The Future of the Welfare State.*

Nurick, John, *Wealth and Power: AIPP's Submission to the Bishops' Committee for Justice, Development and Peace*, Perth: Australian Institute for Public Policy, 1988.

Nurick, John, *Mandate to Govern: A handbook for the next Australian government*, Perth: Australian Institute for Public Policy & Australian Chamber of Commerce, 1987.

Nurick, John, Clifford Orwin, Nathan Glazer, & Wolfgang Kasper, *The Future of the Welfare State*, Critical Issues No. 5, Perth: Australian Institute for Public Policy, 1986.

O'Donnell, Lydia, 'The Social World of Parents', *Marriage and Family Review*, 1983, 9–36.

O'Donohue, Jane, *An Examination of Taxation Arrangements for Couples with Children: Evaluating the Options of Income Splitting*, Social Security Review, Canberra: AGPS, 1988.

OECD (Organisation for Economic Cooperation and Development), *The 1982 Tax/Benefit Position of a Typical Worker in OECD Member Countries*, Paris: OECD, 1986.

Olson, Mancur, *Australia in the Perspective of the Rise and Decline of Nations*, Discussion Paper No. 109, Canberra: ANU Centre for Economic Policy Research, 1984.

Olson, Mancur, *The Rise and Decline of Nations: Economic Growth, Stagflation and Social Rigidities*, New Haven: Yale University Press, 1982.

Orwin, Clifford, 'Welfare and the New Dignity', in Nurick *et al.*, *The Future of the Welfare State*, 23–32.

Oxley, Carol, *The Structure of General Family Provision in Australia and Overseas: A Comparative Study*, Social Security Review, Canberra: AGPS, 1987.

Peden, Joseph R. & Fred R. Glahe (eds), *The American Family and the State*, San Francisco: Pacific Research Institute for Public Policy, 1986.

Piggott, John, 'Statistical Incidence Studies: An Economic Perspective' in *Who Benefits? The Australian Welfare System and Redistribution*, Reports & Proceedings No. 45, Kensington: Social Welfare Research Centre, 1984.

Phillips, Roderick, *Putting Asunder: A History of Divorce in Western Society*, Cambridge: Cambridge University Press, 1988.

Pollard, A.H., 'The Family and the Economy', *The Australian Family*, December 1989.

Pollard, David, *Give and Take: The Losing Partnership in Aboriginal Policy*, Sydney: Hale & Iremonger, 1988.

Popenoe, David, *Disturbing the Nest: Family Change and Decline in Modern Societies*, New York: Aldine de Gruyter, 1988

Postman, Neil, *Amusing Ourselves to Death*, London: Heinemann, 1986.

Raban, Jonathan, *For Love and Money*, London: Collins Harvill, 1987.

Raymond, Judy, *Bringing Up Children Alone: Policies for Sole Parents*, Social Security Review Issues Paper No. 3, Canberra: AGPS, 1987.

Richards, Lyn, *Having Families: Marriage, Parenthood and Social Pressure in Australia*, Ringwood: Penguin, 1985.

Rossi, Alice S., 'Gender and Parenthood', *American Sociological Review* **49** (1984), 1–19.

Rossi, Alice S., 'Sex and Gender in an Aging Society', *Daedalus* **115** (1986).
Rowland, Don T., 'Family Structure' in Kendig, *Ageing and Families*, 17–37.
Sadurski, Wojciech, *Giving Desert its Due: Social Justice and Legal Theory*, Dordrecht: Reidel, 1985.
Saunders, Peter, 'Overview' in Foster & Kendig (eds), *Who Pays?*, 405–407.
Saunders, Peter & Peter Whiteford, *Measuring Poverty: A Review of the Issues*, Canberra: EPAC, 1989.
Sawyer, Peter, *Dolebludging—A Taxpayer's Guide*, Kenthurst: Kangaroo Press, 1986.
Scruton, Roger, *Sexual Desire: A Philosophical Investigation*, London: Weidenfeld & Nicolson, 1986.
Scutt, Jocelynne A. & Di Graham, *For Richer, For Poorer: Money, Marriage and Property Rights*, Ringwood: Penguin, 1984.
Segal, Lynne (ed.), *What is to be done about the Family?*, Harmondsworth: Penguin, 1983.
Sen, Amartya, 'Economics and the Family', *Asian Development Review*, 1983, 14–26.
Smiley, G.W., E.R. Chamberlain & L.I. Dalgleish, *Implications of Marital Separation for Young Children*, Working Paper No. 11, Melbourne: Australian Institute of Family Studies, 1987.
Sowell, Thomas, *Minorities and Markets*, Oxford: Blackwell, 1981.
Sowell, Thomas, *Pink and Brown People and Other Controversial Essays*, Stanford: Hoover Institution, 1981.
Stone, Lawrence, 'The Road to Polygamy', *New York Review of Books*, 2 March 1989, 12–15.
Straus M., & R. Gelles, 'Societal Change and Family Violence from 1975 to 1985 as Revealed by Two National Surveys', *Journal of Marriage and the Family* **48** (1986) 465–79.
Swan, Peter L. & Mikhail S. Bernstam, 'Brides of the State', *IPA Review* **41** (May–July 1987), 22–25.
Swan, Peter. L & Mikhail S. Bernstam, 'Support for Single Parents' in James (ed.), *The Welfare State: Foundations and Alternatives*, 223–235.
Tennison, Patrick, *Family Court: The Legal Jungle*, Victoria: Ashburton, 1983.
Thompson, David, 'The Welfare State and Generation Conflict: Winners and Losers', in Johnson *et al.*, *Workers versus Pensioners*.
Thompson, David, *Selfish Generations: The Ageing of the Welfare State*, Wellington: Allen & Unwin, 1989.
Thornes, B. & J. Collard, *Who Divorces?*, London: Routledge Kegan Paul, 1979.
Toomey, Derek, *Home–School Relations and Inequality in Education*, microfiche, ERIC No. UD024826, 1986.
Toomey, Derek, *Children's Reading and Parental Involvement: Strategies for schools in the research literature*, microfiche, ERIC No. CS008919, 1987.
Trethewey, Jenny, 'What Do Our Futures Hold? The Perspective of Fifty Low-Income Households', paper presented at workshop conference 'The Future of the Household Economy and the Role of Women', University of Melbourne, 1987.
Trivers, Robert, *Social Evolution*, San Francisco: Benjamin/Cummings, 1985.
van Sommers, Peter, 'Male and Female Body and Brain: The Biology of Sexual Differentiation', in Grieve & Burns, *Australian Women: New Feminist Perspectives*, 70–89.
Victorian Women's Consultative Council, *Women in the Home*, Melbourne: Department of Premier & Cabinet, n.d.
Wakefield, Hollida & Ralph Underwager, *Accusations of Child Sexual Abuse*, Springfield: Thomas, 1988.

Wallerstein, Judith S. & Sandra Blakeslee, *Second Chances: Men, Women and Children a Decade After Divorce*, New York: Ticknor & Fields, 1989.
Wallerstein, Judith S. & Joan Berlin Kelly, *Surviving the Break-up: How Children and Parents Cope with Divorce*, London: Grant McIntyre, 1980.
Warren, Neil, *Papers on Taxation and Tax Incidence*, Kensington: University of NSW Centre for Applied Economic Research, 1988.
Whiteford, Peter, *Issues in Assistance for Families—Horizontal and Vertical Equity Considerations*, Social Security Review, Canberra: AGPS, 1986.
Williams, Claire, *Open Cut*, Sydney: Allen & Unwin, 1981.
Willis, Robert J., 'What have we learned from the Economics of the Family?', *American Economic Review* 77 (1987), 68–81.
Wilson, James Q. & Richard J. Herrnstein, *Crime and Human Nature*, New York: Simon & Schuster, 1985.
Winn, Marie, *The Plug-In Drug: Television, Children and the Family*, revised edn, Ringwood: Penguin, 1985.
Wolgast, Elizabeth H., *Equality and the Rights of Women*, Ithaca: Cornell University Press, 1980.
Wynne, Edward A., *Social Security: A Reciprocity System under Pressure*, Boulder: Westview Press, 1980.
Young, Michael & Peter Willmott, *The Symmetrical Family: A Study of Work and Leisure in the London Region*, London: Routledge Kegan Paul, 1973.
Zinsmeister, Karl, 'Brave New World', *Quadrant*, July 1989.

Index